THE NEW
PALGRAVE

PROBLEMS OF THE
PLANNED ECONOMY

THE NEW
PALGRAVE

PROBLEMS OF THE
PLANNED ECONOMY

EDITED BY

JOHN EATWELL · MURRAYMILGATE · PETER NEWMAN

W. W. NORTON & COMPANY

NEW YORK · LONDON

First published in
The New Palgrave: A Dictionary of Economics
Edited by John Eatwell, Murray Milgate and Peter Newman
in four volumes, 1987

The New Palgrave is a trademark of
The Macmillan Press Limited

First American Edition, 1990

ISBN 0-393-02736-8
ISBN 0-393-95861-2 PBK.

W. W. Norton & Company, Inc.
500 Fifth Avenue
New York, NY 10110

W. W. Norton & Company, Ltd.
37 Great Russell Street
London WC1B 3NU

Printed in Hong Kong

1   2   3   4   5   6   7   8   9   0

Contents

Contents

General Preface

The books in this series are the offspring of *The New Palgrave: A Dictionary of Economics*. Published in late 1987, the *Dictionary* has rapidly become a standard reference work in economics. However, its four heavy tomes containing over four million words on the whole range of economic thought is not a form convenient to every potential user. For many students and teachers it is simply too bulky, too comprehensive and too expensive for everyday use.

By developing the present series of compact volumes of reprints from the original work, we hope that some of the intellectual wealth of *The New Palgrave* will become accessible to much wider groups of readers. Each of the volumes is devoted to a particular branch of economics, such as econometrics or general equilibrium or money, with a scope corresponding roughly to a university course on that subject. Apart from correction of misprints, etc. the content of each of its reprinted articles is exactly the same as that of the original. In addition, a few brand new entries have been commissioned especially for the series, either to fill an apparent gap or more commonly to include topics that have risen to prominence since the dictionary was originally commissioned.

As *The New Palgrave* is the sole parent of the present series, it may be helpful to explain that it is the modern successor to the excellent *Dictionary of Political Economy* edited by R.H. Inglis Palgrave and published in three volumes in 1894, 1896 and 1899. A second and slightly modified version, edited by Henry Higgs, appeared during the mid-1920s. These two editions each contained almost 4,000 entries, but many of those were simply brief definitions and many of the others were devoted to peripheral topics such as foreign coinage, maritime commerce, and Scottish law. To make room for the spectacular growth in economics over the last 60 years while keeping still to a manageable length, *The New Palgrave* concentrated instead on economic theory, its originators, and its closely cognate disciplines. Its nearly 2,000 entries (commissioned from over 900 scholars) are all self-contained essays, sometimes brief but never mere definitions.

Apart from its biographical entries, *The New Palgrave* is concerned chiefly with theory rather than fact, doctrine rather than data; and it is not at all clear how theory and doctrine, as distinct from facts and figures, *should* be treated in an encyclopaedia. One way is to treat everything from a particular point of view. Broadly speaking, that was the way of Diderot's classic *Encyclopédie raisonée* (1751–1772), as it was also of Léon Say's *Nouveau dictionnaire d'économie politique* (1891–2). Sometimes, as in articles by Quesnay and Turgot in the *Encyclopédie*, this approach has yielded entries of surpassing brilliance. Too often, however, both the range of subjects covered and the quality of the coverage itself are seriously reduced by such a self-limiting perspective. Thus the entry called '*Méthode*' in the first edition of Say's *Dictionnaire* asserted that the use of mathematics in economics 'will only ever be in the hands of a few', and the dictionary backed up that claim by choosing not to have any entry on Cournot.

Another approach is to have each entry take care to reflect within itself varying points of view. This may help the student temporarily, as when preparing for an examination. But in a subject like economics, the Olympian detachment which this approach requires often places a heavy burden on the author, asking for a scrupulous account of doctrines he or she believes to be at best wrong-headed. Even when an especially able author does produce a judicious survey article, it is surely too much to ask that it also convey just as much enthusiasm for those theories thought misguided as for those found congenial. Lacking an enthusiastic exposition, however, the disfavoured theories may then be studied less closely than they deserve.

The New Palgrave did not ask its authors to treat economic theory from any particular point of view, except in one respect to be discussed below. Nor did it call for surveys. Instead, each author was asked to make clear his or her own views of the subject under discussion, and for the rest to be as fair and accurate as possible, without striving to be 'judicious'. A balanced perspective on each topic was always the aim, the ideal. But it was to be sought not *internally*, within each article, but *externally*, between articles, with the reader rather than the writer handed the task of achieving a personal balance between differing views.

For a controversial topic, a set of several more or less synonymous headwords, matched by a broad diversity of contributors, was designed to produce enough variety of opinion to help form the reader's own synthesis; indeed, such diversity will be found in most of the individual volumes in this series.

This approach was not without its problems. Thus, the prevalence of uncertainty in the process of commissioning entries sometimes produced a less diverse outcome than we had planned. 'I can call spirits from the vasty deep,' said Owen Glendower. 'Why, so can I,' replied Hotspur, 'or so can any man;/ But will they come when you do call for them?' In our experience, not quite as often as we would have liked.

The one point of view we did urge upon every one of *Palgrave*'s authors was to write from an historical perspective. For each subject its contributor was asked to discuss not only present problems but also past growth and future prospects. This request was made in the belief that knowledge of the historical development of any theory enriches our present understanding of it, and so helps to construct better theories for the future. The authors' response to the request was generally so positive that, as the reader of any of these volumes will discover, the resulting contributions amply justified that belief.

John Eatwell
Murray Milgate
Peter Newman

Preface

The term 'planned economy' is typically applied to the economic systems of the Soviet Union, of post-war Eastern Europe, and of the Peoples' Republic of China, which have been more or less copied in a number of Third World countries. The distinctive feature of these economies has been that the material means of production are owned by the state. Although in some cases the state may require decisions to be made according to market signals and may devolve decisions to local production units, ownership ensures that most economic decisions depend on the formation of economic plans by the political authorities.

But whilst this volume is predominantly focused on such economies, they are not its exclusive concern. The economics of planning covers a far wider range of problems. It embodies two quite distinct, though interrelated topics. The first is the study of planned economies given state ownership of the means of production. The second is the economic case for planning whatever might be the pattern of ownership.

In assessing the role of economic planning (whether in centrally planned or mixed economies) the economist has to consider not only the interaction between economics and politics, but also the problem of how an 'efficient' economic system is to be defined. The idea of productive efficiency is fairly straightforward, but the notion of allocative efficiency which is contained in the criterion of Pareto optimality is both weak and inadequate for the major social choices which must be made. Instead, pragmatic assessments of 'the pace of development', 'standards of living' and 'rates of growth' are used to make the case for any particular combination of market and plan. So the general case comes down to 'is it socially acceptable' and 'does it work'.

The formal economic case for planning rests on market failure, whether that failure is due to incomplete markets, the presence of externalities, or transactions costs, or to some more fundamental failure of the price mechanism to achieve social objectives. Since the practical fulfilment of the conditions necessary for there to be no market failure is, in the true sense of the word, incredible, an efficient economic policy requires some consideration of the desirable balance between market and plan.

However, the construction of an efficient economic policy is not just a theoretical problem, but an exercise in practical politics. So the balance is not found along a continuum running from an extreme form of laissez-faire liberalism all the way to the state-directed command economy of war-communism. Instead, it must be devised both with reference to the problems which the market is failing to solve, and the political legitimacy and economic effectiveness of the institutions which take the place of the market. So the problems of planning and of the economic role of the state must be considered in the light of particular historical circumstances, not just on general theoretical grounds.

Alexander Gerschenkron (in *Economic Backwardness in Historical Perspective*) traced the reaction to economic backwardness in the different institutions adopted in relatively backward countries in their endeavours to catch up. American railroads were not constructed in the same laissez-faire spirit as were Britain's railways. Nor were great German banks formed at the end of the 19th century driven by the same market forces as had earlier defined the character of British banks.

The importance of political legitimacy is illustrated by the organization of the British economy during World War II. Britain was far more tightly planned and controlled than was the fascist command economy in Germany. In particular there was stricter direction and more effective utilization of scarce labour resources. The economists of the US Strategic Bombing Survey argued that the key was the greater acceptance of political direction in the democratic state. But detailed controls were only acceptable as long as the national emergency persisted. The end of the 1940s saw the 'bonfire of controls'. Wartime controls were replaced, as Andrew Shonfield pointed out in his *Modern Capitalism*, but a variety of institutional responses to the needs of post-war reconstruction in the 1950s and 1960s. Success appears to have been correlated with some management of the market (in France, Germany and Japan), particularly at the industrial level, rather than reliance on free markets (as in the United States).

The construction of planned economies in the Soviet Union, Eastern Europe, China, and some countries of the Third World followed a quite different path from the various methods of managing accumulation, manipulating the market and expanding the role of the public sector which ebb and flow in capitalist economies. Instead, the socialist economies sought to determine the pattern of production, accumulation, and hence, consumption, by non-market means.

These economies have not been able to sustain a performance comparable to that of the mixed market economies. In the Soviet Union, a relatively backward country was transformed into a major industrial economy, but the mechanisms of extensive heavy industrialization have proved incapable either of applying modern technological advances outside the military sector, or of establishing a standard of consumption comparable to that in advanced capitalist countries. Many features of the Soviet system were reproduced in Eastern Europe, with broadly similar results, and with the burden of imposed political structures.

Experiments with various forms of 'market socialism' have failed to produce any sustained improvement in overall performance, and now consideration of more market driven models, whether West European, American or Japanese, is accompanying political liberalization. Economists are only now beginning to grapple with problems posed by the simultaneous transformation of plan into market and a predominance of state ownership into a predominance of private ownership.

The Editors

Perestroika

A. AGANBEGYAN

The very concept of *perestroika* in its contemporary political and socioeconomic interpretation has emerged in the USSR in connection with the formation of new policies and new thinking, initiated at the Plenary Meeting of the CPSU Central Committee in April 1985. The main guidelines of *perestroika* were charted by the 27th Congress of the Communist Party of the Soviet Union and further developed in the resolutions of the subsequent Plenary Meetings of the CPSU Central Committee and by the 19th All-Union Party Conference in 1988. The concept of *perestroika* is diametrically opposite to the ideas of improving or amending which, in effect, characterize partial evolutionary changes, half-measures. In contrast, *perestroika* embodies qualitative, cardinal changes, those changes being complete, comprehensive rather than partial. *Perestroika* is a revolutionary process of transformation in society.

The term '*perestroika*', coined for the first time in the USSR is now widely used in other countries of the world entering – in our interpretation – the vocabulary of the English and other languages and denoting a system of fundamental changes connected with large-scale transformations in social life. *Perestroika* in the Soviet economy is a most important component part of the entire process of the restructuring of the whole society, including radical transformations in the spheres of ideology, political and legal systems, science, culture and education, foreign policy and so on.

The restructuring of our society is the fate of the people, the question of its survival, its further existence.

The direct cause bringing to life the necessity of the radical restructuring of the Soviet Union was the deterioration of the economic and social situation in the country in the 1970s and early 80s. At that time the rate of economic development slowed down sharply, economic disproportions increased, and the social needs of people ceased to be sufficiently satisfied. Negative trends, which developed at the watershed of the 1970s and the 1980s, resulted in economic stagnation, and the living standards of population began to drop. The country stood at the edge of an economic abyss. Something had to be done, and done fast. *Perestroika* was the answer to the pre-crisis state of the economy. This immediate cause had deep roots. In-depth distortions in the socialist economy and, first and foremost, the administrative-command system of economic management which had emerged during Stalin's rule and was later brought back to life at the time of the Brezhnev stagnation period, were responsible for the stagnation of economy, for low living standards of the people.

Thus *perestroika* in the economy is a radical restructuring of our system, a revolutionary transformation of all economic methods, a fundamental change in the system of planning and management.

What are our objectives? What goals are being pursued by the economic reform?

To begin with, from an economy in which everything is in short supply, in which producers rule supreme, we intend to go over to an economy based on satisfying social needs, where producers strive for the fulfilment of the demands of consumers.

In the economy where everything was in short supply, priority belonged to resource-production goals, while the development of the social sphere was in the background. We want to abandon such a one-sided economic system and turn to an economy working for the good of man, in which high priority belongs to the development of the social sphere and consumer goods and services.

Second, we face the task of radically changing the factors and sources of economic growth, turning from the predominantly extensive type of development to the intensive one. The production orientation of the deficit economy required an increasingly greater amount of resources for the expansion of production. That is why, during the last 15 years, two-thirds of our economic growth was connected with increasing production resources, i.e. it was taking place extensively. Under the new conditions of *perestroika* economic development will be aimed at resolving social objectives, which means that we will have to obtain necessary ways and means for the purpose. It can be done if economic growth proceeds by means of mostly intensive factors – greater efficiency and higher quality. To achieve this it is necessary to make technological progress the main source of our development, to pave the way for the achievements of the technological revolution.

Third, we will have to abandon the administrative-command system suppressing human initiative and to turn to the use of economic mechanisms, far greater use of the market, taking into account economic interests and extending the importance of economic incentives. We must continue to develop towards a democratic economy involving people in the management of economy on a broad basis.

Lastly, we are striving to relinquish the 'closed' economy directed to within the country and separated from the world, and go over to an open economy where our country will join the system of the world economy and the international market.

Obviously we are faced with an enormous and complex economic reform, restructuring all economic linkages. This is not a brief campaign but an extremely serious process of renovation of the economic foundations of society. We intend to implement these transformations in the framework of our socialist economic system, without tolerating hired labour, dividing society into capitalists and working people, with a high degree of social protection of the working people consolidating their confidence in the future.

In his last works written in the 1920s, V.I. Lenin saw the future of the socialist economy as a pluralist economy, in which various forms of ownership (state, cooperative, joint, individual) will co-exist – and all this will be aimed at improving the lives of the people. Later on, Stalin distorted those fundamental Leninist ideas that were based on the Marxist interpretation of socialism as a society of high effectiveness and human wellbeing, a society of social justice and democracy. Our *perestroika* is aimed at reinstating the humanitarian features inherent in socialism, implementing the Leninist model of socialism which was so attractive for millions of people.

In the course of *perestroika* – as will be demonstrated below – we turn to a new model of the socialist economy, a model based on developed market relations, taking into account the economic interests of people, based on material incentives, a model constituting a part of the system of world economy. All this to a large extent brings many features of our economy within reach of the economies of industrially developed Western countries, particularly those of them in which the economic role played by the state is significant and where certain steps aimed at regulating people's incomes and ensuring social protection of the poorer groups of population are implemented.

I refer, first and foremost, to those countries where Social-Democratic governments have been in power for long periods of time – as is the case in Sweden. That is why it is possible and necessary to speak of a certain degree of convergence in the economic development of our country and the developed countries of the West.

Having abandoned the old, distorted model of a socialist economy based on bureaucratic-centralist principles, on concentrating the management of economic life in the hands of the state and neglecting the social interests of the working people, we turn to a new model of a socialist society. In this connection the slogan 'More Socialism' advanced by M.S. Gorbachev in the best way possible expresses the content of our *perestroika*.

What will be the concrete differences between the new socialist economic system emerging in the course of *perestroika* and the economy of the bourgeois countries of the West? The main, fundamental difference is the fact that socialist collective ownership is predominant in the USSR, both as the ownership of the entire people and the ownership of a group, collective. This means that our society will not be divided into the masters owning the means of production and putting money into circulation, and hired labourers. In relation to collective property all workers are in the same social position as co-owners of the property. That is why the income of each worker in our society will be dependent on his or her own contribution, and not on the work of other people hired and paid by others. The ideology of a bourgeois economy where money produces money for its owners, is not predominant in a socialist society. The crucial thing is that income is being produced by one's own work. Obviously, a different approach to the relations of ownership results in a different distribution of incomes. Outwardly it will be expressed by lesser differentiation in the level of incomes and living standards in our country in contrast to Western countries. In the USSR there will be no such gap between wealth and poverty as exists, for instance, in the US.

Existence of public property in various forms makes it possible in a socialist economy to exercise national economic planning through more thorough regulation by the state than in Western countries. But it would be wrong to identify economic centralism in our condition with its concrete historic form implemented as directive planning, the petty guardianship of economic activities by the centre. Centralism can be carried out through the use of more 'flexible', softer methods, by the utilization of economic levers and stimuli – through the centrally adopted system of taxation, centrally established prices for certain key goods, centralized use of the state budget, implementation of the single policy on credits by the USSR State Bank etc. That is why the socialist market in the future model of economic socialism will be, to a large extent, a regulated market.

Let us also note here, that many elements of regulation are widely used by capitalist states, and many countries resort to various methods of national economic planning when indirectly regulating economic processes. In the new model, the entire economic policy of the socialist state will be subordinated to the main goal – growing prosperity of the country's population and better conditions for the development of the individual.

In this connection we will strive to bar unemployment, which is considered to be a calamity for the working people and ensure a higher degree of protection of the social rights of the working people even in comparison with the countries governed by Social-Democratic governments.

Economic *perestroika* in the USSR is being implemented in three main directions integrally linked with each other.

The first direction involves a social reorientation in the development of the economy, a change in the development of the national economy towards an urgent resolution of social objectives, and improvement in the living standards of the population. This is expressed in high priority being given to development of the social sphere and the whole complex of branches of the economy directly aimed at satisfying human needs.

In the first four years of *perestroika* capital investments and other resources earmarked for the development of the social sphere increased twice as fast as expenditures for production purposes, while during the period preceding *perestroika* the ratio was inverse. For instance, during 1961–84 – the period preceding *perstroika* – the volume of housing construction remained at the same level while the population increased by 30%, i.e the volume of housing construction per capita of population significantly dropped. During the years of *perestroika* we succeeded in changing this negative trend and increased the volume of housing construction by 15%. At present our goal is to redouble it so that by the end of the 1990s every Soviet family will be provided with an apartment or a house with all conveniences.

Before the beginning of *perestroika* the share of expenditure in national income and the state budget earmarked for health services and education kept shrinking. During the first four years of *perestroika* it increased sharply. We increased the wages of medical personnel by 30%, of teachers by 40%. The volume of capital investments allocated for the construction of schools and hospitals grew 1.5 times. While during the twenty years preceding *perestroika* the population's mortality was increasing and the average life span dropped from 70 to 68 years; during the first four years of *perestroika* we managed to reverse this trend. The level of mortality began to drop while the average life span increased by more than two years. Radical reform of the school system and broad computerisation of schools are being implemented and the quality of schooling is rising.

We do realize that these are only first steps, and it is imperative to keep on making greater efforts to continue the overtaking development of the social sphere.

The second direction is the conversion of the country's economy to the road of intensive development. Increasing efficiency and better quality rather than the growth of production resources become the decisive factors in economic development. Chief significance here belongs to the utilization of the achievements of the scientific and technological revolution in the national economy. These directions are implemented with the help of new investment and structural policies based, first and foremost, on radical technological reconstruction, retooling and renovation of all branches of the national economy.

Here we also observe positive changes – the increasing efficiency and technological renovation of production. Some time ago, before *perestroika*, almost a quarter of the growth of production was connected with the growing number of workers in production. But workers were in short supply, which resulted in poor quality of labour and fluctuations in manpower. There were not enough people to staff organizations involved in providing services for the population. As a result we had an extremely poor services industry.

In the course of *perestroika* we managed to boost the rate of the productivity of labour 1.5 times, and for the first time in our history all additional growth of production was obtained without increasing the number of workers. This has made it possible to redistribute the labour force to services, redoubling the dynamics of the sphere.

Prior to *perestroika*, an erroneous investment policy was being pursued and the lion's share of capital investments was earmarked for new construction, while the existing stock of machine-tools and equipment was becoming obsolete and almost no efforts were made to renovate it. For years, producers equipped with obsolete machine-tools kept manufacturing obsolete goods. The situation was particularly poor in the civil branches of the machine-building industries.

With the beginning of *perestroika* a study was conducted in the engineering industries. It followed from the result that 71% cent of production in machine-building in our country did not correspond to international standards and should be stopped. During the same year of 1985 only 3.1% of engineering output had been replaced by new production. A programme of fundamental, large-scale reconstruction and renovation of the machine-building industry was developed and its implementation began. This programme has been functioning for three years now (1989). The rate of growth of capital investments in these branches of the national economy was doubled. Already in 1988, 10% of the production of the engineering industries was new. Here we intend to attain an annual rate of 15% during the next few years. Our strategy is to implement in manufacturing modern highly efficient technology in machine-building on a mass scale, and on this basis modernize and reconstruct all other branches of national economy. We intend to double the co-efficent of renovation of machine-tools and equipment in the country's national economy raising it from 3% to 6%.

The third direction, the successful implementation of which is of decisive importance for the solution of scientific, production and scientific-technological problems, is the transition from the administrative system of management to a new integral system based on the use of economic methods of management, the formation of a developed socialist market, greater material incentives and wide involvement of the working people in management.

In the course of extensive preparatory activities three major laws have been adopted – the law on state enterprise, the law on cooperatives and the law on individual labour activities. As follows from the titles of these laws, we are in favour of pluralism in the development of the relations of ownership and keep on looking for new economic forms. State ownership may be represented not only in its own form, but also in lease relations, joint-stock companies, joint ventures with foreign firms, joint state-cooperative enterprises, etc. Almost 75,000 new cooperatives engaged in practically all forms of economic activities and employing over 1.5 million people have been founded in the country over the last two years. Individual labour activities (ILA) began acquiring a wide scope. Over 700,000 people acquired permits for ILA. It goes without saying that this is only a modest beginning. The development of new forms of economic activities and management will continue to expand and deepen.

But most important of all is the fact that in connection with the newly adopted law all enterprises and organizations began working on the basis of new economic conditions – the conditions of self-financing and self-management, under which they themselves have to earn money for paying for their existence and development, distributing the funds they earned in accordance with their needs. Enterprises have received certain economic freedoms, broader rights in the spheres of labour, wages, construction and reconstruction etc. The old system of directives from above has to a large extent been abolished. From the beginning of this year (1989) the process of transition from centrally distributed production goods and resources to wholesale trade has started. This process will be further speeded up next year with the implementation of the reform of wholesale prices throughout the country – the reform being aimed at bringing our domestic prices closer to the level of the prices of the world market and at reducing the sphere of centrally established prices with the corresponding expansion of the sphere of market prices. Three to four years will be required in order to establish a market for production goods where contractual and free prices will be predominant.

At the same time a financial market, or the market called in the West the market for capital, is being developed. To this end a new banking system is being formed, which will take the place of the three existing state banks funded from the state budget and engaged in distributing state funds. This new banking system will comprise a limited number of large specialized state banks (industrial-construction bank, agrobank, savings bank, etc.) and a large far-flung system of commercial and cooperative banks. At present their number is 65, but each week a new bank is being set up. At the head of this system will be the USSR State Bank – the bank of the banks, regulating the circulation of money in the country and shaping the policy of credits. At the same time the banks will be functioning on the basis of self-financing. A draft law providing greater independence for banks is being developed. The banking system in the USSR is in the process of development, and the banks are gradually becoming real banks.

Another emerging branch of the financial market is the securities market. Individual enterprises and cooperatives have begun issuing stocks. Bonds and other securities are issued by the state. Legislation on stockholding activities is being prepared. The adoption of this legislation will be conducive to the development of stockholding forms of enterprise and organizations. The result will be, in all probability, the emergence of a limited market in securities.

In the next few months the foreign currency market will be organized – for the present in the form of an auction. There the country's enterprises and organizations will be able to buy and sell foreign currency they earned at the existing market rate – the relationship between the rouble and other individual hard and other currencies. Such auctions will be held under the auspices of the USSR bank for external economic relations (Vnesheconombank of the USSR).

Administrative obstacles interfering with the free movement of labour forces are being gradually removed. In the course of *perestroika* we want to avoid unemployment, and for this purpose we have developed a system of labour-hiring offices. A network of organizations for retraining and improving skills of personnel, functioning both at the expense of enterprises and the state is being expanded.

In the sphere of foreign economic activities our strategy is to develop external economic relations at a faster rate than domestic production, to assign greater priority to them. To achieve these ends we spare no effort for improving the competitiveness of Soviet goods for the purpose of exporting them. A draft law on increasing the quality of production has been developed, international standards are being widely introduced. Next year we intend to introduce customer tariffs corresponding to the requirements of GATT.

The process of the decentralization of external economic activities is proceeding rapidly. While previously these activities were monopolised by the departments of the Ministry for Foreign Trade, from 1 April 1989 all enterprises, organizations and cooperatives have the right of direct access to the world market including direct contacts with foreign firms.

Over 300 joint ventures have been set up in the USSR as of 1 April, 1989. This number is growing rapidly. This is connected with the liberalization of the conditions for the establishment of such enterprises which have been recently introduced. Foreign partners enjoy broader opportunities in the investment of capital and the management of the joint enterprise. Taxation of joint ventures is being done on the basis of preferential treatment, introducing broader rights in the sphere of hiring workers, level of wages etc. With the creation of a developed market in the USSR the conditions for establishing such enterprises will be significantly improved.

These three guidelines in economic restructuring are the component parts of the new strategy of the CPSU aimed at speeding up the socioeconomic development of the USSR. Acceleration is interpreted not only, and not so much as, a greater pace of economic growth, but rather as ensuring a new quality of this growth – strong social orientation on the basis of greater efficiency of scientific and technological progress and democratic transformations in management.

Acceleration will contribute to raising the socialist economy to a new qualitative level. The advantages of the socialist system of management will acquire an all-round development, and socialism will be again looked upon as a socioeconomic system with a high level of production and best living standards for the people.

The development of the Soviet economy will be connected, to a large extent, with the process of conversion – the transition of many enterprises from defence production to civilian production. In 1989 the USSR announced that it cut defence expenditure by 14.2% and armaments production by 19%. Intermediate-range missiles are being destroyed in accordance with the agreement between the USSR and the US. The Soviet Union unilaterally began to liquidate chemical weapons. Soviet troops have been withdrawn from Afghanistan. The Soviet Union decided unilaterally to cut the size of the Soviet army based in the European part of the USSR by 500,000 men correspondingly putting out of commission ten thousand tanks located there as well as other armaments. This new policy is closely linked with the new defence doctrine of our country. It should also be noted that defence industries in the USSR have always been partly used for the production of consumer goods for the population, and this fact contributes to their conversion at present. The industries of the defence complex will be used for manufacturing equipment for light industry and the food industry. It has also been decided to increase sharply the volumes of the production of consumer goods by the defence complex as production capacities will be released from the manufacturing of armaments.

Positive changes in the development of our economy go side by side with serious shortcomings in the development of the national economy. Here it should be important to understand that at present we have reached the turning-point, the most crucial stage in the implementation of economic reform.

During the early years of *perestroika* we have passed through the preparatory stage when a new concept of management was being developed, some individual experiments conducted, the most glaring shortcomings inherited by us from the stagnation period were being eliminated. 1988 witnessed the beginning of a fundamentally new stage of *perestroika* – the stage of large-scale action, when from words we finally turned to deeds.

Thus at present we have entered the initial stage of the painful transitional period – from the old administrative system of management and from the old structure of the economy to the new system of management and the new economic structure. We still failed in completely destroying the old and abandoning it. It continues to exist in real life, still dominates, though its power is undermined and its back broken. We were leaving the old principles, but still did not accept the new ones. At present there exist only young shoots which do not yet constitute sufficient stimuli for our rapid development. This coexistence of old and new conditions of economic life, when they struggle and oppose each other, strengthens a number of negative trends burdened with our legacy of mistakes inherited from the stagnation period.

Having received a certain economic autonomy from state bodies, enterprises and organizations are still not yet capable of genuinely managing their newly acquired freedom and independence. They are unable to do this because there is no developed market. Industrial goods are still, as in the past, mostly distributed by state departments on a centralised basis and one cannot simply go and buy them. In addition, prices are rigidly centralized. There is no free financial market either. Goods are still not bought, but 'obtained'.

Here lies the drama of the existing transitional situation resulting from the fact that it is impossible to do everything at once.

The contradictory nature of the existing situation when we have, to a large extent, abandoned administrative methods (for instance, rigid control over the level of wages funds at enterprises) and turned to economic regulation of these processes, resulted in the aggravation of some negative processes. For instance in 1988, due to the mistakenly established rules of the regulation of wages and other money bonuses, the money income of the population increased 9 % more than expected. In the system with free prices for consumer goods and services the balance in the market would have been preserved by the corresponding increase in prices. But with us the level of prices for the vast majority of consumer goods is rigidly centralized and, therefore, turnover in current prices increased more slowly than money incomes – by only 6 %; industrial production increased by 4 %, while agricultural production because of the poor harvest grew only by 1 %. *Perestroika* inherited considerable shortages in supply in the consumer market as well as serious disproportions between the market demand of the population and the volume of consumer goods supplied to the market. At present these disproportions are becoming more acute and the shortage of consumer goods increasing.

This disproportion is largely connected with the deficit in the USSR state budget. This deficit is also a part of that heavy burden we inherited, but is increased due to the fact that allocations for the social sphere grew while the growth of capital investments in production did not stop.

As a result the financial situation in the country deteriorated somewhat, and we must implement a series of measures aimed at financial normalization of the country's economy. Recently the government adopted the following measures: it is intended to contain the growth of capital investments in production, and to change the mechanism of regulating the level of wages not allowing the faster rate of growth in comparison with the growth of labour productivity. Some state expenditures will be cut at the expense of lesser allocations for defence and armaments production, and the expenditure for maintaining management apparatus will be lower. It should be noted that the size of the central apparatus including the workers of local and republican management bodies dropped by 600,000 people or 23% in the first four years of *perestroika*. A number of ministries were disbanded and the management structure simplified. But this still was not sufficient, and at present a further reduction of the size of the management apparatus and the expenditures needed for its upkeep is taking place. In this connection of particular importance is the decision to disband the entire system of the Gosagroprom of the USSR (agro-industrial complex) – the largest of all economic management structures existing in the country.

The greatest significance has been given to the provision of a sufficient amount of foodstuffs and consumer goods for the market, as well as services for the population. For the four years of restructuring the volume of agriculture output in the USSR increased by 9% while the money income of the population grew by 25%. As the price of food in the USSR was traditionally kept at a low level, the shortage of a number of industrial consumer goods in the country became more acute.

A developed programme of measures aimed at the transformation of the economic system in agriculture was adopted at the March Plenary Meeting of the CPSU Central Committee. Its intention was to begin a transition to a new agrarian policy in our country. New features in the policy were to encourage pluralism in the relations of ownership in agriculture – in addition to collective and state farms and to other state agricultural bodies small agricultural cooperatives as well as peasants' economic units based on individual labour – family farms – will become increasingly widespread. At the same time there will be a process of integrating agriculture with industry, trade and other spheres of economic activities, large agrofirms and agricultural conglomerates will emerge. There will be a great diversity of joint, mixed forms of managing agriculture when collective farms will largely become associations of peasants' farms or small cooperatives, state cooperative enterprises, etc.

The transition to leasing land to peasants will be of revolutionary character. Land will be leased by organisations, cooperatives, individual families. Land can be leased for long periods of time – 50 years or longer, with the right of inheritance of leased land. A decree on leased land is being developed at the moment, and the movement on leasing land has already started. Taking into account the accumulated experience a draft law on leasing land and agricultural property and machinery is being prepared.

Here the essential thing is a complete independence of grassroots economic units, when they themselves, without any state plans thrust upon them, will decide what they intend to produce, the quantity of agricultural produce and how they are going to use their incomes. Prices will be established on a centralised basis for only the most important agricultural produce, like grain, cotton, meat, milk etc. and this will be done for only that part of agricultural production which will be produced in accordance with the agreements concluded with state bodies. The rest of agricultural produce will be sold through various channels: consumers' cooperative societies, markets, on the basis of agreed prices. All potatoes, vegetables and fruit produced in agriculture will be sold at agreed prices. Thus a market in agricultural produce will gradually emerge, under the regulating influence of the state, this influence being exerted not through direct administrative channels but through indirect economic ones. The formation of such a market will require a reform of purchase prices and the entire price formation system for agriculture. This is planned to be implemented from 1 January, 1991. All these steps are intended to strengthen peasants' incentives to increase the production of food. At the same time, large capital investments will be earmarked for the preservation of agricultural produce and the development of the food-processing industry. A perspective programme of social development of the countryside, improving the living conditions of peasants, was also adopted.

Large-scale steps aimed at the development of light industry and the entire complex of industries producing consumer goods have been adopted. The technological level of these industries had fallen far behind; in addition, developed machine-building industry producing equipment for light and food industries is practically non-existent in the USSR. It has been decided to begin producing contemporary equipment for these industries in the enterprises of the defence industry, the capacities of which have become released in connection with the reduction of armaments production and its reconversion. At the same time a large loan was negotiated with the FRG and Italy for the purpose of acquiring equipment for light and food industries. We intend to reconstruct and develop the whole complex of industries producing consumer goods for the population and fill the market with these goods. Additional steps were also taken for the development of the entire sphere of services for population. While in the past this sphere grew at an annual rate of 4%, it will be growing now at a rate of 10% and more.

In accordance with projections during the next two years the existing acute shortage in supplying the population with food and consumer goods will be eliminated, but more time will be required to provide the market fully.

Only after saturating the market with consumer goods will it be possible to implement the planned reform of retail prices, in the course of which prices for bread, meat and milk products will rise significantly. State subsidies for the production of the above products exceed 60,000 million roubles. The reform of retail prices will be implemented in such a way that the living standards of the population will remain on the same level. Full compensation for additional expenses in connection with higher prices will be paid to the population. The reform itself will be implemented democratically; the draft will be published for the discussion among people; thus the reform will be implemented only if the majority of the population are in favour of new retail prices.

11

Among important unsolved problems a particularly important place belongs to the question of the convertibility of Soviet currency – the rouble. The resolution of this problem will require some time.

We intend to solve this problem, but it is no easy matter. We will have to build our domestic market, increase the competitiveness of Soviet goods, join international economic organisations (GATT, International Monetary Fund, World Bank for Reconstruction and Development, etc.)

A decree on the establishment in the USSR of special economic zones, zones of free enterprise with beneficial conditions for foreign investors is being prepared. In this connection the question of introducing a special second currency system backed from the very beginning by the reserves of convertible currency, gold reserves of the country and export goods is being considered. This second national currency will be immediately convertible and will acquire wide popularity, first and foremost, in business deals connected with economic activities in the special economic zones as well as with the activities of joint ventures.

Permit me to emphasize once again that the economic reform in the USSR is proceeding at a slow pace, encountering many contradictions, somewhat slower and worse than we had expected. But we have already entered the process of economic reform and, as M.S. Gorbachev rightly notes: 'There is no way back'.

Perestroika in the economy, including *perestroika* in economic management, is not a brief, one-time-only campaign, but a difficult and long period of struggle in the transition from old economic forms to new ones. At present the USSR is in the initial stage of the process of fundamental transformation, when both new and old economic forms coexist. In addition, the old burden of large-scale disproportions existing in a previously distorted economy where almost everything was in short supply, inherited by *perestroika*, slows down its development.

Economic *perestroika* is an innovatory process. We have no experience of such transformations. Mistakes committed in the course of *perestroika* are mostly linked with this lack of experience as well as with the survival of old habits in the thinking and actions of people. These shortcomings, caused by past mistakes, create the necessity of taking special steps aimed at the financial rejuvenation of the national economy. Thus every step forward in economic restructuring encounters difficulties, and *perestroika* is proceeding slower than expected. But the changes that have taken place literally in the course of several years in the consciences of people, a clear programme of economic transformations, gradual shifts in the cause of strengthening social development in the management of *perestroika*, and, most important, democratization of entire society – all this inspires optimism and confidence in the success of *perestroika*.

Economic restructuring has not yet become irreversible, its advance is connected to a large extent with the transition to the 13th Five-Year Period (1991–95), the first five-year period based on the workings of the new economic mechanism.

Intensive work aimed at the restructuring of the economy during the coming years and, first and foremost, at the achievement of higher living standards of people, at democratization and transition to economic methods of management, will make *perestroika* irreversible.

Socialist Planning

MICHAEL ELLMAN

The general idea underlying socialist planning is that the market economy is a good system for ensuring micro-economic rationality (e.g. the efficient organisation of production within individual factories) but that it fails to ensure macro-economic and macro-social rationality (e.g. unemployment, poverty, inequality, pollution, wars). Hence to ensure national economic rationality requires using the state as an instrument to manage the national economy in a way analogous to that in which individual firms manage their factories.

There are a number of radically different ideas of how to realize socialist planning, depending on the writer and on the institutional assumptions made. Perhaps the three most important are the traditional Soviet-type model, the indirectly bureaucratically controlled model and the Tinbergenian model. The traditional Soviet-type model is the model traditionally advocated by Communists. The indirectly bureaucratically controlled model is the goal of reform Communists and of many non-Communist economists aware of the political constraints of state socialism. The Tinbergenian model is a Social Democratic model which has been implemented in the Netherlands since 1945 and which is related to practice elsewhere, e.g. France and Japan. In the first model the central authorities attempt to determine directly all production decisions throughout the economy. In the second, current decision making is in principle left to the (state-owned) enterprises and the authorities restrict themselves to the determination of economic regulators (e.g. prices, taxes, exchange rates, rules of enterprise behaviour), investment planning and the main directions of technical progress. In the third, production is carried out mainly by private firms operating in a market economy but government economic policy, utilizing economic levers such as government expenditure, taxes, incomes policy, interest rates, exchange rates etc, plays a major role in the economy. The third model is often referred to as a 'regulated market economy'.

THE TRADITIONAL SOVIET-TYPE MODEL

This model is usually referred to in economic literature by such terms as 'central planning', the 'statist model', the 'command economy', the 'administrative economy', the 'Stalinist model', the 'shortage economy', or the 'administrative-command' model. It was introduced in the USSR in 1930–34 in an unplanned way as a tool of rapid industrialization, as a reaction to the bitter struggle with the peasantry (1929–33) and the economic crisis (1931–33), and under the influence of Marxist–Leninist ideas. Once adopted it remained fundamentally unchanged for decades, although some relatively limited changes did take place. It succeeded the moneyless, fully planned model of 1929–30, which in turn had succeeded the mixed economy model of the 1920s. Under the impact of the great depression in the capitalist world, the widely accepted image of exceptionally rapid economic development in the USSR in the 1930s, and the position of the USSR within the international Communist movement, it became in the 1930s a widely accepted view that this model, combining national economic planning, state ownership of the means of production and rapid economic growth, was a more advanced economic system than capitalism.

After the Second World War this model was adopted throughout the state socialist world, first in Eastern Europe (1949–53) then in China (1953–57) and then in countries such as Vietnam and Cuba. There were naturally some differences between countries in the application of the model. For example, in Poland agriculture was never predominantly collectivized. Nevertheless, there were some important features of the model common to all these countries. Moreover, aspects of the model (e.g. national economic plans, the stress on state ownership of the means of production, the restrictions on the operation of the price mechanism and a negative attitude to private enterprise) were widely copied throughout the world.

The main features of this model have been analyzed by numerous writers. The present author regards the main features of the model as state ownership of the means of production, political dictatorship, a mono-hierarchical system, imperative planning and physical planning.

In this model, the dominant form of ownership is state ownership. The state owns the land, all other natural resources, and almost all the urban enterprises and their productive assets. Collective ownership (e.g. the property of the collective farms) also exists, but plays a subsidiary role and is expected to be temporary. In due course it is expected to be transformed into the higher form of state ownership. Meanwhile the collective ownership is largely formal because of de facto state control. Private property in the means of production (e.g. animals and tools used on the private plots of collective farmers) also persists on a small scale in some sectors, but is frequently subject to official campaigns directed against it (e.g. during the Cultural Revolution in China). The only fully accepted kind of private (or personal) property is that in consumer goods, but even here the state sector receives priority. Those who use state owned consumer goods (e.g. housing) normally receive greater benefits from them (because of their higher quality) than those who rely on privately owned consumer goods.

The political system in which the traditional model is embedded is a dictatorship, that is a system in which the ruling group impose their will on society and deal with opposition (real and imaginary) by repression. This dictatorship was originally known as the 'dictatorship of the proletariat'. This formula expressed the idea that it was a dictatorship of the proletariat, by the proletariat, for the proletariat. The formula 'dictatorship of the proletariat' was abandoned in the USSR under Khrushchev, along with the Stalinist terror which it had been used to legitimate. Under Gorbachev the desirability of independent social organisations, contested elections, pluralism, a 'state based on law', and of a national parliament with some real power and where a variety of opinions could be expressed, were all officially recognised in the USSR. In addition, the Stalinist use of mass terror was denounced and many of its victims rehabilitated. Furthermore, the role of force in the writings of Marx and Lenin was officially criticized. On the other hand, the formula 'dictatorship of the proletariat' and the political practices that go with it, have been retained elsewhere. For example, in China the formula was still orthodox in the late 1980s.

The result of combining state ownership of the means of production with political dictatorship is to create a 'mono-hierarchical' system. This term describes an economy in which the various economic hierarchies are ultimately all responsible to the party leadership. The central economic bodies may be numerous and disunited, the local bodies numerous and at odds with each other and with the central bodies, but ultimately authority flows from the centre to the periphery in accordance with the principle of 'democratic centralism'.

The imperative character of the plans in this model manifests itself in the fact that planning in this model primarily takes the form of orders, binding on the recipient, as in any army or civil service. Characterizing planning in the traditional model, Stalin long ago, observed that 'our plans are not forecasts but instructions'. This identifies planning with the bureaucratic allocation of resources.

Planning in the traditional model is mainly an activity that takes place in physical terms. That is, it is concerned with allocating tonnes of this, cubic metres of that etc. rather than being primarily concerned with allocating financial flows. In this model, the economy is partially demonetized. Although money exists, and there are financial flows corresponding to the real flows, the former are subordinated to the latter. According to the traditional doctrine, the survival of money and financial flows in a socialist planned economy is something of an anomaly which will in due course disappear. Stalin assumed that in the higher phase of communism, when collective ownership would have disappeared and state ownership have become universal, goods would circulate on the basis of direct product exchange (i.e. physical exchange without the intermediation of money). This doctrine was still orthodox in China in the late 1980s.

In this model, the plans are largely long lists of output targets. They are operationalized by two procedures, listing the corresponding investment projects to be completed, continued or initiated, and 'breaking down' the plan to individual enterprises. These lists and 'broken down' production targets become instructions binding on the relevant bodies.

15

Experience of this model in many countries over several decades has shown that it suffers from some fundamental defects, notably in the fields of agriculture, personal consumption, technical progress, hard currency exports and economic freedom. Hence after shorter or longer periods of experience of it, (almost) all the countries which introduced it have embarked on the reform process. During this process private and/or cooperative sectors have reemerged and the role of prices and market relations has increased.

THE INDIRECTLY BUREAUCRATICALLY CONTROLLED MODEL

In this model (sometimes referred to as 'indirect centralization' or 'indirect planning') the role of indirect methods (e.g. prices and taxes) of plan implementation is stressed. Bureaucratic regulation remains of central importance in the economic system, but instead of attempting to implement their goals by means of instructions, the authorities attempt to implement them by adjusting certain economic regulators (e.g. prices, taxes, the rules governing enterprise behaviour, the rate of exchange etc). The classic example of the indirectly bureaucratically controlled model is the New Economic Mechanism introduced in Hungary in 1968. The model which the official reformers in the USSR appeared to have in mind in the late 1980s as the goal of the reforms initiated under Gorbachev was also of this type (although there are numerous differences between the Soviet reforms of the late 1980s and the 1968 Hungarian reforms).

The reduced role of imperative planning in this model reflects the fact that experience has revealed to the top decision-makers and their advisers its inefficiency. On the other hand, a move to a regulated market economy is regarded by the authorities as politically undesirable, socially unacceptable and economically inefficient.

Experience has shown that this model may bring substantial benefits compared to the traditional model. It may lead to a greater tolerance for the cooperative and private sectors, have a favourable effect on living standards, make enterprise management more cost- and market-conscious and expand economic freedom. Nevertheless, it continues to suffer from a number of fundamental problems and cannot be considered a long run terminus for the reform process. The problems it is liable to face, include the following:

1. In this model there is a major role for the central authorities in investment planning. It is argued that current decisions should be left to the enterprises but that much investment should remain planned or at any rate influenced by the state (e.g. by loans and grants). This assumes that investment planning is, or could become, a socially rational process. In fact it is an arena for bureaucratic conflicts which produces typical 'pork barrel' outcomes. Hence investment in this model remains wasteful.

2. Weak control over costs. In the absence of strong competitive pressures, and given the partial persistence of the logic of the former system, the persistence of widespread shortages, a paternalistic owner of the means of production and a common interest by enterprise management and the labour force in raising

16

wages and extracting more resources from the higher bodies, control over costs is weak. This leads to substantial inflationary pressure.

3. The regulation illusion. The intellectual fathers of this model imagine that by suitable manipulation of the levers of indirect control it is possible to ensure that the enterprises take the right decisions from the point of view of the central planners. Experience has shown that although this is possible in some sectors (eg agriculture) in many sectors it is an illusion. The planners are often no more able by indirect levers than they had been previously been able by direct levers, to guide the enterprises to socially rational decisions.

4. The hidden mechanism of recentralization. There is a strong tendency to strengthen the role of instructions and central decision making regardless of the declared aims of the authorities. This is largely a result of two factors. First, the authorities have numerous and partially inconsistent goals. Hence they cannot all be fulfilled at once. Therefore some organization always feels a need to intervene because the goal or goals with which it is concerned are not being achieved. Furthermore, priority among the main goals shifts over time, which appears to require additional interventions. Secondly, there is no adequate mechanism within the model for the reconciliation of economic conflicts because the role of market forces is so small. For example, a conflict between two firms for the output of a third may require administrative intervention since there is no alternative domestic supplier and access to hard currency imports is severely limited.

5. Persistence of shortages. Even though the extent and intensity of shortages in this model is normally less than in the directly planned mode, still many shortages persist and have an adverse affect on everyday life and business efficiency.

6. Redistribution of profits. The logic underlying the introduction of this model is that substantial differences in profitability between enterprises and sectors will emerge as a result of differences in efficiency. In practice, however, there is an observable tendency to redistribute the profits generated by the system by means of changes to prices or taxes, so as to more or less equalize profitability throughout the economy. This ensures that the bureaucratic bargaining process is much more important for the enterprises than their actual economic efficiency.

7. Persistence of the logic of the former system. Although in this model two of the main features of the traditional Soviet-type model (imperative planning and physical planning) have been abolished, the remaining three (state ownership, political dictatorship and a mono-hierarchical system) persist. Hence many of the negative characteristics of the traditional Soviet-type system persist, irrespective of the wish of the authorities to introduce real reforms. The logic of the former system remains partially unchanged because so many of the features of the traditional model have been retained. For example, although in this model entrepreneurship is officially held in high regard, the directors of state enterprises display little of it with respect to dynamic market performance (although they may display a lot of it with respect to obtaining more resources from the authorities, and/or reducing their supply responsibilities or tax obligations). This is entirely natural since they remain cogs in a complex bureaucratic system. They

are appointed, promoted and dismissed by the higher authorities who naturally expect them to respond to official wishes (eg the latest official campaign). Hence in practice the market orientation of the economy is severely limited.

8. Paternalism of the authorities. In this model, as in the traditional Soviet-type model, economic stability plays an important role in the paternalist mode of legitimation. Hence although bankruptcy is officially accepted as an efficiency-raising method of last resort, in practice it happens very rarely. Normally the authorities are very reluctant to let state-owned enterprises actually go bankrupt and their former employees become unemployed and will usually ensure that inefficiency has no adverse consequences by adjustments in prices, taxes, accounting or auditing rules, loans or grants. Hence the budget constraint stays soft, inefficiency and shortage are encouraged and structural adjustment is slow.

9. Restrictions on the cooperative and private sectors. Although one of the features of this model is the greater scope for cooperative and private economic activities, the state sector remains favoured. Hence if the cooperative or private sectors grow 'excessively' the authorities will increase taxes, cut the availability of inputs, tighten up the rules governing private employment, launch official investigations and/or use police measures against the sector, limit the use to which money earned in this sector can be put, restrict the possibilities of employment and investment in this sector, etc. One of the features of this model is the continuous struggle between the state sector, which operates under indirect bureaucratic control, and the non-state sector which is market oriented but operates under strong bureaucratic restrictions.

As a result of all these problems, there is a tendency for the indirectly bureaucratically controlled model to be a transitional stage in the movement from the traditional Soviet planning model to a regulated market economy.

THE TINBERGENIAN MODEL

According to this model, a plan is a consistent numerical exploration of the future which provides data useful for economic policy. It is not a set of instructions, nor does it have to be fulfilled. It is simply part of the policy making process in a regulated market economy which improves the relationship between policy goals and outcomes. This understanding of planning, as a subordinate but useful part of the policy process in a regulated market economy, has been implemented in the Netherlands since 1945. It has been implemented by the Central Planning Bureau, of which Tinbergen was the first director. This has regularly published annual economic plans and macro-economic forecasts and also undertaken a wide variety of policy simulations both for the government and also for independent organisations such as political parties and trade unions.

The simulations made by the Central Planning Bureau in this institutional model make extensive use of econometric model building. This enables maximum use to be made of statistical methods, the available data and computational techniques, makes the relationship between the conclusions and their causes clear, enables alternative policies to be quickly compared, and makes the procedures and conclusions of the Central Planning Bureau seem very authoritative to innumerates. The theory underlying this model was developed by Tinbergen, building on earlier work by Frisch. The best known proposition of Tinbergen's theory is the necessary condition for the achievement of policy goals that there be at least as many instruments as targets. An important conclusion from the later work of the Central Planning Bureau was the view that in the Netherlands (and also in some other countries) in the mid 1970s the balanced budget multiplier was negative. Another important conclusion from the later work of the Central Planning Bureau was the view that the sharp increase in unemployment in the Netherlands in the 1970s was of a structural kind which could not be reduced by demand management.

This style of planning can be considered 'socialist' in the social-democratic sense that it forms an integral part of an organized civil society in which public policy plays a major role. This public policy is aimed at such goals as the provision of public or quasi-public goods (public transport, education and medical care, safe air, water, food and soil), an equitable income distribution, economic growth, industrialisation, the emancipation of formerly underprivileged groups etc. The society recognises and protects negative freedom and fully accepts the usefulness and value of market relations and private ownership, but also looks positively on the state as an active element in attempts to achieve public goals.

The role of the Central Planning Bureau in this model is not unique to the Netherlands. Similar organizations exist in France (*Commissariat Général du Plan*) Japan (Economic Planning Agency) and elsewhere. All three organisations were established shortly after the end of World War II in a political situation in which influential groups wished to introduce the traditional Soviet-type model. All three quickly evolved away from the traditional Soviet-type model and their activities gave a new interpretation to the term 'national economic planning'. Tinbergen's theoretical work linked up this new reality with econometrics and with the theory of economic policy. The French example had a big influence in the UK in the 1960s and in the international economics literature in the 1960s and 1970s. The Japanese example, as part of the 'Japanese model', had a big influence in the NICs in the 1970s and 1980s. The experience both of Eastern Asia and of Western Europe has influenced US policy discussion.

The role of the Central Planning Bureau in this model is similar in some respects to that of academic and private sector policy analysis and forecasting institutes in countries such as West Germany and the USA. The main difference is that as a part of the state apparatus it plays an important role in the social consensus building that plays a key role in policy making in countries such as the Netherlands and Japan.

This model is attractive to significant groups in countries that have had a long experience of the reform process and of attempts to introduce the indirect bureaucratic control model and where influential social groups wish to try the regulated market model. For example, as part of the 1988–89 Polish economic reforms, the Polish central planning commission, a traditional Gosplan type organisation, was abolished and a new central planning office, with forecasting and policy exploration tasks was created in its place. The intention of the Polish authorities was that the new body should have a similar function to the one that the Central Planning Bureau has in the Netherlands. One of the first acts (April 1989) of the new Polish planning organisation was to reach a cooperation agreement with the Dutch Central Planning Bureau. An important aspect of this cooperation agreement was to be an exchange of experiences and opinions about the role of a central planning bureau in a regulated market economy.

The relevance of the Tinbergenian model depends, *inter alia*, on the existence of a government which has wide freedom of manoeuvre in economic policy. To the extent that economic policy is constrained by adherance to rules (e.g. concerning the exchange rate or the rate of growth of the money supply) or the economic situation is primarily determined by external factors (e.g. the world market, the policies of other countries, the wishes of foreign creditors) then the relevance of the model is much reduced. The relevance of the model also requires that the politicians and leading officials believe both that the models of the Central Planning Bureau are a good reflection of economic reality and that discretionary economic policy is desirable.

ASSUMPTIONS COMMON TO ALL VARIETIES OF SOCIALIST PLANNING

All varieties of socialist planning assume that politicians are concerned with the general interest, that discretionary economic policy is desirable, that government economic policy is reasonably effective in achieving its goals, that economic policy is primarily concerned with the achievement of its ostensible goals, that the models of the planners are a reasonable reflection of economic reality, and that society is a flexible entity which can be manipulated by the authorities. All of these assumptions are controversial and none are universally accepted.

BIBLIOGRAPHY

The traditional Soviet-type model
Brus, W. 1972. *The Market in a Socialist Economy*. London: Routledge & Kegan Paul.
Ellman, M. 1978. The fundamental problem of socialist planning. *Oxford Economic Papers*, July.
Grossman, G. 1963. Notes for a theory of the command economy. *Soviet Studies* XV(2), 101–23.
Kornai, J. 1959. *Overcentralization in Economic Administration*. Trans. John Knapp. London: Oxford University Press.
Lisichkin, G. 1988. Mify i real 'nost'. *Novyi Mir*, 11.
Zaleski, E. 1980. *Stalinist Planning for Economic Growth, 1933–1952*. Chapel Hill N.C.

The indirectly bureaucratically controlled model
Abalkin, L. 1989. Kakim byt' novomu pyatletnomu planu? *Kommunist* no. 6 (English translation likely in *Problems of Economics*).
Csaba, L. 1989. Some lessons from two decades of economic reform in Hungary. *Communist Economies* 1(1).

Fehér, F. 1982. Paternalism as a mode of legitimation in Soviet-type societies. In *Political Legitimation in Communist States*, ed. T.H. Rigby and F. Fehér, London.

Hall, J.B. 1986. Plan bargaining in the Hungarian economy: an interview with Dr. Laszlo Antal. *Comparative Economic Studies* XXVIII(2), summer.

Kornai, J. 1986. The Hungarian reform process. *Journal of Economic Literature* XXIV(4), December.

Kornai, J. 1988. Individual freedom and reform of the socialist economy. *European Economic Review* 32(2/3), March.

Laky, T. 1980. The hidden mechanism of recentralization in Hungary. *Acta Oeconomica* 24(1–2).

Novozhilov, V.V. 1970. *Problems of Cost-benefit Analysis in Optimal Planning* (translated from Russian). White Plains, New York: International Arts and Sciences Press.

Swaan, W. 1990. Price regulation in Hungary: Indirect but comprehensive bureaucratic control. *Comparative Economic Studies* 1.

The Tinbergenian model

Het Plan van de Arbeid (Labour's plan). 1935. Amsterdam.

Driehuis, W., Fase, M.M.G. and den Hartog, D. (eds.) 1988. *Challenges for Macroeconomic Modelling*. Amsterdam.

Estrin, S. and Holmes, P. 1983. *French Planning in Theory and Practice*. London.

Griffiths, R.T. 1980. The Netherlands Central Planning Bureau, in Griffiths, R.T. (ed.) *The Economy and Politics of the Netherlands since 1945*. The Hague.

den Hartog, H. and Tjan, H.S. 1976. Investments, wages, prices and demand for labour. *De Economist* 124(1–2).

Hughes Hallett, A.J. 1989. Econometrics and the theory of economic policy: The Tinbergen-Theil contributions 40 years on. *Oxford Economic Papers* 41(1), January.

Killick, T. 1976. The possibilities of development planning. *Oxford Economic Papers* 28(2).

Knoester, A. 1983. Stagnation and the inverted Haavelmo effect: some international evidence. *De Economist* 131(4).

Komiya, R. 1975. Planning in Japan, in M. Bornstein (ed.), *Economic Planning: West and East*. Cambridge, Mass. Reprinted in M. Bornstein (ed.), *Comparative Economic Systems: Models and Cases*, 4th ed. Homewood, Illinois, 1979.

Norwegian issue. 1968. *Economics of Planning* 8(1–2).

Tinbergen, J. 1952. *On the Theory of Economic Policy*. Amsterdam: North-Holland. 2nd ed., 1955.

Tinbergen, J. 1956. *Economic Policy: Principles and Design*. Amsterdam: North-Holland. Rev. ed., 1967.

Tinbergen, J. 1964. *Central Planning*. New Haven.

Tinbergen, J. 1967. *Development Planning*. London: Weidenfeld & Nicholson.

China's Economic Reforms

PETER NOLAN

Background to the reforms. In contrast to other areas of the world of comparable size, for most of the past 2000 years China's huge territory was united, ruled by a centralized imperial bureaucracy. Despite bureaucratic interventions, the peace and unity which this provided permitted enormous long-term pre-modern economic growth with widespread production for profit in the market, which in most products, comprised one enormous free trade area. One of the great historical questions still unanswered, is why this system with such vibrant medieval 'capitalist sprouts' in many parts of China experienced no independent, technological breakthrough comparable to the European Industrial Revolution.

For most of the late 19th and early 20th centuries China's political situation was chaotic, which greatly handicapped economic development. By the 1930s, China was still a poor, underdeveloped economy with the vast bulk of the population working in, and most output contributed by, agriculture. However, rapid growth occurred pre-1949 in a narrow range of modern industries, highly concentrated geographically, especially in Shanghai and in the network of towns spreading down the Yangtse River. Under different conditions, notably more effective state action to assist economic development, the Chinese economy could have advanced much more rapidly than it did pre-1949. However, the dynamism displayed by Chinese capitalism under disadvantageous circumstances, in response to the 'demonstration effect' provided by modern imports and goods produced in 'foreign' factories in China gave evidence of the enormous growth potential of China's economy.

After the 1949 revolution, under the leadership of the Communist Party, China constructed a Stalinist material balance administrative planning system. Over the long-term under Mao, China's planned economy performed well in certain respects. Net material product grew at an annual average rate of almost 6% from 1953 to 1978 (Table 1) which was a strong performance compared both to China's past and to most developing countries. The economic structure shifted rapidly away from agriculture towards industry, and China attained some

22

long-term growth in consumption (the reported average annual growth rate of real consumption per person from 1952 to 1976 was 2.2%) (ZGTJZY, 1988, p. 43). Various measures ensured a low degree of inequality in income distribution enabling China to achieve a high degree of poverty relief from the available consumption fund.

However, these achievements have to be set against serious shortcomings. The Stalinist structure achieved growth in a wasteful fashion, requiring a large and growing amount of capital to produce a unit of output (Table 2). Although initially pursued as a desirable goal, the micro-economic problems of the administered economy compelled long-term priority for heavy industry (Table 1). Industrial labour productivity expanded quite rapidly over the long-term, but only through enormous capital inputs, so that in state industry output per unit of capital fell by no less than 0.7% per annum from 1952 to 1978 (Riskin, 1987, p. 264). In agriculture, rapid increases in capital stock also were accompanied by serious declines in capital productivity. Rapid growth of the rural workforce

Table 1   Key economic indicators, All China (output and income data all at comparable prices)

	Av. annual growth rate (%)	
	1953/78	1978/87
Total social product (gross material product)	7.4	10.8
Gross value of agricultural output	2.9	6.5
Gross value of industrial output[1]	10.6	11.9
of which: heavy industry	13.0	10.0
light industry	8.7	14.1
National income (net material product)	5.7	9.0
of which: agriculture	1.9	6.0
industry	10.5	10.4
construction	5.9	12.8
transport	6.3	9.5
commerce	3.2	9.9
Population	2.2	1.3

Note: (1) Including output produced at village (*cun*) and lower levels.
Source: ZGTJNJ, 1988, 38, 45, 52, and 97.

Table 2   Increase in national income per 100 yuan of accumulation (unit: *yuan*) (current prices)

1953/57	32	1966/70	26	1976/80	24
1958/62	1	1971/75	16	1981/85	41
1963/65	57				

Source: ZCTJNT, 1988, 69

combined with fundamental shortcomings in rural collective institutions to produce stagnant agricultural labour productivity between 1952 and 1978 (Riskin, 1987, p. 271). The reported growth rate of average consumption per person in official statistics almost certainly overstates the real growth of consumption. The available data (see Table 3) show virtually no long-term growth in grain consumption per person and very little in the other main agricultural products. Consumption per person of light industrial products with agricultural raw materials as their main input (especially textiles) was also virtually stagnant. Housing space per person probably didn't increase at all. The main improvement occurred in a narrow range of consumer durables, though the initial base was almost zero and stocks per 100 households in the late 1970s still were extremely low. In the early 1950s China achieved a considerable reduction in the proportion of the population in poverty. However, the low rate of growth of average incomes thereafter meant that there were very limited possibilities for further poverty reduction. With good reason China's post-Mao leadership characterized their own economy pre-1978 as one with 'equality in poverty'.

Moreover, the long-term picture conceals major short-term fluctuations in China's economic performance under Mao. Most notably, after the 'Great Leap

Table 3 Changes in consumption level of the Chinese population

	1975	1978	1987
Value of average p.c. consumption: index, at comparable prices:—			
whole population	71	100	197
urban residents	64	100	176
rural residents	74	100	201
Average p.c. consumption:			
grain (kilograms)	203	196	251
oil (kilograms)	2.4	1.6	5.4
pork (kilograms)	5.1	7.7	14.5
eggs (kilograms)	1.3	2.0	5.6
sugar (kilograms)	1.5	3.4	6.7
cloth (metres)	6.8	8.0	11.3
aquatic products (kilograms)	4.3	3.5	5.5
Average stocks of consumer durables (per 100 people):			
sewing machines	–	3.5	11.0
watches	–	8.5	42.8
bicycles	–	7.7	27.1
radios	–	7.8	24.1
tv sets	–	0.3	10.7
Average amount of housing space p.c. (sq. metres):			
cities	–	4.2	8.5
villages	–	8.1	16.0

Sources: ZGTJNJ, 1988, 801–3.

Forward' (1958–9), output fell precipitously. The average daily availability of food energy per person is estimated to have fallen from 2164 kilocalories in 1957 to just 1535 kilocalories in 1960 (Riskin, 1987, p. 128), a desperately low average figure. The overall impact on China's population was devastating. Establishing the exact magnitudes of deaths from famine is impossible; current estimates for China in 1958–61 range from between 15 to almost 30 million (Riskin, 1987, p. 136). Under Mao the Chinese version of the Stalinist system did well in meeting 'basic needs' in normal times, leading to low mortality rates and high life expectancy compared to other developing countries. However, due to its highly centralized nature, the same system was capable of launching mass movements which could have disastrous results. The great lowering of mortality which the system achieved in normal times has to be set against the huge excess mortality which it produced in 1959–61.

The reforms. Mao Zedong's death in 1976 radically altered the balance of political forces in China. It opened up the possibility for a much wider range of economic analysis and for an honest assessment of the Chinese post-1949 record. There was wide agreement after Mao's death that there were fundamental defects with the over-centralized economic system which China adopted under Soviet influence:

> Such a structure put the national economy in a straightjacket, discouraging initiative in all quarters, causing serious waste of manpower, materials and capital, and greatly hampering the growth of the productive forces. For many years, this was a major cause of the slow pace of the growth of the Chinese economy and the improvement of the living standards of the Chinese people (Liu and Wang, 1984).

Between the historic Third Plenum of the Eleventh Central Committee of the CCP in December 1978 and the late 1980s massive changes occurred. However, there was not a clear programme. Indeed, China's reforms in the 1980s have been likened to a person crossing a river who moves forward from stone to stone without a clear idea of where the next one is since it is hidden under the water ahead.

In the early stages, the pace of advance was much the fastest in agriculture. The agricultural reforms began in the late 1970s with tentative steps to contract land out to groups within the production team, but progressed rapidly by 1983 to full-scale contracting out of collective farmland to individual households. This was, in effect, the largest, most egalitarian land reform in history, since land was mainly divided up among China's 200 million rural households on a locally equal per person basis. 'De-collectivization' did not apply to many types of large agricultural means of production nor to some important collective activities. However, the rural labour process underwent a revolution. Peasants were now working for themselves and could retain any surplus produce or income after meeting state compulsory quotas. The far-reaching changes in rural economic

25

organization provided a breakthrough in people's thinking about the Stalinist economic system.

A considerable contribution to development can be made in labour-surplus countries by small-scale labour-intensive enterprises, as the Japanese and East Asian NICs' experience has demonstrated. Under Mao, in rural areas especially, growth of these activities was confined to only a few types of products (mainly inputs for agriculture), with absolute priority in labour allocation accorded to agriculture. In urban areas growth of the small-scale labour-intensive sector was held in check by tight controls over collective enterprises, including stigmatisation as 'bourgeois' of many of the service activities in which these enterprises could compete. In both town and countryside the slow growth of real incomes also held back this sector, since the products it is able to produce most efficiently are usually wage goods and services.

This sector underwent a revolution in the 1980s. Firstly, the enormous rise in agricultural labour productivity greatly increased the availability of rural surplus labour. Secondly, controls on the collective non-farm sector were relaxed in the early 1980s. Enterprises obtained greatly increased entrepreneurial freedom, and within a short time collective non-farm enterprises operated in a competitive environment. The private sector was legally permitted and from early in the 1980s a relaxed official attitude was adopted towards private labour hiring. As early as 1983 there existed private enterprises with several hundred employees. Indeed, in formerly less prosperous part of China such as Wenzhou, private enterprise became the dominant form of rural non-farm business organization by the mid-1980s (Nolan and Dong, 1989). While the collective enterprise remained dominant in the more advanced areas, such as Southern Jiangsu, a wide variety of new sub-contracting arrangements was introduced. In the small-scale, non-farm sector, as in agriculture, there was tremendous popular support for the increased operation of market forces, which people perceived could for some time only mean an increase in employment opportunities and in family income.

In some respects, the biggest single change in China's political economy after Mao's death was in attitude towards the international economy. Numerous laws were passed with the intention of encouraging foreign investment. Initially, foreign investment was isolated from the rest of the economy in four 'special economic zones', but the way was quickly opened for wider access of foreign investment to China, in which the most important measure was the establishment in 1984 of fourteen 'open coastal cities'. In 1980 China resumed its membership of the International Monetary Fund and the World Bank. These steps were important both in terms of access to capital but also for the considerable weight of policy advice that subsequently flowed from those institutions to the Chinese government. A radical shift occurred too in the 1980s in China's attitude towards foreign trade. Instead of being regarded as a sphere for the exploitation of poor countries, China's leadership shifted to an explicit recognition of the enormous contribution international trade can make to economic advance. China has an abundance of natural resources, a large pool of low-wage, surplus labour, and many areas with strong commercial and manufacturing traditions. Moreover, some potential trade competitors from East Asia were moving into more sophisticated exports with higher value-added per worker as their labour costs rose. China's leaders were acutely aware that she had missed out on a great historic opportunity to expand exports rapidly in the 1960s and 1970s. Given the right set of policies there were considerable opportunities to expand export earnings, even in the more slowly growing world economy of the 1980s. A number of measures were taken to enliven the over-centralized administration of international trade, so that more direct contacts could be established between domestic enterprises and international buyers and suppliers. Alongside some decentralisation of the organization of foreign trade went a considerable devaluation of the *yuan*, and exporting enterprises even were permitted to retain a proportion of the foreign exchange earned from exports. The extent of the 'airlock' between the domestic and the world economy was much reduced compared to the Maoist period. Moreover, the increased role of market forces within the domestic economy meant that domestic enterprises were keener to take advantage of opportunities to profit from international trade.

In the late 1970s over 80% of the value of industrial output was still produced in state enterprises, so that improving their effectiveness was of central importance to the long-term success of the reform. However, their reform proved more difficult to accomplish than that of the collective and private sectors. Nevertheless, considerable changes did occur in the first decade of the post-Mao reforms. The overall objective of the reforms was to increase enterprise autonomy, raising enterprises' efficiency through new incentives to compete in the market place. The attempts to do this can be divided into two phases with the turning point being the 1984 'Decision of the Central Committee on Reform of the Economic Structure'.

In the first, cautious phase the principal changes were in internal enterprise organization, with a return to 'Taylorist' methods of work organization and remuneration. Some adjustment occurred too in industrial relative prices, with the state attempting to bring prices closer into line with costs of production in different industrial sectors. The main method through which it was hoped to increase enterprises' vitality was increased rights to retain profits, which spread rapidly to most state enterprises in the early 1980s. However, this did little to increase enterprise incentives. Given the still fundamentally unreformed nature of the Chinese industrial price system, profits were a poor indicator of enterprise performance, and profit retention became the subject of protracted bargaining between the enterprise and its superior planning authorities. Rather than work to cut costs to raise profits the system placed a premium on cultivating connections to obtain through bargaining a better contracted profit retention share. Beginning in 1983 an attempt was made to circumvent these difficulties by substituting a series of taxes for profit sharing. However, because enterprises and sectors faced unequal market conditions, especially in the form of prices that were more or less divorced from enterprises' costs of production, the crucial tax was the 'adjustment tax' which itself became the subject of protracted bargaining.

By the mid-1980s it was obvious that attempts to reform industrial enterprises would be unsuccessful under the existing price system, and in October 1984 the Central Committee announced that price reform was 'the key to reform of the entire economic structure'. A considerable reduction in state price control occurred in 1985. However, overnight elimination of price control in a system where prices bore little relationship to supply and demand would have produced chaos. Accordingly, the decision was taken to introduce a 'dual track' system, with part of the enterprise output sold at state fixed prices and part at either free market or 'floating' prices (the state determining the boundaries of the 'float'). By 1987, the proportion of non-agricultural consumer goods and industrial means of production sold at state fixed prices had fallen to around 50% and 65% respectively.

The main achievements of the economic reforms. The sharp alteration in China's economic institutions greatly increased competition, shifted resource allocation and considerably increased labour intensity for much of the workforce. This was accompanied by an accelerated growth rate and a much altered growth pattern. The average annual growth rate of net material product rose from its long-term trend of under 6% per annum to around 9% from 1978 to 1987 (Table 1). Moreover, this acceleration in output growth occurred simultaneously with a decline in the annual growth rate of population to only around 1.3% in the 1980s (Table 1). Due to the relatively large number of people entering the reproductive age groups from the mid-1980s to the mid-1990s and the many difficulties associated with trying to implement too harsh a population control policy in the early 1980s, China's natural growth rate of population was rising in the late 1980s (from a low point of 1.1% in 1984 to 1.4% in 1987) (ZGTJZY, 1988, 14), but was still much below the long-term trend rate of the Maoist period.

At least as important as the overall acceleration in the growth rate was the striking change in the balance of growth. Agricultural growth exploded as the rural reforms unfolded. In the early 1980s the average real annual growth rate of agricultural output was close to 10% (ZGTJZY, 1988, 22), an extraordinarily high figure for a country as big as China with limited possibilities to export farm produce. Even over the whole decade the growth rate of net agricultural output was almost three times the long-term rate of the Maoist period (Table 1). These figures shed light retrospectively upon the defects of the commune system. The overall industrial growth rate changed little after 1978. However, major changes occurred in the balance of industrial growth, of which the most striking was the reversal in the growth rates of heavy and light industry, reflecting China's move away from a Stalinist economy. During the reform decade the gross value of light industrial output accelerated to a real annual average growth rate of over 14%, while that of heavy industry declined to around 10% (Table 1).

A number of factors contributed to this. On the demand side urban and rural purchasing power grew rapidly, and the income elasticity of demand for light industrial output was mostly higher for light industry's products than for direct consumption of food. On the supply side, the production of light industrial inputs (e.g. cotton, leather, timber) from agriculture grew rapidly, and much capacity shifted from heavy to light industrial production. Moreover, the overall productivity of capital almost certainly increased (Table 2) so that less output was required of the capital goods industries to produce a unit of final product. The main contribution to improved capital productivity came from agriculture in which the acceleration in real output growth was achieved with stagnant total fixed capital stock (Nolan, 1988). The second important contribution to increased capital productivity came from the rapid expansion of output and employment in labour-intensive non-farm activities. The rapid shift in employment towards the tertiary sector (its share of total employment rose from 11.0% in 1978 to 17.4% in 1987) (ZGTJZY, 1988, p. 17) helped increase the efficiency of resource use through widening markets and better provision of information. Moreover, rapid growth occurred in output and employment in labour-intensive industry, much of which produced light industrial products and often used capital relatively efficiently. The number of workers in rural 'township enterprises' rose from 28 million to 88 million between 1978 and 1987 (ZGTJNJ, 1988, pp. 292–4), while the number employed in urban collective enterprises rose from 24 million in 1980 to 35 million in 1987 (ZGTJZY, 1988, p. 15). The share of the non-state sector in the total gross value of industrial output (at current prices) rose from just 19% in 1978 (ZGTJZY, 1986, p. 48) to over 40% in 1987 (ZGTJZY, 1988, p. 36).

Following a long period of slow export growth and a steadily falling share of world trade, China's export performance improved markedly in the 1980s. In volume terms, China's export growth rate rose from 6% per annum in 1968–80 to 12% in 1980–86 (World Bank, 1988, pp. 242–3), despite the fact that the latter period was one with great difficulties in world trade. China's share of world trade rose from 0.8% in 1978 to 1.7% in 1987, and the ratio of its exports to GNP rose from just 5% in 1978 to 13% in 1987 (Wang, 1989b), a turnaround which both assisted domestic growth and was a reflection of improved domestic supply conditions.

Few nations, let alone those of China's size, have experienced an improvement in living standards in such a short space of time as occurred in China in the 1980s. Chinese data show a doubling of average real material consumption per person between 1978 and 1987 (Table 3). Due to problems with the relative prices used to make the estimates, it is possible that these data somewhat overstate the degree of advance. Nevertheless, the less problematic data in physical units confirm remarkable progress (Table 3). The smallest increase was in grain consumption, but an annual level of over 200 kilograms per person is high relative to other developing countries, and it would be surprising if levels of direct consumption rose much above this. Moreover, the share of 'fine grain' (principally rice and wheat) in peasants' grain consumption rose sharply from 50% in 1978 to around 80% in the mid-1980s (ZGTJZY, 1988, p. 103). The average consumption per person of the principal subsidiary foodstuffs rose extremely rapidly after, at best, stagnation over a long period. For centuries China's average daily calorie intake per person had probably fluctuated around 2000 calories. As population expanded arable area per person declined while labour inputs and yield per hectare increased, leaving output per person more or less constant: in Ishikawa's (1967) graphic phrase China simply moved along the 'subsistence parabola'. In the 1980s China moved sharply away from the parabola, with average daily calorie intake per person rising to over 2,700 in the mid-1980s (Nolan, 1988). A considerable advance occurred in average cloth consumption per person in the 1980s (Table 3). Even more impressive was the doubling in housing space per person (Table 3). Such an advance in housing provision has rarely been seen in any country and certainly not in any of the centrally planned economies, in which housing has been systematically squeezed. However, the most remarkable increased were in consumer durables, produced by better-motivated state enterprises, heavy industry reallocating some of its capacity and the rapid expansion of small-scale, mainly collective, enterprises. Average stocks per 100 households of such items as sewing machines, watches, bicycles, radios and TV sets rose rapidly in the 1980s (Table 3).

Many aspects of great importance to people's quality of life are impossible to quantify. Enormous changes in these areas occurred in the 1980s, mostly in a direction that improved the quality of life. Although the CCP still exercised strong control over social and cultural life, the boundaries of individual freedom widened greatly. A vast array of new cultural possibilities appeared, including access to non-Chinese culture, especially through television. Almost as important as the expansion of cultural freedom was the great increase in freedom of movement in the 1980s. Increased incomes and the availability of food outside state rations tied to place of residence released Chinese people to move about their country, an activity strictly limited pre-1976.

It can be argued that changes in the average living standard is a less important indicator of development than changes in the number and proportion of people in poverty. A wide variety of sources suggests that the Chinese post-1978 reforms were accompanied by a rapid reduction in absolute poverty, partially through the release of production potential in poor areas which the rural reforms made directly possible, partly through 'trickle down' effects to poor people from richer strata and areas, and partly through state policies to use some of the benefits of growth to help disadvantaged areas. The World Bank concludes:

> Using a poverty line based on food intake requirements of 2185 kilocalories per day it is estimated that the proportion of the rural population in poverty declined from 31% in 1979 to 13% in 1982 ...; *the speed and scale of the improvement is probably unprecedented in human history* (World Bank, 1986, 30; my emphasis – P.N.).

Detailed analysis of an individual province such as Anhui shows that almost every county in China obtained some increase in real average income per person between 1978 and the mid-1980s (Nolan, 1988).

Problems and debates. Overall the first decade of China's economic reform since Mao's death was outstandingly successful. However, by 1988 the reforms were far from complete and many problems had emerged. China's economic reform can be divided into two stages, through there is no neat boundary between them. The first stage was characterized mainly by relatively simple institutional changes in which reform was widely welcomed by the producers who were directly affected. This, broadly speaking, applied to the agricultural reforms and the reform of the small-scale, non-farm sector. Due, mainly, to irrationalities in the previous institutional arrangements which had suppressed the growth of, and greatly reduced the efficiency of capital and labour in, these sectors, institutional reform in the labour process and in market relationships produced outstanding results. This underpinned the great improvement in living standards in the 1980s. However, many of these were once-off gains and could not be expected to produce the same rates of growth over a long period. Moreover, in the second phase of reform attention switched to large and medium-sized state-run enteprises. These enterprises are much less flexible than agriculture and small, non-farm enterprises, and their workers and managers form a privileged elite for whom the reforms increase uncertainty. Moreover, in the second stage of the reform it became increasingly clear that a partially reformed economy was associated with a wide range of economic, political and social problems. Indeed, by 1988 most Chinese economists felt China to be in an acute crisis, which was in sharp contrast to the heady successes of the early and mid-1980s. The crisis related to a number of issues which will now be examined in turn.

The politics of reform. China has a huge number of Party and government bureaucrats who have for decades provided direct instructions to enterprises. A radical change in their role was called for under the reforms. Zhao Ziyang declared in 1986:

'Economic departments of the government at all levels should no longer devote their energy to assigning quotas, approving construction projects and allotting funds and materials. Instead, they should do overall planning, implement policies, organise co-ordination, provide services, use economic means of regulation and exercise effective inspection and supervision ... *All personnel of government should fully understand the necessity and historic significance of this transformation*' (my emphasis – P.N.).

However, the old habits proved extremely hard to break. Still in the late 1980s, central and, increasingly, local authorities exercised considerable control over state enterprises, subsidising loss-making enterprises, heavily taxing profitable ones, and setting up new administrative bodies to take over many of the functions formally devolved to enterprises. Only around one-fifth of large and medium-sized state enterprises had gained real freedom from administrative authorities by 1986/7.

China's economic reform of the 1980s destabilized her politics. The reforms had a massive impact on popular consciousness. After decades of stability in basic values tremendous psychological disorientation was caused by a sudden shift away from those values towards an unclear new set of values. On the one

31

hand China's population was told that the old values of 'self-reliance' and 'serve the people' were to be replaced by new values such as 'take the lead in getting rich' and an 'open door' to the outside world. However, simultaneously it was urged to guard against 'decadent bourgeois ideas' and reject 'capitalist filths'. There is a strong analogy with the 19th century '*ti-yong*' debate about western technology (Levenson, 1968): China's rulers hoped then as they did in the 1980s, to benefit from Western technology (*yong*) without absorbing the values (*ti*) that go with it. Moreover, the erosion of traditional values in the 1980s was occurring in the course of a reform which was having a differential impact on different sectors, regions and social strata, causing jealousies and tensions. There is deep concern among Chinese leaders and, indeed, among much wider sections of the population, that China might be thrown into chaos (*da luan*) if the reforms go too fast. A crucial issue, to which it is difficult to gauge the answer, even in the wake of the events of May/June 1989, is the strength of popular feelings which the reforms released for great political democracy and, even, an end to the leading role for the Communist Party.

Agriculture. Agriculture is still the foundation of the Chinese economy, and problems in this sector have wide ramifications for the whole economy. After explosive growth in the early 1980s, China's agricultural growth rate slowed down to around 4% per annum from 1984 to 1987 (ZGTJZY, 1988, p. 23). Given that population was growing at only around $1\frac{1}{2}$% per annum this was far from disastrous. In a poor country of China's size one would not expect a long-term growth rate of farm output per person of much more than 2–3% per annum. However, it was extremely worrying that grain output failed for several years to grow beyond its peak of 1984. State investment in agriculture fell seriously in the 1980s. Moreover, if agriculture is to grow satisfactorily it is necessary to maintain and strengthen cooperation among farm households in respect to a wide range of activities outside direct cultivation of the soil. Poor areas especially experienced a breakdown of village cooperative activities in the late 1980s. However, no issue was more important in analysing the slow down in agricultural growth and the stagnation in grain output than that of price. In the late 1980s the state shied away from allowing a sufficiently large increase in farm purchase prices in general, and grain purchase prices in particular, to stimulate an acceleration in the growth rate of farm output and marketing. The 'social tolerance' of urban workers to the consequential increase in food prices was felt to be low. The 'Polish problem' was never far from the minds of China's leaders. Food subsidies, a small relative increase in farm purchase prices and slow growth of farm output were chosen in preference to a more radical, but politically dangerous alternative.

Loss of control over investment. In order to encourage lower levels to have a greater interest in raising revenues and using it well, the 1980s saw a major decentralisation of budgetary control: the share of 'basic construction investment' (investment in fixed assets by state-owned units) falling outside the central budget rose from 18% in the early 1980s to over 50% in 1981–5 (ZGTJZY, 1986, 73). Partly, this involved decentralization to the enterprise, but it consisted mainly of decentralization to the local authorities. Moreover, an increased proportion of total investment in fixed assets was carried out by collectives and individuals (their share rose from 30% in 1981 to 36% in 1987) (ZGTJZY, 1988, p. 56). Both enterprises and local authorities had long operated in an environment of 'investment hunger' in which there were no penalties for poor returns on investment and many gains to obtaining as much new investment as possible, since prestige and future streams of employment, income and materials flowed from this. In China's partially reformed economy of the 1980s, in which market principles were not fully operational, relaxations of central budgetary control led to a continued rapid expansion of capital construction and neglect of sectors with high social returns, such as education, energy and transport. The structural forces leading to 'over-investment' were strong and it was avoided only during the brief periods when tight, direct central control operated.

Reform of large-scale industrial enterprises. Reform of state enterprises is central to the improved operation of the whole economy. In contrast to small-scale industries and agriculture, the enterprise operators (both workers and managers) were apprehensive about the implications for them of making enterprises more competitive. Moreover, their administrative superiors, especially local authorities, clung tenaciously to control of the enterprises throughout the 1980s. Much interest in the late 1980s focused on ways of trying to separate enterprise ownership from control, with some leading Chinese economists, notably Dong Fureng (Dong, 1990) advocating the joint-stock company as the best method to increase the interest of enterprise employees in reform and reducing outside interference by administrators. A strong school of thought in China believes that a 'capital market' in the form of a stock exchange is a necessary corollary of joint-stock companies, though only tentative moves had been made in this direction by the late 1980s. Experience with setting up stock markets in other developing countries suggests that there will be huge problems obtaining effective corporate disclosure and reporting in the absence of either the necessary tradition or accounting skills, in preventing insider dealing, in avoiding penetration of an embryo market by international organised crime, and in establishing a viable legal framework (Rider and Fung, 1989). Moreover, it is not self-evident that share-ownership via a stock market, as opposed to the various possibilities for non-tradeable share ownership, is the best route to proceed. Evidence from the advanced capitalist economies does not support the proposition that stock markets make a useful contribution to growth, either through gathering together savings, channelling savings to companies with the best investment prospects, or encouraging efficient use of past savings. Indeed, non-stock market economies such as Japan and West Germany have performed better than stock market economies such as the USA or the UK (Singh, 1990).

It is doubtful whether any new policies can attain much improvement in the performance of large-scale industry without a fundamental change in their external setting. Despite the passage of a Bankruptcy Law in 1987 (after long argument) there was virtually no chance of a large state enterprise being declared bankrupt in the late 1980s. Indeed, around 15% of state industrial enterprises made losses but carried on business through state subsidies. Moreover, state administrators, especially local authorities, still removed a substantial portion of the profits from profitable enterprises. Both the 'sticks' and 'carrots' characteristic of capitalist markets were, accordingly, greatly weakened. The budget constraint on state enterprises remained 'soft'. A major reason for this was that the price system still was heavily administered and bore little relationship to supply and demand in either factor or product markets. Accordingly, relying on profits as the criterion of enterprise performance would have produced irrational and unfair results. Unfortunately, gradually reforming prices produces serious problems. The most feasible way to do this is to permit 'dual track' pricing for any given commodity, as China did in the 1980s, gradually raising the proportion sold at free market prices. However, this provides great opportunities for bargaining and corruption in respect to the proportion of output sold at fixed and non-fixed prices and permits those in possession of rights over goods in short supply to benefit from the price differential between parallel markets. That the system should be eventually eliminated is clear, but finding the best pace and method of advance is extremely difficult.

Inflation. For the first time since 1949, China in the 1980s experienced serious open inflation, causing intense debate and great concern among China's economists and policy makers. China's inflation was, in fact, quite moderate compared to most Latin American countries. Indeed, many Latin American countries would be pleased to have as their annual rate of inflation the reported figure of 56% increase in China's 'staff and workers' cost of living index' for the whole period from 1978 to 1987 (ZGTJZY, 1988). However, China's population was not used to inflation and moreover, the rate accelerated in the late 1980s. To some degree China's inflation was 'cost-push'. Increases of the relative price of some formerly low priced heavy industrial inputs did not lead to the hoped for efforts by state enterprises to behave more efficiently and economise on the use of these inputs. When goods were in short supply, and/or where there was a local monopoly in supply, enterprises were able simply to pass on the increases in input prices as increases in final product prices, particularly for that portion of their output sold at free market prices. However, it is not obvious that a change in relative prices accompanied by some freeing of state price control should *ceteris paribus*, result in a rise in the general price level. A major element in China's inflation was failure of macroeconomic management. The rate of growth of the money supply in the 1980s was allowed to accelerate to around thrice the rate pre-1978. A number of factors combined to produce this result, none of which was narrowly economic. Because the state considered it politically impossible to permit urban food prices to rise fully to free market levels it incurred large losses on food sales, grain in particular, to the urban areas. Moreover, such increases as did occur were partially compensated for by state subsidies. Moreover, a relatively large share of state enterprises were running at a loss and were subsidised by the state, nationally or locally. Pre-1978, the state budget had mostly been in surplus, but in the 1980s there was a series of budget deficits (ZGTJZY, 1988, p. 75), with the deficit reaching around 13% of total budgetary expenditure by 1988 (Wang, 1989(a)). Moreover, decentralization of control over banking, with banks coming under intense pressure from local authorities to grant loans, allowed a rapid rise in the supply of bank credit. The demand for funds was insatiable in a 'soft budget' environment where loans were easily available, where bankruptcy for state enterprises was almost unthinkable, and where the real interest rate was mostly negative. A final element in the story is the volatility introduced by the large increase in personal savings in the 1980s. An important reason for the sharp increase in the rate of inflation in 1988 was a vicious circle of panic about an erosion in the real value of these savings by inflation leading to their rapid depletion and a further temporary upward twist to the inflationary spiral.

Inequality. That China is a large country is a truism so important that it bears repetition. The problems of dealing with powerful regional interests is a special one for countries the size of India or China, and it produces the need for political compromises that do not arise in smaller countries such as Taiwan or South Korea, let alone city-states like Hong Kong or Singapore. Moreover, growth in such huge economies, embracing an amalgam of well and badly-located areas, can never hope to be as rapid as in small, well-located countries. Few economies have grown in a spatially balanced fashion. Capital and labour are attracted to well-located areas, albeit that these areas are crowded. This happened in China prior to the impact of Western imperialism as well as under its impact. Despite serious attempts under Mao to control regional inequality, large differences in levels of development existed even in the 1970s. After then, much wider regional differences opened up, with extremely rapid rates of advance is favourably placed areas along the eastern seaboard. Although poor areas' real output and incomes certainly grew under the impact of the reforms, their growth could not match that of eastern seaboard provinces like Jiangsu (see Table 4). China's policy makers in the 1980s attempted to combine increased incentives to well located areas with serious efforts, comparing favourably with those in other large developing countries, to assist growth in backward areas. However, helping poorly located areas is a complex process, without an easy or obvious solution. The vicious circle of poverty in backward areas is extremely hard to break even with plentiful state assistance (see Wang and Bai, 1990).

Under Mao, income differentials in China were low compared to other developing countries. However, major changes occurred to income distribution in the 1980s. These changes were extremely complex. The major change was a reduction in the gap in average income between peasants and urban workers. Within the countryside alongside a sharp fall in the number of people in absolute poverty went relatively fast rates of growth of peasant income in well-located areas. In such areas, the benefits of growth, especially of non-farm employment,

35

Table 4 Jiangsu province: Key economic indicators (all data at 1980 prices)

	Average annual growth rate (%)	
	1953/87	1979/87
Total social product (gross material product)	9.3	15.2
National income (net material product)	7.2	12.0
Gross value of agricultural output of which:	6.6	14.5
industrial output at village (*cun*) or lower level	–	32.2
Gross value of industrial output	12.4	15.7
of which: heavy industry	18.9	14.4
light industry	10.8	16.8
all-people owned	–	10.4
collectively owned	–	22.0
National income per person	8.0 (1952–87)	10.7

Source: JSJJNJ, 1988, Section III

increased the income of most village strata. The overall result was for some increase, but not an 'excessive' one, in rural income inequality as measured by the Gini coefficient (Zhao, 1990). In the urban areas, the persistence of fairly egalitarian remuneration policies in state enterprises led, to a reduction in the reported Gini coefficient in the mid-1980s. A serious problem was that of people who obtained high incomes from 'the contradictions and frictions arising from the transition from one economic system to another' (Zhao, 1989). The opportunities for well placed people in the Party and government to take advantage of the dual-track system to earn high quasi-legal or illegal incomes little related to personal work ability or effort, multiplied following the half-way house of economic reform in the 1980s. These caused great dissatisfaction among the mass of the Chinese population.

BIBLIOGRAPHY
Chinese Statistical Outline (ZGTJZY) (*Zhongguo Tongji Zhaiyao*). 1986. Beijing: Zhongguo Tongji Chubanshe.
Chinese Statistical Outline (ZGTJZY) (*Zhongguo Tongji Zhaiyao*). 1988. Beijing: Zhongguo Tongji Chubanshe.
Chinese Statistical Yearbook (ZGTJNJ) (*Zhongguo Tongji Nianjian*). 1988. Beijing: Zhongguo Tongji Chubanshe.
Dong, Fureng, 1990. Reform of the economic operating mechanism and reform of ownership. In Nolan and Dong (1990).
Ishikawa, S. 1967. *Economic Development in Asian Perspective*, Tokyo: Kinokuniya.

Jiangsu Economic Yearbook (JSJJNJ) (*Jiangsu Jingji Nianjian*). 1988. Nanjing: Nanjing Daxue Chubanshe.

Levenson, J.R. 1968. *Confucian China and its Modern Fate.* Berkeley: University of California Press.

Liu, Guoguang, and Wang, Ruisun. 1984. Restructuring of the economy. In Yu (1984).

Nolan, P., 1988, *The Political Economy of Collective Farms.* Cambridge: Polity Press.

Nolan, P. and Dong, Fureng (eds.). 1989. *Market Forces in China.* London: Zed Books.

Nolan, P. and Fong, Fureng (eds.) 1990. *The Chinese Economy and its Future.* Cambridge: Polity Press.

Riskin, C. 1987. *China's Political Economy.* Oxford: Oxford University Press.

Singh, A. 1990. The stockmarket in a socialist economy. In Nolan and Dong (1990).

Wang, Bingqian, 1989a. Report on the implementation of the state budget for 1988 and on the draft state budget for 1989. *Beijing Review,* 32 (18).

Wang, Hong. 1989b. China's export performance in the 1980s. Cambridge, unpublished mss.

Wang, Xiaoqiang and Bai, Nanfeng. 1990. *The Poverty of Plenty.* London: Macmillan Press.

World Bank. 1986. *China: Long-term development issues and options.* Washington DC: World Bank.

Yu, Guangyan (ed.). 1984. *China' Socialist Modernisation.* Beijing: Foreign Languages Press.

Zhao, Renwei. 1990. Income distribution. In Nolan and Dong (1990).

Nikolai Ivanovitch Bukharin

DONALD J. HARRIS

Nikolai Bukharin is commonly acknowledged to have been one of the most brilliant theoreticians in the Bolshevik movement and an outstanding figure in the history of Marxism. Born in Russia in 1888, he studied economics at Moscow University and (during four years of exile in Europe and America) at the Universities of Vienna and Lausanne (Switzerland), in Sweden and Norway and in the New York Public Library. While still a student, he joined the Bolshevik movement. Upon returning to Russia in April 1917, he worked closely with Lenin and participated in planning and carrying out the October Revolution. After the victory of the Bolsheviks he proceeded to assume many high offices in the Party (becoming a member of the Politbureau in 1919) and in other important organizations. In these various capacities he came to exercise great influence within both the Party and the Comintern. Under Stalin's regime, however, he lost most of his important positions. Eventually, he was among those who were arrested and brought to trial under charges of treason and was executed on 15 March 1938.

At the peak of his career Bukharin was regarded as the foremost authority on Marxism in the Party. He was a prolific writer: there are more than five hundred items of published work in his name, most of them written in the hectic twelve-year period 1916–1928 (for a comprehensive bibliography, see Heitman, 1969). Only a few of these works have been translated into English and these are the works for which he is now most widely known. A brief description of the major items gives an indication of the scope and range of his intellectual interests.

The Economic Theory of the Leisure Class (1917) is a detailed and comprehensive critique of the ideas of the Austrian school of economic theory, as represented by the work of its chief spokesman Eugen von Böhm-Bawerk, but situated in the broader context of marginal theory as it had appeared up to that time. In *Imperialism and World Economy* (1918) he formulated a revision of Marx's theory of capitalist development and set out his own theory of imperialism as an advanced stage of capitalism. This was written in 1914–15, a year before Lenin's *Imperialism*, and is credited with having been a major influence on Lenin's formulation. The theoretical structure of the argument is further elaborated in *Imperialism and the Accumulation of Capital* (1924) by way of a critique of the ideas of Rosa Luxemburg, another leading Marxist writer of that time. *The ABC of Communism* (1919), written jointly with Evgenii Preobrazhensky and used as a standard textbook in the Twenties, is a comprehensive restatement of the principles of Marxism as applied to analysis of the development of capitalism, the conditions for revolution, and the nature of the tasks of building socialism in the specific context of the Soviet experience. This book, taken with his *Economics of the Transition Period* (1920), constitutes a contribution to both the Marxist theory of capitalist breakdown and world revolution on the one hand and the theory of socialist construction on the other. *Historical Materialism: A System of Sociology* (1921), another popular textbook, combines a special interpretation of the philosophical basis of Marxism with what is perhaps the first systematic theoretical statement of Marxism as a system of sociological analysis. In style much of this work is highly polemical and geared to immediate political goals. But it reveals also a versatility of intellect, serious theoretical concern, and scholarly inclination. Arguably, his works represent in their entirety 'a comprehensive reformulation of the classical Marxian theory of proletarian revolution' (Heitman, 1962, p. 79). Viewed from the standpoint of their significance in terms of economic analysis, three major components stand out.

There is, first, the critique of 'bourgeois economic theory' in its Austrian version. Bukharin's approach follows that which Marx had adopted in *Theories of Surplus Value*, which is to give an 'exhaustive criticism' not only of the methodology and internal logic of the theory but also of the sociological and class basis which it reflects. He scores familiar points against particular elements of the theory, for instance, that utility is not measurable, that Böhm-Bawerk's concept of an 'average period of production' is 'nonsensical', that the theory is static. Such criticisms of the technical apparatus of the theory have since been developed in more refined and sophisticated form (see Harris, 1978, 1981; Dobb, 1969). Moreover, certain weaknesses in Bukharin's presentation, such as an apparent confusion between marginal and total utility and misconception of the meaning of interdependent markets, can now be readily recognized. But these are matters that were not well understood at the time, even by exponents of the theory. Bukharin views them as matters of lesser importance. What is crucial for him is 'the point of departure of the . . . theory, its ignoring the social-historical character of economic phenomena' (1917, p. 73). This criticism is applied with particular force to the treatment of the problem of capital, the nature of consumer demand, and the process of economic evolution. As to the sociological criticism, his central thesis is that the theory is the ideological expression of the rentier class eliminated from the process of production and interested solely in disposing of their income through consumption. This thesis can be faulted for giving too mechanical and simplistic an interpretation of the relation between economic theory and ideology where a dialectical interpretation is called for (compare, for instance, Dobb, 1973, ch. 1, and Meek, 1967). But the issue of the social-ideological roots of the marginal revolution remains a problematic one, as yet unresolved, with direct relevance to current interest in the nature of scientific revolutions in the social science (see Kuhn, 1970; Latsis, 1976).

Secondly, Bukharin's work clearly articulates a conception of the development of capitalism as a world system to a more advanced stage than that of industrial capitalism which Marx had earlier analysed. This new stage is characterized by the rise of monopoly or 'state trusts' within advanced capitalist states, intensified international competition among different national monopolies leading to a quest for economic, political and military control over 'spheres of influence', and breaking out into destructive wars between states. These conditions are seen as inevitable results deriving from inherent tendencies in the capitalist accumulation process, at the heart of which is a supposed falling tendency in the overall average rate of profit. Altogether they are viewed as an expression of the anarchic and contradictory character of capitalism. The formation of monopolies is supposed to take place through reorganization of production by finance capitalists as a way of finding new sources of profitable investment and of exercising centralized regulation and control of the national economy. This transformation succeeds for a time at the national level but only to raise the contradictions to the level of the world economy where they can be resolved only through revolutions breaking out at different 'weak links' of the world-capitalist system. The idea of a necessary long-term decline in the rate of profit, and also the specific role assigned to financial enterprises as such, can be disputed. A crucial ingredient of the argument is the idea of oligopolistic rivalry and international mobility of capital as essential factors governing international relations. In this respect the argument anticipates ideas that are only now being recognized and absorbed into the orthodox theory of international trade and which, in his own time, were conspicuously neglected within the entire corpus of existing economic theory. Much of the analysis as regards a necessary tendency to uneven development between an advanced *centre* and underdeveloped *periphery* of the world economy has also been absorbed into contemporary theories of underdevelopment. Underpinning the whole argument is a curious theory of 'social equilibrium' and of 'crisis' originating from a loss of equilibrium. 'To find the law of this equilibrium', he suggests (1979, p. 149), 'is the basic problem of theoretical economics and theoretical economics as a scientific system is the result of an examination of the entire capitalist system in its state of equilibrium'.

The third component is a comprehensive conception of the process of socialist construction in a backward country. These ideas came out of the practical concerns and rich intellectual ferment associated with the early period of Soviet development but have a generality and relevance extending down to current debates both in the development literature and on problems of socialist planning. The overall framework is one that conceives of socialist development as a long-drawn-out process 'embracing a whole enormous epoch' and going through four revolutionary phases: ideological, political, economic and technical. The process is seen as occurring in the context of a kind of war economy involving highly centralized state control, though there is an optimistic prediction of an ultimate 'dying off of the state power'. Room is allowed for preserving and maintaining small-scale private enterprise. The agricultural sector is seen as posing special problems, due to the assumed character of peasant production, which can only be overcome through transformation by stages to collectivized large-scale production. Even so, it is firmly held (in 1919) that 'for a long time to come small-scale peasant farming will be the predominant form of Russian agriculture', a view which Bukharin later abandoned in support of Stalin's collectivization drive. In industry, too, small-scale industry, handicraft, and home industry are to be supported, so that the all-round strategy is one that seems quite similar to that of 'walking-on two-legs' later propounded by Mao for China. An extensive discussion is presented of almost every detail of the economic programme, from technology to public health, but little or no attention is given to issues of incentives and organizational problems of centralization/decentralization which have emerged as crucial considerations in later work.

SELECTED WORKS

1917. *Economic Theory of the Leisure Class*. New York: Monthly Review Press, 1972.

1918. *Imperialism and World Economy*. New York: Monthly Review Press, 1973.

1919. (With E. Preobrazhensky.) *The ABC of Communism*. Harmondsworth and Baltimore: Penguin Books, 1969.

1920. The economics of the transition period. In *The Politics and Economics of the Transition Period*, ed. K.J. Tarbuck, London and Boston: Routledge & Kegan Paul, 1979.

1921. *Historical Materialism, A System of Sociology*. Ann Arbor: University of Michigan Press, 1969.

1924. *Imperialism and the Accumulation of Capital*. New York: Monthly Review Press, 1972.

BIBLIOGRAPHY

Dobb, M. 1969. *Welfare Economics and the Economics of Socialism*. Cambridge: Cambridge University Press.

Dobb, M. 1973. *Theories of Value and Distribution since Adam Smith*. Cambridge and New York: Cambridge University Press.

Harris, D.J. 1978. *Capital Accumulation and Income Distribution*. Stanford: Stanford University Press.

Harris, D.J. 1981. Profits, productivity, and thrift: the neoclassical theory of capital and distribution revisited, *Journal of Post-Keynesian Economics* 3(3), 359–82.

Heitman, S. 1962. Between Lenin and Stalin: Nikolai Bukharin. In *Revisionism*, ed. Leopold Labedz, New York: Praeger.

Heitman, S. 1969. *Nikolai I. Bukharin: a Bibliography*. Stanford: Hoover Institution.

Kuhn, T. 1970. *The Structure of Scientific Revolutions*, 2nd edn, enlarged. Chicago: University of Chicago Press.

Latsis, S. (ed.) 1976. *Method and Appraisal in Economics*. Cambridge and New York: Cambridge University Press.

Lenin, V.I. 1917. *Imperialism, the Highest Stage of Capitalism*. New York: International Publishers, 1939.

Meek, R.L. 1967. *Economics and Ideology and Other Essays*. London: Chapman & Hall.

Central Planning

TADEUSZ KOWALIK

Central planning denotes the total body of government actions to determine and coordinate directions of national economic development. The process of central planning is composed of pre-plan studies and forecasts, formulation of aims for given periods of time, establishment of their priorities (order of importance), listing ways and means, and, eventually, the plan's implementation. Central planning is a term usually associated with Centrally Planned Economies (CPE) as opposed to Private Enterprise (or Market) and Mixed Economies (UN official classification), but it is often used in a broader sense to denote any systematic macroeconomic control by the government. For Tinbergen (1964), central planning means planning by governments, or national planning (in the Netherlands as well as in some other countries there are Central Planning Bureaux, even though these economies cannot be classed with the group of CPEs).

In this broader meaning, central planning takes several different names, specifically: 'direct', 'hierarchical' (Bauer, 1978) or 'centralistic' as practised in most centrally planned economies; 'financial' as in Hungary; 'indicative' as in France.

The term 'planning' often stirs emotions. For some people, especially for many Communist economists, central planning is good by definition. Others use it to denounce socialism and indeed any kind of government intervention as 'planned chaos' (Mises, 1947). The scope and meaning of central planning varies along with changing fashion. When Arthur Lewis confessed 'we are all planners now' (Lewis [1949] 1956, p. 74), it was fashionable to describe any kind of state interventionism as 'planning'. Robbins (1947, p. 68) termed his proposal for a modest anti-inflationary or anti-deflationary fiscal policy as 'overall financial planning'. Since the 1970s, though, general opinion seems to have been increasingly wary of planning, indeed sceptical abouts its effectiveness. Accordingly, even some planners in the state administration who staunchly stood by that idea preferred to cover their activity under less emotionally charged terms (such as 'steering').

Initially, central planning used to be generally regarded as an inalienable feature of socialist economy and hence as the exact opposite of market and commodity production typical of capitalism. It was interpreted as planning in physical units, by central command, based upon a hierarchical structure of national economy which had at its disposal ways and means to enforce decisions by administrative order. Precisely this kind of planning system developed in the Soviet Union, less as a product of any definite concept or vision of socialist economy than as an outcome of many different interacting factors – doctrine and ideology, the specific situation of Russia at that time, and the political ends to which the victorious revolutionary authorities subordinated the economy.

ORIGINS. After the Bolshevik victory in Russia Lenin's writings, apart from the above-mentioned view of planning as the exact opposite of the market (which was shared by many other Marxists), provided two other theoretical contributions to the formidable task of organization of the economy. Following Rudolf Hilferding, Lenin (like Bukharin) described imperialism as an ante-chamber of socialism on account of the steadily accelerating process of production concentration (trusts) and the centralization of banks which were rapidly expanding their control of domestic industries. The German wartime economy with its large-scale combination of latest technology, planning and efficient organization, was viewed by Lenin as something like an archetype for a future socialist economy.

In the period of 'War Communism' (1918–20) the need for planning was repeatedly proclaimed but no national plan could actually be drawn up. It was only towards the end of the period that Gosplan, a planning commission, was created, although its job was modest and only vaguely defined for years thereafter. No firm way could be found to reconcile planning with the New Economic Policy (NEP) introduced in 1921.

The most important accomplishment of the early 1920s was the plan for electrifying all Russia, which was drawn up at Lenin's personal initiative in 1920 and which came to be referred to as GOELRO. That plan provided for the building, within the following 10–15 years, of power stations and related infrastructure in major industrial regions. At that stage, planning was viewed as primarily an engineering rather than economic activity (as can be seen if only from the composition of the commission, which included mostly engineers and agriculture specialists).

From 1925 onwards, Gosplan began to publish each year what were called economy-wide 'control figures' initially for a year only but later for five-year periods. Those figures were regarded as a non-binding set of estimations and forecasts. Their main contribution to the development of planning was that they eventually led up to the design of what is called the balancing method, which juxtaposes demand for goods with their output. The first five-year plans also began to be drafted outside Gosplan.

The Soviet economy became a 'centrally planned' economy only at the time of the First Five-Year Plan (1928/9–1932/3). That was a time of tough internal struggle in the party and one of escalating heroic development programmes. Each new draft version of the five-year plan, beginning with the first one after the Party Congress in December 1927 through to its final approval, set up increasingly ambitious tasks. But the balancing of tasks with resources in the plan was based mainly on overly optimistic (and largely unfeasible) forecasts of labour productivity growth. The party and the state authorities soon began to mobilize the population to over-fulfil the plan, or, more precisely, those targets in the plan which were arbitrarily recognized as the most important ones (priority tasks). Thenceforward, plans became tools for mobilization rather than for balanced allocation of resources. Annual plans often shook up the current five-year plan to accommodate it to these new priorities (or super-priorities).

The First Five-Year Plan (which was officially declared fulfilled in four-and-a-quarter years) generated many bottlenecks and disproportions; this suggested that the pace should perhaps be slowed down – and priorities rearranged, as to some extent was attempted in the final version of the next five-year plan (for 1933–37). At the same time the new plan was even more detailed and its scope expanded significantly (the number of branches comprised by the plan increased to 120 from the original 50). The authors of the first five-year plans apparently did not realize the full institutional and political implications of over-ambitious tasks, the scale of which were in some cases downright unfeasible. In order to rescue those regarded as top priorities (especially those concerning heavy industries and manufacturing), others had to be sacrificed (those relating to standards of living were the first victims). This could only be accomplished by methods typical of wartime economy, that is, highly centralized organization, rigid subordination and discipline, all-embracing rationing, various kinds of coercion, and political mobilization. That was exactly what was attempted during the first two five-year plan periods.

To a considerable extent this amounted to a revival of the methods tried in the period of 'War Communism', including compulsory labour and rationing, however not as formal and lasting institutions like, for example, labour mobilization during the civil war, but either as side-effects of other campaigns (mass deportations during the collectivization drive, purges of the 1930s, etc.), or as emergency responses to situations of extreme penury (rationing) which eventually should make room for allocation of labour and consumer goods through some kind of market (for ideological reasons the term was never used in relation to labour). This was combined with abandonment of the original egalitarianism in incomes policy; increased reliance on material incentives geared to plan fulfilment and piece rates became a distinctive mark of the Stalinist period.

MAIN FEATURES (FORMAL ASPECTS). The first two five-year plans set the general shape for a model of Soviet central planning, transplanted after World War II to communist Eastern Europe. That model survived unchanged through to the mid-1950s (except in Yugoslavia), and in most communist countries it functions to this day in its general outline.

In both its design and implementation stages, central planning is based on a hierarchical pattern of national economy, which in turn presupposes obedience and discipline. Freedom of choice (which is lifted only temporarily or partly) applies to purchases of consumer goods within the existing commodity supply and the state-determined purchasing power, as well as to choice of occupation and workplace within the statutory obligation to be in employment.

Using information on the economy's shape and tendencies at any given moment, the central authority formulates a set of general guidelines of the plan, possibly based on prior special studies and forecasts. The plan's guidelines include such aggregates as the distribution of the national income between accumulation and consumption, the shares and main directions of investment by sectors, the desired rate of overall economic growth etc. These guidelines as a rule are pre-defined by the leading bodies of the ruling party, and are then disaggregated by the government into guidelines for particular industrial ministries and local authorities to produce their own draft plans, which are further disaggregated and communicated to industrial associations and individual enterprises. Government guidelines include two kinds of indices; directives, which are mandatory for local planners in drafting their blueprints (whatever alteration may prove necessary can only be made by a superior agency) and information indices. The enterprise draft plans are then aggregated by industrial associations and branch ministries, and their draft plans are in turn aggregated into a national (or central) economic plan for one or five years which is usually approved by parliament. Only after that are final corrections and adaptations introduced into lower-level plans. This particular procedure of plan construction has been called the 'spindle technique' in reference to textile machines, for guidelines and draft versions first travel from the top downwards, then up, and then again down the hierarchy.

One pivotal point in this procedure is the plan's internal consistency. The idea is to match demand for each particular resource with the level of its supply during the plan period. A whole system of balance sheets (indeed thousands of them) is used for that purpose. Balance sheets set – in physical or equivalent units – available amounts of materials, capacities, energy, labour, as well as financial means (personal income and spending, foreign trade balance, the budget) against anticipated demand in each case.

Plan fulfilment is a fundamental obligation of each economic organization. Managers and, to some extent the workforce as well, are evaluated for their plan performance and rewarded or penalized accordingly. Tasks named in an enterprise plan are both commands by a superior authority and obligations to supply enough resources to safeguard smooth cooperation. Although enterprises are given not only quantitative targets but also qualitative ones (e.g. technological input/output coefficients for materials, power etc, the importance of output–quantity performance is overriding.

ADVANTAGES AND FAILURES. This particular model of planning was conceived in a country with abundant resources of labour (open or disguised unemployment) and primary products; it was applied also in several other countries with large

45

unused capacities. Proving able to mobilize idle resources initially produced very high growth rates, although one cannot take official statistical records at their face value. Determination of obligatory priorities on a national scale enabled countries to concentrate resources and efforts on several selected spectacular tasks. The successful bid to transform the Soviety Union into a superpower in a relatively brief time is perhaps the least debatable success of this planning model.

However, from the mid-1950s onwards centrally planned economies have been coming under growing criticism both from professional economists and from the general public. The criticism became particularly sharp as growth indicators declined and started to affect the (slow anyway) improvement of living standards; the system's weakness in generating and absorbing technological innovations became increasingly evident. However, critical voices – even when acknowledged by political authorities – did not lead, as a rule, to consistent and effective changes in the economic system.

The main lines of criticism of deficiencies of the existing system of central planning can be summarized as follows:

The procedure for building plans outlined above cannot guarantee efficient allocation of resources. The tasks and resources for their implementation are not decided by the central planning agency in a truly 'sovereign' way because such an agency is bound to rely on the supply of information from lower-rank agencies. But that information, apart from some natural delays or mistakes made in its transmission upwards, is often deliberately distorted by enterprises, which use it as a weapon in plan bargaining. Enterprises usually want to wrench as large means and as small tasks as possible from the central economic authority for themselves. Industrial association, indeed even branch ministries, often helps them achieve this purpose. At that stage, too, the main battle for investment funds begins. Enterprises and local authorities try to get 'put on' the plan by deliberately underrating estimated costs of their undertakings. Eventually, the plan is apparently brought into balance, but it has built-in significant disproportions right from its start, which leads to a waste of resources.

Even greater waste results from the centralistic bureaucratic method of controlling the execution of plan tasks, which eventually leads to equating planning with management. The over-taut plan, based as it is on unrealistic assumptions, especially regarding labour productivity growth, can later be 'fulfilled' only by setting up a whole system of ad hoc priorities and superpriorities which makes a reduction of nonpriorities unavoidable. As a rule, the victimized sectors are those related to the sphere of personal incomes or social or municipal services (public transport), the health service, housing, education – treated as residuum.

Once they have been assigned the required resources by the central economic authority, enterprises no longer feel compelled to seek ways of saving materials or energy. Because deliveries of materials and energy are as a rule irregular, enterprises try to provide against such risks by hoarding excessive inventories of materials and reducing employment only reluctantly. Moreover, enterprises are given no effective inducements to seek new technology, indeed even to emulate existing new techniques.

Prices set by the central authority are as a rule rigid and random, reflecting neither costs nor relative scarcities of individual goods. As a consequence, both at the central level and at enterprise level clear criteria of choice are largely absent.

Viewed from the consumer's vantage point, centrally planned economies provide poor-quality goods and a meagre product mix. Their incapability of meeting greater diversification of needs, which inevitably progresses along with increase in income levels, is one of the major reasons for the growth of a 'second economy' (moonlighting, corruption etc).

Over-taut plans, implemented through commands, unavoidably generate an inflated control system and subject the economy to political goals. Subordination of economies to politics is often presented as expression of general (social) interest; in reality this subordination often conceals vested interests of small informal groups. In the process of plan negotiations and rearrangement of priorities in the course of implementation, centralistic administrative planning engenders informal lobbies which exert growing pressure on the central authority. A product of quasi-missionary zeal to develop the production of means of production, the heavy industry lobbies are the strongest of all. Gradually, the central authority is losing its 'sovereignty' to them. Even when the authority begins to appreciate 'harmony' more than 'rush' (Kornai, 1972) it is unable to shed that pressure.

This very role of lobbies goes against the widely held belief that in the centrally planned economies the superior position belongs to the preferences of the central planners. Increasingly concrete decisions are made under growing pressures of various informal vested interest groups. In this situation, criteria of choice cannot be clear or unequivocal, which makes public control of the central planning agency's operations even more difficult. For the same reason, and even more because of the secretive style of work of state agencies, as well as absence or limitation of consumer organizations, environmental groups, independent trade unions, and with restricted press freedom, the central authorities cannot play the part of an umpire reconciling different social interests. Protection of public interest becomes fictitious under these conditions. Thus, when official doctrines proclaim unity of interests, this may simply conceal a growing tendency towards a peculiar kind of 're-privatization' of centrally planned economies.

EVOLUTION AND PROSPECTS. Since the mid-1950s, in the system of central planning as practised in countries of the so-called 'real socialism' two categories of change have taken place.

The growth and mathematization of economics, in particular the expansion of linear programming, operations research, input–output analysis, cybernetics and systems analysis, the wide extension of computer applications etc., have supplied planners with subtler tools for their work. The development of these tools fuelled hopes, already in the 1960s, that planning would proceed 'from balancing the plan towards the choice of optimal plan' (Lange, 1965). 'Planometrics' came into use then, indeed even something like a 'computopia' began to develop.

The second kind of change was more institutional in character. It came along with de-Stalinization, of which economic reform was and still remains a part. Unlike in Yugoslavia, where the economic system was to correspond to an entirely different model of socialist society compared with the Soviet-type one, in the countries belonging to CMEA institutional changes amounted, generally speaking, to a transfer of some economic decision-making to lower-level units, an expansion of material incentives for managers and workers alike, and an extension of market mechanisms.

As a result of the new techniques and of the partial decentralization, central planning has probably become a slightly more efficient tool of economy-wide control. However, all those improvements were ultimately too negligible and inconsistent to stand up to the growing complexity of economy, in particular to offset the depleting reserves of extensive-type growth factors (excess labour, cheap raw materials) by more intensive methods of growth stimulation. The technology gap between CMEA and advanced Western countries, which became clear in the 1960s and has kept widening since then, has not been bridged; if anything, it has continued to widen. Hence, repeated calls for more or less radical economic reform are still the order of the day.

PLANNING AND FREEDOM. Ever since its inception, the question of economic planning has set off disputes about democracy and individual freedom. In its original purely ideological concept, planning used either to be equated with democracy or presented as democracy's exact opposite: suffice it to mention the New Leftist utopia of a social system based on the belief that production and distribution can somehow be planned by the people with a total absence of market and state. The eternal Kingdom of Freedom was to come simply as soon as market and state alike have been abolished.

More elegant, albeit no less utopian, is the free-marketeers' blueprint for rejecting any governmental planning as a threat to efficiency and freedom. Although quite fashionable (and not only in the West), this mode of thinking is nonetheless outside the mainstream of disputes over planning versus freedom.

In fact, most major currents of social thinking have undergone a process of radical re-thinking in the course of recent decades. This holds for liberalism (Mannheim, 1940; Galbraith, 1973; Lindblom, 1977) and for non-Communist socialism (Crosland, 1956; Crossman, 1965; Nove, 1983) as well as for Marxism (Brus, 1975; Horvat, 1982; Kornai, 1985). Whatever differences may divide all these currents of thought, as indeed individual thinkers within each current, all of them are aware of two kinds of threat to freedom – one that comes from all-embracing, hierarchical and bureaucratic planning, and another that comes from the failure to plan anything at all. The market mechanism is regarded as something like a barrier to bureaucratic arbitrariness. But its failures in turn may put at hazard not only economic but even political stability, thereby destroying the foundations of the desired social order. Planning, within given limits, thus turns out to be an indispensable condition of freedom. While making a plea for a polycentric model of economy – both in the sense of providing for different forms of ownership and of decisionmaking – all these currents of thinking believe that society as a whole should have an authentic say (via its representatives) on the main lines of investment and on general rules for national income distribution.

Of course, there is nothing inevitable in the long-run direction this movement will take either in the West or in the East. The chance to create a social order which would be based upon the three main tiers of plan, the market and freedom would be much greater if it were clear that each of these is a necessary condition for high socio-economic efficiency, and that freedom too can be viewed not only as a value in itself but also as a specific kind of production factor. Some authors have questioned this dependence of economic efficiency on political democracy (Gomulka, 1977). However, neither studies of this relationship in many Third World countries (Adelman and Taft, 1967) nor the record of previous reforms in the Communist world supply any definite answer to this question. On the other hand, the analysis of pressures on, and prospects of, the evolution of Communist systems in Eastern Europe has led to a rather persuasive argument (Brus, 1980) that with democratizing internal political relations these systems will be unable to remove (or at least to reduce substantially) central planning's chronic deficiencies, such as insufficient and distorted information flows, negative selection of managerial personnel, chronic investment failures, labour alienation etc. The stagnation threatening the Communist countries presses the ruling groups to more radical reforms which would combine plan, market and freedom. At the same time, repeated setbacks of neoliberal economic policies in the West may well generate fresh and strong public pressure for changes in a similar direction.

BIBLIOGRAPHY

Adelman, I. and Taft, C.M. 1967. *Society, Politics and Economic Development: A Quantitative Approach*. Baltimore: Johns Hopkins Press.

Bauer, T. 1978. Investment cycles in planned economies. *Acta Oeconomica* 21(3), 243–60.

Brus, W. 1975. *Socialist Ownership and Political Systems*. London and Boston: Routledge & Kegan Paul.

Brus, W. 1980. Political system and economic efficiency: the East European context. *Journal of Comparative Economics* 4(1), March, 40–55.

Cave, M. and Hare, P. 1981. *Alternative Approaches to Economic Planning*. New York: St Martin's Press.

Crosland, C.A.R. 1956. *The Future of Socialism*. London: Jonathan Cape; New York: Macmillan, 1957.

Crossman, R.H.S. 1965. Planning and freedom. In R.H.S. Crossman, *Essays in Socialism*, London: Hamish Hamilton.

Davies, R.W. and Carr, E.H. 1974. *Foundations of a Planned Economy 1926–1929*. Harmondsworth: Penguin.

Ellman, M. 1983. Changing views on central economic planning: 1958–1983. *The ACES Bulletin, A Publication of the Association for Comparative Economic Studies* (Tempo, Arizona) 25(1), Spring.

Galbraith, J.K. 1973. *Economics and the Public Purpose*. Boston: Houghton Mifflin.

Gomulka, S. 1977. Economic factors in the democratization of socialism and the socialization of capitalism. *Journal of Comparative Economics* 1(4), December, 389–406.

Horvat, B. 1982. *The Political Economy of Socialism. A Marxist Social Theory.* Armonk, NY: M.E. Sharpe.

Kornai, J. 1972. *Rush versus Harmonic Growth.* Amsterdam: North-Holland.

Kornai, J. 1985. *Contradictions and Dilemmas, Studies in the Socialist Economy and Society.* Corvina: Kner Printing House.

Lange, O. 1965. Od bilansowania do wyboru optymalnego planu (From balancing the plan to the choice of optimal plan). *Nowe Drogi* (Warsaw), No. 2.

Lewis, W.A. 1949. *The Principles of Economic Planning.* London: Allen & Unwin, 1956.

Lindblom, C. 1977. *Politics and Markets. The World's Political-Economic Systems.* New York: Basic Books.

Mannheim, K. 1940. *Man and Society in an Age of Reconstruction. Studies in Modern Social Structure.* London: Routledge & Kegan Paul, 1974.

Mises, L. von. 1947. *Planned Chaos.* Irvington-on-Hudson, NY: The Foundation for Economic Education.

Nove, A. 1983. *The Economics of Feasible Socialism.* London: Allen & Unwin.

Robbins, L. 1947. *The Economic Problem in Peace and War.* London: Macmillan.

Tinbergen, J. 1964. *Central Planning.* New Haven and London: Yale University Press.

Colbertism

D.C. COLEMAN

Colbertism is a term used to describe the economic policies associated with the French statesman, Jean-Baptiste Colbert; and sometimes, confusingly, as a synonym for mercantilist policies in general.

In the course of his account, and denunciation, of the mercantile system, Adam Smith presented it as something foisted upon governments by conspiring businessmen. Extending this view from England to France, he said of Colbert that he had been 'imposed upon by the sophistry of merchants and manufacturers' (Smith, 1776, p. 434). Whatever degree of truth there may be in his account so far as it related to England – and there is some – it wholly misrepresents the mind of Colbert and the nature of Colbertism. Distrusting the self-interest of businessmen as a power for the greater good of society, Colbert believed profoundly that, although their pursuit of profits should be encouraged, the way to ensure that such activities redounded to the greater wealth, and hence power and glory, of France was by regulation and order. So Colbertism was essentially a systematic treatment of economic activities imposed from above by the King through his servant. It could be described as a version of the mercantile system appropriate to an absolutist state. It owed little or nothing to mercantile or manufacturing pressures brought to bear on governments. Although there were some similarities between Colbertism and English mercantilism, both in the ideas which lay behind it and in its outward forms as it affected overseas trade, the creation of Colbertian policies did not in the least resemble the process of bargaining and compromise between Crown and Parliament by which English mercantilism was muddled into existence. For this reason alone the term 'Parliamentary Colbertism', coined by Cunningham and used by him to describe English economic policy, 1689–1776 (Cunningham, 1907, II, pp. 403–68), was singularly inappropriate. It was also inapt for the different reason that Colbertism was distinguished by a concern for the direct control of production which was wholly absent from the English version of mercantilist policies.

The quintessence of Colbertism is strikingly illustrated in Colbert's approach to manufactures. Observing that France had great industrial potential, with many and scattered crafts and substantial manpower, he set about the country's industrial rehabilitation. He used a variety of weapons: subsidies, special tax reductions or exemptions, protection against foreign imports, the encouragement of early marriage and large families, grants of special privileges, and the establishment of *manufactures royales*. Disapproving, for example, of the way in which his countrymen imported and wore the woollen cloth or serges of Holland and England, he set up *manufactures royales* to stimulate their production in France; and in 1667 very sharply increased import duties against the offending English and Dutch imports. Similar techniques were used to promote the making of lace, silk stockings, tapestries, carpets, glassware, tinplate, soap, naval supplies, and cannon. Luxury items and textiles received particular attention. It has been said that 'the greatest industry in France was supplying the wants of the King and his court' (Cole, 1939, II, p. 303). In quantitative terms this was probably untrue but its significance was very real; and such a statement could not possibly be made about English industry. Stimulation demanded regulation. So Colbert established a Code of Commerce, promulgated for textiles elaborate controls covering precise lengths, widths and other details of all types of textiles; established an apparatus of industrial inspection; and insisted upon all labour being organized within the guild structure.

Three points need to be stressed about these measures. First, Colbertism was here a continuation and codification, a new ordering of old practices; it was part of an *étatisme* with medieval roots. Second, at the time that Colbert was imposing these measures on the French economy, their English counterparts were withering away; the last legislative attempt at general regulation of the English cloth industry failed in 1678. Third, Colbert's regulative achievements were continued after his death: Colbertism brought many more detailed regulations in the seventy years after 1683.

Colbert's founding of privileged monopolistic trading companies shows a certain resemblance to the prior establishment of their counterparts in Holland and England. Again, however, the special nature of Colbertian mercantilism is evident both in the preponderance of royal and government finance in the early years of these companies because of inadequate mercantile enthusiasm for them; and in the degree of personal control which Colbert himself exercised, especially over the French East India Company. So far from being a product of mercantile pressures Colbertism ran foul of merchants on more than one occasion. Colbert made himself very unpopular with those of Marseilles, for example, when, obsessed by the need to keep money circulating so that taxes could be paid, he tried to prevent them from exporting coin in order to conduct their trade with the Levant. And the highly protective anti-Dutch tariff of 1667 attracted internal opposition because it so obviously invited retaliation.

The vast regulative apparatus built up by Colbert and his successors showed more contempt than understanding of the role of businessmen. French commercial and industrial advance during the 18th century, though owing something to Colbert's initiating stimuli, continued despite, rather than because of, the perpetuation of Colbertism. Indeed, one of the reasons for the final reaction against it was the extent to which the bureaucratic machine had become both corrupt in its operation and irrelevant to the needs of the French economy. It helped the proliferation in 18th-century France of a congerie of fiscal office-holders and a concomitant trade in offices and privileges functioning in an around an overblown court. Such practices certainly existed before Colbert's day; but just as Colbert brought a new administrative zeal to old economic ideas, so Colbertism came to provide a still more fertile soil for the growth of ancient corruptions. Meanwhile, however, it appealed to other states – Prussia and the German principalities, Russia, Austria, Spain – intent on building up or repairing economic bases for the support of absolutist courts, territorial ambitions, or the urge for military glory. The sorts of mercantilism which they adopted all varied a good deal, despite the common name and some common economic ideas. But those of central, eastern and southern Europe were often much nearer in spirit to Colbertism than to the mercantile system which Smith discerned in England or to the particular variety which the Dutch had erected in Holland. Colbertism was in this sense *sui generis*.

BIBLIOGRAPHY

Cole, C.W. 1939. *Colbert and a Century of French Mercantilism.* 2 vols, New York: Columbia University Press.

Cole, C.W. 1943. *French Mercantilism, 1683–1700.* New York: Columbia University Press.

Cunningham, W. 1907. *The Growth of English Industry and Commerce.* 3 vols, Cambridge: Cambridge University Press.

Smith, A. 1776. *An Inquiry into the Nature and Causes of the Wealth of Nations.* Ed. E. Cannan, New York: Modern Library edn, 1937.

Collective Agriculture

PETER NOLAN

The socialist countries have generally modelled their rural institutions on those of the USSR in the 1930s. For the most part, means of production were owned by the so-called collective, farmwork was 'collectively' organized, and personal income 'collectively' distributed. At their peak, over one-third of the world's farmers worked under this system.

'Socialist' countries have favoured collectives for the following principal reasons.

Firstly, the leadership in most 'socialist' countries initially was afraid of an economically independent peasantry with ideas shaped by individualistic 'petty commodity production'. As Stalin put it: 'a great deal of work has to be done to remould the collective-farm peasant, to correct his individualistic mentality and to transform him into a real working member of a socialist society' (Stalin, 1929, p. 469). Collectives were not intended as independent co-operatives: collectivization was party-led and collectives were subject to considerable external control (see e.g. Davies, 1980; Volin, 1970; Selden, 1982; Unger, 1984). Such a rationale is deeply undemocratic, especially given the peasants' numerical dominance in those countries (see, in particular, Cohen, 1974, ch. 6).

Second, it was believed that state intervention through party-led collectives would improve rural economic performance (see e.g. Stalin, 1929; General Office, 1956). Collectives could raise savings and investment rates through reinvesting income and mobilizing 'surplus' labour for capital construction. Unfortunately, success in these respects can damage labour motivation by reducing current returns to collective labour. Collectives also could provide a vehicle for rapidly introducing new technology. However, this applies to bad as well as good technology – examples of the former are legion in 'socialist' agriculture, including the various programmes in the Soviet Union associated with Lysenko (discussed in Volin, 1970) and the ill-fated introduction of the double-wheeled, double-share plough, in China (Kuo, 1972, ch. 12).

Third, party-led collectives were viewed as a means to attain high farm marketing rates and an outflow of farm sector savings to finance non-farm investment:

> By transferring the disposal of agricultural output from individual peasants to government-supervised collective farm managements, collectivization destroys the basis for the peasants' resistance to the 'siphoning-off' of the economic surplus (Baran, 1957, p. 268).

However, without, for example, adequate supplies of appropriately priced industrial commodities, forcibly raising the rate of farm sector marketings can reduce the growth rate of farm output and the future volume of farm marketings. Moreover, it has proved difficult to achieve a net farm savings outflow due, for example, to agriculture's need for industrial incentive goods and farm inputs (increased, insofar as inputs are inefficiently used and collectivization adversely affects livestock holdings, motive power and fertilizer supplies), and the state's inability to control private market prices (Ellman, 1975; Ishikawa, 1967).

Fourth, it was considered that collectives would prevent 'capitalist' polarization alongside farm modernization, with the majority of peasants become wage labourers (Stalin, 1929; Mao, 1955). Evidence from other developing countries contradicts Stalin and Mao's crude vision of rural class polarization (see, especially, Hayami and Kikuchi, 1981). It indicates too that appropriate state policies (e.g. land reform, provision of education and credit, infrastructure construction, progressive taxation) can mitigate rural class inequalities. Class polarization is not the inevitable accompaniment of rural modernization, nor is collectivization the only way to resolve problems of rural class inequality (e.g. Hayami and Kikuchi, 1981).

Fifth, Lenin, Stalin and Mao all believed that agriculture was characterized by lumpiness and economies of scale (Lenin, 1899; Stalin, 1929; Mao, 1955). In many farm tasks, large scale is indeed an advantage, for example in research, processing, building and maintaining irrigation facilities. However, many modern farm inputs are divisible. Provided they are appropriately priced, credit is available and they have access to lumpy complementary inputs, all farm strata in modernizing areas tend to acquire them (Hayami and Kikuchi, 1981). Moreover, in large agricultural units labour supervision is a major problem (Bradley and Clark, 1972). If a collective's members trust each other and are motivated to work hard for the group irrespective of relative income then labour supervision is not an issue. However, this is rarely the case (Morawetz, 1983) and collective farm managers have had to devise payment systems to motivate farm workers. In certain farm tasks (notably harvesting) it is easy to pay labour according to its product, but for most farm tasks it is more difficult than in industry to devise payment systems that strongly motivate wage labour: farm work often requires a flexible response from the worker which is difficult to anticipate in the payment system; the final produce takes a long time to produce, with different workers' contributions difficult to isolate; work is physically dispersed and production conditions vary greatly from one part of the production unit to another; the main task specializations are seasonal, and permanent minute sub-division of work into easily measurable segments is not generally possible. These problems have meant that under private agriculture, if labour is relatively abundant and capital relatively expensive, the normal outcome is for land to be rented out beyond a certain farm size, so that a relatively high output per acre can be attained through self-operating, self-motivated, rent-paying farmers, rather than cultivated with large number of hired workers. In collective farms, the attempt to supervise large numbers of farm workers has resulted in powerful managerial diseconomies of scale and reduced farm efficiency.

Collective agriculture has not performed well. Collective farms in the USSR in 1929–31 and in China in 1959–61 experienced massive institutionally caused declines in farm output, accompanied by demographic disasters (on the Soviet Union, see Volin, 1970, ch. 10; on China, see Ashton, 1984). It is, indeed, a terrible indictment of collective farming, that the worst famines of the 20th century have occurred under that system. The USSR's long-term growth of farm output has required colossal capital outlays so that by the 1970s, the agricultural sector was absorbing over one quarter of Soviet new fixed investment (Carey, 1976). From the mid-1950s to the later 1970s Chinese farm output per caput was stagnant: 'de-collectivization' of agriculture in the early 1980s was accompanied by a huge rise in farm output (Nolan and Paine, 1986).

The 'socialist' countries' poor agricultural performance is in part attributable to shortcomings in the supply of industrial goods (Smith, 1981). Part is also due to extensive state intervention in collective farms. However, there are fundamental problems in principle even with relatively independent collective farms. Large units (whether state, collective or private) are necessary to undertake activities exhibiting lumpiness or economies of scale. However, for many farm tasks powerful managerial diseconomies of scale exist, and even given favourable policies in other respects, in most circumstances this would prove a barrier to good performance of collective farms.

BIBLIOGRAPHY

Ashton, B. et al. 1984. Famine in China, 1958–61. *Population and Development Review* 10(4), December, 613–45.

Baran, P. 1957. *The Political Economy of Growth*. New York: Monthly Review Press.

Bradley, M.E. and Clark, M.G. 1972. Supervision and efficiency in socialized agriculture. *Soviet Studies* 23(3), January, 465–73.

Carey, D.W. 1976. Soviet agriculture: recent performance and future plans. In USCJEC, 1976.

Cohen, S.F. 1974. *Bukharin and the Bolshevik Revolution*. London: Wildwood House; New York: Knopf.

Davies, R.W. 1980. *The Socialist Offensive: the Collective Action of Soviet Agriculture, 1929–1930*. London: Macmillan.

Ellman, M. 1975. Did the agricultural surplus provide the resources for the increase in investment in the USSR during the First Five Year Plan? *Economic Journal* 85(4), December, 844–63.

General Office of the Central Committee of the Chinese Communist Party. 1956. *Socialist High Tide in China's Villages* (*Zhongguo nongcun de shehuizhuyi gaochao*). 3 vols, Peking: People's Publishing House.

Hayami, Y. and Kikuchi, M. 1981. *Asian Village Economy at the Crossroads.* Tokyo: University of Tokyo Press.

Ishikawa, S. 1967. Resource flow between agriculture and industry. *The Developing Economies* 5(1), March, 3–49.

Kuo, L.T.C. 1972. *The Technical Transformation of Agriculture in Communist China.* London: Praeger.

Lenin, V.I. 1899. *The Development of Capitalism in Russia.* Moscow: Progress Publishers, 1964.

Mao Tsetung. 1955. On the co-operative transformation of agriculture. In Mao (1977).

Mao Tsetung. 1977. *Selected Works of Mao Tsetung.* Vol. V, Peking: Foreign Languages Press.

Morawetz, D. 1983. The kibbutz as a model for developing countries. In Stewart (1983).

Nolan, P. and Paine, S. 1986. Towards an appraisal of the impact of rural reform in China, 1978–85. *Cambridge Journal of Economics* 10(1), March, 83–99.

Selden, M. 1982. Co-operation and conflict: co-operative and collective formation in China's countryside. In Selden and Lippit (1982).

Selden, M. and Lippit, V. (eds). 1982. *The Transition to Socialism in China.* New York: M.E. Sharpe.

Smith, G.A.E. 1981. The industrial problems of Soviet agriculture. *Critique*, No. 14, 41, 65.

Stalin, J. 1929. Concerning questions of agrarian policy. In J. Stalin, *Problems of Leninism.* Peking: Foreign Languages Press, n.d.

Stewart, F. (ed.). 1983. *Work, Income and Inequality.* London: Macmillan; New York: St Martin's Press.

Unger, J. 1984. *Chen Village.* Berkeley: University of California Press.

US Congress, Joint Economic Committee (USCJEC). 1976. *Soviet Economy in a New Perspective.* Washington, DC: US Government Printing Office.

Volin, L. 1970. *A Century of Russian Agriculture.* Cambridge, Mass.: Harvard University Press.

Command Economy

GREGORY GROSSMAN

A command economy is one in which the life-cycle and activity of firms, their adjustment to disturbance, and coordination between them, are typically and in the main governed by administrative means – commands, directives, and regulations – rather than by a market mechanism. Perhaps the most distinctive feature of such an economy is the setting of the firm's production targets by higher directive, often in fine detail. The administrative means rely on planning, budgets, material balances, quotas, rationing, technical coefficients, price and wage controls, and other techniques. While the command principle is likely to clash with the operation of market forces, a command economy may nonetheless contain and rely on the market mechanism in some of its sectors and areas: for example labour allocation or small-scale private production.

The phrase 'command economy' comes from the German '*Befehlswirtschaft*', and was originally applied to the Nazi economy, which shared many formal similarities with that of Soviet Russia. Synonymous or near-synonymous terms are: 'centrally planned economy', 'centrally administered economy', 'Soviet-type economy', 'bureaucratic economy' and 'hierarchy'.

The command economy's conceptual origins go back to the Viennese economist Otto Neurath, who in the years before and after World War I developed an extreme version (to the point of moneylessness) based chiefly on prior experience with wartime economies (Raupach, 1966). Apart from the relatively short-lived Nazi case and even briefer ones under emergency conditions in some other countries, especially in wartime, actual instances of command economies are virtually limited to communist-ruled countries, with the USSR as the prototype and prime exemplar. Thus what follows is mainly inspired by the Soviet example, at the time of writing (1986) still systemically little altered since its appearance in the early 1930s. The means of production are taken to be predominantly state-owned.

A command economy is a creature of state authority, whose marks it bears and by whose hand it evolves, exists, and survives. Except in cases of external duress or mere imitation, it is established for specific purposes or reasons, such as: (1) maximum resource mobilization towards urgent and over-riding national objectives, e.g. rapid industrialization or the prosecution of war; (2) radical transformation of the socio-economic system in the collectivist direction based on ideological tenets and power-political imperatives; (3) not the least, as an answer to the disorganization of a market economy through price control, possibly occasioned by inflationary pressure arising from (1) and/or (2).

It requires a formal, centralized, administrative hierarchy staffed by a bureaucracy; it also needs to be embedded in (at least) an authoritarian, highly centralized polity if it is not to dissolve or degenerate into something else. At the same time, each office or firm and every economic actor within the command structure holds interests which, if only in part, do not coincide with those of superiors or of the overall leadership. This generates important problems of vested interests, principal–agent interaction, incentives, and general enforcement of the leadership's will, and calls for a variety of monitoring organizations (party, police, banks, etc.). The term 'command' must not be taken to preclude self-serving behaviour, bureaucratic politics, bargaining between superiors and subordinates, corruption, speculation and (dis)simulation. On the contrary, such behaviour tends to be widespread in a command economy; yet, the concept of a 'command economy' remains valid so long as, in the main, authority relations and not a market mechanism govern the allocation of resources.

Rational application of the command principle calls for planning, which is basically of two types. Longer-term, developmental planning expresses the leadership's politico-economic strategy (e.g. five-year plans); shorter-term, coordinative planning ideally translates the strategy into resource allocation while aiming to match resource requirements and availabilities for individual inputs, goods, etc., in a disaggregated way for given time periods and locations. Coordinative planning serves, thus, as the basis for specific operational directives to producers and users. A major problem is that detailed planning and the corresponding directives may lack the requisite information, often cannot be effectively coordinated, and owing to their rigidity are peculiarly vulnerable to uncertainty (cf. Ericson, 1983). Information in the command sector tends to flow vertically, up and down, rather than horizontally, between buyer and seller, adding to difficulties of demand–supply coordination. In addition, problems of motivation, accountability (down as well as up), inappropriate decision-making parameters, and divergent interests complicate the procedure. Even at best, this manner of resource allocation can hope to attain only internal consistency (in the sense of effectively matching disaggregated requirements and availabilities) but not a high order of economic efficiency. Economic calculus in quest of efficiency tends to enter more at the project-planning stage than in short-term resource allocation and use.

Though money is used in the command sector (as well as in the household sector), its role as a bearer of options and as the means of pecuniary calculation for decision-making tends to be limited and deliberately subordinated to the planners' will and the administrators' power. Banks and the treasury accommodate the money needs of production, ensuring a soft budget constraint for the individual firm. At the same time, the 'moneyness' of money at the firm level is low, hemmed in as it is by administrative constraints and impediments, including the rationing of nearly all producer goods, and by the widespread 'seller's market' (shortages of goods). This monetary ease plus the seller's market play an important role in ensuring individual worker's job security at the firm level and full employment in the large, while keeping the firm relatively insensitive to money cost.

Producer prices (and most retail prices), wages, prices of foreign currencies, etc., are generally centrally set and controlled, often remaining fixed for long periods of time. Micro-disequilibria abound. The widely perceived dubious meaningfulness of such prices and the administrative allocation of most producer goods in physical terms combine to sustain the traditional system of detailed production plans and directives in terms of physical indicators – yet another bar to more efficient planning and management.

While administrative orders are the rule in a command economy, backed up by greater or lesser degree of state coercion (depending on country and period), Soviet-type economies rely heavily on monetary ('material') incentives to elicit desired individual compliance and performance. A difficulty is that the physical and other indicators to which the material incentives are linked may often be poor measures of social benefit (as seen by the leadership). In any case, liberal resort to such rewards widens the distribution of official earnings and raises questions of permissible limits of income inequality. Yet there may be little choice in that the state must in effect compete with the much higher incomes from the second economy (*infra*). (The Soviet Union during War Communism, Cuba in the 1960s, and the People's Republic of China during some periods before Mao's death in 1976, tended to downgrade material incentives in favour of normative controls, but never did quite abolish them.)

The behaviour of the Soviet-type firm has been much studied. Because its directives ('plan') and the corresponding managerial incentives stress physical output, produced or shipped, and thanks to its low sensitivity to cost and the ambient seller's market, the firm often sacrifices product cost, quality, variety, innovation and ancillary services to its customers, for sheer product quantity. It should be noted that firms in such an economy are largely protected from any product competition, both from the outside world and from other domestic firms, thanks to the climate of administrative controls and the prevalent excess demand for their output. Difficulties with supply, frequent revision of its plans, interference by party and other authorities, and other systemic problems also stand in the way of its more efficient and effective operation. To function at all the firm's management is frequently forced to break rules and even resort to criminally punishable acts.

Such acts, together with ubiquitous and protean illegal activity on private account, add up to a large underground economy characteristic of every command economy. Together with legal private activity (allowed in varying degree in different countries), the underground economy comprises an important 'second economy', which at once supports and supplements the 'first economy' and is inimical to it. While the second economy significantly adds to the supply of goods and services, especially for consumption, it also redistributes private income and wealth, contributes to the widespread official corruption, and generally criminalizes the population (cf. Grossman, 1977).

Command economies have been instrumental in radically transforming societies more or less according to their drafters' intents, in mobilizing resources for rapid industrialization and modernization, at times on a vast scale, and in rapidly amassing industrial power and military strength. Economic growth has been especially marked (though not unparalleled by market economies) where large amounts of un- and underemployed labour and rich natural resources could be mobilized and combined with existing (Western) technology, and where the public's material improvement could be restrained, or even seriously depressed, under strong political control. As these possibilities waned, and as the economies grew in size and complexity, and thus became less amenable to centralized administrative management, rates of growth have tended to decline sharply. At the same time, their shortcomings in adapting production to demand and its changes – providing consumer welfare, effecting innovation, serving export markets – became more apparent and less tolerable. This has led to much discussion and occasional measures of institutional reform.

Some actual reforms have gone so far as to introduce or extend the market mechanism to such a degree that one can no longer regard the economy as a Soviet-type command economy, even if one cannot speak of it as a full-fledged market economy either. Yugoslavia since the early 1950s, Hungary since 1968 and especially since the early 1980s, and post-Mao China, are the most important cases in point; their analysis cannot be undertaken here. Other actual reforms have been of the minor or 'within-system' nature, aiming to decentralize certain types of decision while eschewing the market mechanism and retaining the hierarchical form of organization and the command principle. (Usually the decentralizing measures have been accompanied by a number of other measures relating to organizational structure, prices (still controlled), incentives, indicators, etc.) The Soviet reform of 1965 was of that kind; many similar ones have taken place in other communist countries since the mid-1950s. On the whole, such reforms have had little success in addressing the problems of the command economy. Bureaucratic and political obstacles apart, the attempt to decentralize economic decisions without bringing in a market mechanism almost inevitably leads to economic difficulties. The beneficiaries of devolution of decision-making often lack the necessary information to produce just what the economy requires or to invest to meet prospective needs. Moreover, they may apply the additional power at their disposal to advance particularist causes or to divert resources into illegal channels. Micro-disequilibria mount. Before long, superior authorities step in to recentralize on a case-by-case basis and the reform withers away. The command economy contains a strong immanent – perhaps even congenital – centralizing force (cf. Grossman, 1963; Wiles, 1962, ch. 7).

BIBLIOGRAPHY

Ericson, R.E. 1983. A difficulty with the 'command' allocation mechanism. *Journal of Economic Theory* 31(1), October, 1–26.

Grossman, G. 1963. Notes for a theory of the command economy. *Soviet Studies* 15, October, 101–23.

Grossman, G. 1977. The 'second economy' of the USSR. *Problems of Communism* 26(5), September, 25–40.

Raupach, H. 1966. Zur Entstehung des Begriffes Zentralverwaltungswirtschaft. *Jahrbuch für Sozialwissenschaft* 17(1), 86–101.

Wiles, P.J.D. 1962. *The Political Economy of Communism*. Cambridge, Mass.: Harvard University Press.

Control and Coordination of Economic Activity

BÉLA MARTOS

The particular point of view of the present paper is that it looks upon the economy as a *control system*. This approach was pioneered in the 1950s by Simon (1952), Tustin (1953), Phillips (1954) and Geyer and Oppelt (1957). Lange (1965) attempted an early synthesis. In the 1970s the idea became widespread and developed in two directions. The first and more popular one applied control theoretical models to *economic policy-making*. In this case the structure of the controller is considered to be given and the problem is to find values (time-paths) of the control variables such that the functioning of the economic system be acceptable (most often, stable and/or optimal) according to certain criteria. The second direction is related to the theory of economic systems, and this is where the present paper also belongs. A descriptive and explanatory *theory of economic mechanisms* is aimed at, which might be useful in the choice, change or construction of controllers. Although this research was certainly motivated by, and the findings often applied to, problems emerging in centrally planned economies, with particular reference to mechanism reform in East European countries, the theoretical framework is conceived in a more general setting. This research was initiated by Kornai (1971) and pursued further in Kornai (1980), and Kornai and Martos (1981).

In the first section I present the basic concepts and classifications, followed in the second section by the characterization of the elementary control processes, with the generation and transmission of information and decisions. The final section illustrates the usefulness of this framework by a microeconomic analysis of a non-Walrasian control model.

1. THE ECONOMIC CONTROL SYSTEM

At any point of time (t) an abstract economic system consists of the following ingredients:

A set $\mathscr{A}$ of *agents* (e.g. households, productive firms, banks, government agencies); they are the subjects of the economic activities.

A set $\mathcal{O}$ of *objects* upon which the economic agents act.

The natural, historical, social and economic environment $\mathscr{E}$, which is not a part of, but interacts with, the system.

A set $\mathscr{Y}$ of processes which connect elements of sets $\mathscr{A}$, $\mathcal{O}$ and $\mathscr{E}$ and changes their state.

When speaking about an economic system the first thing we have in mind is a national economy. However, most of the qualifications and methods we use can be applied to systems which are smaller or larger than that (e.g. an industry, a corporation, a region).

For a consistent control-theory approach two kinds of economic processes (elements of $\mathscr{Y}$) must be distinguished:

Real processes ($\mathscr{Y}_r \subset \mathscr{Y}$), which change the state of physical objects. The most important real processes are production, storage, transfer of physical objects among agents, consumption (whether for productive or for final use). The objects of real processes form the set of *commodities* ($\mathcal{O}_r \subset \mathcal{O}$). The set of real processes consists of the real activities of the agents and the external effects of the environment. The former ones depend also on the control processes; the external effects cannot be controlled. The rules which connect the real processes are mostly the laws of nature (or more to the point, technology).

Control processes ($\mathscr{Y}_c \subset \mathscr{Y}$), which change the state of knowledge of the agents and regulate their behaviour. The objects of these processes ($\mathcal{O}_c \subset \mathcal{O}$) are called *signals*. The most important control processes are observation of real processes, signal generation and transmission among agents, and decision-making (the final signal generation) on real activities. A part of the signals may come directly from the environment as far as it is observable.

Since each agent $a \in \mathscr{A}$ performs both real and control activities, it is convenient not only to split the set of activities and objects into two (real vs control) subsets but also to consider each agent as consisting of two units: the *real unit* and the *control unit*, which perform real activities and control, respectively. Needless to say, this splitting of an agent into two units is only a conceptual separation, to which an actual separation of the functions may correspond with some kind of agents (e.g. large firms), but need not in any organized form exist with other kinds (e.g. households).

Finally, to make the dichotomy of the economic system complete, we can divide even the set $\mathscr{A}$ of agents into two subsets: that of *real agents* (or real organizations), $\mathscr{A}_r \subset \mathscr{A}$, whose *main* activities belong to the real processes (like households or productive firms) and that of *control agents* (or control organizations), $\mathscr{A}_c \subset \mathscr{A}$, whose *main* activity lies in information-processing and decision-making (like legislative bodies, local authorities, government agencies).

This classification of the agents requires some further comments. Firstly, there might be borderline agents (e.g. schools) whose classification is ambiguous and will be dependent on the role which they play in a given context. Secondly, the real units (real activities) of the control organizations are often negligible in theoretical considerations (just as the energy input of an electric control device might be negligible compared to the energy input of the physical process it controls). We also will make use of this simplification in the sequel and disregard the real activities of the control agents.

Finally, a few words are in order about the place of *fiduciary goods* (banknotes, accounting money, stocks and bonds), *monetary processes* (emission, exchange, income generation, credit) and *financial organizations* (banks, stockbrokers, tax offices) in the above dichotomy. Since it is not the physical transformation of fiduciary goods which is of economic interest (and hence they cannot belong to the real commodities), they belong to the control sphere by exclusion (in contrast with many other theoretical approaches where money is simply taken as one of the commodities). However, it must be kept in mind that the monetary sphere plays not only a particularly important part in the control of economic activities, but is in many aspects different from the rest of the control processes and obeys laws which are partly similar to the ones valid in the real sphere. A thorough discussion of the consequences of this reasoning would require a separate entry.

The economic control system can also be interpreted in the language of mathematical control theory. In a standard state-space representation of a continuously operating, multivariate, deterministic, externally commanded system, it consists of three equations:

Controlled subsystem:

$$\dot{x} = \Phi(t, x, u, z) \tag{1}$$

Measurement:

$$y = \Psi(x) \tag{2}$$

Controller:

$$u = \Theta(t, y - y^*), \tag{3}$$

where $t \geq 0$ denotes time and the dot above a variable differentiation with respect to time, $x(t)$ is the state vector, $u(t)$ is the control vector, $y(t)$ is the output vector, $y^*(t)$ is the command vector (the normal value of y), $z(t)$ is the vector of external effects on the state and Φ, Ψ and Θ are functions of their arguments as indicated.

The above system is said to be (globally) *viable* with respect to a closed convex subset $\mathcal{K}$ (the viability set) of the state space (the space of xs) if $x \in \mathcal{K}$ for all $t \geq 0$ and any given initial state $x(0) = x_0 \in \mathcal{K}$. If there is a state $\bar{x} \in \text{Int } \mathcal{K}$ and a number $\delta > 0$ such that $x \in \mathcal{K}$ for all $t \geq 0$ and any given initial state

$x_0 \in \mathcal{K} \cap \{x \mid \|x - \bar{x}\| < \delta\}$, that is in the neighbourhood of $\bar{x}$, then the system is said to be *locally viable* at $\bar{x}$ with respect to $\mathcal{K}$.

It was proved by Aubin and Cellina (1983, theorem 5.4.1) that under some continuity, convexity and compactness assumptions there is a feedback rule Θ such that the system (1) to (3) is globally viable. It is to be noted, however, that this is an existence theorem from which no conclusion can be drawn, in this generality, as to how the appropriate feedback rule Θ can be constructed.

The form (1) to (3) is, of course, not the only mathematical form in which a control system can be represented, but it is general enough to cover many important cases and special forms, which are too numerous to list here even partially. I would rather mention systems which are not explicitly represented by the above formulation.

(a) *Intermittently operating systems*. It is frequently the case that, especially in economic applications, the measurement of the state is not done continuously but only at discrete points of time. In this case the value of the control variable remains constant in between. If the observation times are equidistant, the above formulation can easily be transformed to cover this case simply by replacing the differential operator of the left-hand side by a time shift operator $Ex(t) = x(t + 1)$.

(b) *Stochastic systems* arise if x and/or y and/or u represent stochastic processes, and consequently some of the operators, Φ, Ψ, Θ have stochastic values. In the case of a stochastic Φ, the controlled system works erratically; a stochastic Ψ indicates measurement errors; and a stochastic Θ indicates uncertain control behaviour. These are frequent cases in economic systems. (It is to be noted that any random disturbance on z and y^*, i.e. on variables representing the environment, does not make the system stochastic, they are the realizations which enter the functions.)

(c) *Optimum control*, in which case the control rule is not given in the form (3) but is rather a solution to the problem of maximizing a given functional

$$I = \int_0^T \mu(t, x, u)\, dt$$

subject to (1) and some other constraints which require the control variable u to belong to a given set $\mathcal{U}$, and where μ is a scalar function of the arguments.

(d) *Higher-order systems* (as contrasted to externally commanded systems) take different forms:

Self-command (or target modifying) systems produce the command signals y^* themselves.

Learning systems modify the form or parameter values characterizing the operator Θ; a learning mechanism improves the controller.

Self-organizing systems are capable of changing the control structures, the organizations and the interrelations among them both in the controlled subsystem and the controller.

Although it is clear that most economic systems perform such higher-order functioning, their mathematical analysis is difficult and mostly reduced to narrowly specified cases.

2. THE STRUCTURE OF THE CONTROLLER

The controller was typified in equation (3) in a very rough-and-ready way. In actual economic systems the controller has a rather complicated structure, consisting of many different elements which interact in various ways. Some of the elements make simple observations, routine calculations, bookkeeping, and so on; others collect, generate and disseminate important information or make crucial decisions and plans relying on a vast amount of preprocessed information. Some of them work in parallel on different sets of data, and some form interactive or hierarchically ordered groups.

The study of such a structure must begin with the functioning of its constituent elements which are called *transfer elements*. A transfer element is an elementary part of a complex controller which cannot be divided further or has not been in a particular analysis.

There are three subsequent actions in the functioning of a transfer element:

Signal reception. The transfer element receives signals (information) from the observation of real processes, from the environment or from another transfer element. These are the *input signals* of the element.

Signal transformation or signal generation. The transfer element transforms, stores and combines the received signals and thereby generates new ones. The rules by which signals are generated form the *transfer function* of the element.

Signal emission. The transfer element transmits the generated signal (*output signal*) to one or more other transfer elements or to an agent which acts directly on real processes.

In the classification of the elementary control process we apply two criteria both with respect to the kinds of agents who participate in the process: – What kind of agent generates the signal? – Among what kind of agents is the signal transmitted?

With respect to *signal generation* we distinguish three kinds of processes:

Uncoordinated. The signal is generated by the control unit of a single real organization.

Interactive. The signal is generated jointly by the control units of several real organizations.

Centralized. The signal is generated by a control organization or jointly by several control and perhaps real organizations.

With respective to *signal transmission* we also distinguish three kinds of process:

Non-communicative. The signal does not leave the organization where it was generated.

Transactional. The sender and the addressee are two different real organizations, and the signal refers to an (actual or potential) real transaction (usually transfer of a commodity) between the two real organizations (e.g. dispatch of an order, a price quotation, a bill).

Communicative (non-transactional). Any other signal transmission; for example, among more than two real organizations, or whenever a control organization is the sender or the addressee or both.

This dual classification of the transfer elements can be summarized as shown in Table 1. The two empty boxes represent signal generation–transmission combinations which cannot occur. (An interactive signal generation implies some kind of communication, since to generate signals jointly by several real organizations, they must communicate somehow. In the centralized signal generation a control organization takes part, hence it cannot be transactional.)

This simple classification scheme can be applied to elementary transfer units of the controller only. In a complex control process several transfer units are combined which differ with respect to their signal generation and transmission patterns.

Most of the actually existing economic control systems may be called *partially coordinated systems*, in which a considerable part of the decisions are taken by the real organizations in isolation, another part by their interaction (e.g. on the market) and yet another part by different control agents (e.g. legislative bodies, government agencies, banks, trade unions etc.). The problem of analysing (synthesizing) an economic control system consists of the decision about whether one or the other function of the system is (should be) served by this or that kind of transfer unit and how these units are (can be) integrated into a viable or even efficient entity.

An essential feature of the above conceptualization of the structure of the economic control system is that it does not restrict the issue to 'control and coordination of economic activity' from the outside (done exclusively by specialized control organizations) but includes the control functions which work within the real organizations and interact among them. It is also to be noted that the classical distinction between centralized and decentralized control turned out to be insufficient and has been replaced by a more elaborate classification pattern.

Table 1

| | Signal generation | | |
| | Uncoordinated | Coordinated | |
Signal transmission		Interactive	Centralized
Non-communicative	+	∅	+
Transactional	+	+	∅
Communicative (non-transactional)	+	+	+

3. A NON-WALRASIAN CONTROL STRUCTURE

The first economic theory which offered a mathematically rigorous representation of the control mechanism of a national economy is known under the term *General Equilibrium Theory*. Since neither Keynesian macroeconomics in capitalistic systems nor shortage phenomena in socialist economies could have been appropriately studied within the framework of this theory, a new approach emerged under various names: *disequilibrium theory, temporary equilibrium theory, theory of equilibria with rationing, non-Walrasian equilibrium theory*. Without discussing here merits and demerits of these approaches, it is to be noted that – as a rule – there were not based on mathematical control theory.

In what follows I present a non-Walrasian control model differing from the aforementioned approaches in many aspects:

(a) It is not only the (essentially static) equilibrium, its existence and efficiency, which is studied, but rather the dynamics of the trajectories leading to an equilibrium state. Real and control processes run in parallel (out of equilibrium); there is no timeless *tâtonnement* process.

(b) No optimizing behaviour of the agents is assumed; adjustment to exogenous normal values of some output variables is the behavioural rule. When applying this 'control by norm' principle I assume that norms are formed by individual experience or social consent in a long-run process (which is not modelled here), and the norms remain constant along the short- and medium-run adjustment process.

(c) Information and decisions are not centralized as in the hands of an auctioning or rationing agent, but the whole control process is carried out by the control units of real organizations among themselves in an uncoordinated but transactionally communicative way. (This refers only to the particular model variant which follows. In other variants control organizations and coordination also appear.)

(d) Only observable variables are used (no fictitious 'effective demand') and hence the underlying assumptions can be, but generally have not been, empirically tested. (For an exception, see Kawasaki, McMillan and Zimmermann, 1982.)

Still it is to be admitted that this approach has not yet reached the generality and mathematical refinement of general equilibrium and disequilibrium theory.

The model. The economy consists of *n* producers (real organizations), each producing a single commodity. The technology is of the Leontief-type, with constant input coefficients. The environment acts upon the real processes by the final use (private and public consumption, investment) and on the control processes by past experiences, which determine the normal level of inventories (output stocks, input stocks) and backlog orders.

Notation: lower case – *n*-vector; upper case – $n \times n$ matrix; Greek lower case – scalar.

Problems of the planned economy

State variables:
  q – vector of output stocks
  V – matrix of input stocks
  K – matrix of backlog orders
  An asterisk * as a superscript refers to the exogenous normal values of the state variables.
Control variables:
  r – vector of production ($\langle r \rangle$: the diagonal matrix formed from r)
  Y – matrix of commodity transfers among producers
  W – matrix of the transmission of new orders
Other notations:
  $e = [1, 1, \ldots, 1]'$ – the summation vector
  A – the input coefficient matrix
  c – the vector of final uses
  β, γ – control parameters
  $\Gamma(\cdot) = -2\beta\gamma[d(\cdot)/dt] - \gamma^2 \cdot (\cdot)$ – differential operator.
Assumptions:
  1. The final use is constant and semipositive, $c \geqslant 0$.
  2. The input coefficient matrix A is constant and
     (a) non-negative
     (b) irreducible
     (c) productive, i.e. its spectral radius $\rho(A) < 1$.
  3. $\gamma > 0$ (without loss of generality).
The real processes:

$$\dot{q} = r - Ye - c \tag{1}$$

$$\dot{V} = Y - A\langle r \rangle. \tag{2}$$

Equation (1) expresses the change of output stocks as the difference between the amounts produced and that transferred for productive and final use. Equation (2) tells that the change of input stocks equals the material purchases minus the materials used up in production.

The control processes:

$$\dot{K} = W - Y \tag{3}$$

$$\dot{r} = \Gamma(q - q^*) \tag{4}$$

$$\dot{W} = \Gamma(V - V^*) \tag{5}$$

$$\dot{Y} = -\Gamma(K - K^*). \tag{6}$$

Equation (3) describes the bookkeeping (at the supplier) of the backlog of orders; its change equals the difference between the incoming new orders and the deliveries. Equations (4) to (6) are the control equations proper, all of the same (linear) form, describing the assumed behaviour of the agents. The decisions on production level are dependent on the output stocks, the dispatch of orders (by

70

the buyer) on the input stocks, and the deliveries (decided by the supplier) on the backlog of orders, in each case taking the deviation of the actual value from the normal value into account. None of these behavioural rules is at variance with common sense.

It is to be observed, that the transfer elements corresponding to equations (3) to (6) generate all the signals without any coordination; equations (3), (4) and (6) represent non-communicative elements, while there is transactional communication according to equation (5); namely, the orders are transmitted from the buyers to the suppliers.

The viability domain $\mathscr{K}$ for system (1) to (6) may be defined in the following way:

(a) All the variables are uniformly bounded, but the bounds are unspecified.

(b) The variables in q, V, K, r and Y are non-negative, but negative elements of W (withdrawal of orders) are permitted.

Although the theorem of Aubin and Cellina referred to above does not apply here, where we specified the form of the control equations (3) to (6), we can still guarantee local viability in the neighbourhood of the equilibrium state by an appropriate choice of the parameter β.

Theorem. Suppose that the following conditions are met:

(a) Assumptions (1) to (3) hold.

(b) The norms are positive: $q^* > 0$, $V^* > 0$, $K^* > 0$.

(c) $\beta > \max\{|\mathrm{Im}\ \sigma|/(2|\sigma|\sqrt{\mathrm{Re}\ \sigma})| - \sigma^3 + 2\sigma^2 - 2\sigma + 1 \in \text{spectrum of } A\}$ and $\beta > \sqrt{6}/4$.

(d) The initial values at $t = 0$: $(q^0, V^0, K^0, r^0, Y^0, W^0)$ are close enough to the equilibrium state:

$$\bar{q} = q^*, \qquad \bar{V} = V^*, \qquad \bar{K} = K^*,$$

$$\bar{r} = (E - A)^{-1}c, \qquad \bar{Y} = \bar{W} = A\langle (E - A)^{-1}c \rangle.$$

Then the system (1) to (6) is viable for $t \geq 0$ (local viability).

Remark: under (a) the relation (c) is both a necessary and sufficient condition of asymptotic stability.

A detailed analysis of the model and proof of the theorem (extended to varying c) is to be found in a forthcoming book by Martos. Models in a similar vein are analysed in Kornai and Martos (1981).

BIBLIOGRAPHY

Aubin, J.P and Cellina, A. 1983. *Differential Inclusions.* Berlin: Springer.

Geyer, W. and Oppelt, W. (eds) 1957. *Volkswirtschaftliche Regelungsvorgänge im Vergleich zu Regelungsvorgängen in der Technik.* Munich.

Kawasaki, S., McMillan, J. and Zimmermann, K.F. 1982. Disequilibrium dynamics: an empirical study. *American Economic Review* 72, 992–1003.

Kornai, J. 1971. *Anti-Equilibrium.* Amsterdam: North-Holland.

Kornai, J. 1980. *Economics of Shortage.* Amsterdam: North-Holland.

Kornai, J. and Martos, B. (eds) 1981. *Non-Price Control*. Amsterdam: North-Holland.

Lange, O. 1965. *Wstep do cybernetyki ekonomicznej* (Introduction to economic cybernetics). Warsaw: Państwowe Wydawnictwo Naukowe.

Phillips, A.W. 1954. Stabilization policy in a closed economy. *Economic Journal* 64, 290–323.

Simon, H.A. 1952. On the application of servomechanism theory in the study of production control. *Econometrica* 20, 247–68.

Tustin, A. 1953. *The Mechanism of Economic Systems*. London: Heinemann.

Convergence Hypothesis

P.J.D. WILES

This is the doctrine that the Soviet Union and 'similar countries' are becoming and will further become socially and economically similar to the United States and other advanced capitalist countries; or the other way round – so that eventually in either case political differences, and thus foreign policy tensions, will also disappear.

The doctrine takes many detailed forms, but is most often very unspecific. For instance does it mean: that Texan agriculture will be collectivized (each family farm is larger in area than a Soviet *Kolkhoz*); that there will be a stock exchange again in Moscow, where equity shares in Soviet businesses are freely traded; that the *zloty* will be made convertible; that Switzerland will introduce controls over all retail and wholesale prices; that British trade unions will be reduced to the status of Bulgarian trade unions, or vice versa; that Albania will allow a good deal of minor private enterprise; or even that both sides will converge upon self management in a market, *à la Yougoslave*?

The proponents of the doctrine seldom do it the courtesy of bringing it so close to brass tacks. Above all they fail to recognize just how numerous and diverse those brass tacks are. But the core of the doctrine is clear: advanced capitalism is (said to be) moving, through the large corporation (often public) and its intimacy with certain government departments, irreparably away from share-holder dominance, free enterprise and free markets, in respect of all sectors where small enterprise does not dominate; and a new socio-political type is coming to power, nearly indistinguishable in government and business, and very liable to swap jobs (corruptly, let us add). Meanwhile the advanced Communist states are admitting more and more the role of enterprise independence and markets for everyday small decisions; even the quasi-independence of associations of enterprises in larger decisions – the association would correspond to the corporation and the Communist enterprises to its separate, decentralized 'establishments'.

Hungary and France are of course very much further forward in convergence.

A major problem, too, for Convergence theorists and for sceptics alike, is China. Here, right at the bottom of the Communist income scale and without even having first introduced any central planning worthy of the name, 20 per cent of the human race is 'converging' very rapidly indeed. As partly too in Hungary, even private property in the means of production is making a comeback. It is not easy to fit this fact into the ordinary framework of debate.

As to a new socio-political type in power in government and 'business', in the USSR ideology is dying and the typical Party apparatchik is more and more obliged to have had some serious professional training and responsibility within the State machine. Meanwhile the obligatory Party membership of the senior technocrat continues to lie lightly on his shoulders. What then is this type, on both sides? It is above all a professional type: technically educated, pragmatic but accepting the particular value system of the given profession, believing in the rule of reason but unphilosophically confusing it with what was judged reasonable at professional school, striving for a higher 'earned' income as the right of competence in his chosen profession, and naive as to what constitutes the rule of reason in unprofessional matters (which are of course the very great majority of matters). One may think in 1986, as the fathers of Convergence certainly did not think, of the American term Yuppie (Young Upwardly Mobile Professionals). However, in the USSR Yuppies are much more idealistic and critical.

It is clear that every prophecy made about Communism in the previous paragraphs is coming true, and the Convergence theorists deserve praise for this – although it took much longer than they expected. The rule of reason is taking over, and the notion that the Soviet system is a frozen monolith, condemned to remain for ever its unpleasant and highly suboptimal (but rapidly growing!) self, is unfounded. But capitalism by no means shows the predicted unilinear change. Japan in one way ('industrial policy', unnaturally accommodating unions) and France in another (mild planning) used to be the showpieces of convergence from the other side. But recent Japanese financial reforms have tended to open up the country to free trade in money, and French planning is at present being down-graded. Monetarist and supply-sider attacks on the public sector and on taxes in the USA and the UK constitute divergence. So does the new tolerance for very heavy unemployment; even if Communist economic experts talk about the necessity for a little unemployment to discipline labour and create flexibility, the 'target' of Western levels is rapidly receding!

It is, then, capitalism that has 'misbehaved'. And if the rule of reason is eventually restored to economic affairs in the Western world, exactly how far, in so unreasonable a universe, will present divergent trends be reversed? We can at least be sure that protectionism – if that is reason – having flourished even under monetarism, will bloom yet taller under what succeeds it. Indeed under this or that institutional guise, protectionism is common to all systems except capitalist laissez-faire in the 19th century. Then too why should not the rule of reason be 'relaxed' again in the East? Besides, 'reason is and ought to be the slave of the passions': if the value systems of Communism and democratic Capitalism continue to diverge only half as much as now, this is cause enough for the reasonable choice of radically divergent policies and substantially divergent institutions.

These considerations alone give us pause before we can accept the basic optimism of Convergence theory. We pause to note that the seven questions of our second paragraph have not been answered at all. But there is worse – though outside of economics – to follow. Since when did resemblance make for peace? Since when was dissimilarity a cause of war? Especially in this ideological age, is not *minor* dissimilarity, or heresy, a major cause of war? For that matter, do not Third World capitalist countries make war on each other, quite unabashedly, over mere boundary disputes and ethnic irredentas in quite the old style? It is a very long way from convergence in respect of planning and the market, to international peace.

The alleged *aetiology* of convergence could, as set out above, be the existence of an optimal system somewhere in the middle, to which all existing systems gravitate simply because it is better. If, as is often reasonably claimed, the Yugoslav industrial system represents a third pole of equal theoretical importance, then moderate elements of self-management must be added to that optimal goal. But this is all mere wishful thinking: the judgements of politicians and (where they are counted) voters do not coincide all over the world with each other, let alone with the opinions of centre-left economists. An economic system good for some purposes (e.g. full employment, equality) is bad for others (e.g. rational resource allocation, stable prices, labour discipline). As we have seen, people *value* different sets of outcomes differently, and are also confused as to how in practice to obtain them.

But convergence through contact and competition is another matter. Since nearly all people are unthinking materialists, contact (say as an importer and an exporter) will sway them to imitate the at present more prosperous system: capitalism, to which may or may not be attached, in the perception of observers, parliamentary democracy. And this is truer of people living under Communism that of people in the Third World: for the latter are apt to attribute capitalist prosperity to the exploitation of themselves. Sheer economic contact undoubtedly influences Communist leaders in a capitalist direction, if only because of the overwhelmingly unfavourable balance of technological exchange.

Competition is the almost inevitable result of contact: both commercial and military. It goes without saying that competitors in an export market imitate each other, and not only in quality and technology embodied; but even the administrative systems of the enterprises producing the exports will converge on the one that is seen to be superior. Exporting is a sure and genuine source of convergence, that the most hard-nosed Sovietologist must accept. Military rivalry has much the same effects; for a country's forces also 'export' – a threat. But if the convergence of military technology and its maintenance and auxiliary equipment is of obvious relevance to economic systems, that of military doctrine and organization is not our subject. Still less is the convergence of para-military 'exports': training for guerrillas and terrorists, security systems for under-developed countries, espionage.

It can be seen that while high convergence theory is largely (but not altogether) hot air and wishful thinking, there exists a great deal of low-level convergence in fact, all of it easily explicable and much of it very regrettable.

Corporatism

JOSEPH HALEVI

Corporatism is a set of political doctrines aimed at organizing civil society on the basis of professional and occupational representation in chambers called Estates or Corporations. It maintains that class conflict is not inherent in the capitalist system of production and ownership relations. Corporatism has its ideological roots mainly in 19th-century French and Italian Catholic social thought, as well as in German romanticism and idealism. Corporative ideas can be found in eminent European thinkers. Hegel, in his *Philosophy of Right*, thought of a corporate structure in which the Estates constituted the link between civil society and the State (Hegel, 1821). In France, Durkheim put forward a view of corporatism specifically related to the division of labour engendered by modern industry. According to Durkheim, the Corporations' task is to diversify at the level of each industry the general principles of industrial legislation formulated by the political assemblies (Durkheim, 1893).

The Catholic strand appeared first as a response to the social cleavages stemming from the industrialization of Europe. It advocated a return to the corporate form of guild associations of the Middle Ages, which it romantically viewed as based on social harmony. In 1891 the papal encyclical Rerum Novarum took a more reformist approach. It rejected the notion that 'class is naturally hostile to class, and that the wealthy and the working men are intended by nature to live in mutual conflict' (Rerum Novarum, 1891; in Camp, 1969, p. 81). At the same time it recognized the legitimacy of independent workers' unions, although preference was given to the creation of a single organization embracing employers and employees. In practice the Catholic movement opted for the first variant, partly because the industrialists rejected the idea of a single organization and partly because of the strength of the Socialist-led unions.

Where politics were concerned, in countries like Italy and Germany, the Catholics gradually reconciled their corporative social views with parliamentarism. In other instances, the Catholic movement aimed at supplanting parliamentary institutions altogether. In Austria, for example, the alliance between the Social

Christians and the fascist Heimwehr was the basis of the corporative Constitution passed before the assassination of Chancellor Dolfuss, in 1934.

Germany produced an important theoretician of corporatism: Karl Marlo. He wrote a comprehensive critique of liberalism in favour of Estate organizations (Marlo, 1885). His views are a reaction to the radicalization of the working class, which led to the 1848 Revolution. In that year, Marlo proposed to the Frankfurt Parliament that it form a social chamber composed by the representatives of all occupations whose task would be to formulate the social legislation to be approved by the political chamber.

Modern corporatism begins with the idealist jurist and Italian nationalist Alfredo Rocco. In his conception corporatism was an instrument for fostering the productive power of the nation. He considered the Estates to be merely organs of the State.

Italian fascism absorbed Rocco's views from its inception, although it combined them with elements of Catholic corporatism as well as with aspects of the doctrine of revolutionary syndicalism held by Georges Sorel (Togliatti, 1970). The syndicalist component was eliminated in 1926 when Rocco, who had become Mussolini's Minister of Justice, legally recognized the fascist unions only, banning all the others in existence. Under the pressure of the employers' association, Italian Confederation of Industry, shop floor committees, which the syndicalists wanted to retain, were also outlawed. The Italian corporative state was institutionalized when in 1927 a labour charter (Carta del Lavoro) was promulgated and, in 1934, a law was issued establishing 22 Estates. In 1939 their 500 delegates formed the Camera dei Fasci e delle Corporazioni, which replaced the Chamber of Deputies.

Italy's corporative state did not coordinate economic activity. Instead, it enabled the Government to control labour relations by making tutelage over the newly created labour unions legal. It enforced arbitrarion tribunals formed by a judge and two experts, thereby excluding any kind of worker representation even from the fascist unions (Salvemini, 1936; Rossi, 1955).

The rescue operations to save the Banca Commerciale which led to the formation in 1933 of the state-holding IRI (Institute for Industrial Reconstruction) are to be linked to the impact of the Depression on the endemic banking crisis in Italy rather than to any corporative economic programme. Already in 1922, Piero Sraffa pointed out that the frequent crises of Italy's banking system were caused by the fact that banks' activities were based on lending short while borrowing long. Sraffa showed that this was a structural characteristic of the Italian economy (Sraffa, 1922). The Depression magnified the above tendencies and the Government found itself compelled to intervene on an unprecedented scale.

The corporative juridical structure only played an indirect economic role. It legalized, as part of the Estates, a very subordinate form of unionism, while allowing the employers to struggle – within the Estates – for the creation of Consortia which, once approved, became compulsory (Rossi, 1955). Here there is both a similarity and a difference vis-à-vis the German case. The National

Socialist regime pursued a policy of forced cartelization – an objective shared by many industrial groups well before 1933 – but not through a legal system of a syndicalist, corporative character. Workers were organized in a completely separate body called the Labour Front (Neumann, 1944; Kuczynski, 1945).

The juridically more complete nature of Italian corporatism became a reference for populist movements in South America. One important example is the Estado Novo established in Brazil under President Getulio Vargas in the years 1937–46. Following the Italian pattern a Labour Charter was issued. The decree-laws of 1939 legalized government prerogatives over labour unions, which were exercised by the Ministry of Labour.

Unlike Italy, Brazilian corporatism allowed the emergence of strong reformist demands. Although labour relations were governed by norms which prevented the formation of alliances between different groups of workers, the process leading to the corporative state marked also the appearance of formal unionism. Hence in Brazil during the liberal phase (1946–64) populist forces were capable of using institutions designed to control the working class for the purpose of giving political power to labour leaders (Erickson, 1977). Yet the strengthening of corporatism came from the conservative forces themselves, which after the coup d'état of 1964 tightened the controls over labour organizations.

The main element of modern corporatism consists in a detailed network of technical and juridical norms, enforced by ministerial bodies, aimed at controlling the labour movement. A formal system of Estates had either an incidental character (Italy) or was never implemented.

The economic views of the main advocates of corporatism have never reached an analytical dimension. During the 1930s in Italy some discussion took place around the issue of *homo corporativus* versus *homo oeconomicus* (Mancini, Parillo and Zagari, 1982).

BIBLIOGRAPHY

Camp, R. 1969. *The Papal Ideology of Social Reform. A Study in Historical Development, 1878–1967*. Leiden: E.J. Brill.

Durkheim, E. 1893. *The Division of Labour in Society*. London: Macmillan, 1933.

Erickson, K. 1977. *The Brazilian Corporate State and Working Class Politics*. Berkeley: University of California Press.

Hegel, G. 1821. *Hegel's Philosophy of Right*. London and New York: Oxford University Press, 1967.

Kuczynski, J. 1945. *Germany: Economic and Labour Conditions under Fascism*. New York: International Publishers.

Mancini, O., Parillo, F. and Zagari, E. 1982. *La Teoria Economica del Corporativismo*. Naples: Edizioni Scientifiche Italiane.

Marlo, K. 1885. *Untersuchungen über die Organisation der Arbeit*. Tübingen.

Neumann, F. 1944. *Behemoth; the Structure and Practice of National Socialism, 1933–1944*. New York: Octagon Books.

Rossi, E. 1955. *Padroni del Vapore e Fascismo*. Bari: Laterza.

Salvemini, G. 1936. *Under the Axe of Fascism*. New York: Viking Press,

Sraffa, P. 1922. The bank crisis in Italy. *Economic Journal* 32, June, 178–97.

Togliatti, P. 1970. *Lectures on Fascism*. New York: International Publishers, 1976.

Cycles in Socialist Economies

D.M. NUTI

In the Marxist–Leninist project of socialist economy the elimination of cycles in economic activity is the expected result of central planning replacing the 'anarchy' of capitalist markets. *Ex-ante* coordination of the activities of government, households and firms according to a consistent, feasible and efficient plan should, in principle, ensure the continued full employment of labour and other resources along smooth growth paths instead of the recurring bouts of booms and recessions and persistent unemployment characteristic of capitalism.

The experience of those capitalist countries which, especially since World War II, have tried to implement a social-democratic version of this project while maintaining free enterprise does not differ significantly, at least qualitatively, from that of more conventional capitalist economies. Built-in stabilizers and anticyclical management of demand may have reduced the amplitude of fluctuations and the depth of unemployment (though some government intervention has been deemed cyclical because of leads and lags); the individual cost of fluctuations and unemployment has been partly collectivized by the welfare state; but the undesired phenomena have persisted. The same is true for Yugoslavia, a country which has implemented an associationist form of socialism introducing self-management on a large scale but has retained enterprise initiative and markets.

Other countries attempted to implement the Marxist–Leninist project – state ownership, central planning, equalitarianism, 'democratic centralism' under the leadership (and practical monopoly of power) of the communist party, as in the Soviet Union, the East European Six, Mongolia, China, Cuba and the other countries loosely classed as centrally planned economies or CPEs. These countries have been successful in eliminating fluctuations in the degree of labour employment. Full employment of labour was reached in the Soviet Union at the inception of the First Five-Year Plan (1928) as a result of full-scale mobilization of labour and in the other countries in the course of reconstruction after the wars that brought about the new system. Ambitious accumulation policies maintained full employment; the wage pressure generated by labour shortage itself, combined with government commitment to price stability, added sustained excess demand for consumption which contributed further to full employment stability, without any need for specific policies to support it. Full employment has been the by-product of growthmanship. In view of the persistent microeconomic inefficiency of central planning and the underfulfilment of labour productivity targets it can also be said, in a sense, that full employment of labour has been achieved 'by default'. If, however, the decentralization process currently undertaken in most centrally planned economies were to reproduce unemployment tendencies no doubt specific policies would be adopted to restore and stabilize full employment.

Outside labour employment the performance of socialist planning has been less satisfactory than originally expected. In the Soviet Union, since the completion of reconstruction and the launching of accelerated industrialization in 1928, and in the other socialist countries since the corresponding dates in their economic history, fast growth of all performance indicators in peacetime until *circa* 1960 has smoothed small-scale cyclical phenomena, reducing them to fluctuations of positive growth rates rather than of levels of income and consumption. Since then, partly because of the gradual exhaustion of labour reserves and of easily accessible natural resources, partly because of the systemic microeconomic inefficiency exacerbated by the lack of such reserves, a discernible slowdown of growth trends has been accompanied by the appearance of negative rates, i.e. fluctuations of levels as in capitalist countries. Instances range from the early minor case of Czechoslovakia in 1963 to the large-scale income drop of one third in three years in Poland 1980–82.

These phenomena are only partly attributable to exogenous shocks and their echoes, whose persistence in the socialist economy was recognized by Oskar Lange (1969), or to adjustment processes such as accelerator-type movements, whose persistence in the socialist economy had been anticipated by Aftalion already in 1909 and recognized by Notkin (1961) and Coblijc–Stojanovic (1968). Partly – indeed mostly – these phenomena are caused by systemic factors which could be classed under three groups: (i) the lack, or at any rate the slowness, of automatic adjustment feedbacks in the economic life of centrally planned economies; (ii) the acceleration of economic activity towards the end of the planning period – be it a month, a year or five years – to avoid the formal and informal penalties of underfulfilment of targets and to obtain the rewards associated with fulfilment and overfulfilment, followed by slackening at the beginning of the next period; (iii) the presence of political feedbacks, such as popular discontent and unrest resulting from deteriorating economic performance, the changes in political centralization induced by manifestations of unrest, the economic management changes associated with political changes; these phenomena adding up to a systemic mechanism of economic/political cycles.

Markets, like all servomechanisms or homeostatic (self-regulating) devices, are neither costless nor instantaneous but are automatic in their operation; at the cost of unemployment and possibly with a considerable lag, for example, an unexpected contraction in world trade can be gradually accommodated through lower wages and prices than would otherwise have prevailed, lower exchange rate and higher interest rates regardless of government intervention, capital flows etc. Central planning, like manual control, may or may not be faster and cheaper, or more accurate, than automatic servomechanisms, depending on the relative quality of alternative controls and the actual circumstances, but it is never automatic. The experience of centrally planned economies has shown repeated and sometimes glaring instances of inertia and sluggish response to exogenous change, such as persistent accelerated accumulation in the face of rising labour shortages, wage and price stability administratively enforced in spite of rising excess demand for labour and goods, systematic underpricing of imported materials and of exportables in spite of sharpening external imbalance. Reliance on monetary budget constraints and the continued presence of consumers' discretion (if not sovereignty) and some managerial room for manoeuvre make these forms of inertia and delayed response an important handicap for central planners trying to outperform market adjustments. It is precisely inadequate central response to a changing environment (including inadequate ability to innovate institutions and technology) that has given impetus to repeated attempts at reform in the last two decades.

The incentive system typical of central planning, strongly and discontinuously geared to the degree of fulfilment of physical targets, leads to frantic speeding-up of activity (*shturmovshchina* in Russian, literally 'storming') towards the end of the planning period. For monthly plans this haste leads to frequent quality deterioration; for yearly plans 'storming' leads to output being overestimated, or 'borrowed' from the subsequent period (i.e., made up through subsequent unrecorded additional output); so much so that the ratio of December output to that of the following January can be regarded as an index of economic centralization (Rostowski and Auerbach, 1984). For five years plans, 'storming implies a concentration of investment project completions towards the end of the period and a spate of new starts at the beginning, with corresponding fluctuations. Moreover, the generalized growthmanship and emphasis on capital accumulation typical of the centrally planned economy leads usually to the inclusion in investment plans of more projects than can be completed on schedule, through 'investors' (local authorities, ministries, enterprises) underestimating true requirements in order to get a place in the plan and later escalating their demands, and through central planners systematically overestimating capacity and especially labour productivity prospects. Sometimes investment ambition leads to additional investment projects being added after or outside the plan balance (as in Gierek's Poland). As they say in East European literature, 'the investment front widens'. Sooner or later specific or generalized bottlenecks of productive or import capacity slow down implementation and reduce or block new starts. Efficiency falls due to investment resources being frozen for periods longer than economically and technically justified, and possibly because of disruption elsewhere in the economy due to resources being sucked in by investment projects given priority over current operations (a 'supply-multiplier' effect). Capital – i.e.

in Marxian terminology 'dead labour' – is made unemployed instead of live labour. The cyclical pattern of starts and completions of projects, mostly within the plan period but sometimes overstepping it, leads to cyclical patterns of capacity and output endogenously generated by the system and not justified by exogenous factors. These processes have been investigated theoretically and empirically by Olivera (1960), Goldmann (1964 and 1965), Baijt (1971), Bauer (1978), Dahlstedt (1981), Dallago (1982) and above all by Bauer (1982, in Hungarian, forthcoming in English).

Political factors induce cycles in socialist economy directly, through successive leaders trying to reinforce the legitimacy of their rule by appeasing their subjects with short-lived but significant spurts of consumption before the standard growth and accumulation oriented policy typical of socialist governments is resumed and comes up against the constraints discussed in the previous paragraph (Mieczkowski, 1978; Hanson, 1978; Bunce, 1980; Lafay, 1981). The association of economic and socio-political factors is investigated by Eysmontt and Maciejewski (1984), who apply discriminant analysis to a large number of indicators of such factors over time in order to identify – and anticipate – periods of crisis; they do not, however, have a model of the actual interaction of political and economic factors. An attempt at constructing such a model is made by Nuti (1979, 1985): a critical relationship is assumed between political centralization and popular unrest, inverse up to a threshold level and direct beyond it; economic centralization is directly related to political centralization and affects – through its impact on investment policy – the level of shortages and inefficiency which in turn fuel political unrest. A recursive model with lagged variables is shown to simulate the kind of recurring rounds of reform attempts and accumulation drives observable in actual socialist economies. Screpanti (1985) has modified such a model applying catastrophe theory and obtaining a political/economic accumulation cycle similar to that of capitalist economies.

The further progress of economic reform in centrally planned economies towards market socialism is bound to attenuate and ultimately eliminate the systemic types of economic cycles discussed above. However, as Maurice Dobb had already anticipated in 1939, the diffusion of markets instead of solving the instability problems of the centrally planned economy transforms them into those typical of capitalist economies.

BIBLIOGRAPHY

Aftalion, A. 1909. La réalité des superproductions générales. *Revue d'économie politique* 23(3), 201–29.

Baijt, A. 1971. Investment cycles in European socialist economies: a review article. *Journal of Economic Literature* 9(1), March, 56–63.

Bauer, T. 1978. Investment cycles in planned economies. *Acta Oeconomica* 21(3), 243–60.

Bauer, T. 1982. *Tervezès, beruchàzàs, ciklusok.* Budapest: KJK.

Bunce, V. 1980. The political consumption cycle: a comparative analysis. *Soviet Studies* 32(2), April, 280–90.

Coblijc, N. and Stojanovic, L. 1969. *The Theory of Economic Cycles in a Socialist Economy.* New York: IASP.

Dallago, B. 1982. *Sviluppo e Cicli nelle Economie Est-Europee*. Milan: Angeli.

Dobb, M.H. 1939. A note on saving and investment in a socialist economy. *Economic Journal* 43, December, 713–28.

Eysmontt, J. and Maciejewski, W. 1984. Kryzysy społecznogospodarcze w Polsce – ujecie modelowe (Social-economic crisis in Poland – a model approach). *Ekonomista*.

Goldmann, J. 1964. Fluctuations and trends in the rate of economic growth in some socialist countries. *Economics of Planning* 4(2), 88–98.

Goldmann, J. 1965. Short and long term variations in the growth rate and the model of functioning of a socialist economy. *Czechoslovak Economic Papers* 5, 35–46.

Hanson, P. 1978. Mieczkowski on consumption and politics: a comment. *Soviet Studies* 30(4), October, 553–6.

Lafay, J.-D. 1981. Empirical analysis of politico-economic interaction in East European countries. *Soviet Studies* 33(3), July, 386–400.

Lange, O. 1969. *Theory of Reproduction and Accumulation*. Oxford and New York: Pergamon Press.

Mieczkowski, B. 1978. The relationship between changes in consumption and politics in Poland. *Soviet Studies* 30(2), April, 262–9.

Notkin, A. 1961. *Tempy i proportsii sotsialisticheskogo vosproizvodstva* (The rate and proportions of socialist reproduction). Moscow: IEL.

Nuti, D.M. 1979. The contradictions of socialist economies: a Marxian interpretation. *Socialist Register*, London: The Merlin Press.

Nuti, D.M. 1985. Political and economic fluctuations in the socialist system. European University Institute Working Paper No. 85/156, Florence.

Olivera, J. 1960. Cyclical growth under collectivism. *Kyklos* 13(2), 229–52.

Rostowski, J. and Auerbach, P. 1984. Storming cycles and central planning. Discussion Paper in Political Economy No. 52, Kingston Polytechnic.

Screpanti, E. 1985. A model of the political economic cycle in centrally planned economies. European University Institute Working Paper No. 85/201, Florence.

East–West Economic Relations

MARIE LAVIGNE

The decade 1966–75 is usually considered as the golden age of East–West economic relations. Already during the previous decade, i.e. since the end of the cold war, the USSR and the Eastern European countries had increased their trade with the West at an annual rate of growth slightly higher than their total trade. But after 1966 the expansion of trade and cooperation was sustained both by a favourable political climate and by strong economic complementarities between the West (here equated to the OECD countries) and the East (the USSR and the six European countries that are members of the CMEA, or Council for Mutual Economic Assistance; hereafter we shall mention them as CPEs or centrally planned economies, for the sake of brevity).

These years were marked by *détente*, initiated in 1966 with the triumphal visit to the USSR of the French President General de Gaulle. This was not only a bilateral event, but it set the stage for diversified and institutionalized links between Eastern and Western European economies. Later on, in 1972, US President Nixon's visit to Moscow opened the shorter phase of bright US–USSR economic relations which ended in 1975. At the beginning of that year, the Soviet Union unilaterally repudiated the Soviet–American treaty of commerce, as a retaliation for the deprivation of the most favoured nation clause; according to the American legislation just introduced, the clause could not be granted to a country restricting the rights of its citizens to emigrate. Before *détente* came altogether to its end, it was symbolically magnified in the final Act of the Conference for Security and Co-operation in Europe, signed in Helsinki in August 1975. The economic 'basket' of this text was meant to appear as the Charter of East–West mutually profitable relations.

From the economic point of view, the 1966–75 decade was indeed a time of converging interests. The USSR and Eastern European countries had just engaged in economic reforms. They needed to modernize their industries. The Western firms found new markets for selling equipment and turnkey plants. High rates of economic growth, both in the West and in the East, sustained the prospects for increased exports from the East to the West, once the new capacities acquired from the West were put into operation. An era of deepening industrial cooperation, based upon technology imports and reverse flows of manufactured goods, seemed to open.

It was then almost forgotten that even in such a favourable context, East–West trade accounted for less than 3 per cent of world trade. While in 1975 it amounted to slightly under 30 per cent of total trade for the CPEs (slightly more for the USSR and less for the six smaller CPEs taken together), it never exceeded 5 per cent of total trade for the Western countries, except for some non-typical cases (such as Austria or Finland).

The following decade, ending in 1985, witnessed a general shrinking of East–West trade. There was a conspicuous deterioration of the political climate with the invasion of Afghanistan by Soviet troops in December 1979 and, two years later, martial law in Poland. The world economic crisis exerted some adverse effects as well. True, it benefited the USSR as an oil exporter. But the Western recession hampered the export drive of the smaller CPEs. The manufactured goods which they intended to export so as to repay their imports of equipment became less saleable in the East. Thus the imbalance between imports and exports, which had been steadily growing since 1970, could not be corrected through expanded sales. An easier way out was to borrow on Western financial markets. The CPEs were still creditworthy, and the level of international liquidity was high as a result of the inflow of petro-dollars. The total indebtedness of the CPEs culminated in 1981. The subsequent adjustments conducted in 1981–3 (through a decrease in imports and domestic investment) ended up with a marked improvement in the CPEs external financial position and with a decrease in their foreign debt (except for Poland). But the general slowdown of growth in the East, partly due to these adjustments, does not allow for a steep upward trend in East–West trade.

The outlook for East–West economic relations is to be evaluated through the combination of two opposed sets of factors. On the one hand, there are strong interests on both sides pressing for the expansion of trade and cooperation. On the other, equally strong obstacles are hindering such a development. The outcome is probably to be seen in a stabilization of those relations, below the level reached during the 'golden age' decade.

ECONOMIC INTERESTS. East–West trade is sometimes said to be a one-way street. As the magnitudes of shares in total trade show, these relations are several times more important for the East than for the West. However, dependencies are to be found on both sides, with an uneven distribution.

In the West, European countries are the main group of partners. They account for roughly 75 per cent of sales to the East and 90 per cent of imports from the East (figures of 1983). This pattern has been stable since the end of the seventies. In 1970 the share of Western Europe was very similar on the import side, but larger on the export side (about 10 points more). Since then, two major exporters have emerged outside Europe, Japan (for technology) and the United States (for grain, mainly to the USSR).

In the East, the USSR gained a growing share of East—West trade after 1970. From two-fifths of the total trade of the European CPEs with the West, it reached 50 per cent in the mid-1970s and over 60 per cent in the 1980s. This is mainly due to the increase in oil prices after 1973; it allowed the Soviet Union to secure a higher rate of growth of its trade with the West compared with the other CPEs up to 1980, and to avoid the decrease in trade which the other CPEs experienced at the beginning of the 1980s.

The growing concentration of East—West trade on the Soviet Union is an expression of stronger interdependences.

For Western Europe, especially for the large industrial corporations, the USSR emerged in the 1970s as a major purchaser of heavy equipment, whose orders helped to sustain the level of activities and jobs during the recession years. The controversial multi-billion dollars gas pipeline deal concluded in 1981 is a clear demonstration of such interests. When in 1982 the US government tried to oppose the supply of tubes and other equipment for the pipeline, as a retaliation for the Soviet role in the Polish crisis, and also as an attempt to reduce the export capacities of natural gas of the USSR, the European governments backed their firms. Even though the Soviet orders for equipment have substantially declined since then, the Soviet Union remains a huge market.

On the other side, the Soviet Union has become a significant supplier of energy to Western Europe. Fuels now account for about 80 per cent of its sales to the West, from about half that share at the beginning of the 1970s. The major Western European energy importers (Germany, France, Italy) are now dependent for 6–7 per cent of their total energy imports on the Soviet Union. For natural gas alone, their dependence may be above the 30 per cent mark at the end of the 1980s, from about 15–20 per cent a decade earlier. The Soviet Union provides a means of achieving a diversification in energy imports; it is a cheaper supplier for oil and gas because of the distance factor, and may be considered as a more reliable one, than the Third World.

Regarding trade with the United States, the major link is grain. The Soviet Union began to buy large quantities of American grain in 1975–76 and has remained the largest single customer of the United States since then. US sales never again reached the 70 per cent share of Soviet grain imports which they formed in 1979. However, the strength of economic versus political interests is clearly demonstrated by the failure of the grain embargo, which had to be lifted under the pressure of US farmers. The long-term grain sales agreement linking the two countries, first signed in 1975, has not only been renewed but also supplemented with an anti-embargo clause (in 1983).

The Western trade of Eastern Europe lacks these powerful interdependences. The smaller CPEs taken together are on average less involved in trade with the West than the USSR. In 1984, the share of Western trade in their total trade was about 25 per cent (as against 30 per cent for the USSR), and had declined since 1980. But while Bulgaria and Czechoslovakia, much more oriented toward trade within CMEA, have a very low share of their total trade with the West (12–15 per cent), Hungary (34 per cent), Poland, GDR and Romania (30 per cent) are potentially interested in expanding their trade with the West. However, opportunities for that are low. Their supply is made of sensitive goods (steel, chemicals, textiles, manufactured goods, agricultural products), the demand for which is sluggish in the West – and they complain of growing protectionism. For these goods competition is growing on Western markets from the new industrializing countries of the Third World, which in addition are more advanced in some high technology fields (electronics). They can hardly expect concessions from Western countries, for which they provide less promising markets than the USSR. The development of compensation deals is only a marginal way of securing outlets for their goods.

OBSTACLES. In the background of these differentiated economic interests, specific obstacles hinder East–West trade, in the political, institutional (systemic) and financial fields, to which must be added the 1986 developments on the world oil market.

Is East–West trade *political* in essence? In Western Europe, politics and economic relations are regarded as distinct by governments and firms. The lasting failure to find an agreement between the EEC and the CMEA, since the beginning of official talks in 1976, is mainly due to the lack of institutional competence of the CMEA in matters of trade as appraised by the EC Commission (even if on the side of the Commission there is a political concern to avoid strengthening the Soviet-dominated CMEA as an organization). The major involvement of politics in East–West economic relations is related to US policy. The 'linkage' concept of tying economic advantages to Soviet concessions in the political sphere was associated in the 1970s with commercial policies (the granting of the MFN clause) or financial conditions (for access to bank credits). Since the end of that decade it has evolved into a policy of sanctions, first as a retaliation for the Soviet invasion of Afghanistan in 1979 (the grain embargo against the USSR, which was lifted in April 1981, and a tighter control of high technology sales); then as a response to the martial law imposed in December 1981 in Poland. In this last case the sanctions hit Poland (through credit and export restrictions, a suspension of the MFN clause), and the USSR (through attempts to stop the Eurosiberian pipeline deal by preventing the Western European countries from selling equipment to the USSR and from concluding the agreements for the purchases of gas). They were also extended to the other CPEs through a very severe credit squeeze. All these measures culminated in 1982. They proved largely ineffective but generated conflicts within the Western Alliance. The major and lasting field of political pressure is to be found in the embargo on high technology sales to the CPEs, conducted through the Cocom (Coordinating Committee), an informal organization set up in 1949 and including the NATO countries plus Japan. Very active during the years of the cold war, it seemed to be withering in the late 1970s but regained momentum from 1980 on. The present rationale of the Cocom restrictions is threefold: to impose sanctions; to prevent the Soviet bloc from acquiring dual-use technologies (for military as well as civilian ends); to enlarge the scope of controls by restricting high-technology exports of non-Cocom members (Sweden, Switzerland, Austria, and even some Third World countries such as India).

The *systemic* obstacles to trade are related to the specific organization of state trading in the CPEs. The monopoly of foreign trade and the related planning of trade flows remain very rigid in the Soviet Union. Increased flexibility has been introduced in the trade mechanisms of all the other CPEs, where enterprises are gaining easier access to foreign trade transactions. Direct interfirm contacts have been stimulated through industrial cooperation. In all these countries except for GDR, it is now possible to create joint enterprises with foreign equity capital (the experiences remain limited). The state trading system, however reformed, still prevents the CPEs from successfully adjusting to the market requirements in the West.

The *financial* problems of East–West relations are less dramatic than in 1980–81, when the total indebtedness of the USSR and Eastern Europe combined exceeded $80 billion, more than four times its level of the end of 1974. Two countries, Poland and Romania, entered in 1981 a process of rescheduling, which is still going on for Poland. Two others, GDR and Hungary, successfully managed to restore their external accounts in 1982–4. Since then, the Western banks have again been ready to expand their loans not only to the Soviet Union, which has always remained a good risk, but also to the other CPEs, which by all accounts seem more creditworthy than the Third World.

East–West economic relations are finally to be replaced in the broader context of the CPEs' foreign economic relations, including intra-CMEA trade. The move toward closer integration, advocated by the Soviet Union at the Summit meeting of the CMEA in June 1984 and based upon the heavy requirements of the USSR as to its imports from its partners, might well appear as an additional constraint on the expansion of East–West relations by the smaller CPEs.

The fall in oil prices, since the end of 1985, may have strong adverse effects on East–West trade. If the average price of oil is for some time stabilized at half its 1985 level, the Soviet Union will lose at least one third of its export gains in its trade with the West. These losses may be compensated for, in the short run, by cuts in imports and increased borrowing, together with a stronger pressure on the smaller CMEA countries. The latter will thus have to divert to the Soviet market goods exportable to the West. In addition, they too will lose as sellers of refined oil products, with the same consequences as for the USSR. The 'golden age' of East–West trade is definitely not about to be renewed.

BIBLIOGRAPHY

Bornstein, M., Gitelman, Z. and Zimmerman, W. (eds) 1981. *East–West Relations and the Future of Eastern Europe: Politics and Economics*. London: Allen & Unwin.

Economic Bulletin for Europe. 1949 onwards. Geneva: Economic Commission for Europe, United Nations. Each volume contains developments on East–West trade.

Fallenbuchl, Z. and McMillan, C. (eds) 1980. *Partners in East–West Relations, the Determinants of Choice*. New York: Pergamon Press.

Holzman, F. 1976. *International Trade Under Communism, Politics and Economics*. New York: Basic Books.

Lavigne, M. 1979. *Les relations économiques Est–Ouest*. Paris: Presses Universitaires de France.

Lavigne, M. 1985. *Economie internationale des pays socialistes*. Paris: Armand Colin.

Levcik, F. (ed.) 1978. *International Economics – Comparisons and Interdependencies. Essays in honour of F. Nemschak*. Vienna: Springer Verlag.

Marer, P. and Montias, J.M. (eds) 1980. *East European Integration and East–West Trade*. Bloomington: Indiana University Press.

Economic Calculation in Socialist Economies

MICHAEL ELLMAN

The basic method of economic calculation used in the state socialist countries is that of incrementalism, or as it is known in the USSR, 'planning from the achieved level'. The starting point of all economic plans is the actual or expected outcome of the previous period. The planners adjust this by reference to anticipated growth rates, current economic policy, shortages and technical progress. For nearly all products, the planned output for next year will be the anticipated output for this year plus a few per cent added on. The advantages of incrementalism as a method of economic calculation are its simplicity, realism and compatibility with the functioning of a hierarchical bureaucracy. Its disadvantages are that it provides no method for making technically efficient or consistent decisions, nor does it ensure that the population will derive maximum satisfaction from the resources available.

PLANNING AND COUNTERPLANNING. A widely used method of economic calculation is that of planning and counterplanning. If the plan were simply handed down to the enterprises from above, in accordance with the planners' view of national economic requirements but in ignorance of the real possibilities of each enterprise, then it would be unfeasible (if it was too high) or wasteful (if it was too low) or both at the same time (i.e. unfeasible for some products and wasteful for others). Conversely, if plans were simply drawn up by each enterprise, they might fail to use resources in accordance with national economic requirements. The process of planning and counterplanning involves a mutual submission and discussion of planning suggestions, designed to lead to the adoption of a plan which is feasible for the enterprise and ensure that the resources of each enterprise are used in accordance with national requirements.

Unfortunately, the bureaucratic complexity of this procedure militates against both efficiency and consistency.

INPUT NORMS. The main method of economic calculation used to ensure efficiency is that of input norms. An input norm is simply a number assumed to describe an efficient process of transformation of inputs into outputs. For example, suppose that the norm for the utilization of coal in the production of one ton of steel is x tons. Then the efficient production of z tons of steel is assumed to require zx tons of coal.

The method of norms is widely used in Soviet planning, and considerable effort is devoted to updating them. Very detailed norm fixing takes place for expenditures of fuel and energy. Much attention is devoted to the development of norms for the expenditure of metal, cement, and timber in construction. All this work is directed by the department of norms and normatives of Gosplan. Responsibility for elaborating and improving the norms lies with Gosplan's Scientific Research Institute of Planning and Norms.

Nevertheless, the method of norms is incapable of ensuring efficiency. The norms used in planning calculations are simply averages of input requirements, weighted somewhat in favour of efficient producers. Actual technologies show a wide dispersion in input–output relations. Furthermore, given norms take no account of the possibilities of substitution of inputs for one another in the production process, non-constant returns to scale, and the results of technical progress. Thus in general, the method of norms does not make it possible to calculate efficient input requirements, and plans calculated in this way are always inefficient.

The method of norms is not only used in interindustry planning, it is also used in consumption planning. In calculating the volume of particular consumer goods and services required, the planners use two main methods. One is forecasts of consumer behaviour, based on extrapolation, expenditure patterns of higher income groups, income and price elasticities of demand and consumer behaviour in the more advanced countries. The other method is that of consumption norms. The first method attempts to foresee consumer demand, the latter to shape it.

An example of the method of norms, and its policy implications, is set out in Table 1 (see following page).

The table makes clear the logic of the Soviet policy of expanding the livestock sector, and also importing fodder and livestock products. Since the consumption of livestock products is below the norm level, the government seeks to make possible an increase in their consumption.

The method of consumption norms is an alternative to the price mechanism for the determination of output. It is, however, also used in Western countries. It is used there in those cases where distribution on the basis of purchasing power has been replaced by distribution on the basis of need. Examples are, the provision of housing, hospitals, schools and parks. Calculations of the desirable number of rooms, hospital beds and school places per person are a familiar tool of planning in welfare states.

There are two main problems with the norm method of consumption planning. The first is that of substitution between products. Although consumers may well have a medically necessary need for x grams of protein per day, they can obtain these proteins from a wide variety of foods. Secondly, consumers may choose to spend their money 'irrationally', e.g. to buy spirits instead of children's shoes.

Table 1   The Soviet diet

	Norm (kg/head/year)	Per capita consumption in 1976 as % of norm
Bread and bread products	120	128
Potatoes	97	123
Vegetables and melons	37	59
Vegetable oil and margarine	7	85
Meat and meat products	82	68
Fish and fish products	18	101
Milk and milk products	434	78
Eggs	17	72

Source: P. Weitzman, Soviet long term consumption planning: distribution according to rational need, *Soviet Studies*, July 1974, and E.M. Agababyan and Ye.N. Yakovleva (eds), *Problemy raspredeleniya i rost narodnogo blagosostoyaniya* (Moscow, 1979), p. 142.

MATERIAL BALANCES. A material balance is a balance sheet for a particular commodity showing, on the one hand, the economy's resources and potential output, and on the other, the economy's need for a particular product. Material (and labour) balances are the main methods used in calculating production and distribution plans for goods, supply plans and labour plans. Soviet planners take great pride in the balance method and consider it one of the greatest achievements of planning theory and practice. Material balances are drawn up for different periods (e.g. for annual or five year periods), by different organizations (e.g. Gosplan, Gossnab, the ministries) and at different levels (e.g. national and republican). The material balances are also drawn up with different degrees of aggregation. Highly aggregated balances are drawn up for the Five Year Plans, and highly disaggregated balances by the chief administrations of Gossnab for annual supply planning. The aim of the material balance method is to ensure the consistency of the plans.

Normally, at the start of the planning work, the anticipated availability of a commodity is not sufficient to meet anticipated requirements. To balance the two, the planners seek possibilities of economizing on scarce products and substituting for scarce materials; they investigate the possibilities of increasing production or importing raw materials or equipment, or in the last resort they determine the priority needs to be fulfilled by the scarce commodity. Even with great efforts, achieving a balance is difficult. The complexity of an economy in which a great variety of goods are produced by different processes, all of which are subject to continuous technological change, is often too great for anything more than a balance that balances only on paper. Hence it is normal, during the planned period, for the plan to be altered, often repeatedly, as imbalances come to light. Particularly important problems with the use of material balances are the highly aggregated nature of the balances and their interrelated nature.

INPUT-OUTPUT. A wide variety of input–output tables are regularly constructed in socialist countries. Ex post national tables in value terms, planning national tables in value and physical terms, regional tables and capital stock matrices are widely constructed and used. An interesting and important use concerns variant calculations of the structure of production in medium term planning.

Because an input–output table can be represented by a simple mathematical model, and because of the assumption of constant coefficients, an input–output table can be utilized for variant calculations

$$X = (I - A)^{-1} Y.$$

Assuming that A is given, X can be calculated for varying values of Y. Variant calculations of the structure of production were not undertaken with material balances because of their great labour intensity. Variant calculations have a useful role to play in medium-term planning because they enable the planners to experiment with a wide range of possibilities. The first major use of variant calculations of the structure of production in Soviet national economic planning was in connection with the 1966–70 five year plan. Gosplan's economic research institute analysed the results of various possible shares of investment in the national income for 1966–70. It became clear that stepping up the share of investment in the national income would increase the rate of growth of the national income, but that this would have very little effect on the rate of growth of consumption (because almost all of the increased output would be producer goods). The results of the calculations are set out in Tables 2 and 3.

A sharp increase in the share of investment in the national income in the five year plan 1966–70 would have led to a sharp fall in the share of consumption in the national income, and only a small increase in the rate of growth of consumption (within a five year plan period). What is very sensitive to the share of investment in the national income is the output of the producer goods industries, as Tables 2 and 3 show.

Table 2 Output of steel on various assumptions

	Variants				
	I	II	III	IV	V
Production of steel in 1970 (millions of tonnes)	109	115	121	128	136

Source: see Table 3 (following page).

94

Table 3 Average growth rates of selected industries, 1966–1970

	Variants				
	I	II	III	IV	V
Engineering and metal working	7.1	8.2	9.3	10.4	11.4
Light industry	6.3	6.6	6.8	7.0	7.2
Food industry	7.1	7.3	7.4	7.5	7.6

Source: M. Ellman, *Planning problems in the USSR: the contribution of mathematical economics to their solution 1960–1971* (Cambridge: Cambridge University Press, 1973), p. 71.

These results are along the lines of what one would expect on the basis of Feldman's model, but the input–output technique improves on Feldman's model since it enables the effect of different strategies to be seen at industry level rather than merely in term of macroeconomic aggregates.

Another example of the use of input–output for economic calculations concerns the statistical data about the relations between industries contained in the national ex post tables in value terms. In his controversial 1968 book *Mezhotraslevye svyazi sel'skogo khozyaistva*, M. Lemeshev, then deputy head of the sector for forecasting the development of agriculture of the USSR Gosplan's Economic Research Institute, used the Soviet input–output table for 1959 as the basis for a powerful plea for more industrial inputs to be made available to agriculture.

He began by observing that from the 1959 input–output table it is clear that of the current material inputs into agriculture in that year only 23.4 per cent came from industry, while 54.7 per cent came from agriculture itself (feed, seed etc.). He argued that this was most unsatisfactory. In the section on the relationship between agriculture and engineering Lemeshev argued that the supply to agriculture of agricultural machinery was inadequate, in the section on the relationship between agriculture and the chemical industry he argued that the supply of fertilizers was inadequate, and in the section on agriculture and electricity he argued that the supply of electricity to the villages for both productive and unproductive needs was inadequate, and in the section on the relationship between agriculture and the processing industry he argued that the latter was not helping agriculture as it should do, for example, it was sometimes impossible to accept vegetables (although the consumption of these in the towns was well below the norms) because of inadequate processing and distribution facilities. In addition, he argued that the supply of concentrated feed was inadequate and the processing of milk wasteful. In view of the inadequate development of the food processing industry, he argued for the development of processing enterprises by the farms themselves.

The chapter on the productive relations between agriculture and the building industry is an extensive critique of the practice of productive, and housing and communal, building in the villages. Lemeshev argued that the state should take on responsibility for building on the collective farms. The chapter on the relationship between agriculture and transport is critical of the shortage of river freight boats. The chapter on agriculture and investment in agriculture argued that investment in agriculture was inadequate, that in the period 1959–65 there was an unwarranted increase in the proportion of investment in the collective farms which they had to finance themselves, that a greater proportion of agricultural investment should be financed by bank loans, and that as a criterion of investment efficiency the recoupment period is satisfactory. The concluding chapter is concerned with improving the productive relations between agriculture and the rest of the economy. The author argued for improving central planning by the use of input–output, for replacing procurement plans by free contracts between farms and the procurement organs (if a shortage of a particular product threatens then its price can be raised), the elimination of the supply system (i.e. the rationing of producer goods) which hinders farms from receiving the goods they want and sometimes supplies them with goods that they do not want, higher pay in agriculture and the reorganization of the labour process within state and collective farms on the basis of small groups which are paid by results.

This book was a good example of the use of input–output to provide statistical data which can be used, alongside other information, to provide a description of important economic relations and to support a case for important institutional and policy changes.

PROJECT EVALUATION. In the USSR of the 1930s, it was officially considered that there was no problem of project evaluation to which economists could contribute. The sectoral allocation of investment was a matter for the central political leadership to decide. It was they who decided in which sectors and at which locations production should be expanded. These decisions were based on the experience of the more advanced countries, the traditions of the Russian state (e.g. stress on railway building) and of the Bolshevik movement (e.g. stress on electrification and on the metal-using industries) and on the needs of defence. As far as decisions within sectors were concerned, here the main idea was to fulfil the plan using the world's most advanced technology.

The practical study of methods for choosing between variants within sectors was begun by engineers in the electricity and railway industries. The problem analysed was that of comparing the cost of alternative ways of meeting particular plan targets. A classic example of the type of problem considered was the choice between producing electricity by a hydro station or a thermal station.

During Stalin's lifetime, the elaboration by orthodox economists and the adoption by the planners of economic criteria for project evaluation were impossible because they were outside Stalin's conception of the proper role of economists (apologetics). When economists did make a contribution in this area, as was done by Novozhilov, it was ignored. After Stalin's death, however, it became possible for Soviet economists to contribute to the elaboration of methods of economic calculation for use in the decision-making process. An early and important example was in the field of project evaluation. An official method for project evaluation was adopted in 1960, and revised versions in 1964, 1966, 1969 and 1981. In a very abbreviated and summary form, the 1981 version is as follows.

In evaluating investment projects, a wide variety of factors have to be taken into account, e.g. the effect of the investment on labour productivity, capital productivity, consumption of current material inputs (e.g. metals and fuel), costs of production, environmental effects, technical progress, the location of economic activity and so on. Two indices which give useful synthetic information about economic efficiency (but are not necessarily decisive in choosing between investment projects) are the coefficient of absolute economic effectiveness and the coefficient of relative economic effectiveness.

At the national level, the coefficient of absolute effectiveness is defined as the incremental output–capital ratio.

$$E_p = \frac{\Delta Y}{I}$$

where

E_p is the coefficient of absolute effectiveness for a particular project,
ΔY is the increase in national income generated by the project, and
I is the investment cost.

The value of E_p calculated in this way for a particular investment, has to be compared with E_a, the normative coefficient of absolute effectiveness, which is fixed for each Five Year Plan and varies between sectors. In the 11th Five Year Plan (1981–85) it was 0.16 in industry, 0.07 in agriculture, 0.05 in transport and communications, 0.22 in construction and 0.25 in trade.

$$\text{If } E_p > E_a$$

then the project is considered efficient.

For calculating the criterion of absolute effectiveness at the level of individual industries, net output is used in the numerator instead of national income. At the level of individual enterprises and associations, in particular when a firm's own money or bank loans are the source of finance, profit is used instead of national income.

The coefficient of relative effectiveness is used in the comparison of alternative ways of producing particular products. In the two products case

$$E = \frac{C_1 - C_2}{K_2 - K_1}$$

where

E is the coefficient of relative effectiveness,
C_i is the current cost of the ith variant, and
K_i is the capital cost of the ith variant.

If $E > E_n$, where E_n is the officially established normative coefficient of relative economic efficiency, then the more capital-intensive variant is economically justified. In the 11th Five Year Plan, E_n was in general 0.12, but exceptions were officially permitted in the range 0.08/0.10–0.20/0.25.

In the more than two variants case, they should be compared according to the formula

$$C_i + E_n K_i \to \text{minimum}$$

i.e. choose that variant which minimizes the sum of current and capital costs.

It is important not to adopt the rationalist misinterpretation of socialist planning according to which a planned economy is one in which rational decisions are made after a dispassionate analysis by omniscient and all-powerful planners of all the alternative possibilities. In such a system, the adoption of rational criteria for project evaluation would be of enormous importance. Socialist planning, however, is just one part of the social relations between individuals and groups in the course of which decisions are taken, all of which are imperfect and many of which produce results quite at variance with the intentions of the top economic and political leadership.

A good example of the factors actually influencing investment decisions under state socialism is the notorious Baoshan steel plant near Shanghai. The site was apparently chosen because of the political influence of a high-ranking Shanghai party official. The location decision ignored the fact that because of the swampy nature of the site, necessitating large expenditures on the foundations, this was in fact the most expensive of the sites considered. Very expensive, dogged with cost overruns, involving major pollution problems, the whole project was kept alive for some time by a powerful steel lobby. In due course, as a result of a national policy reversal in Beijing, the second phase was deferred and those involved publicly criticized. Judging by its costs of production, it produced gold rather than steel.

In general, the choice of projects owes more to inter-organization bargaining in an environment characterized by investment hunger than it does to the detached choice of a cost-minimizing variant. The development of new and better criteria for project evaluation has turned out to be no guarantee that project evaluation will improve since the criteria are often not in fact used to evaluate projects. Their main function is to provide an acceptable common language in which various bureaucratic agencies conduct their struggles. Agencies adopt projects on normal bureaucratic grounds and then try to get them adopted by higher agencies, or defend them against attack, by presenting efficiency calculations using the official methodology but relying on carefully selected data.

LINEAR PROGRAMMING AND EXTENSIONS. Linear programming was discovered by the Soviet mathematician Kantorovich in the late 1930s. Its relevance for Soviet planning was widely discussed in the USSR in the 1960s and it was widely introduced in Soviet planning in the 1970s. Three examples of its use follow.

PRODUCTION SCHEDULING IN THE STEEL INDUSTRY. Linear programming was discovered by Kantorovich in the course of solving the problem, presented to him by the Laboratory of the all-Union Plywood Trust, of allocating productive tasks between machines in such a way as to maximize output given the assortment plan. From a mathematical point of view, the problem of optimal production scheduling for tube mills and rolling mills in the steel industry, which was tackled by Kantorovich in the 1960s, is very similar to the Plywood Trust problem, the difference being its huge dimensions.

The problem arises in the following way. As part of the planning of supply, Soyuzglavmetal (the department of Gossnab concerned with the metal industries), after the quotas have been specified, has to work out production schedules and attachment plans in such a way that all the orders are satisfied and none of the producers receives an impossible plan. In the 1960s an extensive research programme was initiated by the department of mathematical economics (which was headed by Academician Kantorovich) of the Institute of Mathematics of the Siberian branch of the Academy of Sciences, to apply optimizing methods to this problem. The chief difficulties were the huge dimensions of the problem and the lack of the necessary data. About 1,000,000 orders, involving 60,000 users, more than 500 producers and tens of thousands of products, are issued each year for rolled metal. Formulated as a linear programming problem it had more than a million unknowns and 30,000 constraints. Collecting the necessary data took about six years. Optimal production scheduling was first applied to the tube mills producing tubes for gas pipelines (these are a scarce commodity in the USSR). In 1970 this made possible an output of tubes 108,000 tons greater than it would otherwise have been, and a substantial reduction in transport costs was also achieved.

The introduction of optimal production scheduling into the work of Soyuzglavmetal was only part of the work initiated in the late 1960s on creating a management information and control system in the steel industry. This was intended to be an integrated computer system which would embrace the determination of requirements, production scheduling, stock control, the distribution of output and accounting. Such systems were widely introduced in Western steel firms in the late 1960s. Work on the introduction of management information and control systems in the Soviet economy was widespread in the 1970s but by the 1980s there was widespread scepticism in the USSR about their usefulness. This largely resulted from the failure to fulfil the earlier exaggerated hopes about the returns to be obtained from their introduction in the economy.

INDUSTRY INVESTMENT PLANS. In the state socialist countries investment plans are worked out for the country as a whole, and also for industries, ministries, departments, associations, enterprises, republics, economic regions and cities. An important level of investment planning is the industry. Industry investment planning is concerned with such problems as the choice of products, of plants to be expanded, location of new plants, technology to be used, and sources of raw materials.

The main method used at the present time in the CMEA countries for processing the data relating to possible investment plans into actual investment plans is mathematical programming. After extensive experience in this field, in

1977 a Standard Methodology for doing such calculations was adopted by the Presidium of the USSR Academy of Sciences. The use of mathematical programming for calculating optimal investment plans is an example of the possibilities for efficient control of national economies which the scientific-technical revolution in the field of management and control of large systems is bringing about.

The Soviet Standard Methodology presents models for three standard problems. They are: a static multiproduct production problem with discrete variables, a multiproduct dynamic production problem with discrete variables, and a multiproduct static problem of the production-transport type with discrete variables. The former can be set out as follows:

Let $i = 1, \ldots, n$ be the finished goods or resources, $j = 1, \ldots, m$ be the production units, $r = 1, \ldots, R_j$ be the production technique in a unit, a_{ij}^r be the output of good $i = 1, \ldots, n'$ or input of resource $i = n' + 1, \ldots, n$, using technique r of production in unit j; C_j^r are the costs of production using technique r in unit j; D_i is the given level of output of good i, $i = 1, \ldots, n'$; P_i is the total use of resource i, $i = n' + 1, \ldots, n$ allocated to the industry; Z_j^r is the unknown intensity of use of technique r at unit j.

The problem is to find values of the variables Z_j^r that minimize the objective function

$$\sum_{j=1}^{m} \sum_{r=1}^{R_j} C_j^r Z_j^r \tag{1}$$

i.e. minimize costs of production subject to

$$\sum_{j=1}^{m} \sum_{r=1}^{R_j} a_{ij}^r Z_j^r \geqslant D_i, \qquad i = 1, \ldots, n' \tag{2}$$

i.e. each output must be produced in at least the required quantities

$$\sum_{j=1}^{m} \sum_{r=1}^{R_j} a_{ij}^r Z_j^r \leqslant P_i, \qquad i = n' + 1, \ldots, n \tag{3}$$

i.e. the total use of resources cannot exceed the level allocated to the branch

$$\sum_{r=1}^{R_j} Z_j^r \leqslant 1, \qquad j = 1, \ldots, m \tag{4}$$

$$Z_j^r = 0 \text{ or } 1, \qquad j = 1, \ldots, m, \quad r = 1, \ldots, R_j \tag{5}$$

i.e. either a single technique of production for unit j is included in the plan or unit j is not included in the plan.

In order to illustrate the method, an example will be given which is taken from the Hungarian experience of the 1950s in working out an investment plan for the cotton weaving industry for the 1961–65 Five Year Plan. The method of working out the plan can be presented schematically by looking at the decision problems, the constraints, the objective function and the results.

The decision problems to be resolved were:

(a) How should the output of fabrics be increased, by modernizing the existing weaving mills or by building new ones?

(b) For part of the existing machinery, there were three possibilities. It could be operated in its existing form, modernized by way of alterations or supplementary investments, or else scrapped. Which should be chosen?

(c) For the other part of the existing machinery, either it could be retained or scrapped. What should be done?

(d) If new machines are purchased, a choice has to be made between many types. Which types should be chosen, and how many of a particular type should be purchased?

The constraints consisted of the output plan for cloth, the investment fund, the hard currency quota, the building quota and the material balances for various kinds of yarn. The objective function was to meet the given plan at minimum cost.

The results provided answers to all the decision problems. An important feature of the results was the conclusion that it was cheaper to increase production by modernizing and expanding existing mills than by building new ones.

It would clearly be unsatisfactory to optimize the investment plan of each industry taken in isolation. If the calculations show that it is possible to reduce the inputs into a particular industry below those originally envisaged, then it is desirable to reduce planned outputs in other industries, or increase the planned output of the industry in question, or adopt some combination of these strategies. Accordingly, the experiments in working out optimal industry investment plans, begun in Hungary in the 1950s, led to the construction of multi-level plans linking the optimal plans of the separate industries to each other and to the macroeconomic plan variables. Multi-level planning of this type was first developed in Hungary, but has since spread to the other CMEA countries. Extensive work on the multi-level optimization of investment planning was undertaken in the USSR in connection with the 1976–90 long-term plan. (The 1976–90 plan, like all previous Soviet attempts to compile a long-term plan, was soon overtaken by events. The plan itself seems never to have been finished and was replaced by ten year guidelines for 1981–90.)

THE DETERMINATION OF COSTS IN THE RESOURCE SECTOR. In view of the wide dispersion of production costs in the resource sector, the use of average costs (and of prices based on average costs) in allocation decisions is likely to lead to serious waste. An important outcome of the work of Kantorovich and his school for practical policy has been (after a long lag) official acceptance of this proposition and of linear programming as a way of calculating the relevant marginal costs. For example, in 1979 in the USSR the State Committee for Science and Technology and the State Committee for Prices jointly approved an official method for the economic evaluation of raw material deposits. This was a prescribed method for the economic evaluation of exploration and development of raw material deposits. What was new in principle about this document was that it permitted the output derived from the deposits to be evaluated either in actual (or forecast) wholesale prices or in marginal costs. For the fuel-energy sector, a lot of work has been done to calculate actual (and forecast) marginal costs for each fuel at different locations throughout the country and for different periods. These figures are regularly calculated on optimizing models (they are the dual variables to the output maximizing primal) and have been widely used in planning practice for many years.

COMPARISON WITH THE WEST. An important method of economic calculation in socialist countries is comparison with the West. If a particular product or method of production has already been introduced (or phased out) in the West, this is generally considered a good argument to introduce it (or phase it out) in the socialist countries, subject to national priorities and economic feasibility. Obtaining advanced technology from overseas has always been an integral part of socialist planning. Comparison with the West are particularly important in an economic system which lags behind the leading countries, lacks institutions which automatically introduce innovations into production (i.e. profit seeking business firms), and finds it difficult (because of the ignorance of the planners, stable cost plus prices and the self-interest of rival bureaucratic agencies) to notice, appraise realistically when noticed, and adopt, innovations.

ECONOMIC CALCULATION AND ECONOMIC RESULTS. It is important not to exaggerate the influence of methods of economic calculation on the performance of an economy. The performance of an economy is largely determined by external factors (e.g. the world market), economic policy (e.g. the decision to import foreign capital or to declare a moratorium), economic institutions (e.g. collective farms) and the behaviour of the actors within the system (e.g. underestimation of investment costs by initiators of investment projects). It is entirely possible for an improvement in the methods of economic calculation to coincide with a worsening of economic performance (as happened in the USSR after 1978). Realization of these facts led in the 1970s to a shift from the traditional normative approach (which concentrates on the methods of economic calculation and which regards their improvement as the main key to improved economic performance and the main role of the economist) in the study of planned economies, to the systems and behavioural approaches.

BIBLIOGRAPHY
Birman, I. 1978. From the achieved level. *Soviet Studies* 30(2), April, 153–72.
Boltho, A. 1971. *Foreign Trade Criteria in Socialist Economies.* Cambridge and New York: Cambridge University Press.
Cave, M. 1980. *Computers and Economic Planning – the Soviet Experience.* Cambridge and New York: Cambridge University Press.
Ellman, M. 1973. Changing views on central planning: 1958–1983. *ACES Bulletin* 25(1), Spring, 11–34.

Ellman, M. and Simatupang, B. 1982. *Odnowa* in statistics. *Soviet Studies* 34(1), January, 111–17.

Gács, J. and Lackó, M. 1973. A study of planning behaviour on the national-economic level. *Economics of Planning* 13(1–2), 91–119.

Giffen, J. 1981. The allocation of investment in the Soviet Union. *Soviet Studies* 33(4), October, 593–609.

Kantorovich, L.V., Cheshenko, N.I., Zorin, Iu.M. and Shepelev, G.I. 1979. On the use of optimization methods in automated management systems for economic ministries. *Matekon* 15(4), Summer, 42–66.

Kornai, J. 1967. *Mathematical Planning of Structural Decisions*. Amsterdam: North-Holland.

Kornai, J. 1980. *Economics of Shortage*. 2 vols, Amsterdam: North-Holland.

Kushnirsky, F.I. 1982. *Soviet Economic Planning, 1965–1980*. Boulder, Colorado: Westview, ch. 4.

Lee Travers, S. 1982. Bias in Chinese economic statistics. *China Quarterly* 91, September, 478–85.

Levine, H.S. 1959. The centralized planning of supply in Soviet industry. In *Comparisons of the United States and Soviet Economies*, Washington, DC: Joint Economic Committee, US Congress.

Stalin, J. 1952. *Economic Problems of Socialism in the USSR*. Moscow: Foreign Languages Publishing House.

Standard methodology for calculations to optimize the development and location of production in the long run. 1978. *Matekon* 15(1), Fall, 75–96.

Tretyakova, A. and Birman, I. 1976. Input–output analysis in the USSR. *Soviet Studies* 28(2), April, 157–86.

Fascism

WOLFGANG-DIETER CLASSEN

The term fascism can be applied to historical reality only as an approximation, because the differences between what are called fascist movements and regimes seem to be greater than the similarities, and leave room for many contrary interpretations (cf. de Felice, 1969; Gregor, 1974). Given this restriction the term is applied to both radical populistic mass movements, primarily of the middle classes, and, where they attained power, to the political regimes they created between the two world wars.

The fascist movements emerged as a result of the political, economic and social crisis of the bourgeois societies in European countries after World War I. They propagated an extreme anti-liberal, anti-socialist, nationalist and imperialist (and, in Germany, racial) ideology, and above all, they struggled with militancy and terror against the labour organizations. Where these movements came to power (Italy and Germany) it was by coalition with the bourgeois upper class and thanks to the simultaneous failure of labour organizations to present any effective resistance. The political structure of the fascist regimes was, on the surface, marked by the dictatorial leader, the single party system, the total control of the press and all information sources, massive propaganda campaigns, tendencies toward the coordination of all political, economical, social and cultural institutions from above, and the power of the party militia, the police and the secret police. But behind this surface of strictly hierarchical dictatorship the fascist leaders' disregard for administration, their glorification of struggle and competition as an ideological expression of Social Darwinism led to a lack of constitutionality, to a deficient division of spheres of control and influence between the agencies, and, especially in the later years, to a multiplication of hurriedly erected ad hoc commissariats without any proper plan of coordination. That, in turn, left much room for constant quarrels and boundary disputes between the party leaders, representative of special party organizations (e.g. the SS, the Arbeitsfront in Germany), the army, the state machinery (traditionally the realm of the conservative bourgeoisie) and big industry as rival power blocs.

This disintegration of the regime's power structure often made political decision procedures very ineffective. (With regard to Germany, see Fraenkel, 1941; Neumann, 1944; Broszat, 1969; Hirschfeld and Mommsen (eds), 1980.)

FASCISM AND THE ECONOMY

Fascism did not lead to any original contributions to economic theory except for some elements in the theory of corporatism added by Italian fascists. Positing the primacy of national over individual welfare, the fascist state was to direct economic activities for these purposes. In principle national interests meant economic strength on the basis of private ownership of the means of production, military power as a precondition for imperialistic expansion, independence in the world and autarky. These objectives implied in turn the necessity of rearmament. Thus in fascism the economy became ultimately an instrument of rearmament and autarky objectives; in Germany soon after fascism came to power (1934–5), in Italy during the World Depression that followed a period of relatively liberal economic policy (until 1926–7), in which a free-trade and a deflationary fiscal policy (to balance the budget) was implemented.

To revive the economy after the Depression the fascist regimes utilized deficit-financed government expenditures partly for infrastructural investments (like the Autobahnbau in Germany) but mainly for rearmament. Thus in Germany the total government expenditures as a proportion of gross national product doubled between 1932 and 1938. The armament expenditures as a proportion of GNP rose in the same time from nearly 1 per cent to more than 15 per cent, which in 1938 was 50 per cent of total government expenditure (Erbe, 1958). In addition the regimes tried to stimulate civil economic activities – such as house renovation – by tax reductions and/or pecuniary aid.

Credit policy basically functioned as a means to finance the budget deficit. Because the public debt could not be totally financed from the private capital market, the credit institutions were obliged to absorb the public debt by accepting public treasury certificates. Thus the credit institutions lost their usual function as intermediaries in the private circulation of capital. They served instead as a collecting box of money to cover public debts. Tax credit notes and, in Germany, the so-called Mefo-bills were further financing instruments. The German Reich's debt increased from RM 14 milliard in 1933 to RM42 milliard in 1938, of which RM12 milliard were raised by the Mefo-bills, showing the high proportion of short-term debts. As long as full employment had not been achieved this credit expansion had little inflationary effect.

The control over the volume of investment by prohibiting the distribution of dividends above a fixed level (in Germany, six per cent), by subjecting new issues of shares to the permission of the state and by obliging firms to lend the government all their non-invested excess capital helped in the management of deficit spending.

Falling imports and exports as a result of the Depression and the protectionism of the time led, especially in the fascist countries, to serious tendencies towards an insulation from cyclical trade movements and the creation of a closed economy. A neomercantilistic foreign trade policy became a means of achieving these objectives. Bilateralization of foreign trade, based on clearing and barter agreements accompanied by the use of economic, political and, later, military pressure to attain favourable trade arrangements; import licences; export subsidies; fixing of quotas; control over foreign exchange and high tariff barriers: all these instruments were used to regulate foreign trade totally with regard to the programmes of autarky and rearmament.

Thus, in accordance with the old imperialist aims of big business and as a preliminary to creating the closed '*Grossraumwirtschaft*', German foreign trade shifted from the western to the weak southeast European countries with their large resources of raw materials (Sohn-Rethel, 1973). The volume of German foreign trade with these countries as a proportion of total German foreign trade more than doubled between 1932 and 1938. To get special raw materials German foreign trade with Latin America and northeast European countries developed in the same direction.

Based on growing internal demand Germany experienced rapid economic revival. Full employment had been achieved by 1937–8 from a situation of over 6 million jobless in 1932–3. Although this success served to establish mass loyalty toward the fascist regime, economic development was undoubtedly more for the benefit of the propertied classes and, above all, of big industry, whose profits in 1938 were twice as high as in 1932 (Bettelheim, 1971, p. 232). As a result of the brutal destruction of all traditional independent labour organizations, the prohibition of strikes and the elimination of free wage negotiations, the degree of working class exploitation was increased, scarcely masked by some welfare services. While in Germany wages were fixed at the low level of the Depression year 1932, in Italy they were even cut. In Germany, the index of average weekly real wages reached the level of 1928 only in 1938, yet the average weekly labour time increased from 41.5 hours in 1932 to nearly 47 hours in 1938. Thus the growth of wages is to be seen as the result of rising working hours (Mason, 1977, p. 149). Wages and salaries as a proportion of national income fell from 64 per cent in 1932 to 57 per cent in 1938.

The growing profits were mostly ploughed back into investments. In Germany the gross investment as a proportion of GNP rose from 9 per cent in 1932 to more than 15 per cent in 1938. Although personal consumption increased, total consumption as a proportion of GNP fell from 81 per cent in 1932 to less than 64 per cent in 1938 (Mason, 1977, p. 149). The transformation of the production structure from consumer good industries to those of capital equipment was completely in line with the rearmament programme.

In pursuit of autarky, surrogates for imports and foreign raw materials were increasingly produced, shifting the orientation of many firms' production processes from the world to the domestic market. This often led to a loss of strong world market positions. This process was supported by a cartellization policy which was in contrast to the earlier anti-capitalist slogans of the fascist movement. Moreover, state-run factories were built up to increase the use of low-quality domestic raw materials with correspondingly high production costs. However, self-sufficiency could never be achieved. At the outbreak of the war Germany was still dependent on foreign supplies of oil, iron ore, manganese and many other raw materials (Kaldor, 1945, p. 42).

With the intensification of measures for rearmament and autarky, after full employment had been achieved, beginning in Germany with the declaration of Hitler's 'Vierjahresplan' in 1936, public finances drifted towards a ruinous situation. Inflation was only suppressed by extensive controls of prices and wages. In an attempt to manage critical shortages of raw materials, quota systems were introduced. For the same reason, the employment of the labour force was increasingly controlled and directed. However, these interventions into the running of the economy took place without any proper planning.

Although the outbreak of the war necessitated the further intensification of armaments production German war potential was never fully exploited (Kaldor, 1945). This would have meant the further extension of the average labour time, the employment of more women, the further reduction of consumer good production to the advantage of war production, and total planned economy. The reason the fascist leaders did not force the people to greater sacrifices is to be seen in their interpretation of Germany's defeat in World War I as a result of internal political instability (Mason, 1977).

BIBLIOGRAPHY

Bettelheim, C. 1971. *L'économie allemande sous le nazisme. Un aspect de la décadence du capitalisme.* Paris: Maspero.

Broszat, M. 1969. *Der Staat Hitlers. Grundlegung und Entwicklung seiner inneren Verfassung.* Munich: DTV.

De Felice, R. 1966. *Mussolini il fascista. I: La conquista del potere, 1921–1925,* Turin: Einaudi, 1966; II: *L'organizzazione dello Stato fascista, 1925–1929,* Turin: Einaudi, 1968.

De Felice, R. 1969. *Le interpretazioni del Fascismo.* Bari: Laterza.

Erbe, R. 1958. *Die nationalsozialistische Wirtschaftspolitik 1933–1939 im Lichte der modernen Theorie.* Zurich: Polygraph Verlag.

Fraenkel, E. 1941. *The Dual State. A contribution to the theory of dictatorship.* New York, London and Toronto: Octagon Books.

Gregor, A.J. 1974. *Interpretations of Fascism.* Morristown, NJ: General Learning Press.

Hirschfeld, G. and Mommsen, W.J. (eds) 1980. *Der Führerstaat: Mythos und Realität. Studien zur Struktur und Politik des Dritten Reiches.* Stuttgart: Klett-Verlag.

Kaldor, N. 1945. The German war economy. *Review of Economic Studies* 13(1), 33–52.

Lyttleton, A. 1973. *The Seizure of Power: Fascism in Italy 1919–1929.* London: Weidenfeld & Nicolson.

Mason, T.W. 1968. The primacy of politics – politics and economics in National Socialist Germany. In *The Nature of Fascism,* ed. S.J. Woolf, London: Weidenfeld & Nicolson.

Mason, T.W. 1977. *Sozialpolitik im Dritten Reich. Arbeiterklasse und Volksgemeinschaft.* Opladen: Westdeutscher Verlag.

Milward, A.S. 1965. *The German Economy at War.* London: Athlone Press.

Neumann, F. 1944. *Behemoth. The structure and practice of National Socialism.* 2nd edn, New York: Octagon Books.

Petzina, D. 1967. *Autarkiepolitik im Dritten Reich. Der national sozialistische Vierjahresplan.* Stuttgart: Deutsche Verlagsanstalt.

Sarti, R. 1971. *Fascism and Industrial Leadership in Italy 1919–1940.* Berkeley: University of California Press.

Schweitzer, A. 1964. *Big Business in the Third Reich.* Bloomington: Indiana University Press.

Sohn-Rethel, A. 1973. *Ökonomie und Klassenstruktur des deutschen Faschismus. Aufzeichnungen und Analysen.* Frankfurt am Main: Suhrkamp Verlag. Trans. by Martin Sohn-Rethel as *Economy and Class Structure of German Fascism*, London: CSE Books.

Turner, H.A., Jr. 1985. *German Big Business and the Rise of Hitler.* Oxford and New York: Oxford University Press.

Grigorii Alexandrovic Fel'dman

MICHAEL ELLMAN

Fel'dman was one of the founders of the theory of economic growth under socialism, the economics of planning and development economics. An electrical engineer by profession, he worked in Gosplan from February 1923 to January 1931. It was in this period that his contribution to economics was made. At first he was in the department analysing and forecasting developments in the world economy (he concentrated on Germany and the USA). His first work on the theory of growth was a comparative study of the structure and dynamics of the US economy in 1850–1925 with projections of the Soviet economy between 1926/27 and 1940/41. His most important work ('On the theory of the rates of growth of the national income') was a report to Gosplan's committee for compiling a long-term plan for the development of the national economy of the USSR. It was published in two parts in Gosplan's journal in 1928. A year later Fel'dman published a paper which provides a more popular presentation of how to utilize his ideas to calculate long term plans. The ideas of Fel'dman formed the methodological basis for the preliminary draft of a long term plan worked out by the committee, then headed by N.A. Kovalevskii. This draft was discussed at meetings of Gosplan's economic research institute in February and March 1930. Apart from this serious discussion, during 1930 Fel'dman came under public attack for his ideas. His reliance on mathematics and his lack of fanaticism did not fit in well with the political fervour of 1930. The concrete numerical work of Fel'dman and Kovalevskii in 1928/30 was much too optimistic. It treated as feasible entirely unrealizable goals. The attempt to realize them had disastrous effects on the economy. Unfortunately, the political situation in the USSR prevented Fel'dman from publishing anything on economics after 1930. Even when, in 1933, he reverted from the sensitive subject of socialist industrialization to the problems of capitalist growth, his book was not published.

As far as growth theory is concerned, Fel'dman's work was much in advance of contemporary Western work. He developed a two-sector growth model and

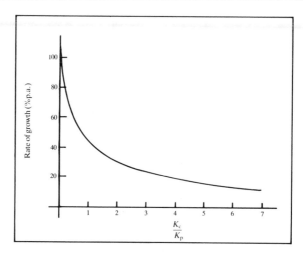

Figure 1 Fel'dman's first theorem, K_c is the capital stock in the consumer goods industry. K_p is the capital stock in the producer goods industry.

showed how different growth rates implied different economic structures. He derived two important results, one about the ratios of the capital stocks in the two sectors, the other about the allocation of investment between the two sectors. The first result is that a high rate of growth requires that a high proportion of the capital stock be in the producer goods sector. This is illustrated in Figure 1. Fel'dman's second theorem is that, along a steady growth path, investment should be allocated between the sectors in the same proportion as the capital stock. For example, suppose that a 20 per cent rate of growth requires a K_c/K_p of 3.7. Then to maintain growth at 20 per cent p.a. requires that 3.7/4.7 of annual investment goes to the consumer goods industries and 1.0/4.7 of annual investment goes to the producer goods industries.

The interrelationship between the two theorems is shown in Table 1, in which Fel'dman explained how any desired growth rate, given the capital–output ratio,

Table 1 Fel'dman's two theorems

$\dfrac{K_p}{K_c}$	$\dfrac{dY}{dt}$ (in % p.a.) (when $K/Y = 2.1$)	$\dfrac{\Delta K_p}{\Delta K_c + \Delta K_p}$
0.106	4.6	0.096
0.2	8.1	0.167
0.5	16.2	0.333
1.0	24.3	0.500

determined both the necessary sectoral composition of the capital stock and the sectoral allocation of investment.

Given the capital–output ratio, the higher the K_p/K_c ratio, i.e. the greater the proportion of the capital stock in the producer goods sector, and correspondingly the higher the $\Delta K_p/\Delta K_c + \Delta K_p$) ratio, i.e. the greater the proportion of new investment in the producer goods sector, the higher the rate of growth. With a capital–output ratio of 2.1, to raise the growth rate from 16.2 to 24.3 per cent requires raising the proportion of the capital stock in the producer goods sector from $\frac{1}{3}$ to $\frac{1}{2}$, and the share of investment in the producer goods sector from $\frac{1}{3}$ to $\frac{1}{2}$.

The conclusion Fel'dman drew from his model was that the main tasks of the planners were to regulate the capital–output ratios in the two sectors and the ratio of the capital stock in the producer goods sector to that in the consumer goods sector. For the former task, Fel'dman recommended rationalization and multi-shift working, for the latter, investment in the producer goods sector.

As far as the economics of planning is concerned, the main lesson to be learned from the Fel'dman model is that the capacity of the capital goods industry is one of the constraints limiting the rate of growth of an economy. There may well be other constraints, such as foreign exchange, urban real wages or the marketed output of agriculture. (Indeed, it is possible that one or more of these is/are the binding constraint/s and that the limited capacity of the producer goods sector is a non-binding constraint.) Economic planning is largely concerned with the removal of constraints to rapid economic growth. Accordingly, a planned process of rapid growth may require that the planners stimulate the rapid development of the producer goods sector.

As far as development economics is concerned, Fel'dman is important because of the argument in his 1928 paper that 'an increase in the rate of growth of income demands industrialization, heavy industry, machine building, electrification...'. When first formulated, this conclusion struck many economists as counter-intuitive and paradoxical.

Fel'dman's work, as is natural for a pioneer, suffers from serious limitations. As far as the theory of economic growth under socialism is concerned, he was an important early contributor, but his work has to be complemented by Kalecki's emphasis on the limits of growth and Kornai's emphasis on the behavioural regularities actually generating the growth process. As for the economics of planning, his arguments have to be complemented by a proper understanding of the role of agriculture, foreign trade and personal consumption and of the danger of an over-accumulation crisis. In development economics, experience in the USSR in the 1930s, India in the 1950s and China in the Maoist period has shown the limitations of a narrowly Fel'dmanite approach.

A brilliant pioneer, Fel'dman's work was ended after only a few years by the Stalinists.

SELECTED WORKS
1927. Soobrazheniya o strukture i dinamike narodnogo khozyaistvo SSha s 1850 po 1925g
i SSSR s 1926/27 po 1940/41gg (Reflections on the structure and dynamics of the

national economy of the USA from 1850 to 1925 and of the USSR from 1926/27 to 1940/41). *Planovoe khozyaistvo* no. 7. Also published as a booklet.

1928. K teorii tempov narodnogo khozyaistva (On the theory of the rates of growth of the national income). *Planovoe khozyaistvo* nos. 11 and 12. English translation in *Foundations of Soviet Strategy for Economic Growth*, ed. N. Spulber, Bloomington: Indiana University Press, 1964, pp. 174–99 and 304–31.

1929a. SSR i mirovoe khozyaistvo na rubezhe vtorogo goda pyatletki (The USSR and the world economy on the eve of the second year of the five year plan). *Na planovom fronte* no. 2.

1929b. O limitakh industrializatsii (On the limits of industrialization). *Planovoe khozyaistvo* no. 2.

1929c. Analiticheskii metod postroeniya perspektivnykh planov (An analytical method for constructing perspective plans). *Planovoe khozyaistvo* no. 12.

1930. Problemy electrifikatsii na novom etape (Problems of electrification at a new stage). In *Na novom etape sotsialisticheskogo stroitel'stva*, vol. 1, Moscow.

BIBLIOGRAPHY

Soviet evaluations. Report of the discussion in Gosplan's economic research institute of February and March 1930. *Planovoe khozyaistvo*, 1930, no. 3, pp. 117–211.

Vainshtein, A.L. and Khanin, G.I. 1968. Pamyati vydayushchegocya sovetskogo ekonomista-matematika G.A. Fel'dmana (In memory of the outstanding Soviet mathematical economist G.A. Fel'dman). *Ekonomika i matematicheskie methody* 4(2).

ENGLISH-LANGUAGE WORKS

Chng, M.K. 1980. Dobb and the Marx–Fel'dman model. *Cambridge Journal of Economics* 4(4), 393–400.

Dobb, M. 1967. The question of 'Investment priority for heavy industry'. Chapter 4 of M. Dobb, *Papers on Capitalism, Development and Planning*, London: Routledge; New York: International Publishers.

Domar, E.D. 1957. A Soviet model of growth. In E.D. Domar, *Essays in the Theory of Economic Growth*, New York: Oxford University Press.

Erlich, A. 1978. Dobb and the Marx–Fel'dman model: a problem in Soviet economic strategy. *Cambridge Journal of Economics* 2(2), 203–14.

Mahalanobis, P.C. 1953. Some observations on the process of growth of national income. *Sankhya* 12(4), 307–12.

Mahalanobis, P.C. 1955. The approach of operational research to planning in India. *Sankhya* 16(1 and 2), 3–130.

Sen, A.K. and Raj, K.N. 1961. Alternative patterns of growth under conditions of stagnant export earnings. *Oxford Economic Papers* 13(1), 43–52.

Tinbergen, J. and Bos, H.C. 1962. *Mathematical Models of Economic Growth*. New York: McGraw-Hill.

Investment Planning

JOSEPH HALEVI

The theories discussed here consist of two complementary formulations originating in India and in the United Kingdom in the 1950s and 1960s. Both deal with investment planning when development starts with virtually no capital goods industry. Thus they represent an expansion of the model of the Soviet economist Fel'dman, since in the latter case the economy did possess an investment sector albeit in a limited dimension (Fel'dman, 1928a, 1928b).

The first approach, due to Dobb (1954, 1960) and to Sen (1960), deals with the choice of techniques and the sectoral distribution of investment and labour. The second approach, elaborated by a number of Indian scholars – Raj and Sen (1961), Naqvi (1963) – is more concerned with the sectoral allocation of investment goods under conditions of stagnant export earnings. The definition of sector is the same as in the Marx-based Fel'dman model with the difference that the capital goods sector itself is divided into two branches. One branch consists of an intermediate sector producing equipment usable only in the consumption goods sector. The second branch is formed by *machine tools* which can reproduce themselves as well as be installed in the intermediate sector.

The emphasis on this kind of structural relations is aimed at providing analytical support to the view that sectoral investment planning by the State is a necessary, although not sufficient, condition for the emancipation from backwardness.

The starting point of both approaches is the historical consideration that colonialism has destroyed the traditional home industries, thereby making expansion dependent on the exports of primary products having low demand elasticities (Raj and Sen, 1961). It is this particular condition which justifies investment priority in the capital goods industry for a growth strategy oriented toward the home market (Dobb, 1967). Industrialization would then imply the creation of capital goods well in advance of any market demand for them, a process called by Dobb *the Accelerator in Reverse*.

Developing economies face the task of investing in a manner largely independent of the preexisting material structure. In this context, indivisibilities of capital equipment – which 'are likely to be significantly large (relatively to the scale of the economy) at early stages of development' (Dobb, 1960, pp. 11–12) – may make the expansion of a certain branch unprofitable although its growth can be of crucial importance for the formation of other industries. State planning of the sectoral allocation of investment performs the role of securing over time the construction of complementary industries.

It must be noticed that some of the views put forward by Dobb and the Indian economists were part of the intellectual climate of the period. In the mid-1950s Prebisch started the debate over the terms of trade between industrialized and underdeveloped countries, arguing the long-term nature of the latter's unfavourable position. Politically, the first meeting of the non-aligned nations, held in the Indonesian city of Bandung in 1955, asserted the necessity to embark on a road privileging the domestic market. Institutionally, sectoral planning by the State seemed to have gained a firm hold also in a non-socialist country as important as India. Practically, the experience of the People's Republic of China suggested that a developing country could reduce the dependency on foreign exchange by building a machine tools industry (Raj, 1967).

Given this cultural and political framework, Dobb's pioneering work has a special place in the theories of planned development. It singled out the fact that the domestic economy of underdeveloped countries does not generate a surplus of wage goods large enough to allow a more or less smooth process of growth. Indeed, with most of the work force employed in subsistence activities, it would be impossible to set in motion the Accelerator in Reverse unless the bottleneck of a limited surplus is widened. The technical form of investment must therefore reflect this initial constraint. In setting forth the answer to the question of the choice of techniques, Dobb challenged the view that 'since a scarcity of capital relative to labour is a usual characteristic of underdeveloped economies, capital investment needs there to take the form of projects of "low capital intensity"' (Dobb [1954], 1955, p. 139).

The gist of his and Sen's argument (Sen, 1960) can be presented as follows:

Consider an economy where fixed capital in the capital goods industry is so small that machines can be thought of as being produced by labour alone. Thus, employment in the capital goods sector multiplied by the productivity of labour – denoted by x – gives the total output of equipment. But employment in the capital goods sector is limited by the surplus produced in the wage goods sector. If 20 people work in the wage goods sector, where the productivity of labour (z) is 20 units per person and the real wage rate (w) is uniform throughout the economy and fixed at 10 units, then 20 people can be put to work in the capital goods sector. The crucial ratio is given by $(z - w)/w$, where $z - w$ is the surplus per unit of labour in the wage goods sector. If the bottleneck in the production of wage goods has to be widened without lowering the real wage, all newly produced machines should be installed in the wage goods sector. On the assumption that these do not depreciate and that each machine employs one worker, total output of capital goods will be equal to the increment in employment in the wage goods sector. The growth rate of the economy is therefore equal to the growth rate of employment in this sector. Given the above mentioned allocation policy, the growth rate is nothing but the productivity of labour in the capital goods sector multiplied by the ratio of the surplus to the wage rate. Hence:

$$g = x(s/w); \quad \text{where} \quad s = z - w. \tag{1}$$

Assuming no production lags, maximization of (1) yields:

$$-(dx/x) = (dz/z)(z/s). \tag{2}$$

According to equation (2), the growth rate would be maximized by using more costly methods of production in the capital goods industry, lowering the productivity of labour in this sector. At the same time, the delivery of improved and more expensive equipment would *ipso facto* raise labour productivity in the wage goods industry. With a positive wage rate – implying a z/s ratio greater than unity – this gain need not be as large as the loss of productivity in the capital goods industry. It is the asymmetrical change in the sectoral productivities of labour which leads to an overall increase in capital intensity.

The results do not change if unassisted labour builds machine tools for the intermediate investment sector. In this case the gains in the intermediate sector multiplied by z/s, should equal the losses in the machine tools industry.

With a construction based on a number of simplifying assumptions, Dobb and Sen provided the rationale for raising the capital intensity of production under conditions of abundant labour supply. Yet the assumptions turned out to be restrictive not so much in relation to traditional theory, but in relation to the scope and objective of the exercise.

Analytically the model does not succeed in giving a criterion for the choice of techniques when the economy embarks on a path of self expansion of the machine tools sector. The only possible observation is that this sector's productivity does not depend on any other branch of the economy, thus there is no constraint on the degree of capital intensity (Johansen and Ghosh, in Dobb, 1960). Dobb's and Sen's results depend very much on the assumptions of no production lags and of immortal machines. In macroeconomic terms, an increase in capital intensity generates a higher growth rate only if the share of investment in national income is raised more than proportionately, which may not be immediately feasible. In the interim period the economy will experience a lower growth rate and a lower share of consumption (Kalecki, 1972a). In turn, the notion of immortal machines becomes untenable whenever Dobb analyses the possibility of drafting the whole of the labour force in the two investment industries for the purpose of building the machine tools sector. If wear and tear is taken into account, as soon as no equipment flows to the wage goods sector its capital stock will shrink and so will the output of consumables. The wage rate will cease to be a parameter, becoming instead a variable conditioned by the proportions in which labour and machines are distributed. Hence, wear and tear and the socially minimum wage rate show the limit of the percentage in which machine

115

tools can be reinvested in their own sector. This is a major structural and social aspect of any process of accelerated accumulation (Lowe, 1976; Halevi, 1981).

Dobb's contribution will remain a classic in the field because it introduced a novel perspective on the reasons for, and the modalities of, socialist-oriented development for the ex-colonial countries. The fact that this approach is no longer followed can only in part be attributed to the limitations outlined above. Perhaps, in addition to the ever present ideological factor, one explanation lies in the change of the historical framework. There are, by now, significant instances in which a process of fast accumulation has taken place hand in hand with the persistence of phenomena such as landlessness and urban poverty. In countries like Brazil, Mexico and India, these are the problems that must be reflected in any planning strategy. The issue is not so much that of building a capital goods sector from scratch, but to conceptualize the economic and political nature of the phenomena (Kalecki, 1972b, 1972c; Taylor and Bacha, 1976).

The second approach, coming mainly from India, is a substantial improvement on the Mahalanobis variant of the Fel'dman model (Mahalanobis, 1955). It uses the same hypothesis of two capital goods industries to discuss the sectoral allocation of machinery imported through a fixed sum of foreign earnings F. Raj and Sen (1961) assumed a negligible amount of equipment in the intermediate investment sector I, and in the machine tools industry M. Furthermore, machine tools are used also for the extraction of raw materials R. The planners can freely choose the initial share of consumption over national income; production coefficients are given. In this context, if F is used to import I goods for the production of consumption goods C, the output of C goods will rise but its absolute increase will tend to nought because raw material requirements will also rise. A constant increment in C goods production can be obtained when F is used to import M goods for the production of I goods and for the extraction of R. In this case raw materials set a limit to the expansion of the I sector output. Finally, the output of consumption goods will grow at a constant absolute rate if M goods are imported in order to produce machine tools to be installed exclusively in the I and R sectors.

The original Raj–Sen paper did not discuss the proportions in which machine tools are reinvested in the M sector itself. In the literature that followed, the point was raised by Naqvi (1963) and later by Cooper (1983). Naqvi noted that reinvestment in the M goods sector would allow for a proportionate growth in C goods also in the presence of a limited amount of import earnings. Moreover he observed that central control of the M goods sector can be used to limit the creation of a luxury goods industry catering for the well to do. Cooper, on his part, argued that planners can more effectively influence the share of consumption by selecting the ratio in which M goods are to be reploughed in their own sector. This is because the share of consumption over national income cannot be freely determined by planners, since it is fixed by the initial distribution of equipment. Planning models based on sectoral relations and on the principle of the Accelerator in Reverse, showed a greater longevity than choice of techniques models. The assumption of given production coefficients did not prevent the analysis of alternative growth paths and the introduction of limiting conditions such as minimum wage rate and stagnant export earnings (Das, 1974). The capital goods–consumption goods model has been used also as a framework for the application of optimal control theory in development planning (Stoleru, 1965), as well as for the analysis of unused capacity caused by a slow growing agricultural output (Patnaik, 1972; Raj, 1975).

Contributions to investment planning using analytically a Marxian sectoral approach have come mostly from Great Britain and from India. The Soviet mathematical economists seem to be more inclined toward generic multisectoral optimization models. This may reflect a belief that a purely capital goods–consumption goods approach ceases to be relevant when a socialist economy possesses a developed industrial structure. Yet, as it emerges from reading the works of some Soviet economists of the mathematical school, generic multisector models cannot give a stylized picture of growth paths (Dadayan, 1981). Indeed, in the Western literature on growth, the crucial issue of the transition between two growth rates – a process called Traverse – is dealt with using an analytical apparatus closer to Marx's sectoral characterization of the economy (Hicks, 1965; Lowe, 1976).

BIBLIOGRAPHY

Cooper, C. 1983. Extensions of the Raj–Sen model of economic growth. *Oxford Economic Papers* 35(2), July, 170–85.

Dadayan, V. 1981. *Macroeconomic Models*. Moscow: Progress.

Das, R.K. 1974. *Optimal Investment Planning*. Rotterdam: Rotterdam University Press.

Dobb, M. 1954. A note on the so-called degree of capital-intensity of investment in under-developed countries. In M. Dobb, *On Economic Theory and Socialism, Collected Papers*, London: Routledge & Kegan Paul, 1955.

Dobb, M. 1960. *An Essay on Economic Growth and Planning*. London: Routledge & Kegan Paul; New York: Monthly Review Press.

Dobb, M. 1967. The question of 'investment-priority' for heavy industry. In M. Dobb, *Papers on Capitalism, Development and Planning*, New York: International Publishers.

Fel'dman, G. 1928a. K teorii tempov narodnogo dokhoda (On the theory of growth rates of the national income). *Planovoe khozyaistvo*, November.

Fel'dman, G. 1928b. K teorii tempov narodnogo dokhoda (On the theory of growth rates of the national income). *Planovoe khozyaistvo*, December.

Halevi, J. 1981. The composition of investment under conditions of non uniform changes. *Banca Nazionale del Lavoro Quarterly Review* 34(137), June, 213–32.

Hicks, J. 1965. *Capital and Growth*. Oxford: Clarendon Press; New York: Oxford University Press.

Johansen, L. and Ghosh, A. 1960. Appendix: notes to chapters III and IV. In M. Dobb, *An Essay on Economic Growth and Planning*, London: Routledge & Kegan Paul; New York: Monthly Review Press.

Kalecki, M. 1972a. The problem of choice of the capital–output ratio under conditions of an unlimited supply of labour. In M. Kalecki, *Selected Essays on the Economic Growth of the Socialist and the Mixed Economy*, Cambridge and New York: Cambridge University Press.

Problems of the planned economy

Kalecki, M. 1972b. Problems of financing economic development in a mixed economy. In M. Kalecki, *Selected Essays on the Economic Growth of the Socialist and the Mixed Economy*, Cambridge and New York: Cambridge University Press.

Kalecki, M. 1972c. Social and economic aspects of 'intermediate regimes'. In M. Kalecki, *Selected Essays on the Economic Growth of the Socialist and the Mixed Economy*, Cambridge and New York: Cambridge University Press.

Lowe, A. 1976. *The Path of Economic Growth*. Cambridge and New York: Cambridge University Press.

Mahalanobis, P.C. 1955. The approach of operational research to planning in India. *Sankhya* 16, December, 3–131.

Naqvi, K.A. 1963. Machine-tools and machines: a physical interpretation of the marginal rate of saving. *Indian Economic Review* 6(3), February, 19–28.

Patnaik, P. 1972. Disproportionality crisis and cyclical growth. A theoretical note. *Economic and Political Weekly* 7, annual number, February, 329–36.

Raj, K.N. 1967. Role of the 'machine-tools sector' in economic growth. In *Socialism, Capitalism and Economic Growth, Essays Presented to Maurice Dobb*, ed. C. Feinstein, Cambridge: Cambridge University Press.

Raj, K.N. 1975. Linkages in industrialization and development strategy; some basic issues. *Journal of Development Planning* 8, 105–19.

Raj, K.N. and Sen, A.K. 1961. Alternative patterns of growth under conditions of stagnant export earnings. *Oxford Economic Papers* 13, February, 43–52.

Sen, A.K. 1960. *Choice of Techniques*. Oxford: Basil Blackwell.

Stoleru, L. 1965. An optimal policy for economic growth. *Econometrica* 33, April, 321–48.

Taylor, L. and Bacha, E. 1976. The unequalizing spiral: a first growth model for Belindia. *Quarterly Journal of Economics* 90(2), May, 197–218.

118

Leonid Vitalievich Kantorovich

V. MAKAROV

Kantorovich made valuable contributions to the theory of welfare and was the founder of the theory of optimal planning of socialist economies. As a professional mathematician, he also made a valuable contribution to a number of sections of modern mathematics. He is regarded (together with G. Dantzig) as the founder of linear programming, the mathematical discipline which has many applications in economics.

L.V. Kantorovich was born on 19 January 1912. He graduated from the Department of Mathematics of Leningrad University in 1930 at the age of 18. Four years later he became Professor of Mathematics at Leningrad University. In 1939, through the publishing house of Leningrad University, he published a small booklet, 'Mathematical methods of organizing and planning production'.

This may be considered a historic document, containing the facts about the discovery of linear programming. The mathematical formulation of production problems of optimal planning was presented here for the first time and the effective methods of their solution and economic analysis were proposed. Thus the idea of optimality in economics was founded scientifically. This booklet and a number of subsequent articles establish Kantorovich together with F.P. Ramsey and J. von Neumann as the founders of the optimization approach to the analysis of economic problems.

His fundamental work, 'The Best Uses of Economic Resources', written in 1942 but published for the first time only in 1959, is a brilliant example of the consistent application of the optimization principle to the analysis of a wide variety of economic problems: the planning of production from the level of the enterprise to the level of the national economy as a whole; a theory of price formation, which includes the principles of price formation not only for goods and services but also for the factors of production, the time factor, the space factor, natural conditions, the conditions of labour application etc.; a theory of economic and social-economic efficiency of economic enterprises.

In fact, Kantorovich developed a powerful tool for the analysis of economic problems from the unified position of global optimum and indeed it is not necessary to find this optimum, it is enough to postulate its existence. In a number of his subsequent articles Kantorovich demonstrated the power of his method for the analysis and improvement of the mechanism of economic management of the socialist economy as a whole and of its components. He proposed methods for calculating wholesale price levels for the branches of the national economy; the value of the norm of effectiveness of capital investments; the norm of depreciation allowances, and the value of transport tariffs, rent payments, etc.

For a number of years Kantorovich showed great interest in the problems of economic dynamics. He proposed, analysed and used in practice a dynamic model of optimal planning. On the basis of this model and its different modifications Kantorovich proposed an original theory of economic evaluation of technical ventures. The essence of this theory is that the economic effect of the introduction of a scientific-technical innovation includes three components: a producer effect; a consumer effect; and an effect which is the result of the increase in general scientific-technical economic potential derived from the innovation. The third component is ignored in usual economic practice which leads to a distorted calculation of the real efficiency of innovations.

Kantorovich was also a world-famous mathematician. He made great contributions to a number of different branches of mathematics, among them the descriptive theory of functions and of sets; the constructive theory of functions; a decision method of solving a wide range of problems concerning the best approximation of functions by polynomials; calculus of variations; functional analysis, where he introduced and studied the class of semiordered spaces (K-spaces); approximate calculation methods; and he developed several effective algorithms as well as a number of other branches of mathematics. This demonstrates his mathematical genius and the vast range of his interests and knowledge.

The author of about 300 scientific works, Kantorovich was awarded the Nobel Prize in economics in 1975.

SELECTED WORKS

1939. *Matematicheskie metody organizatsii i planirovaniia proizvodstva.* Leningrad: State Publishing House. Trans. as 'Mathematical methods of organizing and planning production', *Management Science* 6(4), July 1960, 363–422.

1959a. *Ekonomicheskii raschet nailuchshego isplo'zovaniia resursov.* Moscow: State Publishing House. Trans. by P.F. Knightsfield, ed. G. Morton, as *The Best Uses of Economic Resources*, Oxford: Pergamon, 1965.

1959b. (With G.P. Akilov.) *Funktsional'nyi analiz v normirovannykh prostranstvakh.* Moscow: Nauka. 2nd edn, 1982. 1st edn trans. by D.E. Brown, ed. Dr A.P. Robertson, as *Functional Analysis in Normed Spaces*, Oxford: Pergamon. 2nd edn trans. by Howard L. Silcock as *Functional Analysis*, Oxford: Pergamon, 1982.

1976. *Essays in Optimal Planning.* Ed. L. Smolinski, New York: Wiley.

Labour-Managed Economies

B. HORVAT

Labour management may be understood as a generic concept for all cases when enterprises are managed by those working in them. Institutional forms of such enterprises differ and also the degree of self-management varies. It may be expected that labour-managed firms and economies will behave differently from those run by capitalist or state managers.

The oldest labour-managed enterprises are producer cooperatives. Some of them survived from the Middle Ages; for example, monastic orders and some religious sects (e.g., Hutterites in the USA and Canada). The modern, non-religious equivalent are kibbutzim, which comprise about four per cent of the Israeli economy. They were preceded by various Owenite and Fourierist communities in the 19th century and coexist with a communitarian movement in Europe. Such cooperatives represent not only a specific organizational form but also a specific way of life, different from that of the rest of the community. Small communes in the developed countries and village communities in the non-capitalist environments also belong here.

The modern cooperative movement – cooperatives are just an organizational form of productive enterprises – was born in 19th-century Western Europe. At about the same time the first attempts were made to provide state capital to unemployed workers who were to run their enterprises by themselves (the Ateliers Nationaux of Louis Blanc in 1848).

Since the Paris Commune of 1870 every genuine social revolution has generated strong demands and massive implementation of workers' management. That meant the right of workers to self-management regardless of the ownership of capital (for the history of workers' management see Horvat, 1982, pp. 109–73). Most of these attempts did not survive the revolution itself.

After World War II there was a virtual explosion of various forms of labour management and for the first time an entire national economy (Yugoslavia) was subject to workers' management.

INSTITUTIONAL FORMS. Proceeding from the less inclusive towards more inclusive forms, one may distinguish three pure models:

(1) *Partnership or partial cooperative.* Partners are the founders and the owners of the cooperative. They manage the firm on an equal right basis. They employ other individuals who do not have ownership and management rights. Law and medical firms in the West and frequently organized along such lines.

(2) *Full cooperative.* The firm is owned by all of its members and every member has one vote in management decisions.

(3)*Worker managed enterprise.* Capital is socially owned which means that it is accessible to every member of society on equal terms. All workers participate in management on the basis one man one vote. The organization is based on the distinction between the two types of authority: professional and political. All workers, or their representatives in the Workers' Council, decide on the policy issues. Given the policy thus established, professional coordinators and other experts make their professional decisions. The Workers' Council has, naturally, full access to external expertise. In this way the organization is supposed to combine maximum democracy with maximum efficiency. The participation of all workers means capturing all information that is available within a firm.

Models 1 and 2 are based on collective ownership. Model 3 implies social ownership.

DEGREES OF PARTICIPATION. At around World War I the autocratic organization of typical capitalist firms began to encounter strong resistance. The need to expand war production and avoid strikes induced governments and employers of belligerent countries to experiment with some mild forms of workers' participation. Although similar attempts were made earlier, particularly in Germany, British *joint consultation*, as exemplified in the Whitley councils of 1917, may be taken as a landmark. Joint consulation means that the employer is obliged to consult his employees before making decisions that affect their work and income in some important way. However, the final decision is his.

The next step towards democratization of management was made in Germany after World War I when *codetermination* was introduced. Under the pressure of the 1918 revolution, when German workers demanded the socialization of the economy, the Weimar constitution envisaged codetermination. But this constitutional provision was never enacted. After the last war a series of laws were passed providing for workers' participation on the boards of directors – in some industries on a parity basis – and also reserving the post of the personnel director for the trade union representative. Today all West European countries, and many others as well, have some form of co-determination.

Further development led towards full-fledged *workers' management*. It was both revolutionary and reformist. As a result of a social revolution, workers' management was established in Yugoslavia (1950). The reformist way (called *democracía social de participación plena*), was pioneered by Peru in the 1970s under President Velasco Alvardo, but the development was mostly reversed after his death. The same idea was taken over and more successfully implemented by the Swedes in the 1980s (Meidner, 1978). Genuine democratization of management requires also a change in property relations; workers must have control over invested capital, at least partly. Swedish Wage Earners Funds are financed by a certain percentage of annual gross profits and payroll tax. They buy shares in the companies and are controlled by the unions. That, of course, is not full workers' management. The economy is still privately owned and unions are centralized organizations. But the Swedish reform marks a successful beginning of a reformist transition period.

SOCIAL OWNERSHIP. In the tradition of the First and Second Internationals, Soviet legal theory – and many authors elsewhere – identify state ownership with socialism. Thus the Soviet Civil Code of 1922 distinguishes three types of ownership, in ascending order: private, cooperative and state. The last one represents the basis for socialism. After a while it was discovered that the position of the workers in state firms is no different from that in private firms. Occasionally it may even be worse, since the state is a monopoly employer. Under both regimes the intra-firm hierarchy is preserved and management has autocratic power. Thus one has to distinguish the state ownership that characterizes the social order called *étatism*, from the social ownership which is appropriate for socialism, the latter being a full-fledged worker-managed economy.

Economic and legal theory of social ownership is still in its infancy and is virtually unknown outside Yugoslavia. The basic ingredients of the existing theory are as follows.

As a social category, ownership had three dimensions: *legal, social* and *economic*. In the *formal legal* sense social property is a bundle of rights intended to regulate economic transactions. Traditionally the inventory of such rights consisted of *ius utendi, fruendi et disponendi*. As a result of a long historical process, these right came to be subject to four types of restrictions: (1) market restrictions – cartels are forbidden, monopolies will be broken up, prices are often regulated, etc.; (2) work restrictions – the length of the working day and week is regulated and certain safety measures are mandatory; (3) ecological restrictions; (4) systemic restrictions – the value of productive capital cannot be reduced regardless of the sources of finance. Restrictions 1–3 are common for all modern societies, though they vary in comprehensiveness. Restriction 4 is specific for socialism.

The *social* dimension implies three rights: (1) every member of society has a right to work; (2) every member of the society has a right to compete for any work position if he meets the requirements of the work place; (3) every member of the society has the right of participation in management on equal terms.

Economically social ownership means that income from property (interest, land, mining, location and monopoly rents) belongs to society. Since income is the result of only three factors of production: natural resources, produced resources (capital) and labour – the first two are socially and the last one privately owned – the property right *usus fructus* implies income from live labour exclusively while everything else is capital income. The right (to the product of one's own labour) and the restriction (nothing except the product of labour) is the basis for the principle of distribution according to work. The right to income from capital implies that society is an economic owner of the entire social capital. The attribute *economic* means that formal legal ownership is largely irrelevant as long as the social and economic dimensions of social ownership are preserved. In other words, family farming and smallscale private (in the legal sense) production generally is fully consistent with socialism when it is worker managed and generates income from work only (Bajt, 1968). Income from work includes also income from entrepreneurship.

If we take into account that ownership relations determine particular social orders, then social ownership generates workers' management and distribution according to work (and vice versa) which are the basic constituents of socialism. An historical analysis of social revolutions shows that all of them have been motivated by the quest for justice, which has been interpreted as liberty, equality and solidarity. The three components of justice imply each other and we may take any one as a starting analytical concept. If we take equality as our guiding principle, a society will be considered egalitarian if its members are equal in their fundamental social roles. There are only three such roles: each of us is a producer, a consumer and a citizen. Equality of producers implies workers' management and social property; equality of consumers implies distribution according to work; equality of citizens implies a deconcentration of political power which is a pre-condition for political self-government.

We have arrived at a consistent social theory. Workers' management is a product of historical developments, ethical motivations and organizational solutions required for a society which is about to enter the 21st century. This is the conceptual frame within which we may now proceed to consider the micro and macroeconomics of labour management.

MICROECONOMICS. A few years after the initiation of workers' management in Yugoslavia, an American graduate student, Banjamin Ward, selected it as the subject of his doctoral dissertation. He asked himself what could be the objective function of a worker-managed firm and wound up with the answer that it was not the maximization of profit but the maximization of income per worker (Ward, 1958). This change in assumptions led to some very odd results. For a while Ward's paper passed unnoticed. Then the issue was taken up by Evsey Domar (1966), who considered the Soviet kolkhoz and introduced many inputs and a labour supply function into the analysis. Ward's misallocation effects were considerably weakened but not eliminated. The next step was an attempt at generalization in a book by Jaroslav Vanek (1970). He showed that free entry eliminates misallocation. However, since free entry is a long-run phenomenon, in the short run a labour managed firm will behave inefficiently. Vanek's book broke the silence of the profession. Soon there was a virtual explosion of papers and books and by now the bibliography has accumulated to many hundreds of items. A new discipline was born: the economic theory of labour-managed firms.

Yet, however sophisticated, the later contributions have not departed from the initial methodological framework. It has been taken as an established fact that a labour-managed firm (LMF) is less efficient than a capitalist-managed firm (CMF). Conservatives considered this as proof that capitalism was more efficient than socialism, while radicals tried to discover institutional conditions under which a LMF would catch up in efficiency with the CMF (e.g. reluctance to dismiss colleagues leads to a behavioural asymmetry and a different utility function). In the good neoclassical tradition only allocative efficiency has been discussed; the immensely more important productive efficiency has been hardly touched.

The essentials of the theory are as follows. A capitalist managed firm (CMF) maximizes *absolute* profit. Illyrian firm (IF) maximizes income *per worker*. For reasons to become apparent later I also add the worker managed firm (WMF) which maximizes income per worker *over a planning period*.

Consider a firm with a simple production function with two variable inputs, labour (x_1) and other resources (x_2),

$$q = f(x_1, x_2). \tag{1}$$

There is also fixed cost k, which may be interpreted as depreciation or as a capital tax. Profit appears as

$$\pi = pq - (wx_1 + p_2x_2 + k) \tag{2}$$

where p is the price of output, w is the wage rate and p_2 is the price of the other variable input. If profit is to be maximized, the first order conditions are the familiar marginal equations

$$\frac{\partial \pi}{\partial x_1} = 0, \rightarrow pq_1 = w$$

$$\frac{\partial \pi}{\partial x_2} = 0, \rightarrow pq_2 = p_2. \tag{3}$$

The second order conditions are satisfied if diminishing returns are assumed, as will be done throughout.

An analysis of conditions (3) shows that: (a) an increase in product price increases output and employment; (b) an increase in factor prices decreases output and employment; (c) a change in fixed cost produces no effect, since k does not appear in the conditions; and (d) labour is treated the same as any other resources; there is complete symmetry.

Let us now replace capitalist management by a worker's council. Since wages do not exist, we cannot establish profit. As already mentioned, the objective function is now income per worker

$$y = \frac{pq - (p_2x_2 + k)}{x_1}. \tag{2a}$$

125

Ward was not quite sure that the actual Yugoslav firm maximized y, and so he preferred to talk about the 'Illyrian firm'. The first-order conditions are now

$$\frac{\partial y}{\partial x_1} = 0, \rightarrow pq_1 = \frac{pq - (p_2 x_2 + k)}{x_1} = y$$

$$\frac{\partial y}{\partial x_2} = 0, \rightarrow pq_2 = p_2. \tag{3a}$$

It is evident that the second-order conditions are also satisfied.

We cannot analyse (3a) directly. I shall therefore rearrange terms

$$q - q_1 x_1 = \frac{k}{p} + \frac{p_2 x_2}{p}. \tag{4}$$

It is easy to see that the following is true

$$\frac{\partial}{\partial x_1}(q - q_1 x_1) = -q_1, \, x_1 > 0. \tag{5}$$

A similar analysis now produces the following results: (a) an increase in p reduces the right-hand side of equation (4); in order to preserve equilibrium, the left-hand side must also be reduced, which according to (5) amounts to reducing employment x_1 and, consequently (by virtue of (1) above), output; (b) an increase in the factor price of other resources has the same effect as in the neoclassical firm; (c) an increase in fixed cost k increases output and employment; and (d) factors are not treated symmetrically, since wages do not occur in (3a) and the conditions are structured differently.

The entire exercise is more clearly surveyed in Table. 1.

Table 1   Effects of various changes on output and employment

Type of change	CMF	IF	WMF
Increase in product prices	+	−	+
Increases in wages	−	0	0
Increase in the price of material inputs	−	−	−
Increase in fixed cost	0	+	0

By treating labour differently from material inputs, Illyrians behave in a strange way and impair the efficiency of their firms. When product prices in the market increase, they reduce output. The economy is thus hopelessly unstable. When the government wants to increase employment, it must levy a lump sum tax. The higher the tax, the higher the output and employment. Wage policy is of no use, since Illyrians disregard wages. Because $y > w$, and q_1 (Illyrian) $> q_1$ (capitalist), where q_1 is the marginal product of labour, an Illyrian firm employs fewer workers and produces less than its capitalist counterpart. For the same reason, it uses more capital than necessary. Less employment and higher capital intensity imply, for a given time preference, a smaller rate of growth.

Any meaningful theory must pass two fundamental tests: the verifiability of assumption test and the predictability test. A theory may pass both tests and still not be a correct one. If it fails to pass one or both of them, it is surely not satisfactory. If its assumptions cannot be verified, the theory has no explanatory power; if its predictions are wrong, it is simply useless. The latter test is much simpler and more conclusive, and so we may consider it first. For this purpose we rely on empirical research concerning the Yugoslav economy.

The theory predicts that an increase in price will reduce output. Nothing of the kind has been observed. Increases of price, as signals of unsatisfied demand, have been followed rather quickly by efforts to increase supply.

The theory also predicts that a reduction in k will reduce supply. When the 6 per cent capital tax was abolished in Yugoslavia in the 1960s, no one observed the predicted effect.

The theory predicts that the worker-managed economy will be labour saving. The Yugoslav experience shows, on the contrary, chronic overemployment in the firms.

Where saving and investment are concerned, the theoretical prediction is again wrong. Internal saving of the firm is modest (which is explained by a negative interest rate), but borrowing is enormous, so that the national saving rate oscillates around 35 per cent of GNP (with government accounting for a negligible share). On the other hand, overinvestment tends to contribute to chronic inflation. Social property and planning reduce risks and so increase investment opportunities.

The formal reason for the supposedly perverse behaviour of the Illyrian firm is to be found in the form of the objective function, which is a ratio. If a CMF were assumed to maximize the *rate* of profit, it would display symmetrical perverse effects (Dubravčić, 1970). Alfred Marshall avoided such consequences by distinguishing between the short and the long run; in the short run capital is assumed fixed and so maximizing profit and maximizing rate of profit comes to the same thing. Horvat (1969; 1985) suggested a similar device, which becomes available after a serious methodological error in the existing literature is eliminated. The error consists in deriving dynamic behavioural consequences from static assumptions.

If technology is fixed, we may assume that time does not matter. The resulting traditional static production function implies discovering output possibilities from varying quantities and proportions of inputs. If, however, we accept as a fact of life that technology is changing all the time, output will be a function of inputs *and* time

$$q = f(x_1, \ldots, x_n, t). \tag{6}$$

Marginal product in a production function thus defined is *not* a partial derivative of output with respect to one of the inputs, $\partial q/\partial x_i \neq MP_i$. Thus, the routine maximization procedure is meaningless. Even treating t as a shift parameter will not do. The production function not only shifts in time but also *changes it shape*. Besides, if capacity is not fully used (i.e. less than 3 shifts), which is a normal situation, the returns to variable factors are as a rule increasing.

In Figure 1 the law of variable proportions is operative and marginal product of labour is *diminishing*. With *fixed technology* we examine changes of q due to changes in L. E_0 represents maximum per worker output for technology known at t_0. Since technological progress is a *positive* function of time, marginal product of *dated* labour is *increasing*. Thus new workers, as well as the intramarginal ones, are more productive and per worker income is increasing. In Figure 2 the the production trajectory crosses successive production functions at points of increasingly steeper slopes. The invented perversities of the Illyrian firm disappear.

What the worker managed firms actually do consists in solving dynamic programmes of the following type: maximize total wage income of the currently employed workers over the agreed upon planning period of n years under a set of some six constraints (not all need be binding):

(1) All new workers will be given the same wage.

(2) Wage less than $\bar{w}_t - a_t$ ($\bar{w}_t$ is the average for the economy, a_t = collectively determined welfare factor) will not be tolerated.

(3) Wages higher than $\bar{w}_t + b_t$ are not desirable, because then the social pressure on the firm's funds becomes unbearable (local football club, local welfare programmes, etc.). Besides, progressive taxation drains too many resources away.

(4) Income distributed in wages is progressively taxed, income invested ('profit') is not. Society has no reason to tax its own capital; on the contrary.

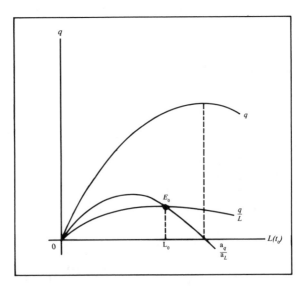

Figure 1   Neoclassical production function (technology fixed).

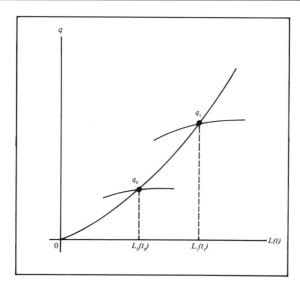

Figure 2 Production trajectory in time (technological progress).

(5) Bank investment loans are given under the condition that c per cent of investment finance is provided out of the firm's funds which serves as a collateral. Thus not all income accrues to wages, but part of it must be saved.

(6) Since capital represents social property, it can only be augmented and never eaten up whatever the source of finance. This solves the problem of the terminal stock of capital.

Once this programme has been solved, the aspiration wages (w^*) become known for the current decision period. The firm now maximizes the short run surplus

$$\max pq - w^*L - (\sum p_i x_i + k). \tag{7}$$

At the end of the accounting period the actual wage is likely to be different, the difference $w - w^*$ depending on the business result. As the actual wage depends on the *ex post* results, it does not appear in the *ex ante* maximization conditions. Since (1) part of income is not distributed, (2) workers are not owners of capital but (3) capital investment is a precondition for increases in wages, it makes no sense to maximize *per worker* surplus or, which is the same thing, total per worker income. Equation (7) is mathematically identical to (2) and so neoclassical efficiency requirements are satisfied as is shown in Table 1.

One additional objection has been raised by Eirik Furubotn and Svetozar Pejović (1970). If workers invest in their firm, they benefit from the increases in wages. If they put their money in the bank, they will collect not only interest but also principal at some future date. Unless the rate of profit is sufficiently higher than the bank rate of interest and the planning horizon sufficiently long, workers will distribute the entire income and investment will be reduced. The objection has some force in the case of cooperatives in a capitalist economy and for this reason the impressive Basque Mondragón cooperative system introduced personal capital accounts for its members. The accounts function similarly to bank deposit accounts. In a fully socialized economy no problem arises. Aggregate investment is a matter of social plans. Whether workers save directly as producers, or indirectly (via banks) as consumers, saving will be used to finance investment. However, worker managers have very strong incentives to save directly as producers because (a) such savings are free of tax while personal incomes and, consequently, savings from such incomes, are progressively taxed (which easily overcompensates the Furubotn–Pejović effect) and (b) the greater are the firm's own funds, the greater is the independence in the decision making. Either bank control is avoided or larger bank loans become available and in both cases worker managers find it easier to expand production and insure their wages against competition.

MACROECONOMICS. Since empirically based macroeconomics is possible only when at least one national economy exists, macroeconomics of worker management is much less discussed and is almost entirely based on the Yugoslav institutions. Consequently, unlike in microeconomics, no well-developed theory – correct or fallacious – has appeared so far. In what follows some of the more important results will be presented.

Business cycles. Even with perfect foresight, adjustments are not instantaneous. Mathematically formulated lagged adjustments lead to characteristic equations with real or complex roots depending on the parameters. Economic parameters seem to be such as to generate complex roots, that is, oscillations. However, even if parameters were to guarantee stability, external shocks (changing weather conditions, changing international environment, etc.) would initiate cycles, as Ragnar Frisch recognized long ago. The procedure may be reversed and, instead of modelling individual processes, an autoregressive scheme for the social product may be assumed right from the beginning and the relevant parameters estimated. For the Yugoslav economy, the parameters appeared significant for two cycle paths: the strongly damped short cycles (3 to 9 quarters) were superimposed over the longer regular ones (10 to 17 quarters) with the multiple correlation coefficient exceptionally high, $R = 0.93$–0.98 (Horvat, 1969, pp. 215–20). This looks very much like Schumpeter's Kitchins and Juglars.

Compared with what is known about business cycles in the capitalist economy, Yugoslav cycles have some specific features. The accelerator is not operative; acceleration or retardation in *production* leads to breaks in investment activity, not the other way round. Inventories are depleted in the upswings and piled up in the downswings. This is explained by the reluctance of worker managers to dismiss their colleagues and the willingness of banks to finance inventory accumulation. The inverse movement of inventories has a significant stabilizing effect. Pressure on prices is less at high rates of growth and greater at low rates. Consequently prices fall or rise more slowly in times of expansion (positive excess demand) and there is inflationary pressure in recession periods (negative excess demand). Either movements of credit do not explain price changes or an increase in money supply reduces prices. This paradox is easily resolved when one remembers that credit stimulates production, expansion of production lowers costs, lower unit costs put less pressure on prices and so it appears statistically that credit lowers prices.

Planning and market, contrary to widespread beliefs, are not antithetical but complementary. Since the market is inherently unstable, planning is indispensable for its normal functioning. On the other hand, in the implementation of economic policy, the market is the most efficient planning device. Within this conceptual framework planning means that strategic proportions (such as the volume, structure and regional allocation of investment) are realized, which is known as 'planning of global proportions'. The social plan, which includes also non-economic goals, is a kind of Rousseau's 'Social Compact'. It has four basic functions: The plan is above all a *forecasting instrument*; by generating information it reduces uncertainty. As such it is an *instrument for the coordination of economic decisions*. The social plan is prepared in a participatory fashion, which implies prior harmonization of development goals of industries and regions. As such it provides the basis for the economic policy and so it serves an *instrument for guiding economic development*. As an elaboration of economic policy, the plan represents an *obligation for the body that has adopted it* and a directive for its organs. Other economic agents are free to make their decisions themselves which, of course, is a precondition for genuine workers' management and a free market.

Distribution according to work. Distribution of income passes through two stages: first the firm earns income and then it distributes income among the workers. Workers themselves decide on the internal distribution of income (the structure of wages and the share of accumulation). Total income earned depends on their work and entrepreneurship, but also on general market conditions. It is the duty of the planning authorities to equalize starting business conditions for all firms. This may be done in the following way (Horvat, 1982, pp. 263–82). All plants are classified into relatively homogeneous industry groups comprising twenty or more units. It may be assumed, for statistical reasons, that all industry groups are about equal in terms of effort and entrepreneurship and so average per worker income ought to be equal for all groups. If that is achieved, intragroup wage differences reflect exclusively distribution according to work. It remains to establish an objective standard for the measurement of average group incomes. Since capital is social, the planning authorities charge a uniform interest rate. Land, mining and locational rents are extracted in the usual way. An occupation, which is performed under approximately the same conditions throughout the economy, is taken as a standard unit. Incomes of all firms are expressed in such units using each firm's own wage differentials as weights. If wages thus aggregated differ from one industry group to the other, the planning authorities must adjust policy instruments in order to achieve the highest possible degree of equality. The remaining (extra) profits represent monopoly rents and are subject to progressive income taxation. Although industry averages are about equal – unless there is some reason for stimulating the development of a particular industry – differences between individual firms may be great and that provides incentives for work effort and entrepreneurship.

Finally, we may mention two classical problems – optimum distribution of income and optimum investment – which have proved analytically intractable under individualist or étatist institutions of privately or state owned economies. If firms and states are hierarchically structured and autocratically managed, there is in principle no possibility for interpersonal comparisons. If, however, all concerned participate in the decision making and a consensus is achieved, there is no possibility of improving upon such a solution. In a class structured society, consensus is in principal impossible. The higher the wages, the lower the profits and vice versa. In a classless society it is at least logically admissible.

BIBLIOGRAPHY

Bajt, A. 1968. Social ownership – collective and individual. Reprinted and translated in *Self-Governing Socialism: A Reader*, Vol. 2, ed. B. Horvat, M. Marković and R. Supek, New York: Sharpe, 1975.

Domar, E.D. 1966. The Soviet collective farm. *American Economic Review* 56, September, 734–57.

Dubravčić, D. 1970. Labour as an entrepreneurial input: an essay in the theory of producer cooperative economy. *Economica* 37, 297–310.

Furubotn, E. and Pejović, S. 1970. Property rights and the behaviour of the firm in a socialist state: the example of Yugoslavia. *Zeitschrift für Nationalökonomie* 30, 431–54.

Horvat, B. 1969. *Business Cycles in Yugoslavia*. Trans. H.M. Kramer, New York: M. Sharpe, 1971.

Horvat, B. 1982. *The Political Economy of Socialism*. New York: M. Sharpe.

Horvat, B. 1985. The theory of the worker managed firm revisited. *Journal of Comparative Economics*. (The basic idea was first propounded in 'Prilog zasnivanju teorije jugoslavenskog poduzeća', *Ekonomska analiza*, 1967, 7–28.)

Meidner, R. 1978. *Employee Investment Funds*. London: Allen & Unwin.

Vanek, J. 1970. *The General Theory of Labour-Managed Market Economies*. Ithaca, New York: Cornell University Press.

Ward, B. 1958. The firm in Illyria: market syndicalism. *American Economic Review* 48(4), September, 566–89. In B. Ward, *The Socialist Economy*, New York: Random House, 1967.

Oskar Lange

TADEUSZ KOWALIK

Lange was born on 27 July 1904 in Tomaszow Mazowiecki, near Lodz, into the
family of a German-born textile manufacturer, and died on 2 October 1965 in
a London hospital following thigh surgery. He studied law and economics in
Poznan and Cracow. His main tutor was Adam Krzyzanowski, liberal and
Anglophile. In 1929 Lange studied in London and in 1934–5 in the United
States, mostly at Harvard and Berkeley. He lectured in statistics and economics
in Cracow (1927–37), Chicago (1938–45) and Warsaw (1948–65). Politically
involved since his youth, he was active at the Independent Socialist Youth Union
in the interwar period. During World War II he pushed the cause of
Soviet–American rapprochement and socialist–communist cooperation. He
served as the first ambassador of the Polish People's Republic in Washington
(1945–6) and as the Polish delegate to the UN Security Council (1946–7). Later
he was member of parliament and member of the State Council in Poland.

Lange's special position in economic theory rested on his profound knowledge
of its main currents, both of Marxist economics and Western academic economics
(above all the neoclassical) and later both of capitalist and centrally planned
Eastern European socialist economies. This induced him to make several attempts
at a 'major synthesis' and to undertake political actions for a rapprochement
between the West and the communist world, for peaceful coexistence and
economic cooperation.

CAPITALISM AND ECONOMICS. The capitalist economy was Lange's chief research
concern from his early youth until the end of World War II. His primary interests
included the study of business cycles and the evolution of capitalism. His PhD
thesis was a study of business cycles in the Polish economy 1923–7 (1928), and
he won the title of docent (assistant professor) for a statistical study of the
business cycle (1931). These were among the chief topics of his lectures at United

States universities, mainly in Chicago. Early in the war he studied, together with L. Hurwicz, ways of empirical verification of business cycle theories. Although he became a leading authority on this subject (cf. his review, 1941a, of Schumpeter's book and, 1941b, of Kalecki's cycle theory), he never produced a complete theory of his own. His studies of the business cycle led him to econometrics, a discipline he helped create (during World War II he edited the quarterly *Econometrica*). His textbook of econometrics (1959), the first of its kind in Eastern European countries, recapitulates his studies of business cycle and of market mechanisms, in addition to an outline of programming theory based on Leontief's input–output tables and on Marxian reproduction schemata.

The evolution of capitalism interested him both as a scholar and as a political writer. Initially he believed that the development of large corporations marked a transition from 'the anarchical freemarket capitalist economy to a consciously planned economy' ([1929] 1973, p. 70), that is, to an organized capitalism. But with the Great Depression those hopes vanished. Monopolies and government intervention, he concluded, cause chaos and disarray in the economy and lead eventually to a collapse of capitalism and the victory of socialism ([1931] 1973). Soon, however, he came to the conclusion that 'it was not capitalism but the worker movement which collapsed during the crisis' resulting in a 'stabilization of capitalism' ([1933] 1973, p. 63).

Just before and during the war Lange often argued that capitalism cannot possibly be reconciled with economic progress in the long run. But at the same time he looked for ways of reforming capitalist structures to turn them into mixed-type economies – calling for a socialization of the monopolies which he regarded as threats to political democracy and which he blamed for generating unemployment.

During his stay in the United States, Lange published a number of contributions exploring and developing, as well as criticizing, the standard economics which was, and continues to be, taught at most universities in the West. Those studies fall roughly into two categories: the first was 'pre-Keynesian' from the point of view of general approach, while the other was closely connected with the absorption of the 'Keynesian Revolution' by traditional economics.

In one major study (1936b, 1937b), Lange tried to explore the relationships between interest theory and the theory of production factor cost. Using a strongly simplified model (one final commodity produced by labour and one capital good, free competition, 'neutral' role of money, risk is neglected), Lange unfolded a theory of interest which in many of its points came close to that of Frank Knight, even though in his concept of money capital ('as a general command over means of production') he was influenced more strongly by Schumpeter and Marx.

Lange is regarded as one of the founders of 'modern welfare economics' (Graaff, 1957). Following Bergson's pioneering study (Burk, 1938), Lange listed (1942a) theorems which do not require interpersonal comparability of utility as well as those which do. The study of optimal distribution of incomes must be based on *a priori* hypotheses concerning marginal utility of incomes for different persons.

For welfare economics propositions it is not necessary that utilities of individuals must be measurable as long as these utilities can be ordered.

The next and probably most important group of studies concern Keynesian theory's relationship to the mainstream of Western economic thinking. In a (1938b) study, Lange explores the internal logic of Keynes's theory investigating the mutual relations between interest rate, propensity to consume, marginal efficiency of capital, investment, and national income. In Lange's model, elasticity is the all-decisive concept. Using this concept and some of Walras's ideas, Lange outlined a 'general theory' of which the Keynesian theory was one particular case. That special case occurs when elasticity of liquidity preference to income is close to zero or when it is infinitely great in relation to the rate of interest. Then, the rate of interest does not depend on the marginal efficiency of capital or on propensity to consume. When the elasticity of liquidity preference to the rate of interest is close to zero, then the classical and neoclassical theory, stressing the dependence of money demand on income alone, holds. Keynes approved Lange's interpretation of his theory as following 'closely and accurately my line of thought' (Keynes, 1973, p. 232n). Lange's exposition of the notion of multiplier (1943a) was more modest in its intention.

Analysing Say's Law (1942b), Lange made one of the first ever attempts to overcome what was called the dichotomy of the pricing process. In traditional neoclassical theory, commodity prices were determined under the assumption that money is just 'a worthless medium of exchange and a standard of value' (1942b, p. 64), and hence of a barter economy. Only later, on prices determined in this way, were pecuniary prices 'superimposed'. Accordingly, the substitution of money for commodities and vice versa was ignored completely. That was the gist of the assumption that total demand is identically equal to the total supply of commodities. Thus, the theory of money must start with the rejection of this contention (of Say's Law) and investigate conditions and processes leading to equilibrium of total demand with total supply. For this purpose, money must be included in the theory of general equilibrium.

These studies prepared the ground for a more ambitious synthesis. In his previous studies, Lange had already studied questions and problems asked by Keynes (this partly holds also for the theorists of imperfect competition and for Schumpeter) and tried to resolve them in his own fashion, relying on mathematical tools of general economic equilibrium as developed and modified by Henry Schultz, R.G.D. Allen and Paul Samuelson, but especially by J.R. Hicks.

That undertaking found its most complete and systematic exposition in Lange's (1944a) book, which sums up his theoretical work during his American period. The book is something like a restatement of the theory of general economic equilibrium in which money is incorporated explicitly as part of this theory. Substitution between money and goods is the key concept for understanding processes of equilibrating and disequilibrating the national economy. As Lange puts it, 'The interest in the problem and the recognition of the crucial importance of substitution between money and goods were inspired by Lord Keynes. For the tools of analysis the author is heavily indebted to Professor J.R. Hicks' (1944a, p. vii).

But Lange's book was an outcome as much of theoretical as of practical disputes over general economic policy. His main point of interest was the belief, which survived repeated attacks from Keynesians, that price flexibility – and in particular flexible prices of production factors, mainly of labour – is a condition of full utilization of production factors. Defending the Keynesians' position on this matter, Lange intended to reach both the general public and sophisticated, mathematically minded economists who refuted Keynes's language of aggregate concepts as too unscientific.

With such different audiences in mind, Lange composed his exposition at two or even three levels of difficulty. The main body of the book is 'as simple as possible' and in colloquial non-mathematical language full of socio-political corollaries. Only in the numerous footnotes did he present technical details. The final part of the book, called 'The Stability of Economic Equilibrium' and published as an appendix, is in rigorous mathematical language and is addressed to the narrower group of specialists.

The book's main message can be summarized in the following way. There are three ways in which money can affect economic equilibrium under flexible prices:

(1) If the overall amount of money is constant, the fall in prices of a factor leads at first to a fall in other prices and to a growth in purchasing power of the existing stock of money. An excess supply of money arises. This, in turn, drives up demand for goods and checks prices from falling further. As other prices are falling less quickly than that of the factor under consideration, demand for this factor increases. Along with that, the amount of loanable funds grows, which causes a fall of the interest rate. This, then, encourages investment and results in employment growth. This is the case of the effect of money being *positive*.

(2) When the overall amount of money is determined by credit creation and changes in step with the changing demand for money (cash balances), the effect of money can be said to be *neutral*. In this case, the mechanism of automatic maintenance and restoration of equilibrium no longer works. The stock of money shrinks in proportion to the falling demand for cash balances and an excess money supply develops. The purchasing power of the stock of money remains unchanged. In consequence, the fall in prices is not checked by a rise in the purchasing power of the stock of money and interest rates do not fall. The excess supply of the production factor under consideration is not being absorbed.

(3) Money has a *negative* effect when its amount shrinks more than proportionately to falling demand for cash balances. Banks, for example, react to the fall in prices by demanding loan repayment. A shortage of money is then felt in the market. Pessimism, growing uncertainty, etc., foster this development. Then, a fall in the given production factor's price (e.g. wages) causes an even more dramatic fall in prices of other goods, which leads to an even larger excess supply of the production factor than was the case originally (e.g. to even higher unemployment).

Lange's general conclusion from his analysis was quite pessimistic:

Only under very special conditions does price flexibility result in the automatic maintenance of restoration of equilibrium of demand for and supply of factors of production. These conditions require the combination of such a responsiveness of the monetary system and such elasticities of price expectations as produce a positive monetary effect, sensitivity of intertemporal substitution to changes in interest rates ..., absence of highly specialized factors with demand or supply dependent on strongly elastic price expectations, and finally, absence of oligopolistic or oligosonistic rigidities of output and input. To a certain extent, the absence of a positive monetary effect may be replaced by the stabilizing influence of foreign trade ... (1944a, p. 83)

On the whole, Lange regarded price flexibility as 'a workable norm' of long-run but not necessarily short-run economic policy during the long period between the 1840s and 1914. However, the favourable conditions which prevailed during that period belong to the remote past. The oligopolization process, the deteriorating investment oppostunities, the tendency towards unemployment caused by new technology applications, along with the bad experiences of the two world wars and the Great Depression – all these made any automatic attainment of equilibrium and stability a very unlikely prospect.

This conclusion prompts the question: what significance does the general economic equilibrium theory have for economic theory and for economic policy? Several years later, Lange compared that theory, which deals with very unlikely contingencies, to the case of an ape trying to write the Encyclopaedia Britannica. While probability calculus does not preclude such a possibility, we should ask ourselves if dealing with such an unlikely case is not an utterly futile exercise.

Price flexibility was the last fruit of Lange's study of the general equilibrium theory. To what extent his subsequent silence on this subject was due to the fact that, after 1945, he found himself in an entirely different environment, and to what extent due to his disenchantment with the theory, is difficult to say. Anyway, his economic thinking in later years took an unexpected turn. Contrary to his attitude in public life, as a philosopher of science Lange was rather conservative-minded believing that 'science does not progress ... by the wholesale rejection of old theories and the devising of new ones, but by arduous work of enriching and improving existing scientific achievements' (1970, pp. 80–81). Accordingly, he put a great deal of effort into showing that the so-called Keynesian Revolution was no revolution at all; and that it should be viewed as a contribution merely 'enriching and improving scientific achievements'. But when he accomplished that job, Lange dropped the synthesis he had worked out with such a great expense of effort only to choose an alternative paradigm.

After World War II, however, Lange only sporadically resumed his study of capitalism, mainly to consider whether capitalism is able to resolve economic problems of backward countries (to which his answer was emphatically negative

(1957)) or prospects for disarmament and economic cooperation between the Council for Mutual Economic Assistance countries and the capitalist West.

LANGE–BREIT MODEL OF SOCIALIST ECONOMY. Lange first manifested himself as a socialist writer in his book (1928) on Edward Abramowski (1868–1918), whose ideology Lange called 'constructive anarchism'. In those ideas, Lange emphasized Abramowski's resentment of government interventionism, pitting it against the ideas of English Guild Socialism and of Austro-Marxism, both of which had strongly influenced Lange himself. Lange advocated especially the idea of industrial self-government, of separating the economy from political power, and the decay of the state as an institution of class domination though not of an instrument of coercion.

Together with Marek Breit (1907–42), he write the first outline of a socialist economy's functioning ([1937] 1973) in the chapter of a collective book, *Economy – Polity – Tactics – Organization of Socialism* (1934). It was the product of a group of left-wing socialists, led by Lange, and committed to the revolutionary reconstruction of a system in Poland which would be different from the Soviet model of polity and economy.

The Lange–Breit model, or the 1934 model (cf. Kowalik, 1970 and 1974; Chilosi, 1986) is one version of a corporate market economy under socialism. It rests on the following rules. Plants should go public, or be 'socialized', in his terminology, by transferring private ownership titles to a Public Bank and by organizing the national economy into Public Trusts by industrial branches. Trusts would be the basic units of the economy and endowed with a great deal of autonomy. The decisive say in their boards would belong to workers, who would be organized into 'an appropriate system of worker councils'. Trust autonomy is limited by the Public Bank's supervision and coordination functions or, more exactly, by the functions performed by a uniform and monopolistic bank system. Basic planning instruments would include accumulation fund management and trust financing. The Public Bank would also watch if trusts and companies subordinate to them abided by management rules, in particular by rules of 'rigorous' price and cost accounting. Plants run at a loss would be closed down. Plants failing to record an average surplus would forfeit their right to get loans not only for expansion but even for ordinary capital replacement, and hence they would decline. Both trusts and plants would be obliged not only to remit their production costs but also to achieve a certain accumulation, the rate of which would be established by the Public Bank and subsequently redistributed for investment and for subsidizing public utilities (which may be run at a loss).

Since trusts would hold virtually monopoly power in the market, as all public plants would by law belong to some trust, Lange and Breit perceived the danger of charging excessive prices and cutting output rates. They realized that such a policy might become quite popular among employees of any given trust who might hope to get their wages increased. To forestall monopoly practices, they therefore proposed to oblige trusts to take on all job-seekers applying to them. If price increases resulted in higher wages in any given trust, employees from other trusts would swarm to it so that the increased wage fund would have to be redistributed among a larger number of employees. The underlying purpose of that obligation, then, was to deter trusts from driving up prices.

As the two authors did not consider the question of inflation, they did not say why excessive wage increases by one trust should not set off an avalanche of price increases if other trusts attempted to forestall an exodus of their own workforce. Nor did they envisage possible consequences of the indivisible nature of means of production and of possible consequences of delays in market adaptation. Moreover, the Public Bank's investment policy would be based on workforce migration in reaction to changing demand, price fluctuations, and subsequently price changes. This was to be something like an automatic indicator of demand intensity for individual goods.

The Public Bank would further control capital imports and exports, whereas a 'foreign trade office' created by the trusts concerned would be in charge of goods sales and purchases abroad. The Public Bank would also be authorized to transfer capital assets from trust to trust. .

The private sector, which is consistently referred to as the 'non-socialized', i.e. non-public, sector of the economy, was to remain 'broad', consisting of private farms holding less than 20 hectares of land, crafts shops, business enterprises with less than 20 people on their payrolls, as well as retail trade shops. However, because economies of scale were expected to impart higher efficiency to larger companies, the private sector would be 'a relic on the way out'. The two authors said nothing about credit policies toward this sector, but the Public Bank would conduct a discriminatory kind of policy toward profit-making small capitalist businesses (up to 20 employees) designed eventually to bring about their demise through taxes. Lange and Breit recommended that the Public Bank should levy taxes equal to the accumulation rate, which was supposed to reduce owners' incomes to the level of managers' salaries. The two authors failed to take account of the role of risk and innovation.

Nor is it clear how the two authors thought plants (which they preferred not to call enterprises) would be managed, or how trusts would be organized and what prerogatives the latter would have. They merely said workers organized in a system of worker councils would have the decisive say and that trade unions and worker cooperatives were best suited to create trusts. Nor did they propose any clear procedure for appointing the Public Bank's board of management, which was expected to make the socialist economy a planned economy.

Designed as an alternative model to the command-planning system then existing in the Soviet Union, the Lange–Breit concept was largely reminiscent of Bolshevik concepts from before the period of wartime communism or right after it (trusts, worker councils, a single state-owned bank, a long-run policy of farm collectivization), modified by an emphasis on separating political authority from economic organization, on impartial economic criteria, and on recognizing consumer preferences as the foundation of investment policies.

THE THEORY OF MARKET SOCIALISM. The next model of socialist economy, which I propose to call the classical, Lange presented in a study (originally published as two articles, 1936a, 1937a, and in book form, with Taylor, 1938b). It was devised only two or three years after publishing the Lange–Breit model. But this period brought up an immense improvement of Lange's analytical expertise.

On a Rockefeller Foundation Grant, Lange studied at Harvard, Berkeley and Chicago, and at the London School of Economics. He was strongly influenced by Schumpeter, under whose tutorship he worked at Harvard during most of his two-year scholarship, and he took part in a famous seminar (The Economics Club) led by the Austrian-American economist. That influence surfaces in many of Lange's studies, including his study *On the Economic Theory of Socialism*, especially in the economic justification of socialism. That study, or at least its main body, was written at Harvard and must have been heatedly discussed there. At that time he also became intellectually involved with the brothers Alan and Paul Sweezy, economists and socialists of a similar orientation to that of the visitor form Poland. He also had working contact with W. Leontief.

On the Economic Theory of Socialism expresses Lange's long-lasting conviction that neoclassical economics, especially welfare economics, is best suited to serve as a foundation of a theory of socialist economy.

The classical model, of course, is theoretically more sophisticated and more accurate in its purely economic aspect, but perhaps at the cost of giving less specific treatment to institutional aspects than the 1934 model. That was probably due to the chief purpose of that study, namely to disprove Mises' argument about a theoretical and practical (practical, according to Hayek and Robbins) unfeasibility of economic calculus in socialism because of the absence of a genuine market (prices) for capital.

Many formulations in that classical study indicate that a socialist society's general outlines of economic organization were similar or identical in both the early and classical models. In particular, this is true of the separation of political power from economic management, of its three-level structure – the centre, the branches organized in trusts, individual plants – and of the similar powers of the Central Planning Board (CPB) and the Public Bank. In both models, the centre is expected to react to changes in market factors (prices and wages) and, correspondingly, to changes in employment in the early model or to changing inventories and emerging shortages in the classical one. The CPB, basically, is to imitate the market. The early model was clearly more 'market-oriented' because all prices of goods and services were to be determined by the market. Accordingly, there would be no difference between actual market prices and calculated prices as set by the CPB.

Perhaps the most important difference between the early and the classical models was his new emphasis that

'the real danger of socialism is that of a bureaucratization of economic life, and not the impossibility of coping with the problem of allocation of resources'. He reassured himself by pointing out that the same danger existed in monopolistic capitalism and that 'officials subject to democratic control seem preferable to private corporation executives who practically are responsible to nobody'.

When he became aware of that danger, which would exist even in a market-dominated brand of socialism, he embarked on a long quest for what he called in the title of one article (1943b), 'The Economic Foundations of Democracy in Poland'. In the classical study he had already put forward the idea of a Supreme Economic Court whose function would be to safeguard the use of the nation's productive resources in accordance with the public interest, in particular to declare as null and void any CPB decision which was incompatible with adopted management rules.

During World War II Lange suggested a number of ideas for better safeguards for democracy, either by substantiating the injunction to take account of consumer preferences (and hence limiting the central economic authority's prerogatives) or by devising institutional guarantees for democratic control of decision-making bodies, or by indicating limits to the socialization of property.

There were a number of highlights of the evolution of Lange's views during that period.

In his letter to Hayek in 1940 (Kowalik, 1984) Lange gave a more accurate, and perhaps slightly different, description of the CPB's prerogatives for pricing goods and services:

Practically, I should, of course, recommend the determination of prices by a thorough market process whenever this is feasible, i.e. whenever the number of selling and purchasing units is sufficiently large. Only where the number of these units is so small that a situation of oligopoly, oligopsony, or bilateral monopoly would obtain, would I advocate price fixing by public agency. . . .

Accordingly, he recommends socialization of industries only in areas where there is no automatic competitive market process.

Later in 1942–3 he departed even further from his classical model toward a mixed economy. In his review of Dickinson's book (1942c), he had the following idea of how to prevent the central authority's arbitrariness in determining the accumulation rate. With reference to Lerner's observation of the dependence of interest rates not only on the quantity of capital involved but also on investment rates, Lange thought that if saving was ceded to individual consumers, accumulation rates could be made to reflect consumers' preference. His 1936–8 model should be improved in this way, he said.

In his two public lectures in Chicago on The Economic Operation of a Socialist Society ([1942] 1975) Lange tacitly dropped what was perhaps the chief feature of his classical model, namely the central authority's prerogative of setting and reviewing prices as a road towards equilibrium. He made only a passing remark about such a possibility, and only in reference to *future* prices the centre may impose on production managers in order to ensure stable forecasting (which is as a rule erratic in a capitalist economy).

141

But perhaps the greatest change in his concept of the desired shape of socialism can be found in his article on the economic foundations of democracy in Poland (1943b). The title alone shows that a commitment to furnish solid economic foundations for 'Poland's democratic order' was the point of departure in designing future political transformations. In that article, Lange envisaged the socialization only of key industries (which necessarily include banks and transport). This would put an end to the power of 'the socially irresponsible monopolistic capitalism'. Having said this, he cautions that care should be taken to prevent the socialized key industries from becoming a foundation for 'an equally dangerous' threat to democracy in the form of too much economic power being concentrated in the state bureaucracy along with privileges arising from this.

But private farms, crafts shops and minor but also medium-sized industries were all to remain areas of private initiative and enterprise. So broad a field of action for private entrepreneurship was, on the one hand, to be one foundation of democracy, and, on the other, it was to preserve 'the kind of flexibility, pliability and adaptiveness that private initiative alone can achieve'. This is the reason for which the development of a private sector is to be one of the chief guidelines for the socialized financial policy. The private sector then appears to have been a permanent element of the new model Lange proposed for Poland.

This proposal had its counterpart for the United States in the lengthy essay written with Abba P. Lerner on a democratic programme for full employment (1944b).

The changes in Lange's views of socialist economy during the war years were evidently so substantial that they could be used to compose an alternative version of a market socialism, compared with which his classical model can indeed be described as 'quasi-centralistic' (Pryor, 1985). The extent of those changes may have been the reason why he dropped his previous plan to revise his classical study:

> The essay is so far removed from what I would write on the subject today that I am afraid that any revision would produce a very poor compromise, unrepresentative of my thoughts. Thus, I am becoming inclined to let the essay go out of print and express my present views in entirely new form. I am writing a book on economic theory in which a chapter will be devoted to this subject. This may be better than trying to rehash old stuff ([1945] 1975).

FROM IDEA TO REALITY. Indeed, Lange gave an entirely new expression to his view of socialist economy. But by an ironic twist of history (to which he was fond of referring) he did that only when his views changed in an entirely different direction, namely when he embarked on the search for a rationale for the command-type economy and subsequently for ways of reforming it.

The evolution of Lange's views of socialism in the postwar years is much harder to follow because he became so deeply involved in politics. Not only the form but also the substance of his views were often influenced by tactical considerations and by the changing measure of freedom of expression accorded to scholars in social science. The freedom was broad prior to 1948, virtually extinct in the early 1950s, considerable in the latter half of that decade, and gradually curtailed later on.

The main change in Lange's theoretical approach was that he switched over from a micro- to a macro-economic approach. Whereas he had previously based his argument on the general equilibrium theory, after 1945 he relied on a Marxian reproduction model. The new approach was first presented in the report he submitted to the International Statistical Conference (1947) on practical economic planning and optimal resource allocation. In it he tried to confront Eastern European economic practices with welfare economics. His point was that the centre's main decisions resulted from a desire to industrialize the country as rapidly as possible. The economic successes those countries had scored up to them were due to full employment and to the liquidation of monopolies which worked as powerful checks on their national economies in the past. Economic choices were a second-rate matter in the period of reconstruction, but as those countries are moving into a phase of development more sophisticated choices may have to be made. Marginal analysis may in such events prove useful, provided it is carried out in categories adequately reflecting reality. Although Lange talked about practical planning in descriptive rather than theoretical terms and although he did not then reject marginal analysis, F. Perroux said:

> Je note que le théoricien socialiste a complètement changé de méthode. Il a autrefois essayé de montrer qu'une économie socialiste peut fonctionner à peu près comme isolée des unités économiques de marché, sur la base de calcul... Il fonde aujourd'hui sa thèse sur les macrodécisions de l'Etat. Il le fait paradoxalement au moment précisément où tout le monde est d'accord sur la nécessité du 'breakdown of the aggregate quantities' (1947, p. 172).

The new theoretical approach was given more clearcut contours in a booklet (1953) in which Lange commented on Stalin's famous work on socialist economy in the USSR. The reasons for which Lange wrote that book, in which he extolled the Stalin work as 'a momentous event in the history of science with far-reaching practical consequences', are somewhat puzzling. He did it, probably, for two reasons. First, he was convinced that the Stalin work marked a turn from economic voluntarism toward respect for the inexorable laws governing economic life, toward a rehabilitation of efficiency and greater consideration of social needs. Indeed, the first studies written by Polish theorists who later became revisionists did find some support in Stalin's work. The second reason that prompted him to write the booklet must have been his view of the evolution the communist economies were undergoing due to industrialization. He believed that not only the Stalinist terror but also the main body of practical devices applied then, as well as the functioning of the economy itself at that time, were all determined by political considerations, specifically by militarization and the forceful industrialization bid (1943c). Lange often defined the centralistic command model as wartime economy. But he hoped that industrialization, with the subsequent emergence of an educated working class and socialist intelligentsia, would create a good social base for democracy and decentralization of management. Presuming that industrialization entailed democratization, he believed the future of the 'Polish economic model' depended on how mature and experienced society will be. This is why he was unwilling 'to design any new model from behind the desk'. In 1956–7 he refused to give his permission for the publication of a finished translation of his classical work of 1936–8 because he did not want to lend his support to the 'socialist free-marketers'. But it is unclear whether he regarded the market-oriented model of socialism as premature or as invalidated by the progress made in economic theory and practice (1967).

TOWARD A MAJOR SYNTHESIS. Lange's lifelong ambition to produce a synthesis can be seen to have differed in scope, so that a 'minor' and a 'major' synthesis can be distinguished in it. His earliest endeavours included an attempt to incorporate the method of partial equilibrium into the general equilibrium theory developed by the mathematical school (1932). In later years he wrote a series of studies commenting on various aspects of the Keynesian theory to reduce it eventually to a particular case of general equilibrium theory.

Several times during his life Lange prepared himself to produce his major synthesis. He did have the indispensable background for such a job, not only on account of his economic versatility (he was intimately familiar with all the main currents and schools in economic theory, and with the 'three worlds') but also because he felt at home in several other disciplines such as statistics and econometrics, history and sociology, praxiology and cybernetics.

The first outline for a major synthesis came in his article 'Marxian Economics and Modern Economic Theory' (1935). Its chief argument was that these two currents are in fact complementary. Their advantages and drawbacks arose from the different specific tasks each of them was supposed to do. Marxian economics was designed to furnish the revolutionary movement with guidance for rational policies, defining as it did the lines and limitations of the evolution of capitalism; modern economic theory, for its part, was expected to provide a foundation for capitalist management. But equilibrium theory, which was designed to serve precisely this purpose, was actually universal in character, so after some adaptation it could be used for day-to-day management of socialist economy, a job Marxist economics was ill-suited to do. For some time Lange thought his synthesis should be based on marginalist economics, the categories of which seemed useful for presenting problems of class structure. Clinging to 'Marxist semantics' was to him a sign of traditionalism and conservative attitudes.

In the late 1950s he began to work on a three-volume treatise on political economy which would rest on two tiers – historical materialism and the principle of rationality. He managed to finish the first volume ([1959] 1963) on method and half of the second one ([1966] 1971a).

Late in his life cybernetics became his fascination. Using the theory of systems self-regulation and self-control, Lange gave an interpretation of the chief categories, wholes and parts, of dialectical materialism ([1962] 1965a). He also wrote an introduction to economic cybernetics (1965b), and to the theory of optimal decisions. (1971b).

SELECTED WORKS

1928. Koniunktura w zyciu gospodarczym Polski 1923–27 (The business cycle in Poland). In *Przewroty walutowe i gospodarcze po wielkiej wojnie* (Currency and economic upheavals after the Great War), Kraków.

1931. *Statystyczne badanie koniunktury gospodarczej* (Statistical investigation of the business cycle), Kraków.

1932. Die allgemeine Interdependenz der Wirtschaftsprognosen und die Isolierungsmethode. *Zeitschrift für Nationalökonomie* 4(1).

1934. (With Marek Breit.) Droga do socjalistycznej gospodarki planowej (The road to the socialist planned economy). In *Gospodarka–polityka–taktyka–organizacja socjalizmu* (Economy–polity–tactics–organization of socialism), Warsaw.

1935. Marxian economics and modern economic theory. *Review of Economic Studies* 2(3), June, 189–201.

1936a. On the economic theory of socialism, Part I. *Review of Economic Studies* 4(1), October, 53–71.

1936b. The place of interest in the theory of production. *Review of Economic Studies* 3(3), June, 159–92.

1937a. On the economic theory of socialism, Part II. *Review of Economic Studies* 4(2), February, 123–42.

1937b. Professor Knight's note on interest theory. *Review of Economic Studies* 4(4).

1938a. The rate of interest and the optimum propensity to consume. *Economica* 5, February, 12–32.

1938b. (With Fred M. Taylor.) *On the Economic Theory of Socialism.* Ed. with an introduction by Benjamin Lippincott, Minneapolis: University of Minnesota Press.

1941a. Review of J. Schumpeter, *Business Cycles: A Theoretical, Historical and Statistical Analysis of the Capitalist Process. Review of Economic Studies* 23(4), November, 190–93.

1941b. Review of M. Kalecki, *Essays in the Theory of Economic Fluctuations. Journal of Political Economy* 49(2), April, 279–85.

1942a. The foundations of welfare economics. *Econometrica* 10(3–4), July–October, 215–28.

1942b. Say's Law: a criticism and restatement. In *Studies in Mathematical Economics and Econometrics*, ed. O. Lange et al., Chicago: University of Chicago Press.

1942c. Review of H.D. Dickinson, *Economics of Socialism. Journal of Political Economy* 50(2), April, 299–303.

1943a. The theory of the multiplier. *Econometrica* 11(3–4), 227–45.

1943b. Gospodarcze podstawy demokracji w Polsce (Economic foundations of democracy in Poland). In *Ku gospodarce planowej* (Towards a centrally planned economy), London.

1943c. *Working Principles of the Soviet Economy.* New York: Russian Economic Institute.

1944a. *Price Flexibility and Employment.* Bloomington: Principia Press.

1944b. (With Abba P. Lerner.) The American way of business. In *Problems in American Life, Teaching Aids for the Social Studies*, Washington, DC: National Council for the Social Studies.

1947. The practice of economic planning and the optimum allocation of resources. In *Proceedings of the International Statistical Conference*, Vol. V, Washington, DC.

1953. *Zagadnienia ekonomii politycznej w swietle pracy J. Stalina 'Ekonomiczne problemy socjalizmu w ZSRR'* (Problems of political economy in the light of J. Stalin's work, 'Economic problems of socialism in the USSR'), Warsaw.

1957. *Dlaczego kapitalizm nie potrafi rozwiazaé problemu krajów gospodarczo zacofanych* (Why capitalism is unable to solve the problems of backward countries), Warsaw.

1959. *Introduction to Econometrics*. Oxford and London: Pergamon Press.

1963. *Political Economy*. Vol. 1: *General Problems*. Oxford and London: Pergamon Press.

1965a. *Wholes and Parts. A General Theory of System Behaviour*. Oxford and London: Pergamon Press.

1965b. *Introduction to Economic Cybernetics*. Warsaw: Państwowe Wydawnictwo Naukowe.

1967. The computer and the market. In *Socialism, Capitalism and Economic Growth, Essays Presented to M. Dobb*, ed. C.H. Feinstein, Cambridge: Cambridge University Press.

1970. *Papers in Economics and Sociology*. Trans. by P.F. Knightsfield, Oxford: Pergamon.

1971a. *Political Economy*. Vol. II. Warsaw: Państwowe Wydawnictwo Naukowe.

1971b. *Optimal Decisions, Principles of Programming*. Oxford: Pergamon.

1973. *Dziela* (Works). Vol. I. Warsaw: Polski Wydawnictwo Ekonomiczne.

1975. *Dziela* (Works). Vol. II. Warsaw: Polski Wydawnictwo Ekonomiczne and Państwowe Wydawnictwo Naukowe.

BIBLIOGRAPHY

Bergson, A. 1967. Market socialism revisited. *Journal of Political Economy* 75(5), October, 655–73.

Burk, A. [pen-name of Abraham Bergson] 1938. A reformulation of certain aspects of welfare economics. *Quarterly Journal of Economics* 52, February, 310–34.

Chilosi, A. 1986. Self-managed socialism with 'free mobility of labor'. *Journal of Comparative Economics* 10(3), September, 237–54.

Graaff, J. de V. 1957. *Theoretical Welfare Economics*. Foreword by Paul A. Samuelson, Cambridge: Cambridge University Press.

Keynes, J.M. 1973. *Collected Writings*. Vol. XIV: *The General Theory and After*. London: Macmillan; New York: St Martin's Press.

Kowalik, T. 1970. Oskara Langego Wczesne modele socjalizmu (O. Lange's early models of socialism). *Ekonomista* 5, 965–1000.

Kowalik, T. 1974. Zur klassischem Modell des Sozialismus. In *Sozialismus, Geschichte und Wirtschaft, Festschrift für Eduard Marz*, Vienna: Europaverlag.

Kowalik, T. 1984. Review of A. Nove, *The Economics of Feasible Socialism. Contributions to Political Economy* 3, 91–7.

Lavoie, D. 1985. *Rivalry and Central Planning: The Socialist Calculation Debate Reconsidered*. Cambridge: Cambridge University Press.

Perroux, F. 1947. Comments on Lange's paper. In *Proceedings of the International Statistical Conference*, Washington, DC, Vol. V, 172.

Pryor, F.L. 1985. *A Guidebook to the Comparative Study of Economic Systems*. Englewood Cliffs, NJ: Prentice-Hall.

Lange–Lerner Mechanism

TADEUSZ KOWALIK

This is a designation commonly used to denote a market-oriented socialism model devised by Lange, who later amended it after public discussion with Lerner. The first, fundamental part of Lange's study was published together with A.P. Lerner's (1936) critical remarks in the same issue of the *Review of Economic Studies*, while the second part appeared together with Lange's reply to Lerner (1937). Later on, Lange made the changes necessary to publish his study (together with F.M. Taylor's essay) in book form (1938). The term is occasionally used in a less restricted sense, to bring out the similarity of Lange's and Lerner's views on other matters concerning market socialism.

The mechanism of socialist economy in the Lange–Lerner blueprint was based on the following assumptions. It has its institutional framework in the public ownership of means of production (for simplicity, the private sector is omitted) and in the free choice of consumption and employment (job and workplace), while consumer preferences – 'through demand prices' – are the all-decisive criterion of both production and resource allocation. Under these assumptions, an authentic market (in the institutional sense) exists for consumer goods and labour services. But prices of capital goods and 'all other productive resources except labour' are set by a Central Planning Board (CPB) as indicators of existing alternatives established for the purpose of economic calculation. So, apart from market prices, there are also 'accounting prices'. Both categories of prices are used by enterprise and industry managers, who are public officials, in order to make their choices.

Production managers in charge of individual enterprises or entire industries make autonomous decisions about what and how much should be produced and how it should be done, while prices are set as parameters outside the enterprises or industries. But since profit maximization has by definition ceased to be a direct goal of economic activity, to ensure that they can achieve effects close to those achieved in free-market economy, production managers must obey two rules. First, they must pick a combination of production factors under which average cost is minimized, and second, they must determine a given industry's total output at a level at which marginal cost is equal to product price. The first rule was expected to eliminate all less efficient alternatives. In combination with the second rule, insofar as it concerns plant managers, it performs the same function as the free-market economy desire to maximize profit. This leads to minimization of production costs. The second rule compels production managers to increase or cut the output of a whole industry in accordance with consumer preferences, which is a substitute for free entry in a free competitive economy.

These rules lead to an economic equilibrium by the trial-and-error method first described by Fred M. Taylor (1929). The CPB acts like an auctioneer, initially watching the behaviour of economic actors in reaction to a price system it picks at random or – perhaps the best solution – to the historically inherited prices. The behaviour of the system is measured by the movement of inventories of goods. If there is too much of some product at a given price, then its inventory grows, and vice versa. This is regarded as information that the product price should be cut or increased, respectively. This procedure is applied as many times as is necessary to reach equilibrium, providing that this process does in fact converge to the system of equilibrium prices. Accounting prices, then, are objective in character, just like market prices in a competitive system, the difference being that in this case the CPB performs the role of the market.

The same trial-and-error way toward equilibrium could also be applied in two other models of socialist economy, one providing for a decreased consumer influence on production programme, the other presupposing none at all.

In its extreme version, which for sociopolitical reasons Lange deems untenable, the model might provide no freedom of choice for either consumption or employment. Production plans would be decided by the CPB officials' scale of preferences. In such a version all prices are basically accounting prices. Consumer goods are rationed, while the place and kind of employment are imposed by command. If production managers keep to the above-mentioned rules, and if the CPB keeps to the parametric price system, then economic calculus is possible even in this version, while prices are not arbitrary but reflect the relative scarcity of factors of production.

There is an intermediate model, which provides for freedom of consumption decisions but only within a production plan established on the ground of CPB preferences. In this case, accounting prices of producer and consumer goods reflect the CPB's preference scale, while production managers would rely on them in their decision-making. Market prices for consumer goods would be set by supply and demand. But Lange rejects even this system as undemocratic, saying that the dual system of prices could be applied only when there is widespread agreement that checking the consumption of some products (say, alcohol) while promoting the consumption of other goods (say, cultural services) is in the public interest.

But the CPB might conceal its preferences and resort to rationing production goods and resources. Society can defend itself against such practices by creating a supreme economic court which would be entitled to declare any unconstitutional CPB decision as null and void. In Lange's view, any decision introducing rationing would be unconstitutional.

Interestingly, Lange rejects these two versions of socialist economy on account of the potential hazards they carry for democracy, and says not a word about democracy's possible link with economic efficiency.

Lange considers the distribution of national income in three aspects.

Wages would be differentiated by seeking a distribution of labour services that would maximize society's wealth in general. This happens when differences in marginal disutility of work in different trades and workplaces are offset by wage differences. Wage differentials can be treated as converses of prices paid by employees for differing work conditions, as a simplified form of buying free time, safety or pleasant work (which is easy to imagine assuming that all employees get the same earnings but pay different prices for doing different jobs; the easier and safer a given job, the more one has to pay for it). In this sense, the wage differentiation rule can be brought into harmony with egalitarianism.

Apart from wages paid to employees, each consumer is paid a public dividend as his or her share of capital and natural resources. At first Lange was inclined to distribute such dividends proportionally to wages. But as Lerner point out that such a policy would impart added attractiveness to the hardest jobs, Lange changed his mind, saying there should be no link between procedures for public dividend distribution and wage differentials.

The distribution of national income between consumption and accumulation, said Lange, would not be arbitrary when only consumers' individual savings decide the rate of accumulation. But if savings are 'corporately' determined – and Lange at first thought that was typical of a socialist economy – then there would be no way of preventing the CPB from being at least partly arbitrary in its decisions.

Emphasizing that resource allocation is guided by formally analogous rules in both socialist and free competitive economies, Lange argued that real allocation in socialism would be different from and more rational than that in capitalism. In his static analysis, he considered the following factors as decisive in judging the relative performance of the two systems. Greater equality of income distribution enhances society's well-being (in the subjective sense, that is, as a sum total of individual satisfactions). Second, socialist economy makes allowances in its calculus for all the services rendered by producers and for all the costs involved, while a private entrepreneur does not care for benefits that do not flow into his own pocket nor for costs he does not have to pay: 'Most important alternatives, like life, security, and health of the workers, are sacrificed without being accounted for as a cost of production' (1938, p. 104).

Even the possible flaws that Lange conceded might appear in a socialist economy, such as the arbitrary setting of the rate of accumulation or the danger of bureaucratization of economic life, would be milder than under capitalism, he argued.

But the ultimately decisive economic argument in favour of socialism, Lange believed, was the general waste and endogenous tendency toward stagnation generated by modern capitalism's monopolistic tendencies. This question, though, goes beyond the scope of the often-criticized static analysis underlying

Lange's classical model. Leaving aside the now enormous critical literature, let us try to answer the question of what Lange himself saw as his model's limitations.

Lange anticipated possible charges by critics in the second part of his study, in his discussion of 'The Economist's Case for Socialism':

> The really important point in discussing the economic merits of socialism is not that of comparing the equilibrium position of a socialist and of a capitalist economy with respect to social welfare. Interesting as such a comparison is for the economic theorist, it is not the real issue in the discussion of socialism. The real issue is *whether the further maintenance of the capitalist system is compatible with economic progress* (1938, p. 110).

But as he develops this general idea, Lange clearly uses an asymmetrical kind of argument. Having presented free competitive capitalism as the system which generated 'the greatest economic progress in human history', Lange proceeds to show (among other things, by referring to Keynes) that the source of that progress is drying up because of the progressive concentration and monopolization of production. His main point is that corporations, which are capable of controlling the market, attempt to avoid losses due to capital depreciation caused by innovation, and hence they try to check progress in technology. Neither a return to free competition nor government control can effectively eliminate this tendency. The only effective solution, then, is the socialization of big capital, the introduction of socialism.

But will socialism ensure rapid technical progress? Will the abolition, via socialization, of capitalist monopolies' well-known tendency to check technological progress automatically dismantle all the barriers to innovation? Or will it amount to substituting new barriers for old? Will the two rules for managers be sufficient to guarantee the adoption of state-of-the-art production techniques? In his classic study, Lange never even asked such questions and only much later did he become aware of them.

Toward the end of his life (in a latter to the present writer dated 14 August 1964), Lange wrote:

> What is called optimal allocation is a second-rate matter, what is really of prime importance is that of incentives for the growth of productive forces (accumulation and progress in technology). This is the true meaning of, so to say, 'rationality'.

BIBLIOGRAPHY

Lange, O. 1936–7. On the economic theory of socialism. Pts I–II. *Review of Economic Studies* 4, Pt I, October 1936, 53–71; Pt II, February 1937, 123–42.

Lange, O. and Taylor, F.M. 1938. *On the Economic Theory of Socialism*. Ed. and with an introduction by Benjamin Lippincott, Minneapolis: University of Minnesota Press. Reprinted, New York: McGraw-Hill, 1964.

Lerner, A.P. 1936. A note on socialist economics. *Review of Economic Studies* 4, 72–6.

Taylor, F.M. 1929. The guidance of production in a socialist state. *American Economic Review* 19, March, 1–8.

Vladimir Ilyich Lenin

MEGHNAD DESAI

Vladimir Ilyich Ulyanov, who wrote and gained fame under the pseudonym Lenin, was born in April 1870, the second son of a Russian provincial official in Simbirsk (now Ulyanovsk). After the arrest and execution of his elder brother Alexander in 1887 for alleged terrorist activity, Lenin became increasingly active in political study groups at Kazan, Samara and St Petersburg (now Leningrad). He same to identify himself with the Marxist rather than the populist (Narodniki) stream in these study groups. He played an active part in the early theoretical debates between these two streams on the future course of Russia's economic and political development. At the time of the founding of the Russian Social Democratic Labour Party (RSDLP) in 1898, he was already known as its best young theorist. A split in the RSDLP took place in 1902 and Lenin became identified as the leader of the majority (Bolshevik) faction. He spent much of the early years of the 20th century in exile in London, Paris and Zurich. He returned to Russia in April 1917 after the February Revolution had initiated the post-tsarist phase of Russian politics. Lenin, unlike his fellow party members, correctly foresaw the instability of the political situation in which an unelected liberal democratic cabinet uneasily shared power with the federation of popularly elected factory committees (Soviets). He launched the Bolsheviks on a strategy of revolutionary rejection of the government and a platform of peace in the World War at any price. His analysis proved correct when in November 1917 the Bolsheviks won a majority in the All Russian Congress of Soviets and took power. Lenin led the communist government from that day until illness forced his withdrawal from active politics in March 1923. He died in January 1924.

Lenin's economic writing is extensive, comprising books, pamphlets, newspaper articles and occasional speeches (see Desai, 1986, for a full bibliography). His contributions can be placed under three headings: analysis of Russia's capitalist development in the period 1880–1900; the analysis of the developments in world capitalism in the period 1900–1916, where his concept of imperialism as a form of monopoly capitalism was an innovation; and lastly as a Marxist policy maker during the period 1917–23.

THE DEVELOPMENT OF CAPITALISM IN RUSSIA. Lenin's book of this title published in 1898 is a substantial piece of work which traces the growth of commercial relations and specialization in agriculture leading to an erosion of the traditional communal forms. On the industrial side, Russia's late arrival entailed an active role for the Tsarist state in fostering industrialization and an influx of foreign capital to finance the development. This meant that Russia, although a newly industrializing country in the 1890s, had a larger proportion of its industrial labour force in large factories than older industrialized countries like Britain. Lenin saw these as predictable consequences of rapid capitalist growth which made any going back to pre-capitalist communal forms of village organization impossible. The growth of large factories also meant concentration of workers in a few places, facilitating their combination in trade union activities. These economic circumstances – the growth of commercial relations in the countryside and of concentrations of the urban proletariat – dictated for Lenin the political strategy of a socialist party which hoped to win power by mass organization. Lenin's theory of the development of the democratic political movement follows the economic stages quite closely. In this sense he can be said to have developed an economic framework for a Marxist political theory. *The Development of Capitalism in Russia* is even to this day the only comprehensive economic history of a country from a Marxist perspective.

IMPERIALISM, THE HIGHEST STAGE OF CAPITALISM. In 1916, Lenin wrote his well-known economic pamphlet of this title. The background was provided by World War I, which had broken out two years previously with enthusiastic participation by the working people of various combatant nations and the connivance of the socialist parties. The 'betrayal' by the workers and their political leaders was one factor in Lenin's urge to explain these events. The second urge was perhaps provided by a desire to integrate the facts of a war into a Marxist theory of the long-run development and eventual breakdown of capitalism.

Marx had predicted a tendency for the rate of profit to fall as capitalist development proceeded. Among the forces which may counteract this tendency was an increasing concentration in industry and the emergence of larger industrial units. In 1907, Hilferding in his *Finance Capital* had provided a theory and empirical evidence for the increasing integration of bank finance and industrial capital. The formation of trusts and cartels was helped by banks willing to finance mergers and controlling and interlocking equity holdings. Marxist economists saw the 20th century as entering a monopoly phase of capitalism in contrast to the competitive phase that Marx had written about.

Lenin's achievement is to add to the Marx–Hilferding account an international economic and political element. One part of his theory came from Hobson's

Imperialism. As an underconsumptionist, Hobson linked the fight over African and Asian territory in the last decades of the 19th century among European nations to the search for outlets for surplus which could not be sold at home. Hobson took the view that this imperial search was irrational. Lenin, as a Marxist, saw the irrationality as a systematic functional element in a world of monopoly capital economies each of which was trying to stave off the falling rate of profit by exporting. The battle for markets could not however take place in a politically neutral context as envisaged by competitive economic theory. Large cartels and monopolies gave a few leading bankers and industrialists influence with the political governments of their country. The battle for markets thus became a struggle between developed capitalist nations for territory. It was the struggle for territory as a surrogate for markets which led to military confrontation between the major industrial nations and hence war. War was not however predicted to be a satisfactory solution to the problem of markets or of profitability. It was likely in Lenin's view to be the harbinger of proletarian uprising against the system in these countries which would end it.

Thus Lenin blends international political developments into a Marxian theory of capitalist development. Imperialism in Lenin's definition is the entire set of unequal economic relations between capitalist countries – between rival mature capitalist countries fighting for markets as well as between mature countries and developing economies which become their markets. Formal political control by one nation over another is not a necessary element in Lenin's view of imperialism. Although immensely influential in the interwar years due to Comintern orthodoxy, this theory has come under some attack recently (Warren, 1980). It lacks a coherent analytical theory of how monopoly capital differs from competitive capitalism and its empirical predictions proved only temporarily true when a series of political uprisings took place in Europe after World War I. These uprisings did not mature into a full-scale collapse of capitalism, which continues seventy years after Lenin foresaw its highest phase as having been achieved.

SOCIALIST ECONOMIC POLICY. As the first Marxist to lead a government, Lenin had to formulate practical economic policy. Given the notorious lack of discussion of socialist economic policy in Marx's writings, Lenin had to improvise. Two notions stand out as his distinctive contribution to this area. First, his description of post-revolutionary Russia as a transitional state from capitalism to socialism. During this transition, state capitalism was seen by Lenin as an advance upon private capitalism in as much as the political state was not a capitalist one but a workers' state. Lenin used the wartime German economic organization as the ideal of a fully integrated single economic unit which a planned socialist economy could beneficially emulate. Second, in the return to normality after the Civil War – in his pamphlet 'The Tax in Kind' – Lenin sketched a theory for the role of trade in reviving economic activity. The key was to move from a forced requisition of food surpluses to a policy of tax in kind and encouraging exchange. A revival of agriculture was required for an industrial revival but the terms of trade between the two sectors was a crucial policy variable in this respect. Trade is seen as an antidote to economic bureaucracy in this pamphlet. It was this pamphlet that inaugurated the New Economic Policy which could be said to have lasted from 1921 to 1929.

SELECTED WORKS

1898. *The Development of Capitalism in Russia.*

1916. *Imperialism: the Highest Stage of Capitalism.*

1921. *The Tax in Kind.*

Collected Works. 45 vols. Trans. of the 4th enlarged Russian edn, Moscow: Progress Publishers, 1960–70.

BIBLIOGRAPHY

Desai, M. 1986. *Lenin as an Economist.* London: Lawrence & Wishart.

Warren, B. 1980. *Imperialism: Pioneer of Capitalism.* London: New Left Books.

Abba Ptachya Lerner

TIBOR SCITOVSKY

Lerner was one of the last of the great non-mathematical economists and certainly one of the most original, versatile and prolific members of the profession. Born in Romania in 1905, raised from early childhood in the Jewish immigrant quarter of London's East End, he went to rabbinical school, started work at 16, working as tailor, capmaker, Hebrew School teacher, typesetter, and then founded his own printing shop. When that went bankrupt at the onset of the Great Depression, he enrolled as an evening student at the London School of Economics to find out the reason for his shop's failure. There, his outstanding logical faculties soon became evident and won him all the available prizes and fellowships, one of which took him to Cambridge to study with Keynes. He published many major articles already as an undergraduate, was appointed temporary assistant lecturer at the London School of Economics in 1935, assistant lecturer in 1936, and in 1937 a Rockefeller fellowship took him to the United States, where he remained, although his reslessness kept him from settling at any one university for more than a few years. He died in 1982.

Lerner was a lifelong socialist, advocate of market pricing for its allocative efficiency, and believer in private enterprise, whose offer of private employment he considered an essential safeguard of individual freedom. That unusual combination of principles accounts for Lerner's loneliness and political isolation. In his economics, however, he knew how to reconcile those principles. His reconciliation of the first two made him into one of the founders (along with Oskar Lange) of the theory of market pricing in the decentralized socialist economy, and he sought to reconcile the first and third principles by advocating what he called socialist free enterprise: 'the freedom of both public and private enterprise to enter any industry on fair terms which, in each particular case, permit that form to prevail which serves the public best'.

Although Lerner's ambition was to improve the economy, not economics, he made many, often fundamental contributions to economic theory, mainly in the fields of welfare economics, international trade and macroeconomics but also in the theories of production, capital, monopoly, duopoly, spatial competition and index numbers. Furthermore and hardly less important, he made generous use of his geometrical skill and genius for exposition in tidying up and clarifying other people's ideas. As a result, a number of important economic theorems and ideas, though first stated by others, became the profession's common property in Lerner's simpler and clearer formulations. An important example of that is the well-known rule that marginal cost pricing is a condition of welfare optimality. Another example is his definitive proof (Lerner, 1936) that in the two-country, two-commodity model, export and import duties have identical consequences if their proceeds are spent in the same way.

In welfare economics, one of his first articles (Lerner, 1934) not only introduced the notion that monopoly is a matter of degree, whose extent is best measured by the excess of price over marginal cost, but in the process also provided the first complete, comprehensive and clear statement and discussion of the nature and limitations of Pareto optimality, and of the equality between price and marginal cost and between price and marginal value product as necessary conditions of optimality. All that, along with Lerner's many papers on market pricing under socialism, was restated, elaborated and extended in his 1944 *The Economics of Control: Principles of Welfare Economics*.

That work, Lerner's best book, became and remains the most comprehensive non-mathematical text on welfare economics. Although written in the style of a handbook, with its propositions presented as rules for the planners and plant managers of a decentralized socialist economy to follow, the book is better described by the second than by the first half of its title. For most of those rules are nothing but the first-order conditions of optimality, presented with great care, clarity and completeness but without a hint at the practical obstacles in the way of putting them into actual practice. As a text on welfare economics, however, it is exceptionally meticulous and complete, it extends the scope of the welfare principle from resource allocation narrowly defined to taxation, macroeconomics and international trade and finance, and it contains the first logically based analysis of distributional optimality. Moreover, since a socialist economy, for Lerner, meant the use of private enterprise in some sectors, State-owned plants in others, depending on which was the more efficient in each, his guidebook for socialist planners also discusses why and when perfect competition leads to optimality and why and when real-life competition falls short of being perfect.

In the field of international trade theory, Lerner derived Samuelson's celebrated factor-price equalization theorem 15 years before Samuelson in a 1933 unpublished seminar paper printed only 19 years later (Lerner, 1952). His elegant and ingenious resolution of a 19th-century controversy over the identity of import and export duties has already been mentioned; he devised (Lerner, 1932 and 1934b) the standard geometry of the two-country, two-commodity model, which is well known from a whole generation of textbooks; and he was the first to raise and deal with the question of 'optimum currency areas' in his 1944

Economics of Control.

Most of Lerner's innovations in microeconomics and international trade theory were so basic and so useful that they promptly became integral parts of every economist's standard equipment. That is why it is hard to appreciate, at this late stage, the striking originality and elegant simplicity of his logic. One gets a glimpse of that by looking at his almost unknown proposal of how to counter OPEC's raising of the price of oil (Lerner, 1980). He proposed the imposition of a variable import duty on oil (which he called extortion tax), whose level would always match the producer's profit margin, thereby rising and falling with the oil price and being higher on imports from high-priced and lower on those from low-priced producers. Since such a tariff would make consumers face much larger price changes than those decided upon by OPEC and much greater price differentials than those set by the different oil exporters, it would also make consumers' responses to those price changes and differentials correspondingly greater, thereby raising the price elasticity of demand for oil as it appears to producers. That would lower OPEC's monopoly power and so its profit maximizing monopoly price, and it would increase the rewards and the temptation for OPEC members to break up the coalition by defecting from it.

In macroeconomics, Lerner did as much as anyone to clarify, extend and popularize Keynes's *General Theory*; he was the first to recognize the inflationary implications of employment policies, the first to analyse in depth and in detail the causes and nature of inflation, and to propose a remedy for stagflation.

Lerner wrote the first article (Lerner, 1936b) to make Keynes's employment theory simple and generally intelligible, and in two short papers clarified Keynes's 'user cost' and 'marginal efficiency of capital' concepts (Lerner, 1943b and 1953). He wrote an interesting book (Lerner, 1951) to summarize and significantly extend Keynes's employment theory; he published an enlightening paper to explain the *General Theory*'s obscure chapter 17 (Lerner, 1952b), thereby clearing up the complex role wage rigidity plays in rendering underemployment equilibrium possible; and he was the person best to elucidate the relation between macroeconomics and microeconomics by representing them as the two limiting cases of a more general type of economic analysis (Lerner, 1962).

Next to his work on welfare economics and international trade theory, Lerner's best known and most shockingly new contribution was his introduction of the idea of 'functional finance' (Lerner, 1943; also restated in Lerner, 1951, and in his 1944 *Economics of Control*), whose advocacy of Keynesian employment policies exposed the latter's logical implications and revolutionary nature. To careless readers, it also seemed like a wildly inflationary doctrine, although Lerner's concern over inflation and over the inflation effects of employment policies antedate everybody else's by many years.

Lerner's extensive work on inflation began with his distinguishing between low and high full employment (Lerner, 1951). High full employment is that beyond which further demand expansion presses against supply limitations and creates overspending (demand-pull) inflation; low full employment is the employment level below which the price level is stable. Levels of employment between the low and high full-employment levels create administered (cost-push) inflation, owing to labour's excessive bargaining strength. His 'low full employment' therefore is a forerunner (by 17 years) of Friedman's 'natural rate of unemployment'.

Lerner's theoretical papers on inflation contain many pioneering insights. One is his sharp analytic distinction between overspending or excess-demand inflation and administered or excess-claims inflation (Lerner, 1958 and 1972), of which the former does, but the latter (according to him) does *not* call for fiscal and/or monetary restraint. He later added a third category, expectational inflation (Lerner, 1972), which he also called defensive inflation to differentiate it from the aggressive nature of excess-claims inflation – arguing that incomes policy is effective against the former but ineffective against the latter. Another and well-known distinction which Lerner was the first to draw was that between expected and unexpected inflation (Lerner, 1949).

Since Lerner's heart was in reform, not in analytic niceties, his many discussions of inflation were just a preamble for working out a plan to control the main economic problem of his time, stagflation, that is, the combination of unemployment and inflation, which he considered characteristic of administered or excess-claims inflation. Restrictive policies were to him an inadmissible cure for that type of inflation, because he considered the creation of unemployment a prohibitive cost. Incomes policies he judged ineffective against all but expectational inflation, and he was too ardent a believer in the pricing mechanism to argue for wage and price controls. He wanted to stabilize the general price level without impeding the free movement of individual prices and wages. To accomplish that, he devised and, with David Colander's help, worked out in detail a scheme, called Market Anti-Inflation Plan, better known as MAP (Lerner, 1980b), for rationing the right of firms to raise the 'effective price' of their output, that is, the sum of profits and wages entering the price of their products (value added). The scheme would give every firm the right to increase its value added in the proportion of the estimated rise in the economy's overall productivity, but it would also allow them to sell their unused rights or the unused portion of their rights (in a market created for the purpose) to those other firms that want to increase their wages and/or profits (value added) in greater proportion.

Lerner developed his Market Anti-Inflation Plan gradually and published it at several stages and in several versions before it reached its final form in 1980. It was his last major contribution to economics and a fitting end to his career, because it well illustrates both the strengths and the weaknesses of his extraordinarily fertile and original mind. It is bold, elegant, ingenious and impeccably logical, with meticulous attention to every conceivable detail and exception, but combines those qualities with a slightly utopian flavour, all of which have characterized just about all of Lerner's many proposals for reform.

For their sheer novelty and stark logic Lerner's arguments and policy proposals usually took people aback, but he was utterly unwilling and perhaps also unable to soften their impact in the interests of their easier acceptability. He was well aware of the reasons for the hostile reception of virtually all his recommendations but believed, with some justification, that as time wore off their shocking novelty, they would become more acceptable and politically feasible. Lerner's MAP could well be the best remedy for stagflation but many less good remedies will first have to be tried and prove ineffective in order to render MAP politically acceptable.

SELECTED WORKS

1932. The diagrammatical representation of cost conditions in international trade. *Economica* 12, August, 346–56.

1934a. The concept of monopoly and the measurement of monopoly power. *Review of Economic Studies* 1, June, 157–75.

1934b. The diagrammatical representation of demand conditions in international trade. *Economica* NS 1, August, 319–34.

1936a. The symmetry between import and export taxes. *Economica* NS 3, August, 306–13.

1936b. Mr. Keynes' 'General Theory of Employment, Interest and Money'. *International Labour Review*, October, 435–54.

1943a. Functional finance and the federal debt. *Social Research* 10, February, 38–51.

1943b. User cost and prime user cost. *American Economic Review* 33, March, 131–2.

1944. *The Economics of Control: Principles of Welfare Economics.* New York: Macmillan.

1949. The inflationary process: some theoretical aspects. *Review of Economics and Statistics* 31, August, 193–200.

1951. *Economics of Employment.* New York: McGraw-Hill.

1952a. Factor prices and international trade. *Economica* NS 19, February, 1–15.

1952b. The essential properties of interest and money. *Quarterly Journal of Economics* 66, May, 172–93.

1953. On the marginal product of capital and the marginal efficiency of investment. *Journal of Political Economy* 61, February, 1–14.

1958. Inflational depression and the regulation of administered prices. *Joint Economic Committee Print,* Conference on Economic Stability and Growth, March.

1962. Macro-economics and micro-economics. In *Logic, Methodology and Philosophy of Science: Proceedings of the 1960 International Congress,* ed. E. Nagel, P. Suppes and A. Tarski, Stanford: Stanford University Press.

1972. *Flation: Not Inflation of Prices, Not Deflation of Jobs.* New York: Quadrangle Books.

1980. OPEC – a plan – if you can't beat them, join them. *Atlantic Economic Journal,* September, 1–3.

1980. (With D.C. Colander.) *MAP, A Market Anti-inflation Plan.* New York: Harcourt, Brace and Jovanovich.

For a representative collection of Lerner's best writings, see D.C. Colander (ed.), *Selected Economic Writings of Abba P. Lerner,* New York: New York University Press, 1983. That volume contains most of the articles cited here and also has Lerner's complete bibliography.
For other, more detailed appraisals of Lerner's contribution to economics, see:

Samuelson, P.A. 1964. A.P. Lerner at sixty. *Review of Economic Studies* 31, June, 169–78.

Scitovsky, T. 1984. Lerner's contribution to economics. *Journal of Economic Literature* 22, December, 1547–71.

Sobel, I. 1979. Abba Lerner on employment and inflation: a post-Keynesian perspective. In *Essays in Post-Keynesian Inflation,* ed. J.H. Gapinski and C.E. Rockwood, Cambridge, Mass.: Ballinger.

Mao Zedong

PETER NOLAN

Mao Zedong [Mao Tse-tung] (1893–1976) led the Chinese Communist Party (CCP) in its revolutionary struggle pre-1949 and was pre-eminent in the post-revolutionary leadership for most of the period from Liberation (1949) until his death. The degree to which Mao personally dominated China's post-revolutionary development is illustrated by the dramatic changes that have occurred since his death. It seems reasonable to speak of a 'Maoist model' to characterize China's development path for much of the period from 1949 to 1976.

There were a number of influences underlying this model. Nationalism was central to Mao's thinking. He was proud of China's historical achievements and angry at her humiliations in the century before 1949. He wished to build a powerful modern economy so that China would 'never again be an insulted nation'. China's cultural tradition permeated Mao's thought; his analysis of problems in terms of 'contradictions' owes as much to the traditional Chinese dialectic of *yin* and *yang* as to Marxism.

The Leninist–Stalinist application of Marxism in the USSR also influenced Mao (not always positively). From this tradition he accepted the notion of a post-revolutionary vanguard party overseeing all aspects of socio-economic life. From it too he absorbed the view of a 'socialist' economy as the antithesis of capitalism, i.e. no private ownership of the means of production and economic decisions determined not by market forces but by planners' administrative directions ('with us plans are primary and price is secondary . . . the law of value has no regulating function'). The adverse consequences of administrative planning under Mao were the same as those in economies with similar systems (e.g. low incentives for technical progress or to improve the range and quality of products; high incentives to hoard resources).

Mao was convinced of the possibility (and desirability) of changing popular consciousness, so that the main force motivating social action might become collective interests rather than personal gain. Although he wanted modernization and material progress, Mao stood outside the Marxist–Leninist tradition in thinking that 'socialist' values ('fighting self' and 'serving the people') might be more successfully developed among poor people ('poor people want change, want to do things, want revolution') and in the villages more easily than in the 'corrupting' cities. For Mao, Liberation marked the beginning of a long process of both economic development and 'permanent revolution' in China's class relations.

Mao's economic policies may be examined under four headings: (1) population; (2) economic growth; (3) rural institutions; (4) the international economy.

After 1949 Mao initially considered population control unnecessary. He was persuaded eventually of the problems of rapid population growth, but a sustained campaign to control population growth was not implemented until the 1970s, so that China's population grew rapidly for most of the 1950s and 1960s.

Although Mao did not produce a rigorously formulated theory of economic growth, certain aspects of his thinking on this question can be identified. He considered a high rate of investment a necessary condition of rapid growth. Administrative planning via physical controls, direct control over the urban wage bill, and the CCP's influence on rural collectives' income distribution, together permitted a high rate of investment – China's 'accumulation' rate stood at over 30 per cent of national income in most years from 1957 to 1976.

Mao's writings suggest that under him China broke away from the heavy industry emphasis of other 'socialist' countries. Unfortunately, the high investment rate, microeconomic inefficiency, slow technical progress and a vicious circle of self-expansion within the capital goods sector, together helped produce an alarming fall in the incremental output–capital ratio from the 1950s to the 1970s. From 1949 to 1957 heavy industry's investment share rose rapidly, and thereafter generally absorbed 45–55 per cent of state units' 'basic construction investment'. Many Chinese economists (when permitted) criticized the system that produced this result, but Mao refused to make the sweeping changes required to shift away from the heavy industry basis.

Mao considered microeconomic relationships to be important for economic growth. He argued that in a cooperative environment 'workers will look upon the enterprise as their own and not the cadres''. This, he believed, would release the vast areas of human creativity left untapped by capitalism's antagonistic class relations. For Mao, a socialist enterprise was one in which workers had a powerful say in enterprise decision making, managers and technicians discarded their 'haughty airs' and participated in manual labour, the competitiveness of piece rates was replaced by time rates, differences in basic wages were kept within strict limits, and the proportion of income allocated 'according to need' rose over time. With the partial exception of Yugoslavia, these utopian ideas had not received such attention in the 'socialist' countries since the first months of War Communism in the USSR.

Despite their intrinsic problems, in a different setting such policies might have produced better results. However, in China they were often crudely applied (e.g.

'integrating' managers and technicians with ordinary workers by forcing them to wear dunces' hats in public) and were practised in enterprises with negligible independence and whose workers experienced little long-term growth of real income. These caused serious motivational problems.

The CCP led China's peasants through land reform and on to establish rural collectives which were the basic framework of economic activity for most Chinese people from the mid-1950s to the early 1980s. Mao though they were an appropriate setting for developing 'socialist' values, avoiding the class conflict of 'capitalist' agriculture, and supporting disadvantaged peasants. He believed too that collectives would benefit from economies of scale. It was to prove much harder to develop 'socialist' values among peasants than Mao had anticipated. The CCP waged a constant, unsuccessful battle to 'cut off the tails of capitalism' in the villages. Moreover, in certain areas of farmwork (especially labour-intensive crop cultivation) powerful managerial *dis*economies of scale appeared. Farm efficiency was adversely affected too by state control over key collective decisions, such as the allocation of income between accumulation and consumption. As a result, the micro-level problems were even worse in the countryside than in the cities.

Mao was afraid that extensive contact with the international economy would make China 'dependent' on outside forces. In the 1950s China built a comprehensive industrial system. Trade was viewed as a necessary evil. Exporting firms were denied direct contact with world markets; it made no difference to them whether their products succeeded or failed internationally. Unsurprisingly, China's export performance from the late 1950s to the late 1970s was poor. Mao did not wish China to have a high level of imports, confident that she could produce domestically most of the products she required and could be virtually self-sufficient in technical progress. He did not permit foreign investment in China or China's acquisition of long-term debt. The economic costs of Mao's extreme position were high.

In the early 1970s, as China emerged from the isolation of the Cultural Revolution, Western economists were increasingly sympathetic to China. Development economics textbooks commonly included a brief section on the 'Maoist model'. While arguing against its transferability to different political systems, it was usually praised for its alleged achievements in combining quite rapid overall growth with the elimination of mass poverty and more equal income distribution than in most developing countries.

Since Mao's death, the mass of newly available statistical and anecdotal information has led to a major reappraisal of the Maoist epoch. There have been shocking allegations of mass starvation after the Great Leap Forward (1958–9) during which Maoist policies were applied in their purest form. China's official statistics show that its population fell by about 14 million from 1949 to 1961, suggesting a demographic disaster. Many Western observers enthused about Mao's utopian goals in the Cultural Revolution but it became clear that these had been pursued in a deeply repressive fashion, involving the imposition of one man's vision upon an increasingly unenthusiastic population. The end of Maoism was greeted with huge relief at all levels of Chinese society.

It can now be seen that the Chinese economy in the mid-1970s was in a state of crisis. Rapid population growth over two decades, an excessively high and unbalanced accumulation rate, pervasive microeconomic inefficiency, and isolation from the world economy, combined to produce little measured improvement in average living standards from the mid-1950s to the late 1970s, and in certain important respects (e.g. housing, cotton cloth, edible oil, entertainment) the situation had deteriorated. Despite some success in ensuring that a basic minimum consumption standard was provided, when Mao died there still were wide regional income disparities and a sizeable minority of the Chinese population was abjectly poor.

These problems were illuminated by the results of the post-1978 economic reforms, which dismantled many important aspects of the Maoist model. After 1978 average living standards rose dramatically and the proportion of the population in poverty declined sharply. It is impossible not to attribute these achievements (and important new problems) to the massive institutional reform (especially that in the countryside), the increased impact of market forces, expanded contact with the international economy, and alterations in the state's investment policy.

It is not surprising that the attractiveness of Mao's development model waned rapidly after his death. Perhaps the most fitting epitaph is that provided in 1978 by the elderly economist Chen Yun:

Had Chairman Mao died in 1956, there would have been no doubt that he was a great leader of the Chinese people, a respected, loved and outstanding great man in the proletarian revolutionary movement of the world. Had he died in 1966, his meritorious achievements would have been somewhat tarnished but still very good. Since he actually died in 1976, there is nothing we can do about it.

SELECTED WORKS
Selected Works of Mao Tse-Tung. Vols I–V, Peking: Foreign Languages Press.

Market Socialism

W. BRUS

Market socialism is a theoretical concept (model) of an economic system in which the means of production (capital) are publicly or collectively owned, and the allocation of resources follows the rules of the market (product-, labour-, capital-markets). With regard to existing socialist economies the term is often applied more loosely to cover both systems which tend to approximate it in the strict sense (as the Yugoslav system in the aftermath of the 1965 reform), as well as those which replace commands and physical distribution of producer goods by financial controls and incentives as instruments of central planning ('regulated market', as in the Hungarian 'new economic mechanism' after the 1968 reform).

INTRODUCTION. Marx's political economy had for a long time been interpreted to hold that socialism is incompatible with the market. Market relations, even in their simplest form of commodity exchange between two self-employed producers, are presented in *Das Kapital* (Marx, 1867) as a nucleus out of which – logically and historically – capitalism emerges. The market forms an indispensable link between economic actors when they are apparently separated from each other (by private ownership), and the social nature of their activity is hidden, revealing itself and being verified only through exchange; the overall outcome is then an ex post resultant of a multitude of spontaneous actions, with the negative consequences becoming the more pronounced the more developed the truly social character (interdependence) of the economic process. Socialism – according to this line of thought – makes the market redundant and overcomes its shortcomings as an allocation mechanism by bringing into the open the social nature of work, assigning it directly ex ante to a particular role in the economic process through the 'visible hand' of planning, which secures full utilization of resources, free of cyclical fluctuations. Above all, socialism removes the absurdity of having, side by side, unsatisfied needs, and excess capital and labour.

After the Russian revolution of 1917, when the shape of socialist economic systems became a practical problem, basic elements of the marketless concept of socialism found their way into programmatic documents of the Communist parties. Any application of the market mechanism was presented as only a temporary concession, to be justified mainly by the immaturity of the socio-economic conditions that required a longer transition period between capitalism and socialism, especially in underdeveloped countries with dominant peasant agriculture and other types of 'petty commodity production' (Communist International, 1929). At the same time, however, the social-democratic wing of Marxism began to recognize the relevance of the market for the operation of a socialist economy (Kautsky, 1922).

Theoretical debates on market socialism acquired a new dimension in the interwar period, particularly after republication by F.A. von Hayek (1935) of an article by L. von Mises published originally in 1920, which categorically denied the possibility of rational economic calculation under socialism, because exchange relations between production goods and hence their prices could be established only on the basis of private ownership. Among the many attempts at refutation of this view (Taylor, 1929; Dickinson, 1933; Landauer, 1931; Heimann, 1932), probably the best known is that by Oskar Lange (1936–7). Similar ideas had been developed in the same period by Abba Lerner (1934–7), hence the often used designation of 'Lange–Lerner solution'.

Lange not only denied the purely theoretical validity of von Mises' stand (by pointing to Barone's (1908) demonstration of the possibility of dealing with the question through a system of simultaneous equations), but also tried to present a positive solution. This was to consist of a 'trial and error' procedure, in which the Central Planning Board performs the functions of the market where there is no market in the institutional sense of the word (or – it may be added – where market imperfections threaten the parametric function of prices). In this capacity the Board fixes prices, as well as wages and interest rates, so as to balance supply and demand (by appropriate changes in case of disequilibrium), and instructs managers of socialist enterprises (and entire industries) to follow two rules: (1) to minimize average cost of production by using a combination of factors which would equalize marginal productivity of their money unit-worth; (2) to determine the scale of output at a point of equalization of marginal cost and the price set by the Board.

The emphasis in the elaboration of the 'trial and error' procedure was, in the first place, on proving socialism to be capable of allocating resources in a way equivalent to a purely competitive market system. But it acquired much wider significance as an attempt to construct a normative model of market socialism. However, in the latter interpretation – as a normative solution – the model of a socialist market economy becomes more vulnerable to practical tests of validity than would a model of a capitalist market economy. The real behaviour of actors in capitalist markets is by no means determined by the propositions of general equilibrium theory, whereas socialist managers are to be *instructed* to follow the textbook rules, with all the ensuing consequences of iteration processes which may not only operate with considerable time-lags and oscillations, but may not be convergent at all. This explains to some extent the inclusion into the model of a number of features which would distinguish it from a standard 'free market'. In Lange's presentation the main such feature is the determination of the rate of accumulation, not by market processes but directly ('arbitrarily') by the Board, which establishes also the rules of distribution of the social dividend from publicly owned capital and land (with a proviso that this should not affect the choice of occupation).

In addition, the 'trial and error' procedure assumes that actual markets are limited to consumer goods and labour only, while the functions of the market for production goods are performed by the Board itself (market *simulation*). Moreover, in a generalized version, even these assumptions may be dropped. The Board may impose its own scale of preferences on the composition of consumer goods output, even ration goods and assign people to their jobs, but it can still apply the 'trial and error' procedure to derive accounting (shadow) prices of production goods provided that there is no rationing outside the sphere of distribution of consumer goods and labour, i.e. at least a simulated market for production goods must exist. Thus, the market may be understood in Lange's model as a 'computing device of the pre-electronic age' for solving a system of simultaneous equations, as that author himself emphasized in his last article (Lange, 1965), in which the relative merits of the computer and the market are weighed very carefully, with the market in an institutional sense being judged by no means superior on all scores, particulary with regard to long-term dynamic problems.

Market socialism in the above form was to be capable of combining the allocative efficiency of competitive conditions (secured by the Board's rules, which ought to preclude oligopolistic and monopolistic behaviour), with welfare maximizing income distribution (by eliminating inequalities stemming from private ownership of capital and land) and internalization of externalities (by inclusion of all alternatives foregone into comprehensive social cost calculations). An economy operating on the principles of this model was to be open to innovations without generating cyclical fluctuations. The main difficulty considered – the danger of bureaucratization of economic life – was assessed (by Lange) as not greater than that under monopolistic capitalism, and perhaps even more containable under socialism due to democratic control over public functionaries.

This concept of market socialism came under heavy criticism from two opposite sides: from those who disputed the validity of the socialist component in the market system, and those who disputed the market component in the socialist system. The first kind of criticism, mainly following Hayek (1940) has concentrated on the unlikelihood of creating the informational and motivational foundations of market-type managerial behaviour without the background of private ownership which provides the necessary stimuli (expected returns) and constraints (financial responsibility) to innovative decisions involving risk. Schumpeter (1942) denied the relevance of the charge by pointing to the divorce between ownership and management under modern capitalism, but the empirical evidence from communist countries suggests that this is indeed a most serious issue. The second type of criticism, apart from that of general ideological nature, has concentrated on the market-type behaviour postulated in the model and directed toward static efficiency, and the overriding exigency of a dynamic process with full utilization of resources which it is claimed can be satisfied only through direct central planning – otherwise, strong elements of instability would become inherent in the system, along with deviations from the postulated pattern of income distribution (Dobb, 1939; Baran, 1952). Independently, the rationale of relying on market mechanisms of allocation in the face of large-scale dynamic problems was widely questioned in the Soviet debates in the 1920s (Erlich, 1960), as well as in the East European countries and in China after World War II. Lange himself acknowledged the need to re-examine his model from the point of view of long-term economic dynamics, oscillations, and income effects (Lange, 1947 and 1965). As for the informational and motivational weaknesses stemming from elimination of private ownership, the problems involved had not attracted much attention in communist countries until the last quarter of the 20th century, when they surfaced quite distinctly in connection with difficulties encountered in the course of various attempts to reform the economic system by increasing the role of actual markets.

THE COMMAND SYSTEM. The history of economic institutions in communist countries could be interpreted as displaying a certain tendency toward broadening the scope of operation of the market; but changes have been slow, and by the mid-1980s most communist countries still adhered to the essentials of the orthodox Soviet system based on commands and physical allocation of producer goods. The command system introduced in the USSR in the early 1930s was transplanted after World War II to all other communist countries (including China and Cuba), which might be taken as evidence that it was regarded as a general model and not as a reflection of Russian conditions peculiar to that time. Prior to that the Soviet Union went through so-called 'war communism' (during the civil war, 1918–20), when circumstances of extreme penury precipitated an attempt to switch to a moneyless economy with resources and products distributed *in natura* (it was this system which first prompted von Mises to challenge socialism's capacity for rational economic calculation). Later came the period of 'the new economic policy' (NEP), (1921–28/9), when the market was allowed to function relatively widely, but only as a temporary expedient of transition from capitalism to socialism. The first five-year plan (1928–32) and forced collectivization of agriculture marked the end of this period; the command economic system was installed as corresponding to the stage of socialism (a lower stage of communism).

The principles of the compound system as a model do not eliminate the market completely, but they relegate it to the peripheries of the state-owned (or fully state-controlled, as in the case of nominally collective farms and other cooperatives) production sphere. Freedom of choice of consumer goods – outside public consumption – combined with freedom of choice of occupation and jobs means that economic relations between the state and the households have to go through some kind of market with an active role for money. Prices, wages and interest rates on savings and personal loans etc., affect choices made by households as labour suppliers, consumers and savers. Free sales of agricultural produce above the state-quotas, particularly from individual plots cultivated by members of collective farms (as well as by many state employees) constitute another important segment of the market in the command system. In practice, however, all these segments are subject to restrictions, such as rationing, forced labour, curbs on labour mobility, constraints on the scale of individual farming etc. During the Stalinist period these restrictions were very severe, at some points overshadowing the elements of the market. However, the general tendency since 1953 has shown a gradual removal of restrictions, which makes the model's assumptions more meaningful.

Within the production sphere of the command system, the market does not function as an allocative mechanism. This role belongs to the Plan, which is meant to decide in a direct way not only major macroeconomic issues of growth, structure of productive capacity and income distribution, but also detailed schedules of current output and input, together with directions of flows between production units and toward the consumption sphere – predominantly in physical terms. Plans in the command system are in fact commands. The supply of production factors and intermediate goods is limited by rationing (allocation orders), and performance is assessed by plan-fulfilmen yardsticks. Money is used within the production sphere for aggregation and accounts-control purposes, and the forms of exchange transactions (sales, purchases, prices, credit) between enterprises are used in the same way. However, money remains *passive*, i.e. calculations and transactions in money terms follow the physical flow of resources and intermediate goods decided by the Plan (Brus, 1961); this means also that although among the targets and limits of the Plan financial goals (costs, profit, etc.) figure as well, the latter are subordinated to the physical indicators, and the financial position of enterprises is adjusted (through subsidies, dual price systems, differentiated product taxes, etc.) in such a way as to enable them to fulfil the physical tasks – the 'soft budget constraint' (Kornai, 1980). Thus, the production sphere is separated from the market elements outside it (relations between the state and the households, and among the households), and consumers' choices are not transmitted to the producers via the market mechanism, but filtered through planners' preferences. Similarly, the domestic economy is separated from foreign markets, both Western and intra-Comecon, by the 'monopoly of foreign trade' which operates through import and export quotas and adjusts the financial position of importers and exporters via a 'price equalization mechanism' (Wiles, 1969).

Consequently the command system fails to provide even the minimum conditions for Lange's 'trial and error' procedure: it can accommodate some kind of market in the consumption sphere with the possibility of finding equilibrium prices for consumer goods, but it eliminates the market within the production sphere, where goods are rationed and prices are arbitrary. Obviously, the separation between the two spheres can never be complete; the feedback effect is particularly noticeable via wages which have – under normal circumstances and with all reservations due to imperfection of labour markets anywhere – to reflect supply and demand, while at the same time constituting the major component of cost calculations that enter in one way or another into the considerations of the planners.

THE YUGOSLAV EXPERIMENT. Market socialism first appeared as a practical challenge to the command system in the early 1950s in Yugoslavia, after the Stalin–Tito break. The primary motives of this challenge were not economic, although the economic difficulties arising from originally the most complete (for Eastern Europe) and – paradoxically – voluntary transplantation of the command system to a small country without resources on the Soviet scale, played a considerable part. The Yugoslav Communit Party searched mainly for political and ideological self-determination vis-à-vis the hitherto unquestioned authority of Stalin in the communist world. It was found in the concept of self-management, presented as an embodiment of this strain in Marxian ideas which emphasizes socialism as a social order which overcomes alientation of labour by placing means of production under control of 'associated direct producers' (Ljubljana Programme, 1958).

Contrary to Soviet doctrine, nationalization came to be regarded here as only the first step towards the socialization of the means of production, because even a socialist state is merely an indirect representative of the producers who remain wage labourers until they themselves decide how to use the means of production entrusted to them, and how to allocate the income generated. The process of socialization is thus tantamount to consistent development of self-management in every unit of the economy (and in other spheres of social life); the direct economic involvement of the state has to be curtailed gradually through decentralization of decision-making, not only with regard to current operations of enterprises, but also with regard to capital investment. The functions of the national plan are in principle only indicative, confined basically to provide information and framework for (voluntary) coordination, and to counteract monopolistic and oligopolistic behaviour; direct allocation of resources by state organs is an exception, for cases such as development aid to particularly backward regions or emergency measures in acute social situations. Otherwise the economy is to be regulated by the market, a *socialist* market – its participants being not private (individual or corporate) employers of labour, but associated producers, workers' collectives.

The process of implementation of these ideas was gradual and by no means straightforward. The problems of de-controlling prices and foreign economic relations, both essential for creating competitive conditions, proved to be particularly difficult. Despite numerous retreats in the field of prices, and reimpositions of controls on foreign operations, production in Yugoslavia ceased to be regulated by commands and input rationing, and money assumed an active role with prices tending to clear the market. Isolation from the outside world diminished substantially. In 1965 the country was launched into what was supposed to become the decisive stage of development of self-management and market socialism: the responsibility for 'expanded reproduction' (i.e. for the main bulk of capital investment) was to be shifted from the state budget to the self-managed units, which were to be free to decide about the shares of retained and distributed (as personal incomes) earnings, and about the use of the retained part. The mechanism of financial intermediation in the process of re-allocation of investment funds between sectors and areas was to be provided mainly by the network of commercial banks, with only a marginal role for the state budgets at various levels.

Yugoslavian market socialism aroused considerable interest and gave fresh impetus to theoretical debates, for example, to confrontations of this concept with the 'Lange–Lerner solution' (Bergson, 1967). The behaviour of Yugoslav-type labour-managed firms was equated with (or held sufficiently similar to) cooperatives maximizing net income per member. Using assumptions of perfect competition, several authors beginning with Ward (1958) argued that a labour-managed firm pursuing its objective function will tend to settle for a lower level of output and employment, and higher capital intensity, than would a capitalist firm in analogous conditions, and that it will even display a 'perverse' price-elasticity of supply (diminishing output and employment when the price of the product rises, and vice versa). Most of these peculiarities disappear however when imperfections of the market are taken into account. The labour-managed firm will try then to establish a maximum price (depending on the conditions of entry), and vary its output according to the movement of demand at that price, that is, in a 'normal' way (Lydall, 1984).

Nevertheless, empirical evidence suggests that the attempt to combine market mechanism with self-management of the Yugoslavian kind generates problems unknown either to capitalist market economy or to full-fledged cooperatives operating in a market environment. They stem mostly from the fact that the workers' share in the enterprises' results is not based on any form of personal property rights, which they may carry with them, but exclusively on employment; upon termination of employment their stake disappears. This affects attitudes toward the distribution of returns between current personal incomes (for consumption or private savings), and collective investment; in particular, older workers and those without prospects or willingness to stay on the job will have a low propensity to invest out of the enterprise's income. The self-management organization of the economy also presents problems with regard to investment in other existing enterprises (there can be no sharing in profits), or in establishing new firms, especially in other sectors and regions (such firms become, as a rule, independent self-managing units). Absence of capital markets in which firms might participate directly puts even greater pressure on the banking system as a substitute. In the post-1965 period the banks were expected to establish themselves as fully fledged financial intermediaries, but the actual position proved rather disappointing, for reasons related at least to some extent to the specific features of the Yugoslav political system.

The one-party state used its power to impose a variety of formal and informal controls, for example through the so-called self-management compacts. Decentralization of state functions substantially enhanced the power of local organizations (particularly at the level of national republics and autonomous regions) which led to strong autarkic tendencies that not only had a disruptive effect on the unity of the national market, but also made it easier to overrule the commercial principles of operation (e.g. of the banks) by politico-administrative interference. This adversely affected the conditions of competition, especially as perennial balance of payments constraints frustrated the hopes of bringing competitive pressure from outside. At the same time, difficulties in promoting active participation in self-management of the workforces of large organizations gave rise to the so-called 'basic organizations of associated labour' (BOAL) – autonomous decisional and accounting units which may correspond to entire small or medium enterprises but form only self-contained parts of a large one. Excessive fragmentation resulted in some cases, especially as links between workers' income and performance on a BOAL scale led to differences in remuneration for the same kind of work. In general, incentives linked to performance, particularly under imperfect markets, engendered problems that had been largely overlooked in Lange's model. This had assumed not only the viability of simulating perfect competition but also the existence of a motivational structure capable of inducing economic actors to observe fully the Board's rules, without any individual material stimulation beyond compensation of disutilities (the implicit interest in increasing the social dividend belongs to a different category of incentives). The scale and direction of change in income differentials – inter-enterprise, inter-sectorial, inter-regional – became a major issue not only in the Yugoslavian case but also in overall analysis of market socialism in comparison with both contemporary capitalist market economies and command systems.

For a considerable time Yugoslavian market socialism proved capable of combining fast growth with significant welfare gains that were unmarred by the shortages and glaring maladjustments so characteristic of command systems. However, the end of the 1970s and the beginning of the 1980s brought substantial deterioration in this respect (slowdown of growth, high unemployment, accelerated inflation, fall in real earnings), which prompted renewed scrutiny of the effectiveness of the Yugoslavian model. In Yugoslavia itself the principle of self-management was not subjected to open debate, although the question of property rights was raised again (Bajt, 1982), and the role of political factors was quite widely recognized. With regard to the plan–market relationship, the predominant view seemed to be that the market had actually not been given a true chance, but accusations that excessive 'marketization' had precluded effective macroeconomic planning were also made (Mihailovič, 1982).

THE HUNGARIAN REFORMS. From the mid-1950s pressure to extend the role of the market began to manifest itself in countries belonging to the Council for Mutual Economic Assistance (CMEA), including the Soviet Union; towards the end of the 1970s a similar tendency appeared strongly in China. The reasons were basically economic – dissatisfaction with the performance of the economy under command systems, although in several cases (Hungary before the 1956 revolution, Poland in 1956–7 and again in 1980–81, Czechoslovakia in 1968) the presumed linkages between marketization of the economy and pluralization of the polity played an important part. Economic reforms – as the blueprints of the attempted changes came to be called – failed in most of the CMEA countries, or were reduced to rather secondary modifications within the framework of the command system. The failure was usually explained in academic literature by political resistance of the ruling elites, vested interests of the administrative state – and party – apparatus, coupled with reluctance on the part of the rank-and-file and managers to trade-off security for stronger incentives linked to efficiency. Difficulties of substance in devising and implementing a sufficiently consistent reform were mentioned less frequently, but they were certainly important and interacted with all other factors. By the mid-1980s among the CMEA countries only Hungary, where the 'new economic mechanism' (NEM) was introduced in 1968, could be regarded as actually outside the confines of command systems – despite the fact that the idea of market-oriented economic reforms kept returning in one form or another in most of the countries of the Soviet bloc, especially in response to crises. In 1981, during the existence of the independent trade union Solidarity, a wide ranging design of self-managed market socialism was worked out in Poland. A much more circumscribed reform, introduced after the suppression of Solidarity, met with a number of difficulties of both economic and political nature. China, having successfully revived the market mechanism in agriculture, embarked in 1984 upon a major programme of economic reform in industry and trade.

Conceptually, the Hungarian 'new economic mechanism' of 1968 is distinct from the Yugoslav market socialism, not only in leaving out self-management, but also in having a different relationship between the plan and the market. The principle of central planning is upheld, while the methods of realization are changed, with the market assigned an active role not only in relations between the state and the households (where the restrictions appearing in the practice of command systems are consistently removed), but also within the state production sector itself. Obligatory output targets for enterprises are abolished, as are physical allocations of production goods from the centre. Thus, enterprises are freed from hierarchical administrative commands and exposed to market-type self-regulatory mechanisms in their current operations, with profit as the main criterion and source both of incentives for the workforce (wage rises dependent on financial viability plus profit-sharing fund for bonuses) and of self-finance for autonomous investment. Prices, both in the consumption and production spheres, are meant to clear the market; but only some prices are allowed to fluctuate freely, and the most 'important' are fixed by state bodies, with other prices moving only within an established range. Isolation of internal from external markets is also lifted, again with substantial indirect controls retained. Thus, the question of incentives apart, the 'new economic mechanism' as a model meets the Lange–Lerner requirement for the 'trial and error' procedure of establishing prices of production goods. Where it falls short of the Lange–Lerner solution is in the investment sphere: not only the rate of accumulation, but also the allocation of the *main bulk* of investment funds among sectors, areas and large individual projects is determined directly by the Board, whereas equilibrating supply of and demand for capital through appropriate variation of the interest rate takes a secondary place (only with regard to crediting enterprises' autonomous investment, which is considered secondary).

The capacity of the Board to harmonize economic activity on a micro-level with the general provisions of the plan is therefore supposed to rest on: (i) the macroeconomic framework created by the Board's fundamental decisions concerning distribution of national income (including principles of remuneration) and investment allocation; (ii) determination of 'rules of behaviour' for enterprises (success criteria and their incentive consequences) in such a way as to direct local interests onto a path convergent to general interests; (iii) fiscal, monetary and price policies which would effectively support (i) and (ii), in the first place by securing the parametric character of the 'indices of available alternatives' (Lange, 1936–7), viz: prices, wages, interest and tax rates. The primacy of the plan so conceived means not only abandonment of direct forms of control, but elimination of central control as such over many aspects of economic activity (recognition of broad 'zones of indifference' as far as planners' preferences are concerned). The interaction between an effective central plan and a market mechanism which requires enterprises to adjust to general rules and conditions makes the model of *central planning with regulated market mechanism* (Brus, 1961) an approximately adequate description of the concept of the 'new economic mechanism'.

These economic reforms were introduced in Hungary under mixed political circumstances. On the one hand, the party leadership became firmly committed to them, although the opposition was strong enough to force partial retreat from the principles of the reforms in the period 1973–8. On the other hand, the Soviet bloc offensive against the Czechoslovakian reforms of 1968 was an important adverse factor, among other things because it contributed to the abandonment of economic reforms elsewhere, leaving Hungary an exception within CMEA. The operation of the new economic mechanism was clearly affected by this, as Hungary had to adjust accordingly the management of her relations with other member-countries (particularly with the USSR), and with the CMEA as a whole. All this diminished the capacity of the new mechanism to respond to the deteriorating external conditions caused by the oil shocks of the 1970s and the Western recession. Hungary, poorly endowed in fuel and raw materials and at the same time highly dependent on foreign trade, was the worst hit country in Eastern Europe by the fall in the terms of trade, and the growing difficulties of exporting to the West.

Under the circumstances the performance of the Hungarian economy in the 1970s could be judged as relatively favourable, particularly in maintaining equilibrium on the domestic market. This was due in the first place to the successful development of genuinely cooperative activity combined with private initiative in agriculture, where the provisions of the reforms produced the greatest advantage. With a rather broad consensus of opinion both among the political leaders and professional economists, the inconsistencies and retreats in implementation of the new economic mechanism began to be corrected at the end of the 1970s.

The most pertinent question however was whether, or to what extent, the failure of the systemic changes to live up to expectations was due to deviations from the 1968 blueprint, or to deficiencies in the blueprint itself. Special significance was attached to the search for reasons why, instead of applying the general rules and rigours of the market to state enterprises, the widespread practice was to tailor financial norms in such a way as to keep every enterprise afloat (cooperative enterprises were treated differently). This phenomenon, which replaced the former bargaining with the higher authorities over output targets and input allocations by new forms of bargaining over financial conditions, was noticed in the early stages of the reforms and attributed to the ideologically motivated microeconomic job-security commitment (Granick, 1975). However, the Hungarian debates at the beginning of the 1980s linked this also with the limitations on the investment activity of enterprises that was imposed by the principle of earmarking the main bulk of investment decisions for the central planner. An enterprise unsuccessful in its given line of business has only a very limited prospect on its own for restructuring or branching out if substantial capital outlays are involved, and this often narrows down the range of options to the stark choice between complete closure and subsidization, the latter course being that almost invariably taken.

Apart from the obvious softening of the 'budget constraint', with all ensuing consequences for the maintenance of pressure for efficiency in enterprises, and for distortions in market relations, this increased the enterprises' dependence on their administrative supervisors. In conjunction with criticism of the poor quality of many investment decisions taken by the centre (particularly when genuine *political* control is missing for lack of pluralism), this line of analysis convinced a substantial body of opinion in Hungary of the necessity to go beyond the product market (and the labour market in its existing form) to the creation of a *capital market*. Suggestions considered in Hungary in the first half of the 1980s envisaged a gradual and cautious movement along these lines, with a substantial part of investment ('infrastructural') still in the hands of the centre, and careful control over institutions of financial intermediation (commercially acting banks in the first place, but also direct issuance of bonds, and even equity shares in prospect). Nevertheless, the debates pointed clearly away from the mixed model of central planning cum regulated market mechanism, towards full-fledged market socialism, in which allocation of capital is accomplished through market instruments, with the rate of interest equilibrating supply and demand, as in Lange–Lerner. In similar vein, the *labour market* should provide the means to arrive at the equilibrium level of wages through the process of bargaining between management and the workforce; the latter – lacking the countervailing power of independent trade unions – would be able to make use of widely opened job-opportunities outside the state sector ('second economy') as a market instrument of pressure.

CONCLUSIONS. Thus, the evolution of both the Yugoslav self-management system and of the Hungarian economic reforms brings back on the agenda most of the problems debated theoretically in connection with the Lange–Lerner model of market socialism. Assuming that institutionalization of the capital market proves feasible in the framework of predominantly public ownership, the old question arises again of whether such a market, even with the help of fiscal and monetary tools of state intervention, is capable of securing continuously a macroeconomic level of demand appropriate for sustained economic growth with full employment, a goal that is regarded as an essential feature of socialism. Moreover, as any realistic concept of market socialism has to include incentives that are in some way linked to performance, capital markets and labour markets of the type referred to above must strongly affect the pattern of income distribution and of wealth as well. However, the assumption of the compatibility of capital markets with public ownership cannot be taken for granted, not only in view of the theoretical reasons advanced in the past, but to a considerable degree in the light of the practical experience of communist countries, where few instances of the relative success of fledgling capital markets can be found exclusively outside the state sector, whereas attempts to use them within that sector (e.g. the Yugoslav 'social sector') largely proved a failure. The effort to re-examine in principle the position of public ownership in close connection with the postulated enhancement of the role of the market (Tardos, 1982), and particularly the search for institutional solutions which would effectively cut the umbilical cord linking public enterprises with state administration, may also be regarded as indicators that these are topical issues. On the other hand, by the mid-1980s there were no signs of any of the communist countries moving in the direction of pluralization of the political system, which was regarded by some as providing a chance by which to reconcile central planning with the market mechanism (Brus, 1975).

In the last quarter of the 20th century market socialism remains an active issue not only in the context of economic reform in communist countries, but also in the broader context of reappraisal of the validity of the socialist idea in general, faced with the growing challenge of new realities and new attitudes (Nove, 1983).

BIBLIOGRAPHY

Bajt, A. 1982. O nekim otvorenim pitanjima drustvene svojine (On some open questions of social property). *Pregled* 72(11–12), 1345–80.

Baran, P. 1952. National economic planning, Part 3, Planning under socialism. In *A Survey of Contemporary Economics*, Vol. 2, ed. V.B. Haley, Homewood, Ill.: R.D. Irwin.

Barone, E. 1908. Il Ministerio della Produzione nello stato collectivista (Ministry of Production in a Collectivist State). Trans. in *Collectivist Economic Planning*, ed. F.A. Hayek, London: George Routledge & Sons, 1935, 245–90.

Bergson, A. 1967. Market socialism revisited. *Journal of Political Economy* 75(5), October, 655–73.

Brus, W. 1961. Ogólne problemy funkcjonowania gospodarki socjalistycznej (General problems of functioning of a socialist economy). Trans. in *The Market in a Socialist Economy*, ed. A. Walker, London: Routledge & Kegan Paul, 1972.

Brus, W. 1975. *Socialist Ownership and Political Systems*. London and Boston: Routledge & Kegan Paul.

Communist International. 1929. *Programme of the Communist International*. London.

Dickinson, H.D. 1933. Price formation in a socialist community. *Economic Journal* 43, June, 237–50.

Dobb, M. 1939. A note on savings and investment in a socialist economy. *Economic Journal* 49, December, 713–28.

Erlich, A. 1960. *The Soviet Industrialization Debate*. Cambridge, Mass.: Harvard University Press.

Granick, D. 1975. *Enterprise Guidance in Eastern Europe. A Comparison of Four Socialist Economies*. Princeton: Princeton University Press.

Hayek, F.A. (ed.) 1935. *Collectivist Economic Planning*. London: George Routledge & Sons; New York: A.M. Kelley, 1967.

Hayek, F.A. 1940. Socialist calculation: the competitive solution. *Economica* 7(26), May, 125–49.

Heimann, E. 1932. *Sozialistische Wirtschafts- und Arbeitsordnung*. Potsdam: A. Protte.

Kautsky, K. 1922. *Die proletarische Revolution und ihr Programm*. Stuttgart: I.H.W. Dietz Nachfolger; Berlin: Buchhandlung Vorwärts.

Kornai, J. 1980. *Economics of Shortage*. Amsterdam, New York and Oxford: North-Holland.

Landauer, C. 1931. *Planwirtschaft und Verkehrswirtschaft* (Planned economy and exchange economy). Munich and Leipzig: Duncker & Humboldt.

Lange, O. 1936–7. On the economic theory of socialism. In O. Lange and F. Taylor, *On the Economic Theory of Socialism*, ed. B. Lippincott, Minneapolis: University of Minnesota Press, 1948.

Lange, O. 1947. Przedmowa do polskiego wydania (Preface to the Polish edition). In *Dzieta* (Collected Works), Vol. II, Warsaw: Państwowe Wydawnictwo Ekonomiczne, 1973.

Lange, O. 1965. The computer and the market. In *Socialism, Capitalism and Economic Growth. Essays Presented to Maurice Dobb*, ed. C. Feinstein, Cambridge: Cambridge University Press, 1967.

Lerner, A. 1934. Economic theory and socialist economy. *Review of Economic Studies* 2, 51–61.

Lerner, A. 1936. A note on socialist economics. *Review of Economic Studies* 4, 72–6.

Lerner, A. 1937. Statics and dynamics in socialist economics. *Economic Journal* 47, 253–70.

Ljubljana Programme. 1958. *Program Saveza Komunista Jugoslavije* (The programme of the League of Communists of Yugoslavia). Belgrade.

Lydall, H. 1984. *Yugoslav Socialism. Theory and Practice*. Oxford: Clarendon Press.

Marx, K. 1867. *Capital*. Vol. I, London: Progress, 1970.

Mihailovič, K. 1982. *Ekonomiska stvarnost Jugoslavije* (The economic reality of Yugoslavia). Belgrade.

Mises, L. von. 1920. Die Wirtschaftsrechnung im sozialistischen Gemeinwesen. In *Collectivist Economic Planning*, ed. F.A. Hayek, London: George Routledge & Sons, 1935; New York: A.M. Kelley, 1967.

Nove, A. 1983. *The Economics of Feasible Socialism*. London: George Allen & Unwin.

Schumpeter, J.A. 1942. *Capitalism, Socialism and Democracy*. 5th edn, London: George Allen & Unwin, 1976.

Tardos, M. 1982. Development program for economic control and organization in Hungary. *Acta Oeconomica* 28(3–4), 295–316.

Taylor, F. 1929. The guidance of production in a socialist state. In O. Lange and F. Taylor, *On the Economic Theory of Socialism*, ed. B. Lippincott, Minneapolis: University of Minnesota Press, 1948.

Ward, B. 1958. The firm in Illyria. *American Economic Review* 48(4), September, 566–89.

Wiles, P. 1969. *Communist International Economics*. Oxford: Basil Blackwell; New York: Praeger, 1969.

Material Balances

GREGORY GROSSMAN

A material balance is a simple planning device developed (if not originated) early in Soviet planning for the purpose of equating prospective availabilities of a given good and its prospective requirements over the plan period (or at some target date in case of a stock). It occupies a central role in Soviet-type planning. The phrase, a literal rendering of the Russian *material'nyi balans*, is somewhat inexact and possibly confusing inasmuch as each of the two words has a variety of meanings in English. A more exact term would be 'sources-and-uses account' for a flow or 'balance sheet' for a stock. As such, material balances have counterparts in planning and management the world over.

In Soviet-type planning, a material balance is typically constructed *ex ante*. It can pertain to any good or resource requiring planners' attention or administrative disposition; thus, 'balances' are drawn up not only for material products, but also for labour, capacity, foreign exchange, etc. While it can be drawn up at any level of the hierarchy of a command economy and by any relevant organizational entity, these alternatives carry important economic, bureaucratic, and even political implications in a Soviet-type economy. 'In the course of preparing the annual plan . . . the USSR State Planning Commission draws up [some] 2,000 single-product balances, the State Commission for Supply – up to 15,000, and the ministries – up to 50,000' (*EKO*, August, 1983, p. 26). Though there may be some duplication in terms of goods between these figures, they nonetheless do suggest the magnitude of the annual task, especially if one bears in mind the interconnections.

In Soviet-type practice a material balance not only has the passive purpose of checking requirements against availabilities, but forms the operational basis for specific production or import directives to designated organizations and firms, and for specific acquisition permits to designated users of the good. Note that nearly all producer goods are administratively allocated (rationed) to users.

A material balance may take the following form (adapted from Levine, 1959):

Table 1 Material balance for good X for (year)

Sources	Uses (distribution)
1. Current production – by major producing organizations, firms	1. For production – by organizations, firms
2. Imports	2. For construction – by organizations, firms
3. Other sources	3. For household sector ('market fund')
4. Beginning-year stocks – by organizations	4. For export
5. Total sources	5. To central reserve stocks
	6. End-year stocks at suppliers – by organizations, firms
	7. Total uses (distribution)

Two kinds of questions arise: (a) operational – how is the balance initially compiled and 'balanced', and later adjusted for outside effects (from other balances) and the extent to which successive iterations are required to converge? (b) policy – the bounds and degree of aggregation of a 'good', the organizational locus and level of compilation, etc.?

Little is known about the initial compilation. There must be serious problems of the requisite detailed information in the case of many goods, given that the preparation of the annual plan extends over most of the pre-plan year (and often into the plan year). Thus, the database may anticipate the plan year by one-and-a-half to two years whose projection is obviously subject to uncertainty. A common problem is the uncertainty of going-on-stream of capacity under construction. Also, the data may not be very accurate to start with, given the cat-and-mouse game that firms and other subordinates play with their superiors. What is more, the thousands of balances are being drawn up simultaneously, often by different organizations or subdivisions, with the obvious difficulty of mutual coordination.

The 'balancer' must take into account – in addition to technical parameters – political and other high-level decisions, existing economic programmes, bureaucratic politics, and the usual pressure to squeeze more out of the economy's resources. Corruption is not unknown. The work is largely done manually and inevitably to some extent subjectively. While computers are beginning to be used, the input–output techniques – which in principle is eminently suitable for the purpose – seems to be applied for the grosser computations and checks, not for the drawing up of operational, short-term material balances. The main reasons are that the sectors in even the largest matrices are too aggregative for the material balances, and the data underlying the technical coefficients are not current enough.

Among the balancer's technical parameters, pride of place is occupied by the 'norm' – a disaggregated input–output ratio, which assists the compiler in filling in parts of both sides of the account. Much effort goes into computation of the norms, given their crucial role in the preparation of plans and the issuing of specific assignments. They are supposed to be 'scientific', i.e. representing the best applicable engineering practice (note: for technical rather than economic efficiency), but given their enormous number and informational problems, this remains an ideal. In the event, the balancer must employ short-cuts and resort to optimistic assumptions in order to achieve equality of requirements and availabilities while under pressure to deliver high ('taut') production targets. A common and much criticized short-cut is simply to raise output targets of all producers by a uniform percentage, with corresponding adjustments of the norms.

The weakest link in the material balance method is coordination among the many balances to achieve a reasonably internally consistent plan for the whole economy or a sector thereof. (Montias, 1959, discusses this at length.) Even if the implicit inter-industry matrix is close to triangular, every iteration is a major undertaking under the actual conditions. Aggregating the goods would simplify the iteration process, but would not suit well the demands posed by detailed production assignments and allocation orders. So would the holding of ample reserve stocks, which are not always there or accessible. In fact, adjustments and corrections tend ordinarily to be carried to only a few adjoining balances.

The overall annual plan that emerges is typically of low internal consistency (not to say, economic efficiency), causing considerable difficulties to those charged with its implementation and necessitating continual further correction and adjustment during the plan year, with the same effect.

BIBLIOGRAPHY

Levine, H.S. 1959. The centralized planning of supply in Soviet industry. U.S. Congress, Joint Economic Committee, *Comparison of the United States and Soviet Economies* I, Washington, DC.

Montias, J.M. 1959. Planning with material balances in Soviet-type economies. *American Economic Review* 49, December, 963–85.

Vasily Sergeevich Nemchinov

M.C. KASER

Born the son of a State Bank messenger in Grabovo, Russia, on 2 January 1894, Nemchinov graduated from the Moscow Commercial Institute between the February and October Revolutions of 1917, but joined the Communist Party only in 1940 on appointment as Director of the K.A. Timiryazev Agricultural Institute, the Statistics Faculty of which he had headed since 1928. He showed courage in prohibiting from his Institute the pseudo-genetics ('Michurinism') of T.D. Lysenko, but when at Stalin's instigation mainstream genetics were condemned in 1948 he was forced from the directorship. The Academy of Sciences (to which he had been elected in 1946) then made him chairman of its Council for the Study of Productive Resources, a post retained (with a chair at the party's Academy of Social Sciences) until his fatal illness. In 1958 he established the first group in the USSR to study mathematical economics (from 1963 the Central Economic Mathematical Institute) and was posthumously awarded a Lenin Prize for elaborating linear programming and economic modelling for the USSR. He died in Moscow on 5 November 1964.

The research embodied in Nemchinov (1926) and (1928) was distorted to justify Stalin's coercion of the peasantry: his data on rural social stratification gave cover to 'liquidation of the kulaks as a class' (though Nemchinov had avoided the term 'kulak'); his measurement of absolute gross harvest (Nemchinov, 1932) was used to extort deliveries from collective farms. As soon as Stalin died, Nemchinov campaigned for the publication of official statistics and for more sophisticated techniques to utilize them – cybernetics had been damned as a pseudo-science serving capitalist interests. His organization of experimental national and regional input–output tables led him to question the meaningfulness of administered pricing, and his last book (1962) sought, as his widow put it (Nemchinova, 1985, pp. 202–21), 'a broad-based system of social valuations . . . as a single, internally consistent set of values'.

SELECTED WORKS

1926. O statisticheskom izuchenii klassovogo rassloenniya derevni (On the statistical study of rural class stratification). *Bulleten' Ural'skogo oblastnogo statisticheskogo upravleniya* (Bulletin of the Urals Regional Statistical Administration) 1. Reprinted in *Selected Works*, Vol. 1, 44–62.

1928. Opyt klassifikatsii krest'yanskikh khozyaistvo (Experience from the classification of peasant households). *Vestnik statistiki* (Statistical bulletin) 1. Reprinted in *Selected Works*, Vol. 1, 85–120.

1932. Vyborochnye izmereniya urozhainosti (Sampling measurement of yields). *Narodnoe khozyaistvo SSSR* (National economy of the USSR) 5–6. Reprinted in *Selected Works*, Vol. 1, 128–60.

1962. *Ekonomiko-matematicheskie metody i modeli* (Methods and models of mathematical economics). Moscow: Sotsegiz. 2nd (posthumous) edn, 1965. Reprinted in *Selected Works*, Vol. 3, 138–476.

1967–9. *Izbrannye proizvedeniya* (Selected Works). 6 vols, Moscow: Izdatel'stvo Nauka.

BIBLIOGRAPHY

Nemchinova, M.B. 1985. The scientific work of Vasily Sergeevich Nemchinov (on the 90th anniversary of his birth). *Matekon. Translations of Russian and East European Mathematical Economics* 21(2), Winter, 1984–5, 3–25; translation of an article in *Ekonomika i matematicheskie metody* (Economics and mathematical methods) 20(1), 1984.

Viktor Valentinovich Novozhilov

HOLLAND HUNTER AND ROBERT W. CAMPBELL

Novozhilov was born in Khar'kov in 1892, and died in Leningrad in 1970. He was instrumental, along with the mathematician Leonid Vital'evich Kantorovich, in reviving a mathematical approach to economic theory in the USSR after Stalin's death, and in laying a basis for a modern theory of value and allocation.

Educated at Kiev University before the revolution, Novozhilov taught at several institutions in the Ukraine, but from 1922 lives in Leningrad, teaching and working in research institutes. From 1935 he taught at the Leningrad Polytechnical Institute, and from 1944 until 1952 was also professor and head of the Department of Statistics at the Leningrad Engineering-Economics Institute. His work with project-making institutes involved Novozhilov in the issue of capital intensity choices, which became the basis for his doctoral dissertation. In illuminating the question of effective allocation of capital among competing projects, he developed a more general theory for allocation of all resources, the centrepiece of which was the concept of 'inversely related expenditures' (*zatraty obratnoi sviazi*) equivalent to opportunity cost. His analytic framework was dynamic, incorporating capital allocation over time, as well as the impact of depreciation and obsolescence.

His original and elegant theoretical ideas were presented in papers published in 1939, 1941, 1946 and 1947 that were largely ignored. The most comprehensive exposition of Novozhilov's ideas is a book he was finally able to publish in 1967, which illustrates his ideas on investment choices and the time factor in economics, places his innovative approach in its doctrinal context, and defends it against domestic and foreign critics. His economic theory is expounded within the limits of political orthodoxy. Novozhilov took the structure of demand as given (by the Party), which enabled him to spell out resource-allocating criteria for the Soviet economy very similar to those familiar in the West, except that with the demand blade of the scissors held fixed, only the supply side cut the paper. By casting the resource allocation problem in terms of minimizing labour input (direct and indirect) he sought to preserve Marx's labour theory of value. Both his contribution and the absence of an explanation of demand were soon recognized abroad (see Grossman, 1953; Campbell, 1961).

In the mid-1950s, when V.S. Nemchinov organized a revival of serious economic analysis in the USSR, Novozhilov, along with Kantorovich, was a central figure in training a new generation of economists. The three men were awarded Lenin Prizes in 1965. As a result of the pioneering work of Novozhilov and Kantorovich, the basis for a correct and comprehensive theory of value has already been to hand for four decades. If Soviet reformers now want analytic guidance, they can draw most of their basic theory from Kantorovich, and get useful ideas from Novozhilov as well.

Additional biographic and bibliographic details, and interpretations of Novozhilov's work may be found in Campbell (1961), Ellman (1973), Grossman (1953), Holubnychy (1982), and Petrakov (1972).

SELECTED WORKS

1939. Metody soizmereniia narodnokhoziaistvennoi effektivnosti planovykh i proektnykh variantov (Methods of co-measuring the economic effectiveness of variants in planning and project-making). *Trudy Leningradskogo industrial'nogo instituta* (Papers of the Leningrad Industrial Institute), No. 4.

1941a. Metody izmereniia narodnokhoziaistvennoi effektivnosti proektnykh variantov (Methods of measuring the national economic effectiveness of project variants). Dissertation for the doctoral degree, awarded in 1941.

1941b. Praktikuemye metody soizmereniia sebestoimosti i vlozhenii (Methods used in practice for co-measuring current outlays and investments). *Trudy Leningradskogo politekhnicheskogo instituta* (Papers of the Leningrad Polytechnical Institute), Leningrad, No. 1.

1946. Metody nakhozhdeniia minimuma zatrat v sotsialisticheskom khoziaistve (Methods of finding the minimum expenditure in a socialist economy). *Leningradskii politekhnicheskii institut imeni M.I. Kalinina*: *Trudy* (The Leningrad Kalinin Polytechnical Institute, Papers), No. 1.

1947. Sposoby nakhozhdeniia maksimuma effekta kapitalovlozhenii v sotsialisticheskom khoziaistve (Methods for finding the maximum effect of capital investments in the socialist economy). *Trudy Leningradskogo finansovo-ekonomicheskogo instituta* (Papers of the Leningrad Financial Economic Institute), Vypusk III (Issue 3).

1967, 1972. *Problemy izmereniia zatrat i rezul'tatov pri optimal'nom planirovanii* (Problems of Cost-Benefit Analysis in Optimal planning). Moscow, 1967. 2nd edn, 1972. Trans. (with title as shown), White Plains, New York: International Arts and Sciences Press, 1970.

1972. *Voprosy razvitiia sotsialisticheskoi ekonomiki* (Questions of the development of socialist economics). Moscow.

BIBLIOGRAPHY

Campbell, R.W. 1961. Marx, Kantorovich, and Novozhilov: Stoimost' versus reality. *Slavic Review* 20(3), October, 402–18.

Ellman, M. 1973. *Planning Problems in the USSR; The Contribution of Mathematical Methods to Their Solution, 1961–1971.* Cambridge and New York: Cambridge University Press.

Grossman, G. 1953. Scarce capital and Soviet doctrine. *Quarterly Journal of Economics* 67, August, 311–43.

Holubnychy, V. 1982. V.V. Novozhilov's theory of value. In *Soviet Regional Economics: Selected Works of Vsevolod Holubnychy*, ed. I.S. Koropeckyj, Edmonton: Canadian Institute of Ukrainian Studies, University of Alberta.

Petrakov, N.I. 1972. Nauchnaia i pedagogicheskaia deiatel'nost' V.V. Novozhilova (The scientific and pedagogical work of V.V. Novozhilov). In Novozhilov (1972).

Planned Economy

ALEC NOVE

'Planning; planned: Intended, in accordance with, or achieved by, a careful plan made beforehand'. This is the Chambers Dictionary definition. Of course in this sense we all plan, whenever we think carefully of what we might do in the future. All economic decision-making relates to the future, since all transactions take time, and in the course of time some circumstances might have changed, and so plans are frequently unfulfilled, or have results different from the original intention.

However, we will have in mind here the deliberate actions of *public* authorities, primarily the state, while referring from time to time also to plans made in the private sector. Plans can be of many kinds. The Soviet version is *'directive* planning' or command planning. The authorities issue binding instructions to subordinate management, telling it what goods and services to provide, from whom to obtain the required inputs, and, as we shall see, much else besides. Then there is *indicative* planning, when the state uses influence, subsidies, grants, taxes, but does not compel. There is also *sectoral* planning, which concerns, for instance, a road network, urban rapid-transit, the coal industry, the national health service. This need not be related to any overall plan for the economy as a whole.

Then there are differences in purpose, reason, objectives. One is to impose the centre's priorities, to replace or combat spontaneous market forces, i.e. deliberately to achieve what would not otherwise occur. This applies most evidently to a war economy, but also to Stalin's economic strategy of the Thirties, with its mass mobilization of material and human resources to create a heavy-industrial base in the shortest possible time. On a less drastic scale these considerations also apply to programmes of rapid development in some Third-World countries, that is, to conscious attempts to transform a country's political economy. In such cases the market is seen as an enemy, to be limited or combated (as in Preobrazhensky's phrase about the battle between 'primitive socialist accumulation and the law of value'), and the same was at least partly true in war economies in the West: prices were fixed, materials allocated, free-market deals in controlled commodities were treated as black-market criminal offences.

However, other kinds of public-sector planning have, or need have, no such hostility to the market, can and do coexist with it. The motive to plan them relates partly to what may be called public goods (e.g. the road network, street lighting, rubbish collection), and partly to externality-generating sectors, where the profit-and-loss account of the enterprises concerned constitutes a misleading criterion even on narrowly economic grounds, and/or where private and the more general interests conflict. Examples are many: thus urban public transport, docks, airports, are in the public sector even in the United States. Environmental protection is another important factor: thus in a number of countries deforestation threatens ecological disaster, while in the North Sea it is essential to act to preserve fish stocks, while short-term private profit dictates the cutting of trees and overfishing respectively. There are also natural monopolies, where competition is unnecessary or wasteful: electricity, water, posts, until recently also telephones, are examples; the choice here lies between a regulated private monopoly and state ownership and control. The choice may be influenced also by considerations of public policy. Thus if it is desired to provide a comprehensive postal or telephone service, to supply all houses with pure water, and even remote Scottish islands with electricity, then clearly the public-service aspects must be given some priority: it has always been evident that some of the above activities cannot be profitable.

Some confusion is engendered by the inability to distinguish between *responsibility* for provision of a good or service and the way in which it is provided. Thus, to cite some examples, the public authorities must ensure that city rubbish is collected and disposed of, but this no more requires the rubbish collectors to be public employees than responsibility for road-building requires those who build the roads to be civil servants!

Then there are sectors to which economic profitability considerations may be held not to apply at all: education, health, pensions, are widely held to be the proper subject of planning and provision by public authorities.

Finally, there is the species of planning designed to facilitate and encourage the operation of market-orientated private enterprise. This ranges from infrastructural investment to what is usually called indicative planning, which is not compulsory or imposed, but which helps to fill a most evident gap in the pure free-market doctrine, which is concerned with large-scale investment. Long ago G.B. Richardson (1960) pointed out that, on the assumptions of perfect competition and perfect markets, it is hard to imagine how or why investment should take place, since the profitable opportunity is, by definition, equally visible to all the competitors. Therefore imperfect knowledge and/or collusion, neither of which is in the model, are preconditions for investment. The important role of the state in the success of the South Korean and Japanese export-orientated strategies is inexcusably ignored by the *laissez-faire* ideologists, who can see the success and attribute it wholly to free-market entrepreneurship. Planning of this sort, reinforced by unofficial pressures and fiscal incentives, could be described as a form of state-organized collusion. In addition there is the role of the state in ensuring macro-balance, or taking counter-cyclical action, which used to be accepted quasi-universally as necessary, though this is now vigorously questioned by the revived *laissez-faire* school, which considers that the economy is basically self-righting.

So only in one of its versions is planning to be seen as in inherent contradiction with the market; in all the others they supplement each other, or plans are actually made operational *through* the market.

SOCIALIST PLANNING. Socialist planning has a long history. Generations of socialist thinkers, including Marx and his followers, contrasted the deliberate planning that would occur under socialism with the 'anarchy' of capitalism, in which production was for profit, not for use. The 'associated producers' would join together to discuss what is needed and how best it could be provided. As Engels put it, they would compare the useful effect of products with the time necessary to produce them.

Some, for example Kautsky and Lenin, saw a socialist society of the future as if it were one giant enterprise, a single all-embracing factory or office. There would be no 'commodity production', that is, production will be for use, not for exchange. Labour would, when applied, be 'directly social', that is, its use will be validated not *ex post*, through the market, but *ex ante*, by the all-embracing plan, which will express society's needs. Costs would be measured in terms of what was seen as the one ultimately scarce resource, human effort.

Critics, such as Barone and L. von Mises, pointed out some major weaknesses in this approach to socialist planning: the number of calculations required would be enormous, the economic criteria for decision-making would be lacking without meaningful prices. Yet, with but few exceptions, socialists in the marxist tradition persisted in their belief that such planning would be 'simple and transparent' (Marx), that 'everything would be simple without the so-called value' (Engels); 'capitalism had so simplified the task of accounting and control ... that any literate person can do it' (Lenin), 'The society of the future will do what is called for by simple statistical data' (Bukharin).

Planning in practice proved to be very complicated indeed. It must be emphasized that it did serve its purpose when that purpose was analogous to that of a war economy: to concentrate resources for the priority objectives determined by the central political authority. When the war did break out, the USSR's survival, after initial military disasters, was in no small degree made possible by the ruthlessly-imposed priority of military requirements. In Western countries too, though in lesser degree, central controls were tight, resources were allocated, and the resultant bureaucratic deformations had much in common with Soviet-type planning. Yet these must be seen as a cost, in the circumstances a necessary cost, of imposing the priorities of war. It was Lange who once likened the Soviet planning system to a war economy, *sui generis*.

In normal times, the priorities become more diffuse, also more numerous. The growth of the economy itself presents new problems and challenges. A Soviet scholar remarked that, if the size of the economy grows six-fold, the number of links to be planned grows to the square of that (or any other) number, i.e. 36-fold, and indeed this can be seen as one expands the number of items included in an input–output table.

The Soviet economy today contains several hundreds of thousands of enterprises, in mining, manufacturing, agriculture, construction, transport, distribution, catering, services. The large number is not due to their excessively small size. On the contrary, it has been argued that Soviet agricultural and industrial establishment are too large, certainly much larger than is the case on average in Western capitalism. Because neither production nor the supply of inputs is based on horizontal, market-type relations, each of these hundreds of thousands of enterprises needs to receive, from some unit in the planning hierarchy, specific instructions as to what to produce, what materials to obtain and from whom, while other plan targets relate to labour productivity, wages, costs, material utilization, investment, technical progress, fuel economy and much else besides. The number of identifiably different products and services, fully disaggregated, has been estimated as upwards of twelve million. The sheer scale of the task of the planners is probably *the* most important source of inefficiency and imbalance. Though Soviet experience shows that a planned economy of this type can function, this same experience strongly supports Barone's conclusion, arrived at in 1908, before there was any practical example to study: it would be difficult but not quite impossible to arrive at a 'technically' balanced plan, that is, one where the needed inputs match the intended output, but *quite* impossible to see how one could approach an *economic* optimum. Thus it is indeed very hard for those institutions responsible for material allocation to ensure that the needed inputs are provided, but they seldom have the practical possibility or the information to ensure that the inputs are those which are most economical.

This is but one of the difficulties attributable to the sheer scale of the required coordination between multi-million plan-instructions. Academician Fedorenko quipped that next year's plan, if fully checked and balanced, might be ready in approximately 30,000 years time.

It is necessary to distinguish between *long-term* and *current* planning. The long- (or medium) term plan looks forward to the end of a quinquennium, or in some instances as much as fifteen years; thus in 1985 some targets were published relating to the year 2000. These plans are necessarily highly aggregated, and contain broad objectives relating primarily to productive capacity (and so to investment), rather than to the product mix, which will be adapted to requirements which cannot be foreseen in advance in detail. A long-term plan must be balanced in an input–output sense, and planners proceed by so-called material balances for major products, ensuring that planned availability matches planned utilization. These plans are not yet operational, that is, they have no 'addressee': no specific enterprise is instructed to act. Or rather the addressee is the planning and administrative mechanism itself. It is true that there have been proposals, and even decisions, about the need to incorporate enterprises'

189

own quinquennial plans into this process, and indeed to make these plans stable and to relate various norms and incentives to them. However, this has not been possible in practice. Indeed, stable 'micro' plans for five years ahead are surely an impossibility, when even annual plans are notoriously unstable, being altered repeatedly during the period of their currency to cope with the unexpected or to correct errors belatedly identified.

The drafting of the relatively aggregated 'unaddressed' longer-term plans does not present an impossible task, there being only several hundred items. It is the operational annual plan, broken down by quarters and by months, which presents formidable problems. It is drafted in the last few months of the previous year. According to one Soviet source, output plans are made for about 48,000 products, which implies that on average each will contain about 250–300 sub-products or varieties. To go into greater detail would cause inordinate delay. But since each of the 48,000 requires numerous inputs, which must be provided through the allocation mechanism, and since every enterprise must receive specific plan-instructions relating to output and inputs, even in relatively aggregated form the burden on the planners is huge. The essential task of coordination is rendered the more complicated by the fact that responsibility is necessarily shared by numerous separate planning departments and economic ministries.

CENTRALIZED PLANNING. The centralized planning model is based upon the supposition that 'society' (i.e. in practice the planning agencies, under the authority of the political leadership) knows or can discover what is needed, and can issue orders incorporating these needs, while allocating the required means of production so that the needs are economically met. It is worth noting that in some sectors this supposition is close to reality. Thus electricity is a homogeneous product, power stations are interlinked into a grid, information on present and estimated future needs is best assessed at the centre, as it also is in many Western countries. The centre is also the obvious place for decision-making on armaments production. However, a very wide range of goods and services, both producers' goods and consumers' goods, are supplied in a wide variety of types, models, sizes, to serve specific needs. Choice of technique, decisions on new products, possible alternative uses of agricultural land, are matters on which the centre has little relevant information which could serve as a basis for micro-commands. Also it is an evident fact that management possesses vital information as to the production potential of the enterprise, and the planners must rely on an upward flow of proposals and suggestions if they are to issue the correct orders. 'Many if not most commands in a command economy are written by those who receive them', remarked a wise Hungarian, in conversation.

Devolution of authority is thus not only necessary, but inevitably occurs, since plans are frequently late, contradictory, aggregated, and their implementation requires much managerial ingenuity, which frequently has to stretch the boundaries of legality. But the system lacks any criterion for managerial decision-making other than the plan-targets to which management's bonuses and promotion prospects are related. Since prices do not, in either theory or practice, reflect supply-and-deman relationships, relative scarcities or demand intensity, profitability cannot serve as a rational criterion for micro decision-making. Furthermore, because of lack of time and imperfect knowledge, the planners are compelled to proceed on the basis of past performance, introducing the so-called ratchet effect: output targets in the next plan period will be a little higher, costs a little lower, than in the previous period, and indeed all concerned proceed on the assumption that no major changes in past supply or delivery arrangements are likely to occur. It is this which enables the system to function, but Soviet sources understandably criticize these methods, since they are not only conservative, but stimulate undesirable behaviour by management. The latter, judged by plan-fulfilment, seeks a plan easy to fulfil and avoids doing too well in case the following year's target is set too high. Fears of supplies not arriving, and of arbitrary plan changes, also stimulate hoarding of labour and materials, and over-application for inputs.

Attempts to fulfil aggregate plan targets, in roubles, tons, square metres or whatever, engender some familiar distortions, when management produces not for the customer but for plan-fulfilment statistics. This can generate the sort of waste which is typified by the building industry (whose plan is in roubles spent) trying to use the dearest possible materials, and metal goods which are unnecessarily heavy to 'clock up' the necessary plan tonnage. It proves to be remarkably difficult to express a plan for heterogeneous products in any unit of measure which does not result in unintended distortions. The weak position of the customer is due to two causes: the supplier is a *de facto* monopolist, and there is a chronic tendency for shortages to occur, which finds expression in a 'take-it-or-leave-it' attitude on the part of the supplier. But perhaps the most fundamental cause is the one already mentioned: the model requires the centre's plans to incorporate requirements in a degree of detail which is impossible in the complex multi-product real world, and yet it is these necessarily aggregated plan-targets which serve as the basis for micro-economic activity of enterprises, since they are judged by their fulfilment of these targets.

Initiative is likewise (unintentionally) frustrated. It is not only that management is risk-averse, since risk-taking is not as such rewarded. It is that any new action requires not only motivation but also information and means. Thus innovation, whether in product design or in production methods, is frequently rendered impossible because the required machines or materials are not obtainable, these being allocated by remote bureaucratic offices.

While enterprises are supposed to operate on so-called 'economic accounting', in fact money and prices generally play a passive role, priority being given to plan-fulfilment indicators. The absence of any built-in incentive to economize has meant the proliferation of compulsory cost-cutting and material-economy plans, which can conflict with the objective of providing what the customer requires. While citizens are free to spend their wages on goods in state shops at state-fixed prices, there is no direct economic link or feedback from these prices to the wholesale prices received by the producing enterprises.

Such a planning system as this becomes increasingly unable to cope with the challenges of what has come to be known as 'intensive growth', that is, growth based on the more efficient use of scarce resources. However, this same system does give to the political authorities, that is, party and state officials, a high degree of control over material and human resources. There also has developed a kind of informal social contract with the masses: security of employment, toleration of slackness at work, prices of necessities and rents kept low. Any major changes, towards some species of 'market socialism', would thus encounter considerable resistance at all levels of society.

MARKET SOCIALISM. The Hungarian New Economic Mechanism (NEM), introduced in 1968, sought to overcome the deficiencies of the Soviet model by the limited use of the market mechanism as the basis of current enterprise operations. That is to say, enterprises made their own output plans, based upon negotiated contracts with customers, and purchased their inputs without having to apply for an administered allocation. The 'addressed' current obligatory plan was eliminated. State plans were now to be concerned mainly with investment, that is, with the creation of new capacity and structural change. Prices, market forces, profitability, were to play a major role in guiding the actions of management. However, state-owned enterprises remained under the ultimate authority of economic ministries, and, as also in the Soviet Union, party officials can issue orders on almost any subject.

Hungarian experience can only be seen as a partial test of the viability and effectiveness of the 'market-socialist' model, and this for a number of reasons. One of these has little to do with the model itself: Hungary was hard hit by adverse terms of trade in the Seventies, and the resultant strains led to adverse effects on living standards and to the imposition of tighter controls than was envisaged within the logic of the model, and this included controls over prices. Another 'external' factor was that Hungary trades mainly with other communist-ruled countries, and this trade is predominantly based on annual inter-governmental bilateral deals, a procedure inconsistent with the 'market' logic of the NEM. But there were other problems, which may highlight some contradictions inherent in 'marrying' the principles of market and of socialism. Thus the market requires competition, but there is little competition in Hungarian industry, partly because it is a small country with few producers, but also because of mergers. Competition in turn generates winners and losers, but the commitment to full employment and the pressures from the unsuccessful result in there being no bankruptcies: the loss-makers receive a subsidy, while extra taxes are levied on those judged to be too successful. For all these reasons, the micro-economic logic of the NEM's 'mix' of plan and market has had only limited success.

The success is particularly visible in two sectors: agriculture and distribution (trade, catering, services). In agriculture cooperative (collective) farms are freed from compulsory delivery quotas, freed also from the need to apply to the planners for authority to purchase their inputs (usually they are able to buy them without any permits). There is much more autonomy, much less outside interference, than in the USSR, and also greater flexibility in providing incentives for peasants, and in allowing scope for peasants' private activities as well as for non-agricultural activities of the farms themselves. Since agriculture is notoriously unsuitable as an object of central planning, this is indeed a sector which benefits from reliance on decentralization and the market. Trade and catering benefited both from realistic pricing (persistent shortages of many goods in the USSR were at least in part due to the tendency to under-price them), and also from the legalization of a sizeable private sector: thus many shops and restaurants in Hungarian cities are either privately owned or leased from the state by private operators. Competition has a visible effect on quality and service. Private ('second economy') activities are legal also in construction, repairs, transport (private taxis are allowed) and a range of small-scale manufacturing. In the USSR most of these activities would be illegal, but a sizeable underground second economy exists there also. Thus in Hungary one can observe both the advantages and difficulties which arise when plan and market are allowed to coexist – though of course the particular 'mix' that exists in Hungary is not the only possible one.

It is noteworthy that Poland and China have formally adopted a model which resembles the Hungarian NEM, though one difference concerns agriculture: in Poland the bulk of the peasantry have remained private smallholders, while in China the 'household responsibility system' introduced after 1979 has effectively decollectivized the peasantry. In the Polish case the serious economic difficulties which persist have been an obstacle to the implementation of these reforms. In China the resolution adopted in October 1984 explicitly asserts the need to recognize the role of market forces as well as of state planning, and, along with greater freedom for peasant agriculture, petty private trade and ownership have been legalized. This is a 'mix' reminiscent of NEP in the Soviet Union in the early Twenties. However, it is too soon to conclude that the Chinese have a new and durable plan model. One of their leaders remarked that, while managers must be allowed to show enterprise and spread their wings, and they had been confined to too small a cage, there must be a cage: 'otherwise the bird will fly away'. There appear to be considerable differences of opinion among Chinese party leaders as to the meaning of present policies. Is the use of the market, and the opening to foreign capital, a temporary phase, as NEP was in Russia, with some sort of real socialist planning to follow? Or is the mix between plan and market a long-term model of socialist planning? The rapid growth of income inequalities, the corruption of many officials, a speed-up in inflation, could lead to a counter-attack, to the reimposition of more central planning. This is not the place to speculate on such matters, only to note that the Chinese are still seeking their own model.

Yugoslavia's combination of plan and self-management was also based in principle on the use of the market mechanism. The micro-economy was to function on the basis of contractual relations between self-managed enterprises, guided by material advantage and by realistic free-market type prices. The problems related to self-management are treated elsewhere (see MARKET SOCIALISM). Yugoslavia's economy has run into serious difficulties, not least because the necessary minimum degree of central planning was absent. Tinbergen wisely remarked that under conditions of self-management, 'it can be convincingly shown that in an optimum order some tasks must be performed in a centralized way and cannot therefore be left to the lowest levels' (Tinbergen, 1975).

Part of the problem was republic–regional fragmentation, complicated by a long history of local nationalisms, so that each republic tended to make its own investments, to keep its own earnings from exports, to run its own finances, which helped to disintegrate the economy of what is, after all, a small country. There is a moral here of wider application about regional planning powers; a regional authority will tend to divert resources for the use of its own region, even if it harms others, if it has the power to do so. But this is but one aspect of a more general problem: the interests of the parts do not necessarily add up to the interests of the whole. There are economies (and diseconomies) of scale, and externalities, which cannot be ignored. Furthermore the self-management model itself tends to encourage excessive income distribution and discourage labour-intensive investments, a situation which can and did give rise to serious unemployment combined with accelerating inflation. The latter was also due to lack of adequate control over credits issued by the (numerous) banks, and to what for several years was a negative real rate of interest.

Yugoslav experience does not prove that either self-management or the market mechanism was wrong. It does strongly point to the need of economic powers at the centre, not only to ensure macro-economic balance but also to devise and enforce the 'rules of the game' for the micro-economy. It also demonstrates the limitations and dangers of 'socialist *laissez-faire*'. If the USSR's economy is stifled by all-embracing central controls, then Yugoslavia shows the consequences of having no systematic central controls at all.

This criticism can be extended to some early models of a decentralized socialist economy, such as that of Oskar Lange and Abba Lerner. These do contain a Central Planning Board, but it is imagined as functioning only via the fixing of parametric prices, to which management is supposed to react in accordance with the best neoclassical principles. Intended to show, in reply to critics (notably Mises), that socialist planners do not require to solve innumerable simultaneous equations, Lange's counter-model contained neither growth nor indeed any plan at all. Nor, of course, did the world of Mises. What was shown was that equilibrium with efficient allocation would be possible, on the abstract assumptions common to both protagonists. It is worth reminding oneself of Kornai's dictum: few indeed are those who take decisions on the basis only of information about price (especially when, in taking investment decisions, the relevant prices are those of the future).

Those critics of socialist planning who emphasized the alleged impossibility of solving too many simultaneous equations had grounds for alarm when the computer, programming, input–output techniques, appeared to make the impossible possible. After all, whereas in a capitalist planless society there was and could be no operational objective function, a centrally planned economy could – it might be supposed – use the new techniques to arrive at the most economically efficient way of achieving the objectives defined by the supreme political authority, which is simultaneously in command of the economy. Indeed some members of the Soviet mathematical school explored in very interesting ways how that might be attempted, and Kantorovich, who received the Nobel prize for his pioneering work on linear programming, proposed a system of plan-valuations which could be used in calculations designed to achieve optimal allocation (and had to defend these valuations from criticism from dogmatic defenders of the labour theory of value).

It turned out that progress along this route was disappointingly slow. We can now see more clearly why. Firstly, the 'objective function' proved to be operationally indefinable, despite efforts by able mathematical economists to define it. What could be the objective basis for an optimal plan, what could be the criterion by which to judge if any given plan were optimal? The objectives of the political leadership cannot serve as such a criterion, since (as one Soviet economist remarked) it seeks advice as to what the plan objectives should be, and would not thank those economists who replied that its wishes were their criterion. Any real society generates numerous inconsistent objectives, and in a one-party state these are also present, and find expression within the one party. Then the 'curse of scale' must again be emphasized. Botvinnik, the former world chess champion, estimated that the number of possible moves in a chess game exceed substantially the number of words spoken by all human beings since the Pyramids were built. A chess board has only 64 squares, and rules of the game are known. An economy or a society has many more, and the human 'pieces' play different games and dispute about the rules. So even if one day a chess grandmaster might have trouble beating a chess-playing computer, the idea that computers could replace markets and make Soviet-type centralized planning 'efficient' is surely a chimera. It is true that computers can aid the centre in making calculations. They have numerous uses at micro, i.e. decentralized levels, as a source of data, or in design bureaux, etc. However, one can scarcely imagine that the centre can administer through a computerized programme a fully disaggregated micro-plan for millions of products, distributed among hundreds of thousands of enterprises. Not only would there be too much information to handle (and check), but decisions involving quality, or judgement as to uncertain outcomes can hardly be left for computers. Scale is also a hindrance to the use in practice of prices based on central computerized programmes (the 'objectively determined valuations' of Kantorovich). At the operational disaggregated level there is no such thing as *the* price of 'agricultural machinery' or 'ball-bearings', or 'footwear': there are hundreds or thousands of different products under each of these heads, which need to be provided, and priced, for different requirements or preferences.

PLAN AND MARKET. Plan and market have been seen as incompatible opposites, both by dogmatic socialists and by dogmatic anti-socialists. However, a strong case can be made for the proposition that a mix of the two is essential in any modern society. True enough, a long list can be made of distortions and deficiencies directly attributable to planning. Disastrous indeed have been some comprehensive redevelopment schemes devised by well-meaning urban planners, and some of the housing has later had to be dynamited. Planning foreign trade in a number of countries, especially in the Third World, has been a means of personal enrichment for those entitled to issue import licences. Development plans have sometimes been grandiose and wasteful. From these and similar experiences some have drawn the conclusion that planning is 'bad', that reliance on the market mechanism will provide the right answers to all economic problems, and that state intervention should confine itself to controlling the money supply and to providing a minimum range of so-called public goods, such as defence and lighthouses. Conversely, socialists see that the operation of the free market generates excessive income inequalities, gives rise to monopolistic abuses, to trade-cycles, to unemployment. The market inspires acquisitiveness, substitutes conflict (between classes, and also between competitors) for the desired harmonious cooperation.

Yet both sets of dogmatists appear to be mistaken. The evils which they have noted do indeed exist, and require to be explicitly recognized and combated. The difficulties faced by centralized marketless socialism have already been discussed at length, and it is hard to see how decentralization could be envisaged without some sort of market mechanism which would link the parts together. *Laissez-faire*, the belief that virtually all public-sector planning or provision is either harmful or unnecessary, ignores much of what did or does happen in the real non-textbook world.

Investment is clearly one relevant sector. Given the degree of uncertainty facing private investors, their understandable desire for security, the attraction of high interest rates (and the negative effect of such high rates on would-be borrowers), it would seem to be a remarkable act of faith to imagine that investments, especially in the longer term, could be rational, let alone optimal. Various forms of indicative planning, reinforced by the state's own investment plans (e.g. in infrastructure), become an important contribution to guiding private investment decisions. As already mentioned, the South Korean government played a key role in the process of developing highly successful exporting sectors. If interest rates are (say) 15 per cent, whose private concern should it be to think about (for instance) the consequences for Great Britain of the exhaustion of North Sea oil or gas supplies by the end of the century? It requires ideological obstinacy of a high order not to see that an energy plan might be desirable, in the national interest. The devotees of 'methodological individualism' go so far as to assert that there *is* no national interest, distinct from the individual interests of the citizens. Even on so extreme an assumption it must still be recognized that individual or sectoral interests can conflict with one another; the elementary example of many people wishing to park cars in a narrow street is but one of many instances when people literally get in each others' way, and public authority has to sort out the mess. One returns, too, to examples cited earlier concerning external effects. Docks, airports, rapid-transit systems, have wide-spreading effects – on industrial profitability, property values, congestion, etc. – which do not show up in their respective profit-and-loss accounts. It does seem absurd to assert that the Washington or Montreal (or Moscow, or Munich, or Budapest) metros should not be part of a transport plan for their respective cities, or should not be provided because – as is the fact – they do not 'pay'. But the 'methodological individualists' are plainly mistaken. In virtually any institution, from the state to a firm or a university, it is frequently possible for the perceived interest of the part to conflict with that of the whole. While it is too complex and time-consuming to attempt to 'internalize' all externalities, it is essential to try to identify contradictions and conflicts of interest when these are important, and not to evade the issue by pretending that – with appropriate legal and institutional arrangements – they will not exist. State intervention is one form of dealing with these problems, in the general interest.

Businessmen, especially at times characterized by uncertainty and high interest rates, have a short-time horizon. Thus Nobel laureate Wassili Leontief wrote: 'Our [US] business man investor expects to get back his capital in about four-and-a-half years. So really he is not very worried about what will happen beyond these four and a half years' (*The Federalist*, March 1985, p. 66). This is not necessarily in the long-term interest of the firm, let alone of the entire economy or of society.

Some extreme anti-planners need reminding of the fact that trade-cycles existed even when trade-union powers were minimal, that chronic unemployment may be as irrational a waste of resources as anything that happens in a centrally planned economy. The notion that labour markets 'clear' but for remediable imperfections is surely a myth derived from general-equilibrium analysis. Real competition *requires* unused capacity, necessarily involves winners and losers, otherwise how could competition actually proceed? This is apart from the serious danger of technologically induced long-term unemployment, which may pose a major threat to overall stability. Yet to combat unemployment by an expansionary policy can engender accelerating inflation unless consideration is given to an incomes policy, itself part of a plan.

It is true that, in the effort to plan and control, major errors have been and could be committed. However, to take one last example, the fact that dreadful mistakes in town-planning have occurred does not prove that no town-planning powers should reside in public authorities.

The whole subject remains highly controversial, and ideologies of both left and right heavily influence both policies and theoretical formulations. At present in many Western countries it is the advocates of planning that are fighting a rearguard battle.

BIBLIOGRAPHY

Nove, A. 1983. *The Economics of Feasible Socialism*. London: Allen and Unwin.
Richardson, G.B. 1960. *Information and Investment*. London and New York: Oxford University Press.
Tinbergen, J. 1975. Does self-management approach the ultimate order? In *Self-Governing Socialism*, ed. B. Horvat et al., New York: IASP, 226.

Planning

RAJIV VOHRA

Formally, planning in an economic context can be identified with a constrained maximization problem. The objective, whether it is simply social welfare or multiple individual utilities, is maximized subject to the resource and technological constraints. It needs to be emphasized that the planning problem is not simply one of characterizing the solution to the maximization problem but also of defining a computational procedure to obtain the solution. A planning process can be defined as an iterative procedure which, through successive approximations, finds a solution to the maximization problem.

The literature on planning processes goes back at least to the debate of the 1920s and 1930s on the possibility of economic calculation in a socialist state. While the formal versions of the welfare theorems, as presented by Arrow (1951) and Debreu (1954), were not available then, it was fairly well recognized that the competitive mechanism would, in equilibrium, satisfy the marginal conditions in terms of the equality of prices and the relevant rates of substitution and that this would constitute an efficient method of allocating resources. In what seems, at least in retrospect, to be an argument one may well be tempted to make if one was aware of the second welfare theorem, Mises (1922) argued that since the markets for capital goods, and hence their prices, would not exist in a socialist economy, it would be impossible for such an economy to allocate its resources rationally. However, Pareto (1897), in comparing the market to a computing machine, had already pointed out that a procedure similar to the competitive process of the market could be used to determine a plan. His argument had been further elaborated by Barone (1908). The focus of Mises's criticism was somewhat changed by Hayek (1935) who did not rule out the theoretical possibility of a planned economy being able to allocate resources rationally. The scepticism was centred around the ability of the planning authority, say the Central Planning Board (CPB), to solve the 'hundreds of thousands' of equations necessary to achieve the objective. Partly in response to this criticism, iterative processes were presented, in what are now famous papers by Taylor (1929) and Lange (1936–7), to show that a planned economy could allocate resources in much the same way as the competitive system. They formalized a planning process which would follow the competitive rules to allocate resources; the trial and error method for finding the optimal allocation was similar to Walrasian tâtonnement. The arguments presented by the sceptics were turned on their head; the planned economy could play the competitive game just as well as the market, perhaps better.

While, in the classical environment, a process which imitates the competitive market has the clear advantage of leading, in equilibrium, to a Pareto optimal allocation, the dynamic properties of such a process were analysed much later. Samuelson (1949) showed that in a linear economy, such a mechanism led to indefinite oscillations. Arrow and Hurwicz (1960) rigorously formalized Lange's process, for an economy with a single utility function, and showed that strict concavity of the utility function and the technological constraints were crucial in establishing the convergence of the dynamic process.

In the subsequent development of this literature considerable attention has been paid to developing processes which converge to an optimal plan. Other criteria for comparing different processes have also been formalized (see for example Hurwicz, 1960, and Malinvaud, 1967) and we shall discuss these in more detail in section 1. At this stage it is, however, worthwhile to point out that a planning process which mimics the competitive process has considerable appeal. In the classical environment it leads to an allocation which is Pareto optimal. It also retains the attractive informational processing properties of the competitive mechanism; the CPB is not required to collect all the information on the economic environment nor does it need to solve the entire programming problem by itself since various stages of the optimization process are conducted at the individual level. Subsequent literature on planning processes has, quite justifiably, concentrated on processes which are in some sense decentralized. Processes applicable to non-classical environments have also been formulated.

There is also a considerable literature on general allocation processes in which the CBP is not assigned a distinguished role (see for example Arrow and Hurwicz, 1977). In this essay we shall concentrate only on planning processes. In particular, we consider an economy with many firms and a CBP. Except for the section on public goods where we consider many consumers, the CPB is assumed to have the objective of maximizing a single utility function. Section 1 will set out the model and the criteria which may be used to compare different processes. Processes designed for the classical environment are considered in section 2. Sections 3 and 4 deal respectively with economies with increasing returns and with public goods. Due to limits on space, we shall not deal with other non-classical environments that have also been studied in the literature on allocation process (see for example section III of Hurwicz, 1973). Another important aspect of planning which is not covered here is that of incentive compatibility. Moreover, the discussion is not intended to cover all the details of the processes under consideration and the reader may find it useful to consult the cited papers. Notable among the surveys in this area are Heal (1973), Hurwicz

(1973) and Tulkens (1978).

1. THE FORMAL MODEL AND DEFINITIONS. We shall consider an economy with k commodities, indexed by l, and $n+1$ agents, n firms and the CPB. Agents will be indexed by

$$i, i = 1, \ldots, n, n+1.$$

We shall also find it convenient to index the firms by $j, j = 1, \ldots, n$. Firm j's technology is represented by production set $Y^j \subseteq R^k$. The environment of firm j is simply $e^j = Y^j$. The CPB has a continuous utility function $U: X \to R$, where X is the consumption set. The aggregate endowment of the economy is denoted $\omega \in R^k$. The economic environment of the CPB is $e^{n+1} = (X, U, \omega)$. The economy can be described in terms of its environment $e = (X, (Y^j), U, \omega)$.

D.1. A *program* (x, y) consists of a consumption plan $x \in X$ and a collection of production plans $y = (y') \in Y = \prod_j Y^j$.

D.2. A program (x, y) is said to be *feasible* if $x = \sum_j y^j + \omega$.

D.3. A program (x, y) is said to be *Pareto optimal* if it is feasible and there does not exist another feasible program $(\bar{x}, \bar{y})$ such that $U(\bar{x}) > U(x)$.

A planning process is an iterative process in which messages are exchanged between the firms and the CPB. Agent i chooses a message m^i from a set M, taking into account the environment and the messages received in the previous period. Let m_t^i refer to agent i's message in time period t and

$$m_t = (m_t^1, \ldots, m_t^j, \ldots, m_t^{n+1}).$$

The response of agent i may then be defined in terms of a response function $f^i: M^{n+1} \to M$, where M^{n+1} refers to the $n+1$ fold cartesian product of M and

$$m_{t+1}^i = f^i(m_t; e).$$

An equilibrium message is simply defined as a stationary message. The equilibrium of the process is determined by an outcome function h which translates the equilibrium message into the equilibrium program or plan. We can now formally define these concepts:

D.4. Given an environment e, a *planning process* is defined as $\pi = (M, f, h)$ where $f: M^{n+1} \to M$ and $h: M^{n+1} \to X \times Y$.

D.5. An *equilibrium message* for a process π is an $m \in M^{n+1}$ such that $m = f(m; e)$.

D.6. An *equilibrium program* (or an *equilibrium plan*) for a process π is a program (x, y) such that $(x, y) = h(m; e)$ and m is an equilibrium message.

We shall now discuss some of the desirable properties that a planning process may have. These properties may be broadly classified in terms of the performance of the process and its informational efficiency. We begin by presenting the performance criteria introduced in Malinvaud (1967).

Clearly convergence to a Pareto optimal allocation is a requirement that any planning process ought to satisfy.

D.7. A process π is said to be *convergent* if an equilibrium program exists and is Pareto optimal, i.e. as $t \to \infty$, $\mathrm{Lim}_t \, h(m_t; e)$ is Pareto optimal.

Malinvaud also stresses the importance of the following properties which may, in practice, be even more important if the process needs to be terminated before equilibrium is reached.

D.8. A planning process $\pi = (M, f, h)$ is said to be *feasible* if $f(m, e)$ and $h(m, e)$ are non-empty and $h(m, e)$ is feasible for all $m \in M^{n+1}$.

D.9. A planning process π is said to be *monotonic* if $U(x_{t+1}) \geqslant U(x_t)$ for all t, where x_t is the consumption plan corresponding to $h(m_t; e)$. It is *strictly monotonic* if it is monotonic and $U(x_{t+1}) = U(x_t)$ implies that $h(m_t; e)$ is Pareto optimal.

Hurwicz (1960) and (1969) formalized the notion of informational efficiency associated with a process. His definitions are applicable to general allocation processes in which a CPB is not assigned a distinguished role and we shall suitably modify his concepts to apply specifically to planning processes. The definitions which follow are aimed at formally defining a decentralized process, a definition which is intended to include but not be synonymous with the competitive process. An important characteristic of the competitive system is that initial information is dispersed among the agents; firm j knows only its own environment Y^j while a consumer knows only his or her utility function and endowment. A process in which the ith agent's response functions depends only on e^i is said to be *external*. A process is *anonymous* if the agents do not know the source of their messages. Since there is only one planning authority, this requirement may not be relevant for the firms; if certain kinds of messages are transmitted only by the CPB the firms would know the source of these messages. As far as the CPB is concerned, it would be desirable if messages did not have to be identified with particular firms. In particular, if the aggregate response of the firms is all that the CBP needs to determine its message this must be considered a significant advantage. Clearly, this would be a stronger requirement than anonymity and a process satisfying this requirement will be called *aggregative*. Another informational requirement that Hurwicz (1969) imposes on a decentralized process is that the message space M be R^k. Calsamiglia (1977) considers a somewhat less restrictive condition on the amount of information that needs to be transmitted. He defines a process to be *point valued* if M is some finite dimensional Euclidean space.

D.10. A process $\pi = (M, f, h)$ is *informationally decentralized* if it is external, aggregative and point valued, i.e. if

$$m_{t+1}^j = f^j\left(\sum_{)j(} m_t^j, m_t^j, m_t^{n+1}; e^j\right),$$

$$m_{t+1}^{n+1} = f^{n+1}\left(\sum_j m_t^j, m_t^{n+1}; e^{n+1}\right)$$

and

$$M = R^s,$$

where $\sum_{)j(} m^j$ refers to the summation across the messages of all except the jth firm and s is a positive integer.

While most of the planning processes in the literature are external and aggregative, many of them are not point-valued in the above sense. In particular, Malinvaud's (1967) process is one in which the agents transmit point-valued messages in every time period but the response of the CPB depends also on the messages received in the past. Such a process would not be informationally decentralized according to the above definition; however, there is something to be said for making a distinction between messages and memory, and between a process in which messages at each point in time are infinite dimensional and one in which finite dimensional messages are transmitted but the CPB has a memory of past messages. Processes of the latter variety have also been termed decentralized and while this may not be unreasonable, it has led to some confusion (see Cremer, 1978).

2. THE CLASSICAL ENVIRONMENT. In this section we discuss planning processes designed for the classical environment in which there are no externalities, production sets are convex and the utility function is quasi-concave. In this setting, the competitive allocation has the attractive welfare properties that it is Pareto optimal and any Pareto optimal allocation can be sustained as a competitive allocation with a redistribution of initial resources. In an economy with a single utility function, a competitive allocation is unambiguously optimal.

We begin by considering Lange's process as formalized by Arrow and Hurwicz (1960). As mentioned earlier, the Lange–Arrow–Hurwicz (LAH) process is closely related to the Walrasian tâtonnement. Arrow and Hurwicz consider the following process: the CPB announced prices p and the firms choose profit maximizing production plans. The CPB computes a consumption plan to maximize $U(x) - px$. The prices are then varies in proportion to excess demand.

Arrow and Hurwicz formulate the planning problem as a programming problem and apply the gradient method (or method of steepest ascent) to find its solution. They formulate their process in continuous time in the activity analysis framework. We now formally describe the LAH process in its discrete version, as transposed by Malinvaud (1967) to the model presented in section 1 above. Given prices p, firms choose their profit maximizing plans the the CPB chooses the consumption plan which maximizes $U(x) - px$. The price of a commodity is then increased by an amount proportional to its aggregate excess demand, the coefficient of proportionality being a positive constant ρ, provided this change does not make the price negative. The responses of the agents can now be defined formally:

(i) $y_t^j = \{y_t^j \in Y^j \mid p_{t-1} y_t^j \geqslant p_{t-1} z \text{ for all } z \in Y^j\}$ $\qquad j = 1, \dots, n,$

(ii) $x_t = \{x_t \in X \mid U(x_t) - p_{t-1}x_t \geqslant U(z) - p_t z \text{ for all } z \in X\}$,

(iii) $p_{t,l} = \max\left\{0, p_{t-1,l} + \rho\left(x_{t-1,l} - \sum_j y_{t-1,l}^j - \omega_l\right)\right\}$ $\qquad l = 1, \ldots, k$.

It is clear that in order for the process to be convergent, a Pareto optimal allocation must exist. This in turn will be guaranteed if, for example, all the production sets and the consumption sets are compact. The assumption that the above mappings are all single-valued, i.e. there is a unique production plan that maximizes profits for each firm, given p and a unique consumption plan that maximizes $U(x) - px$, also turns out to be important for the convergence properties of the process. While the process is continuous time is convergent (see Theorem 12 in Arrow and Hurwicz, 1960), Uzawa (1958) showed that the discrete version of the LAH process converges only approximately. The following result is the version presented in Malinvaud (1967).

Theorem 1. If there is a unique Pareto optimal allocation $(\bar{x}, \bar{y})$ and the functions defined by (i) and (ii) are single-valued, the process defined by (i), (ii) and (iii) is approximately convergent in the following sense: for any $\varepsilon > 0$, there exist ρ_0 and t_0, both depending on ε, such that if $p \leqslant p_0$, then for $t \leqslant t_0$ the distance between $h(m_{t;e})$ and $(\bar{x}, \bar{y})$ is no greater than the distance between $h(m_{t-1}, e)$ and $(\bar{x}, \bar{y})$, and for $t \geqslant t_0$, the distance between $h(m_t; e)$ and $(\bar{x}, \bar{y})$ is no greater than ε.

It is easy to see that this process is not feasible since, out of equilibrium, aggregate excess demand for some commodities may be positive. There is also the problem that since the function $\rho(\varepsilon)$ is not known and it is not possible, given some ε, to choose the value of ρ to be most efficient.

Malinvaud (1967) proposes two other processes which are feasible, monotonic, and convergent but are not decentralized according to D.10 since the CPB is required to remember the messages conveyed by the firms in the past. Malinvaud's first process is designed only for a linear economy and is based on Taylor's (1929) proposal. Each firm is assumed to have a set of fixed coefficient techniques that can be operated under constant returns to scale. The CPB announces prices corresponding to which firms respond with a cost minimizing technique. The CPB then solves the open Leontief model to obtain prices which would make firms' proposed techniques earn zero profits and a consumption plan which maximizes utility at these prices. This process is then shown to satisfy Malinvaud's criteria under certain conditions. Malinvaud's second process covers a more general environment and we shall now discuss this in somewhat more detail.

This process is an application of the Dantzig–Wolfe (1961) decomposition algorithm to the planning problem. The CPB builds up an approximation of the firms' production sets based on messages received from them in the past. At each stage firms reveal their profit maximizing production plans, given the prices conveyed by the CPB. Assuming that all the production sets are convex, the CPB can construct a subset of a firm's production set by taking the convex combination of all the production plans revealed by that firm in the past. The

CPB then solves the programming problem of maximizing utility subject to the resource constraints and the technological constraints as given by its construction of the firms' production sets. In the next stage the shadow prices obtained from the programming problem are announced as prices and the process continues. For the process to start it is assumed that the CPB has initial information about at least one feasible production plan for each firm.

We can now define the process formally. Let Δ denote the $k-1$ dimensional simplex and $Y_t^j = \text{Con}(y_1^j, \ldots, y_{t-1}^j)$, where Con denotes convex hull. Let $(\bar{x}_t, \bar{y}_t)$ denote the allocation which solves the programming problem at t, i.e.

$$(\bar{x}_t, \bar{y}_t) = \left\{ (x, y) \in X \times Y \mid x_t \leqslant \sum_j y_t^j + \omega \text{ and } U(x_t) \geqslant U(z) \right.$$

$$\left. \text{for all } z \in \sum_j \text{con}(Y_t^j) + \omega \right\}.$$

We shall say that $p \in \Delta$ *supports* the allocation $(\bar{x}_t, \bar{y}_t)$ if

    (a) $U(x) \geqslant U(\bar{x}_t)$ implies $px \geqslant p\bar{x}_t$,

    (b) $y \in Y^j$ implies that $py \leqslant p\bar{y}_t^j$ for all j.

The process is defined by the following equations:

    (i) $y_t^j = \{ y \in Y^j \mid py \geqslant p\bar{y} \text{ for all } \bar{y} \in Y^j \}$, $j = 1, \ldots, n$.

    (ii) $p_t = \{ p \in \Delta \mid p \text{ supports } (\bar{x}_t, \bar{y}_t) \}$.

The plan at stage t is simply defined as $(\bar{x}_t, \bar{y}_t^j)$.

The following assumptions are sufficient for this process to satisfy Malinvaud's criteria. (A1) X is closed, convex and bounded from below. $U(x)$ is continuous, quasi-concave and locally non-satiated. (A2) Y^j is convex and compact for all j. (A3) the CPB knows a feasible program (x_1, y_1). We can now state

Theorem 2 (Malinvaud, 1967). If (A1), (A2) and (A3) are satisfied the process defined by (i) and (ii) is feasible, monotonic and convergent.

To see that this process is feasible notice that, given (A2), (i) always has a solution and, given (A1) and (A2), the programming problem, for any t, has a solution and this solution constitutes the plan for that time period. We can appeal to the second welfare theorem (see, for example Theorem 6.4 in Debreu, 1959) to assert that (ii) also has a solution. Monotonicity is an obvious property of this process since the constraint sets in the programming problem of time t are contained in the constraint sets of time $t+1$. Convergence is established by considering a limit argument, using the fact that all the plans lie in a compact set. We refer to Malinvaud (1967) for the proof.

As the above theorem shows, this process has better performance properties than the LAH process. However, its information requirements are much stronger. The CPB is required to have memory and to know of a feasible allocation. It also solves a rather complicated programming problem at each stage. Moreover, to implement the plan the firms are instructed to follow the production plans

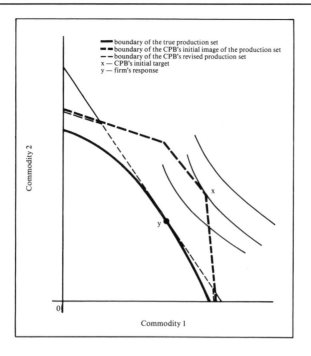

boundary of the true production set
boundary of the CPB's initial image of the production set
boundary of the CPB's revised production set
x — CPB's initial target
y — firm's response

Commodity 2

0

Commodity 1

Figure 1

computed by the CPB. While these plans are consistent with profit maximization, a specific instruction has to be issued to each firm. But this problem can be avoided in the simpler case where all production sets are strictly convex. In this case, the equilibrium plan can be implemented simply by announcing shadow prices and letting the firms find their unique profit maximizing production plans.

Weitzman (1970) proposed a process which is in a sense a dual of Malinvaud's process. The CPB has a belief about a firm's production set, which is not necessarily correct, and, given these imaginary production sets, it solves the programming problem and provides each firm with a production plan as a target. If the firm finds that this target is not feasible it responds with an efficient plan and a corresponding marginal rate of substitution. The CPB then constructs a new production set which is the intersection of its previous one with the half space determined by the firm's announced efficient plan and marginal rate of substitution. The CPB again solves the programming problem and announces new targets (see Figure 1). Not only is this process convergent, if the production sets are polyhedral, convergence is achieved in a finite number of steps. However, it is not feasible since the CPB's targets may not be feasible for the firms.

Another process which uses production quotas rather than prices as signals is one due to Kornai and Liptak (1965). Their process is formulated for a linear economy in which the CPB's utility function is separable among the firms' outputs. The CPB allocates resources to the firms which respond with rates of substitution and the CPB reallocates resources in response to the value of the allocated resources at the shadow prices. They model the interaction between the CPB and the firms as a game and show that the process is convergent.

3. INCREASING RETURNS. Heal (1969) proposed a non-price gradient process which locates local maxima even for economies with increasing returns. The CPB allocates the inputs among firms which then respond with efficient output levels and marginal productivities. The CPB then reallocates the inputs towards the firms with higher marginal productivities. The process can be most easily understood in the simple setting in which all firms produce an identical output using m primary resources. Departing from our notation of section 1, we shall denote by y_i the amount of output produced by firm i and by f_i firm i's production function. The amount of input j used by firm i is denoted x_{ij} and the technological constraints may be stated as follows:

$$y_i = f_i(x_{i1}, \ldots, x_{im}) \quad i = 1, \ldots, n, \quad x_{ij} \geq 0, \quad \text{for all } i \text{ and } j.$$

Let R_j denote the aggregate endowment of the jth resource. The resource constraints can be stated as

$$\sum_i x_{ij} \leq R_j \quad \text{for all } j.$$

The objective of the planning process is to find x_{ij} to maximize $\sum_i y_i$ subject to the technological and resource constraints. Let f_{ij} denote firm i's marginal productivity of the jth input and let a dot over a variable denote its rate of change. The process starts with the CPB allocating x_{ij} to the firms subject to the resource constraints. The CPB then raises the allocation of input j to a firm if its marginal productivity is greater than a certain average productivity and lowers it if it is lower than the average, subject to the non-negativity constraints. Formally, the rate of adjustment is determined by the following equations.

$$\dot{x}_{ij} = f_{ij} - \text{Av}(K_j)f_{ij}, \quad \text{if } i \in K_j \quad 0 \text{ otherwise},$$

where $\text{Av}(K_j)f_{ij}$ denotes the average of f_{ij}'s contained in the set K_j. The set K_j is constructed (see Heal, 1969) so that the non-negativity constraints are not violated in applying the adjustment equations and it satisfies the following property

$$K_j = \{i \mid x_{ij} > 0 \quad \text{or} \quad x_{ij} = 0 \quad \text{and} \quad f_{ij} > \text{Av}(K_j)f_{ij}\}.$$

K_j includes firms with positive allocations of input j or firms with a zero allocation but a marginal productivity higher than the average.

We can now state the following theorem, which applies to the simple model we are considering but also extends to the more general case where firms produce different commodities.

Theorem 3 (Heal, 1969). If all f_i have continuous, finite first derivatives and the initial allocation is feasible, the process defined above is feasible and monotonic. Moreover, every limit point of the process satisfies the necessary conditions for Pareto optimality. If the initial allocation is not a local minimum, then the limit points are to local minima.

To see that the process is feasible, notice that

$$\sum_i \dot{x}_{ij} = \sum_{i \in K_j} \left[f_{ij} - (1/K_j) \sum_{i \in K_j} f_{ij} \right] = 0, \qquad \text{for all } j.$$

Thus, if the initial allocation is feasible so are all other allocations. To establish monotonicity, we consider

$$\dot{y} = \sum_i \sum_j f_{ij} \dot{x}_{ij}$$

which can be written as

$$\dot{y} = \sum_j \sum_{i \in K_j} f_{ij} \left[f_{ij} - (1/|K_j|) \sum_{i \in K_j} f_{ij} \right] = \sum_j \sum_{i \in K_j} \left[f_{ij} - (1/|K_j|) \sum_{i \in K_j} f_{ij} \right]^2 \geq 0.$$

Thus, $\dot{y} \geq 0$ and $\dot{y} = 0$ if and only if $f_{ij} = f_{kj}$ for all i and $k \in K_j$ for all j. It is easy to see that the equality of f_{ij} for all i in K_j is the necessary condition for optimality. This implies that y increases monotonically except when the necessary conditions for optimality are satisfied. In particular, if the initial allocation is not a local minimum, the equilibrium allocation, arrived at through monotonic increases, cannot be a local minimum. Hori (1975) showed that the convergence to a point of inflection is unlikely in a well defined sense. A discrete version of this gradient process would also be approximately convergent in the sense described in Theorem 2 above.

Since this process requires the CPB to respond with allocations to firms, the informational requirements are much stronger than those of a price guided process in which a common price vector is given out to the entire production sector. In the general case where firms produce many commodities the CPB uses marginal valuations not only to allocate inputs but also output combinations to each firm (see Heal, 1973, ch. 8). However, unlike the Malinvaud or the Weitzman process, the CPB is not required to have a memory. It is also possible to modify this process to take advantage of the informational efficiency which is characteristic of the price guided processes. Such a mixed planning process was formulated by Heal (1971) and is similar to one proposed by Marglin (1969). In Heal's (1971) process the CPB allocates resources to the firms and also provides them with prices of the final goods. The firms inform the CPB of their profit maximizing output bundles and also of the marginal productivity of the inputs. The CPB reallocates inputs as in the previous process and announces new output prices which reflect the marginal rates of substitution in consumption. The performance of this process is similar to that of the previous one with the important difference that the CPB does not determine the complete allocation at each step. The substitution of one output for another is carried out by the firms depending on the common price vector for outputs announced by the CPB. Aoki (1971a) proposed a mixed planning process which combines the LAH process with Heal's (1969) process. He considers an economy with increasing returns in which there is one input such that if this is fixed, each firm faces decreasing returns with respect to all the other inputs. The CPB allocates this input to the firms in accordance with its marginal profitability and the LAH process is then used to allocate all the other resources. This process is clearly more complex since the LAH process is used at each step in which the essential input is reallocated, but it does converge to a local maximum.

Another approach to planning in economies with increasing returns is the modified LAH process. Arrow and Hurwicz (1960) showed that their process could deal with linearities and non-convexities if the Lagrangian is suitably modified so that it becomes strictly concave and the gradient method is then applied to locate a saddle-point of this concavified Lagrangian. There is, however, a significant difference. The modified Lagrangian expression is no longer a sum of functions each involving a different variable and it is no longer simply possible to determine demands and supplies given the prices. The CPB and firms need the entire price schedule and this makes this modified process less informationally decentralized than the original LAH process.

All the processes that we have so far considered in this section, depending as they do on first order properties of the relevant functions, cannot guarantee convergence to a global optimum. They also seem to be less informationally decentralized than processes for the classical environment. The natural question to be raised at this stage is whether it is possible to formulate a decentralized process which converges to a global optimum in an environment with increasing returns. Calsamiglia (1977) showed the answer to this question is no. He begins by making a rather important point about the interpretation of a local maximum. He provides an example of an allocation which is a local maximum but does not satisfy aggregate production efficiency. While at a local maximum it is not possible to make marginal changes to increase utility, it may be possible to increase utility simply by reorganizing production among the firms to produce more of each commodity. But, as he then proves, even in simple economies with increasing returns there does not exist a decentralized process which converges to a global optimum.

It is, however, possible to construct a process which has nice convergence properties at the cost of giving up decentralization as defined in D.10. This was shown by Cremer (1977). He considers a quantity–quantity algorithm in which the CPB, as in Malinvaud (1967) and Weitzman (1970), possesses a memory and builds up successive approximations of the firms' production sets and solves the programming problem. This process is in many respects similar to Weitzman's process. Convexity of the production sets was used crucially in Weitzman's process to ensure that when the CPB constructs a new production set, by considering the announced marginal rate of substitution, it knows that no point above the corresponding hyperplane need be considered again. In the presence of increasing returns this is no longer true and in Cremer's process firms do not respond with marginal rates of substitution. The CPB only knows that if a firm responds with a feasible production plan then all production plans which are greater than it can be ruled out of further consideration. Figure 2 shows how the CPB revises its information about the firm's technology. It is assumed that

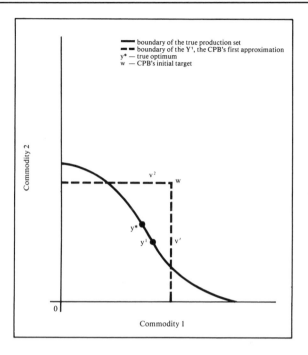

Figure 2

the CPB knows that the optimal production plan $y^* \leqslant w$. It announces w as a target. If this is not feasible the firm responds with some y^1 which is feasible and strictly less than w. The CPB then knows that it must now consider only points less than or equal to either v^1 or v^2. If the utility at v^2 is higher than at v^1 the CPB considers its new approximate production set to be the set of all points in Y^1 but equal to or less than v^2. Under certain boundedness conditions it can be shown that this process converges to a global optimum. Since the targets are not necessarily feasible nor is the process.

4. PUBLIC GOODS. This section draws heavily on Tulkens (1978). We begin by considering the simple setting of an economy with a single private good y and a single public good z. There are n consumers with continuously differentiable and strictly quasi-concave utility functions $U^i(x^i)$, where $x^i = (y^i, z^i)$. The public good is produced according to the technology of the form $w = g(z)$, where w represents the private good input and g is assumed to be convex. A feasible allocation $((x^i))$ satisfies the conditions that

$$\sum_i y^i + w = \sum_i \omega_i, \qquad z^i = z \quad \text{for all } i \quad \text{and} \quad w = g(z).$$

Lindahl (1919) in his positive solution to the public goods problem proposed a process, the convergence properties of which were analyzed by Malinvaud (1971). The Lindahl process concerns a two-consumer economy in which the public good is produced under constant marginal cost γ. Each consumer is assigned a share, θ^i in the price of the public good so that $\theta^1 + \theta^2 = \gamma$. Consumers take as given their personalized prices or unit taxes θ^i to determine their demands for the public good. The supply of the public good is made equal to the lower of these two demands and the CPB adjusts the unit taxes by raising the tax on the consumer with the higher demand and lowering it for the other. The process continues as long as the utilities of both the consumers rise. Malinvaud (1971) showed that utilities would not rise monotonically till the two demands become identical and, therefore, this process does not converge to a Lindahl equilibrium. He suggested a modification which ensures convergence to a Pareto optimal allocation (though not necessarily to a Lindahl allocation). In this modified process the CPB announces not only unit taxes but also lump-sum taxes, T^i such that $\sum_i T^i = 0$. Let $d^i(\theta^i, T^i)$ refer to consumer i's demand for the public good and $\bar{d}$ the corresponding average demand. The CPB adjusts i's unit tax in proportion to the difference between d^i and $\bar{d}$. Supply is made equal to the average demand and T^i is adjusted to compensate i for the change in θ^i. Formally the adjustment equations are, (i) $\dot{\theta}^i = a[d^i - \bar{d}]$, for all i, (ii) $\dot{T}^i = -(1/n)\sum_i d^i\dot{\theta}^i$, for all i, where a is a positive constant. While this process converges to a Pareto optimal allocation, it is neither feasible nor monotonic.

An alternative would be to consider a process in which the CPB responds with quantities rather than prices. The Malinvaud–Drèze–de la Vallée Poussin (MDP) process, formulated by Malinvaud (1970–71) and Drèze and de la Vallée Poussin (1971), is a quantity guided process in which the CPB announces an allocation and the agents respond with rates of substitution. Starting with a feasible allocation, the firm reports its marginal cost γ and each consumer reports his or her marginal rate of substitution of the public good for the private good π^i. The adjustment take place according to the following differential equations, (i) $\dot{z}_t = \dot{z}_t^i = a(\sum_i \pi_t^i - \gamma_t)$, for all i, (ii) $\dot{w}_t = \gamma_t\dot{z}_t$, (iii) $\dot{y}_t^i = -\pi_t^i\dot{z}_t + \delta^i a(\sum_i \pi_t^i - \gamma_t)^2$ for all i, where a is a positive constant and $\delta^i \geqslant 0$ for all i and $\sum_i \delta^i = 1$.

Since the process starts at a feasible allocation, (ii) ensures that the process is feasible. It has also been shown that it converges to an allocation at which the first order conditions for optimality are satisfied, i.e. the sum of the marginal rates of substitution equals the marginal cost. The MDP process is also monotonic. To see this, consider

$$\dot{U}^i = U^iy^i(\dot{y}^i + \pi^i\dot{z}).$$

Using (i) and (ii) this can be rewritten as

$$\dot{U} = U^iy^i\delta^ia\left(\sum_i \pi^i - \gamma\right)^2 \geqslant 0.$$

While the MDP process converges to some Pareto optimal allocation depending on the choice of the distribution profile $((\delta^i))$, Champsaur (1976) has shown that the process is neutral in the sense that given any initial allocation and any Pareto optimal allocation which is Pareto superior to this allocation, there exists a distribution profile with which the MDP process converges to the given optimum. A discrete time version of the MDP, with the same performance properties, was provided by Champsaur, Drèze and Henry (1977).

Malinvaud (1970–71) and Drèze and de la Vallée Poussin (1971) also extend the MDP process to an economy with many private and public goods by considering the MDP process as described above for public goods and a quantity guided process for the private goods. Another alternative, considered in Aoki (1971b), Malinvaud (1972) and Champsaur, Drèze and Henry (1977), is to construct a process which combines the MDP process with a price guided process for private goods. These processes, however, have to deal with a well known problem, namely one of ensuring convergence of a price guided process in an economy with many consumers without making the gross substitutability assumption.

Aoki (1971b) considers an economy with many private and public goods and many firms and consumers. He avoids the income distribution problem by specifying a social welfare function. The CPB announces prices of the private goods and quantities of the public goods. Firms maximize profits and report input demands and marginal costs for public goods. The CPB increases private goods prices according to the difference between marginal utilities and prices and the public goods levels are adjusted according to the difference between marginal utilities and marginal costs. This process is feasible, monotonic and convergent.

Malinvaud (1972) formulates a price guided process for allocating not only private goods but also public goods. The gross substitutability assumption is avoided by specifying individual incomes as proportions of aggregate income and revising them during the process (notice that Malinvaud's, 1971, price guided process also made use of lump-sum transfers). This process converges locally but is neither feasible nor monotonic.

Champsaur, Drèze and Henry (1977) present a process which combines in a sequential way an MDP process for public goods allocation with a price guided process for private goods allocation. Given public goods' levels a price guided process is used to allocate private goods. Then keeping fixed the levels of all except one numeraire private good, the MDP process is applied to allocate public goods. This process is shown to be feasible, monotonic and convergent to some Pareto optimal allocation.

Given the difficulty in using a price guided process when there are many consumers, it is perhaps not surprising that a satisfactory process which converges to a Lindahl equilibrium has not been established, although some results are available in this direction (see Milleron, 1974).

BIBLIOGRAPHY

Aoki, A. 1971a. An investment planning process for an economy with increasing returns. *Review of Economic Studies* 38, 273–80.

Aoki, A. 1971b. Two planning processes for an economy with production externalities. *International Economic Review* 12, 403–413.

Arrow, K. 1951. An extension of the basic theorems of welfare economics. In *Proceedings of the Second Berkeley Symposium*, ed. J. Neyman, Berkeley: University of California Press.

Arrow, K.J. and Hurwicz, L. 1960. Decentralization and computation in resource allocation. In *Essays in Economics and Econometrics in Honor of Harold Hotelling*, ed. R.W. Pfouts, Chapel Hill: University of North Caroline Press; reprinted in K.J. Arrow and L. Hurwicz (1977).

Arrow, K.J. and Hurwicz, L. (eds) 1977. *Studies in Resource Allocation Processes*. Cambridge and New York: Cambridge University Press.

Barone, E. 1908. The Ministry of Production in the collectivist state. In *Collectivist Economic Planning*, ed. F.A. von Hayek, London: Routledge, 1935; New York: A.M. Kelley, 1967.

Calsamiglia, X. 1977. Decentralized resource allocation and increasing returns. *Journal of Economic Theory* 14, 263–83.

Champsaur, P. 1976. Neutrality of planning procedures in an economy with public goods. *Review of Economic Studies* 43, 293–300.

Champsaur, P., Drèze, J.H. and Henry, C. 1977. Stability theorems with economic applications. *Econometrica* 45, 273–94.

Cremer, J. 1977. A quantity-quantity algorithm for planning under increasing returns to scale. *Econometrica* 45, 1339–48.

Cremer, J. 1978. A comment on 'decentralized planning and increasing returns'. *Journal of Economic Theory* 19, 217–21.

Dantzig, G.B. and Wolfe, P. 1961. The decomposition algorithm for linear programs. *Econometrica* 29, 767–78.

Debreu, G. 1954. Valuation equilibrium and Pareto optimum. *Proceedings of the National Academy of Sciences* 40, 588–92.

Debreu, G. 1959. *Theory of Value: An Axiomatic Analysis of Economic Equilibrium*. Cowles Foundation Monograph No. 17, New York: Wiley.

Drèze, J.H. and de la Vallée Poussin, D. 1971. A tâtonnement process for public goods. *Review of Economic Studies* 37, 133–50.

Hayek, F.A. von. 1935. The present state of the debate. In *Collectivist Economic Planning*, ed. F.A. von Hayek, London: Routledge; New York, A.M. Kelley, 1967.

Heal, G.M. 1969. Planning without prices. *Review of Economic Studies* 36, 346–62.

Heal, G.M. 1971. Planning, prices and increasing returns. *Review of Economic Studies* 38, 281–94.

Heal, G.M. 1973. *The Theory of Economic Planning*. Amsterdam: North-Holland.

Hori, H. 1975. The structure of the equilibrium points of Heal's process. *Review of Economic Studies* 42, 457–67.

Hurwicz, L. 1960. Optimality and informational efficiency in resource allocation processes. In *Mathematical Methods in Social Sciences*, ed. K.J. Arrow, S. Karlin and P. Suppes, Stanford: Stanford University Press. Reprinted in Arrow and Hurwicz (1977).

Hurwicz, L. 1969. On the concept and possibility of informational decentralization. *American Economic Review* 59, 513–34.

Hurwicz, L. 1973. The design of resource allocation mechanisms. *American Economic Review* 58, 1–30; reprinted in Arrow and Hurwicz (1977).

Kornai, J. and Liptak, T. 1965. Two-level planning. *Econometrica* 33, 141–69.

Lange, O. 1936–7. On the economic theory of socialism. *Review of Economic Studies*. Reprinted in *On the Economic Theory of Socialism*, ed. B. Lippincott, Minneapolis: University of Minnesota Press, 1938.

Lindahl, E. 1919. Just taxation – a positive solution. In *Classics in the Theory of Public Finance*, ed. R.A. Musgrave and A. Peacock, London and New York: Macmillan, 1958.

Malinvaud, E. 1967. Decentralized procedures for planning. In *Activity Analysis in the Theory of Growth and Planning*, ed. M.O.L. Bacharach and E. Malinvaud, London: Macmillan; New York: St. Martin's Press.

Malinvaud, E. 1970–71. Procedures pour la détermination d'un programme de consommation collective. *European Economic Review* 2, 187–217.

Malinvaud, E. 1971. A planning approach to the public goods problem. *Swedish Journal of Economics* 73, 96–112.

Malinvaud, E. 1972. Prices for individual consumption, quantity indicators for collective consumption. *Review of Economic Studies* 34, 385–406.

Marglin, S.A. 1969. Information in price and command systems of planning. In *Public Economics*, ed. J. Margolis and H.K. Guitton; London: Macmillan.

Milleron, J.C. 1974. Procedures to a Lindahl equilibrium corresponding to a given distribution of income. Paper presented at the European Meeting of the Econometric Society in Grenoble.

Mises, L. von. 1922. *Socialism*. London: Jonathan Cape (1936).

Pareto, V. 1896. *Cours d'économie politique*. Vol. I, Lausanne.

Samuelson, P.A. 1949. Market mechanisms and maximization. In *Collected Scientific Papers of Paul A. Samuelson*, ed. J.E. Stiglitz, Cambridge, Mass.: MIT Press, 1966.

Taylor, F.M. 1929. The guidance of production in a socialist state. *American Economic Review* 19, 1–8. Reprinted in *On the Economic Theory of Socialism*, ed. B. Lippincott, Minneapolis: University of Minnesota Press, 1938.

Tulkens, H. 1978. Dynamic processes for public goods: an institution-oriented survey. *Journal of Public Economics* 9, 163–201.

Uzawa, H. 1958. Iterative methods for concave programming. In *Studies in Linear and Non-Linear Programming*, ed. K.J. Arrow, L. Hurwicz and H. Uzawa, Stanford: Stanford University Press.

Weitzman, M. 1970. Iterative multi-level planning with production targets. *Econometrica* 38, 50–65.

Evgenii Alexeyevich Preobrazhensky

MICHAEL ELLMAN

An Old Bolshevik and a distinguished Marxist theoretician, Preobrazhensky was born in 1886. He joined the Russian Social Democratic Workers' Party (which split into Bolshevik and Menshevik factions) in 1903 and became a professional revolutionary, being repeatedly arrested and twice subject to internal exile. He led the local party organization in the Urals during the October revolution. In 1918 he was a member of the Left Communist group within the party which opposed the treaty of Brest Litovsk. He played an active role in the Civil War. He was a full member of the Central Committee and also Central Committee Secretary in 1920–21. In 1921–2 he was critical of NEP (New Economic Policy). He was worried about concessions to the peasantry and their implications for rural stratification and Soviet power. A signatory to the Platform of the 46 (October 1923), he was an active oppositionist in 1924–7; he was expelled from the party in December 1927 and exiled to Siberia. Under the influence of Stalin's move to the Left, he broke with the Opposition and in July 1929 accepted Stalin's leadership. He attended the Seventeenth Party Congress (1934) where he praised Stalin and collectivization, denounced both himself and Trotsky, and advocated unity and unconditional acceptance of the party line and Stalin's leadership. Arrested in 1935, he served as a prosecution witness at the trial of Zinoviev in 1936. Arrested again in 1936, he was not brought to a public trial, probably because of his refusal to confess to non-existent crimes. He was shot in 1937.

Preobrazhensky was the author of a large number of books and articles. They covered the exposition of Marxist–Leninist theory, financial and monetary questions, economic policy in France and economic policy in the USSR. Preobrazhensky's most original and important work concerned the problem of building socialism in a backward, overwhelmingly agrarian country.

Marx and Engels did not analyse how a future socialist economy would be organized and strongly opposed utopian socialism with its speculations divorced from current reality. Nevertheless, from their criticism of the anarchy of production under capitalism and their analysis of the views of rivals in the socialist movement, it is possible to draw inferences about how they expected a socialist economy to function. At the end of the 19th century Marxists had worked out some preliminary ideas for the transition to socialism and the organization of a socialist economy, as can be seen, for example, from the 1891 Erfurt Programme of the German SDP and Kautsky's *Das Erfurter Programm* (Stuttgart, 1892) which is a commentary on it. They assumed, however, that the country concerned would be predominantly working-class and have a highly developed industry. In the 1920s, however, the Bolsheviks found themselves in power in a predominantly agrarian country at a low level of economic development. How should they build socialism in these circumstances? It is in answering this question that Preobrazhensky made his main contribution.

In *Novaya ekonomika* (1926a) he argued that just as capitalist accumulation had required an earlier period of original accumulation (*Capital*, Vol. 1, part VIII), so socialist accumulation would require an initial phase of original *socialist* accumulation. That is, economic growth on the basis of investment generated within industry would have to be preceded, in backward Russia with its limited industrial apparatus, by a period of economic growth on the basis of investment resources obtained from outside the state sector. He generalized his argument into a fundamental law of socialist accumulation which runs as follows:

The more backward economically, petty-bourgeois, peasant, a particular country is which has gone over to the socialist organization of production, and the smaller the inheritance received by the socialist accumulation fund of the proletariat of this country when the social revolution takes place, by so much the more, in proportion, will socialist accumulation be obliged to rely on alienating part of the surplus product of pre-socialist forms of economy and the smaller will be the relative weight of accumulation on its own production basis, that is the less will it be nourished by the surplus product of the workers of socialist industry. Conversely, the more developed economically and industrially a country is, in which the social revolution triumphs, and the greater the material inheritance, in the form of highly developed industry and capitalistically organized agriculture, which the proletariat of this country receives from the bourgeoisie on nationalization, by so much the smaller will be the relative weight of pre-capitalist forms in the particular country; and the greater the need for the proletariat of this country to reduce non-equivalent exchange of its products for the products of the former colonies, by so much the more will the centre of gravity of socialist accumulation shift to the production basis of the socialist forms, that is, the more will it rely on the surplus product of its own industry and its own agriculture.

As methods to obtain investment resources from the non-state sector (predominantly peasant agriculture) Preobrazhensky recommended the state monopoly of foreign trade, price policy, railway tariffs, taxation and state control of the banking system. He paid particular attention to the advantages of price policy as opposed to the use of coercion.

Preobrazhensky's analysis was very controversial when it was first published and led to a very heated debate. The reason for this is that the political basis of the Soviet regime in the 1920s was the precarious compromise between the Bolsheviks and the peasantry represented by the New Economic Policy. In addition, economic policy was based on the encouragement by the Bolsheviks for the peasants to 'enrich yourselves'. It was hoped that the development of peasant agriculture, in a mixed economy in which the commanding heights were in the hands of the state, would provide the food, raw materials, exports, internal market and labour force necessary for Soviet economic development. Hence Preobrazhensky's argument, with its presentation of the case for accumulation at the expense of peasant agriculture, was both politically and economically very disturbing. In particular, the analogy with original capitalist accumulation was distinctly ominous. According to Marx, original capitalist accumulation was based mainly on force, in particular on the use of force to expropriate the land from the peasantry. In the minds of the supporters of NEP, Preobrazhensky's analysis raised the spectre of a revival of the methods of War Communism.

Preobrazhensky's ideas evolved over time. In a paper of 1921, the very year the NEP was introduced, he anticipated an armed conflict between the Soviet state and the kulaks. He regarded this as inevitable and argued in good Stalinist style that 'the outcome of the struggle will depend largely on the degree of organization of the two extreme poles, but especially on the strength of the state apparatus of the proletarian dictatorship'. He concluded his argument, which was published at a time of serious famine and disease, partly caused by the class-war policies of the Bolsheviks, by warning his readers 'to prepare for everything that will ensure victory in the inevitable class battles that are to come'. In a paper of 1924, the thesis about the inevitable conflict between the state and the peasantry still plays a central role, but economic levers (e.g., price policy) rather than coercion, play the key role in resolving the conflict in the interests of socialist accumulation.

In a paper of 1927, attention has shifted to the conditions for growth equilibrium. The Harrodian conclusion about the essential precariousness of dynamic equilibrium is reached. The lesson is drawn that 'The sum of these contradictions shows how closely our development towards socialism is connected with the necessity – for not only political but also for economic reasons – to make a break in our socialist isolation and to rely in the future on the material resources of other socialist countries.'

In an unpublished paper of 1931 he criticized overinvestment and pointed out the danger of an 'overaccumulation crisis'. His argument that 'socialism is production for consumption's sake' was unacceptable during the frenzy of the Soviet Great Leap Forward and was condemned as heretical. His position in 1931 seems to have been similar to that of Rakovsky, another Left Communist intellectual, who in an article of 1930 warned against the coming Soviet economic crisis (which shook the whole economy in 1931–3) and stressed the wasteful and inefficient methods of Stalinist industrialization.

The accumulation that Preobrazhensky theorized about was *socialist accumulation*, that is, accumulation leading to the development of socialist relations of production. It is entirely natural, for example, that the imaginary author of Preobrazhensky's book *From NEP to Socialism* (1922), which takes the form of lectures supposedly given in 1920, is simultaneously a university professor and a fitter in a railway workshop. This reflected Preobrazhensky's expectation that the division of labour would be sharply reduced under socialism.

Preobrazhensky's work has had an enormous influence throughout the world. In the USSR in the 1920s he played a major role in the debate about the main directions of economic policy. In the West he was rediscovered in a famous paper in the *Quarterly Journal of Economics* (1950) and has been much discussed ever since. In the Third World his ideas play an important role in theoretical discussions and policy debates. He is rightly considered one of the outstanding Marxist economists of the 20th century.

SELECTED WORKS
1920. (With N.I. Bukharin.) *Azbuka kommunizma*. Petrograd. Trans. as *The ABC of Communism*, Ann Arbor: University of Michigan Press, 1966.
1921. *Bumazhnye den' gyi v epokhu proletarskoi dictatury* (Paper money in the epoch of the proletarian dictatorship). Tiflis.
1922. *Ot nepa k sotzializmu*. Moscow. Trans. by B. Pearce as *From NEP to Socialism*, London: New Park Publishers, 1973.
1926a. *Novaia ekonomika*. Moscow. Trans. by B. Pearce as *The New Economics*, Oxford: Clarendon Press, 1965.
1926b. *Ekonomika i finansy sovremennoi frantsii* (The economics and finances of contemporary France). Moscow.
1930. *Teoriia padaiushchei valiuty* (The theory of a depreciating currency). Moscow.
1931. *Zakat kapitalizma*. Moscow. Trans. as *The Decline of Capitalism*, New York: M.E. Sharpe, 1985.
1980. *The Crisis of Soviet Industrialization*. Ed. D.A. Filtzer, London: Macmillan; New York: M.E. Sharpe. (This book of selected articles contains on pp. 237–40 a select bibliography of Preobrazhensky's works.)

BIBLIOGRAPHY
Day, R. 1975. Preobrazhensky and the theory of the transition period. *Soviet Studies* 27(2), April, 196–219.
Erlich, A. 1950. Preobrazhenski and the economics of Soviet industrialization. *Quarterly Journal of Economics* 64(1), February, 57–88.
Erlich, A. 1960. *The Soviet Industrialization Debate*. Cambridge, Mass.: Harvard University Press.
Filtzer, D. 1978. Preobrazhensky and the problem of the Soviet transition. *Critique* 9, Spring-Summer, 63–84.
Millar, J.R. 1978. A note on primitive accumulation in Marx and Preobrazhensky. *Soviet Studies* 30(3), July, 384–93.

Prices and Quantities

A. BRODY

These are the most directly and readily observable attributes of commodities (goods and services produced for and exchanged on the market). Both price and quantity relate to a unit (piece, bushel, barrel, pound etc.), established usually by commercial practice as the customary unit of reckoning.

The intrinsically numerical character of prices and quantities renders accounts and statistics, the incessant measurement of the stream of commodities, feasible. This preoccupation is motivated by and yields motivation to business and economic interests. It also seems to be responsible for the profound drive to develop economic theories with the aid of mathematical tools, applied already successfully to the exigencies of natural sciences.

The units of measurement are manifold on the various markets and are also arbitrary to a certain extent. If the units undergo any changes, say, when measuring in grammes instead of ounces, then the numerical magnitude of both prices and quantities changes accordingly. Nevertheless this change in their numerical expression must not alter the total value (volume) of a given amount of commodities so measured: if the unit is doubled then the price of the new unit doubles likewise but the numerical expression of the quantity is halved.

This interdepencence of prices and quantities prompted an historically early perception of their parallel, dual character. To this was soon added the appreciation of the mutual effect they exert on each other in the market. As Smith (1776) explained: if the quantity brought to market surpasses the effective demand, that is if an oversupply exists, this will depress prices. On the other hand, a high or excessively profitable price will induce a stepped up production of the commodity in question, possibly also a reduction in its effective demand. This skew-symmetric relationship, with quantities acting negatively on prices while prices influence quantities positively, has remained the popular wisdom of everyday economics up to the present day.

Later investigations and descriptions pointed to the existence of different mechanisms; be it the 'target farmer' in Third World countries who reacts to a

218

rise in prices by reducing the quantity brought to market, or instances of administratively guided economic situations where the economic agents try to minimize their productive effort once prices are fixed. Still the basic form of interdependence in the market, as elucidated by Smith, remained valid in the majority of economic transactions and gained popular and scientific sanction and consensus.

Smith argued that there was a more or less perfect functioning of the 'invisible hand' of the market forces that promotes equilibrium (equality of production and consumption, prices and costs) on almost all markets almost all of the time. Equilibrium therefore came to be seen as the normal state of affairs: the productive effort geared to match effective and solvent needs of the society. Random shocks, whether caused by changes in taste, technology or circumstances, were believed soon to be adjusted to. Hence the general prescription to economists (and politicians): not to interfere with this near perfect mechanism and not to tolerate obstacles, constraints, monopolies hampering the smooth operation of markets.

Here the economic profession split for the next two centuries. Economists less convinced about the fairness and impartiality, optimality and efficiency of markets and worried also about the historically emerging adverse tendencies, started critical investigations. They still accepted equilibrium as a theoretical tool of reasoning yet became increasingly aware of certain inadequacies observed on the market. With Ricardo (1817) and Marx (1867) the school of the labour theory of value came into being. This school maintained that prices and quantities are regulated in last instance by the respective amounts of live and congealed labour bestowed on the production of the commodities in question. They were interested mainly in long run tendencies in the economic circumstances of whole societies and used equilibrium reasoning to spell out these tendencies and also as a critical tool against existing imperfections. They were also responsible for developing more clearly the dual categories of value-in-use and value-in-exchange: the extensive and intensive attributes of commodities. Marx particularly excelled in developing economic terminology in decidedly dual categories with analogous and parallel reasoning for price-type and quantity-type theorems as, for instance, the process of production and the process of realization, surplus product and surplus value, technical and organic composition of capital etc. This he considered as the main achievement of his approach.

> The best thing in my book is: 1. the emphasis on the dual character of labour, right in the first chapter, according to whether the labour is expressed in use value or exchange value (this is the basis of the whole understanding of facts).

The other school, less critical about the market and seeking rather the perfection of market mechanisms, has been interested more in short run responses of the economic system, looking for local and particular explanation of the actual behaviour found on the diverse markets. They maintained that prices and quantities are determined by the marginal adjustments needed to adapt to equilibrium; thus prices, in particular, depend on marginal costs and quantities will be determined by maximizing profits. Among others it has been mainly

Pareto (1896) and Marshall (1920) who honed the economic arguments to the textbook precision of present-day economics.

With Böhm-Bawerk (1896) the battle between the two schools became exacerbated and they spared no argument in refuting 'inimical' standpoints. This confrontation remained heated and mostly unjust on both sides, harbouring a sometimes implicit, sometimes explicit, political content roughly dividing the two camps into evolutionary and revolutionary protagonists.

Considering its strictly theoretical merits the feud, nevertheless, resembles the altercation in mechanics: Newton's followers starting from equilibrium considerations and in search of the *causa efficiens*, while d'Alembert's disciples fight for an optimizing approach and are looking for the *causa finalis*, the aim and purpose of motion. It took much time and pain to acknowledge finally the basic equivalence of the two seemingly inimical and antagonistic approaches.

A similar insight has been injected into economics by von Neumann (1937). The theoretical roots of his approach to and model of General Economic Equilibrium can be found partly in earlier unifying efforts in mathematical economics and partly in thermodynamic reasoning.

As a pioneer in mathematical economics Walras (1874–7) had already developed a model to determine the prices and quantities of a given economic system simultaneously. By establishing $2n$ equations in the $2n$ unknowns, n prices and n quantities, he claimed the problem to be theoretically solved.

The idea was brilliant, the set-up ingenious, the proof incomplete. By counting equations it is not possible to prove existence and uniqueness of a mathematical solution. Even in the relatively simple case of linear equations where all the unknowns appear in their simplest form, multiplied only by some coefficients and then added up, the equations may be inconclusive. They may be contradictory, not permitting any solution at all. They may also be redundant and allow multiple solutions. And even if a solution exists and is unique we cannot exclude on *a priori* grounds some negative elements. Yet negative prices or negative quantities are usually meaningless in an economic context and cannot be accepted as genuine solutions.

These perplexing problems were eliminated finally by von Neumann in the following way.

Let $A = \{a_{ik}\}$ be the matrix of commodity inputs, $i = 1, 2, \ldots, m$ required to sustain one unit of the process $k = 1, 2, \ldots, n$ and similarly $B = \{b_{ik}\}$ the matrix of outputs yielded by the respective processes. Then, given p prices and x quantities (or 'intensities of production') pAx and pBx will express the total value of inputs (respectively, outputs). Thus $\lambda = \lambda(p, x) = pBx/pAx$ represents the rate of interest (as a relation of proceeds to advances in the process of realization, or the rate of possible growth as a relation of commodities produced to commodities consumed in the production process).

Analysing the gradients of this function leads to the following dual conclusion: If $\partial\lambda/\partial x = (pB - \lambda pA)/pAx$ is non-positive, that is if

$$pB \leqslant \lambda pA \qquad (1)$$

then λ cannot be further increased by any variation of x and hence will be maximal. If inequality obtains in (1) for any k, then $x_k = 0$ because the process operates at a loss and should be discontinued.

If on the other hand, $\partial\lambda/\partial p = (Bx - \lambda Ax)/pAx$ is non-negative, that is if

$$Bx \geqslant \lambda Ax \qquad (2)$$

then λ cannot be further diminished by any variation of p and hence will be minimal. If inequality obtains in (2) for any i, then $p_i = 0$ because the commodity is produced in a superfluous quantity and thus turns into a 'free' good.

Von Neumann now proved that the function $\lambda(p, x)$ has a 'saddle point' for positive prices and quantities, where the maximal rate of growth equals the minimal rate of interest. Thus he succeeded in solving the economic problem of equilibrium by defining a so-called potential function and replacing equations by inequalities. Existence and positivity of prices and quantities in equilibrium still permit multiple equilibria, in a double sense.

Firstly, as can be seen, every multiple of the equilibrium price system yields the same equilibrium value and likewise every multiple of the equilibrium quantities is again a system in equilibrium. Thus only proportions and not absolute magnitudes are determined. Yet by choosing, as Walras did, one of the prices as 'numeraire' and expressing all the others as multiples of this 'numeraire' – and fixing one of the quantities as the reference unit – the system can be made wholly determinate.

Secondly, there are certain cases – they could be called 'degenerate' – where true multiplicity of entirely different solutions may emerge. This problem can sometimes be remedied by a small perturbation of the initial data. Yet, it now appears that the possibility of multiple equilibria cannot be ruled out *ab ovo*, because they may appear in real economic systems just as well.

The theoretically decisive root of von Neumann's approach can be found in phenomenological thermodynamics, especially with Gibbs (1875), whose treatise 'On the Equilibrium of Heterogeneous Substances' synthesized classical thermodynamics and opened the way for physical chemistry. He applied first a 'max-min' criterion for equilibrium: maximizing entropy and minimizing energy, just as von Neumann maximized the growth rate and minimized the rate of interest, and he seems to have been the first to apply inequalities as well as equations in the description and analysis of equilibrium.

Von Neumann was fully aware of the analogy and stressed it when setting up his potential function $\Phi(X, Y)$, to be maximized by quantities X and minimized by prices Y:

> A direct interpretation of the function $\Phi(X, Y)$ would be highly desirable. Its rôle appears to be similar to that of thermodynamic potentials in phenomenological thermodynamics; it can be surmised that the similarity will persist in its full phenomenological generality (independently of our restrictive idealization).

Von Neumann's original notation followed the then accepted usage in physics:

X for 'extensive magnitudes', that is quantities, and Y for 'intensive magnitudes', that is prices. The gradients of a potential function (the partial derivatives according to the variables) spell out the 'force field' in physics, and the vanishing of those gradients is the necessary requirement of equilibrium. In the von Neumann model, as in thermodynamics, theoretical considerations induce a complex 'saddle point' problem: instead of simply maximizing the potential function the saddle point can be found only through minimizing by some and maximizing by other variables.

It is not pure coincidence that this thermodynamic approach proved to be so fertile in handling economic problems. New investigations in the axiomatic foundation of thermodynamics indicate (Giles, 1964, p. 26) that 'any experimentally verifiable assertion of thermodynamics can be expressed in terms of states with the aid of the operation + and the relation → alone'.

Though the axioms related to the permitted → transformations may turn out slightly differently in economics – there is important work undertaken concerning variously formulated basic axioms, Debreu (1959) being a powerful and articulate example – it is evident that the mathematical structures underlying the two scientific disciplines are closely similar.

The new approach, because of the unification of criteria of optimality with criteria of equilibrium, did much to bridge the gap between the two opposing schools of economic thought. Both found their basic ideas tolerably well reflected in the set-up of the von Neumann model and hence a new round of revision and even partial reconciliation could be started.

One should stress: it has been surely the 'restrictive idealization' that facilitated the general acceptance of the new approach. The model only encompasses linear processes with a linear combination of inputs, resulting in a likewise linear combination of commodities. It represents, furthermore, only the production of freely reproducible commodities, that is: it does not contain any external constraints on the scale of production. Such a model keeps data and computational requirements relatively modest and is also easy to grasp.

With matrix notation now universally accepted this convenient shorthand made the model mathematically transparent. The very simple statement of dual equilibrium, $\lambda pA = pB$ and $\lambda Ax = Bx$, could not possibly be simplified further.

We now have an almost complete mathematical theory of so-called 'matrix pencils', that is matrices of the form $A + \lambda B$. It is interesting to note that Weierstrass (1867) reported on his investigations concerning this form in the same decade in which most of the ingredients, indispensable for our topic to take its present shape, were published. Marx, Walras, Gibbs and Weierstrass made known their results in the same decade not only independently but without having the slightest notion about each other.

With the advent of computers, also pioneered by von Neumann, matrices with several thousands of rows and columns became manageable and this permitted and motivated an ever-broadening use and proliferation of a family of models having their theoretical and mathematical source in the von Neumann model.

Some very important and justly famous models were developed in the next decades. Being all equivalent in a mathematical sense to the Neumann model, as it has been demonstrated in most instances by the respective authors themselves, they can and should be considered as mathematical variants of the latter: input–output analysis, as proposed by Leontief (1941), linear programming, as investigated by Dantzig (1947) and Kantorovich (1940), the neo-Ricardian model set up by Sraffa (1960) and finally two-person game theory, an earlier product of von Neumann (1926), reaching broader scholarly circles only with the von Neumann–Morgenstern (1944) volume. (The last contains a further generalization to n-person games.)

In spite of the mathematical equivalence those models have been developed mostly independently and have roots in widely different economic considerations. Sraffa's approach, a careful and consistent restatement of Ricardo's value theory, proved to be particularly important. The underlying idea, if possible, is even more simple here. In a self-replacing system where, in the absence of growth, $\lambda = 1$, with no joint products, hence $B = 1$, the prices can be determined unequivocally by the postulate: the inputs required to reproduce the respective commodities have to be defrayed from the proceeds of selling the same commodities. Hence the proportions of prices and quantities are determined by the dual system of equations

$$pA = p \quad \text{and} \quad Ax = x. \tag{3}$$

Still in the more realistic cases, when extended reproduction and joint products have to be admitted, the description and solution is more rigorously and easily furnished by embedding the Sraffa system in a general von Neumann model.

Considering also the neo-Marxian restatement of labour theory as furnished by Brody (1970) and Morishima (1973), exploiting the Leontief model, where

$$p(A + \lambda B) = p \quad \text{and} \quad (A + \lambda B)x = x \tag{4}$$

and B interpreted as a stock-input matrix, a certain consensus seems to be reached.

According to the neoclassical exposition of Hahn (1982), all the schools would compute the same numerical magnitudes for prices and quantities for an economic system in equilibrium. They would accept the same system of equations, though they would interpret those equations differently. Deeper and yet unreconciled differences emerge only when abandoning the critical point of equilibrium.

With painfully won reconciliation in sight, a new theoretical attack on equilibrium reasoning takes shape. Kornai (1971), collecting all the critical observations and deeply influenced by the inadequacies of economic systems which endeavour to replace the market by equilibrium computations, declared: the equilibrium school 'has become a brake on the development of economic thought'.

Paradigms – and equilibrium thinking is one such, with a domain much broader than economics alone – are seldom damaged by criticism. They may be done away with only by new and more powerful paradigms. Hence they rather thrive on objections – and all the internal problems already emerged with Smith who implicitly or explicitly maintained that equilibrium (i) exists, is (ii) optimal, is (iii) pursued and is also (iv) achieved.

Existence has been proved yet under 'restrictive idealization' in linear models, but by a shrewd mind, knowing that it is permitted to approximate most functions, however, complicated, linearly by taking their derivatives in the neighbourhood of the point analysed. (This may be achieved by taking a series expansion and neglecting terms of higher order.) The isomorphism of matrices and operators has been also well known to the pioneers of operator theory. So it is no wonder that all the models introduced are wide open to further generalization. Here non-linear programming, with Kuhn and Tucker (1956) and Martos (1975) and non-linear input–output models with Morishima (1964) have to be mentioned, also the success in generalizing the Neumann model by Medvegyev (1984) and applying operator calculus with Thijs ten Raa (1983). An increasing unification with linear and non-linear systems theory and with modern non-equilibrium thermodynamics can be safely predicted.

Optimality has also ethical, social, psychological and political connotations because one has to propose an entity (growth rate, utility, satisfaction, equity etc.) to be optimized. In this respect our subject belongs to the domain of welfare economics. Mathematically, the question is fairly simple: equilibrium and optimality can be made to correspond because solving equations is equivalent to minimizing the errors of the solution. That is: the solutions of $Ax = b$ and $Ax = r$ with $\Sigma(r - b)^2 \to$ minimal are the same if they both exist.

Ethical, political, and other convictions will of course always influence scholars in choosing and developing their topics but, luckily, they do not play any role in proving or refuting theorems and corollaries.

Stability, the question whether equilibrium can or cannot be achieved, if pursued, and maintained, once achieved, is the most interesting question in the forefront of present research. The stability analysis of economic systems, performed by methods borrowed again from physics and also thermodynamics: analysis of the eigenvalues of the response matrix, negative definiteness, discussion of the second partial derivatives, the le Chatelier–Braun principle etc., indicate that both market and planning systems are usually stable, yet seldom asymptotically stable, and if asymptotically stable the speed of convergence is usually very slow.

Stability means that a given deviation from equilibrium will now grow without bound: if the deviation is initially small it will not become infinite. This secures the feasibility of the system, its ability to function; yet a system may be stable and perform very poorly. Even asymptotic stability, that is achieving the decline and vanishing of discrepancies, is an unsatisfactory criterion in economic matters because by the time the equilibrium point is reached or approximated it may be already displaced by changes of the system itself.

In reality economic systems move not in slowly changing equilibrium states but along so-called transients, a succession of non-equilibrium positions. Thus we are still far from an acceptable theory of economic motion. The models introduced spell our requirements of equilibrium but not the actual forces bringing, or not bringing the system to equilibrium. Still, certain inroads have been made by models of cycles, for example, Kalecki (1935), Goodwin (1967) and Brody (1985).

But perhaps more important than analysis seems to be the task of synthesis. Acknowledging that neither plan nor market can avoid economic fluctuations, the quest for controlling prices and quantities in a smoother and more efficient way is understandable. Questions of optimal control in linear and non-linear systems emerge and once approximately solved the search will go unavoidably deeper: how to control the position of equilibrium itself, how to become master of structure and technology. To shape interdependence itself in a conscientious manner, to influence the outcome of technological and structural change is the next item on the agenda of mathematical economics.

BIBLIOGRAPHY

Böhm-Bawerk, E. 1896. Zum Abschluss des Marxschen Systems. In *Festgaben für Karl Knies*, Berlin. Translation in *Karl Marx and the Close of his System* by Eugen Böhm-Bawerk, ed. P. Sweezy, Reprints of Economic Classics, New York: A.M. Kelley, 1966.

Brody, A. 1970. *Proportions, Prices and Planning*. Amsterdam: North-Holland.

Brody, A. 1985. *Slowdown: Global Economic Maladies*. Beverly Hills: Sage.

Dantzig, G. 1947. Maximization of a linear function of variables subject to linear inequalities. In *Activity Analysis of Production and Allocation*, ed. T.C. Koopmans, New York: Wiley; London: Chapman, 1951.

Debreu, G. 1959. *Theory of Value: an axiomatic analysis of economic equilibrium*. Cowles Foundation Monograph No. 17, New York: Wiley.

Gibbs, J.W. 1875. On the equilibrium of heterogeneous substances. *Transactions of the Connecticut Academy* III, October 1875–May 1876 and May 1877–July 1878. (See also *The Scientific Papers of J. Willard Gibbs*, New York: Dover, 1961.)

Giles, R. 1964. *Mathematical Foundations of Thermodynamics*. Oxford and New York: Pergamon Press.

Goodwin, R. 1967. A growth cycle. In *Socialism, Capitalism and Economic Growth*, ed. C.H. Feinstein, Cambridge: Cambridge University Press.

Hahn, F. 1982. The neo-Ricardians. *Cambridge Journal of Economics* 6(4), December, 353–74.

Kalecki, M. 1935. A macrodynamic theory of business cycles. *Econometrica* 3(1), July, 327–44.

Kantorovich, L.V. 1940. Ob odnom effektivnon metode reshenia nekotorih klassov extremalnih problem (On an efficient method to solve some classes of external problems). *Dokladi Akademii Nauk SSSR* 28.

Kornai, J. 1971. *Anti-Equilibrium. On economic systems theory and tasks of research.* Amsterdam and London: North-Holland.

Kuhn, H.W. and Tucker, A.W. (eds) 1956. Linear inequalities and related systems. *Annals of Mathematics Studies* No. 38, Princeton: Princeton University Press.

Leontief, W. 1941. *The Structure of American Economy 1919–1929*. New York: Oxford University Press.

Marshall, A. 1920. *Principles of Economics*. 8th edn, New York: Macmillan, 1956; London: Macmillan, 1964.

Martos, B. 1975. *Nonlinear Programming. Theory and Methods.* Amsterdam: North-Holland.

Marx, K. 1867. *Capital.* Vol. I, Moscow: Foreign Languages Publishing House, 1961.

Medvegyev, P. 1984. A general existence theorem for von Neumann economic growth models. *Econometrica* 52(4), July, 963–74.

Morishima, M. 1964. *Equilibrium, Stability and Growth: a Multi-sectoral Analysis.* Oxford: Clarendon Press.

Morishima, M. 1973. *Marx's Economics. A Dual Theory of Value and Growth.* Cambridge and New York: Cambridge University Press.

Neumann, J. von. 1928. Zur Theorie der Gesellschaftsspiele (On the theory of games of strategy). In *Collected Works*, Oxford: Pergamon Press, 1963; New York: Macmillan.

Neumann, J. von. 1937. A model of general economic equilibrium. In *Collected Works*, Oxford: Pergamon Press, 1963; New York: Macmillan.

Neumann, J. von and Morgenstern, O. 1944. *Theory of Games and Economic Behavior.* Princeton: Princeton University Press.

Pareto, V. 1896. *Cours d'économie politique.* In *Oeuvres Complètes*, Geneva: Librairie Droz, 1964–7.

Ricardo, D. 1817. *Principles of Political Economy and Taxation.* In *Works and Correspondence of David Ricardo.* Vol. 1, ed. P. Sraffa, Cambridge: Cambridge University Press, 1951; New York: Cambridge University Press, 1973.

Smith, A. 1776. *An Inquiry into the Nature and Causes of the Wealth of Nations.* Ed. E. Cannan, London: Methuen, 1961; Chicago: University of Chicago Press, 1976.

Sraffa, P. 1960. *Production of Commodities by Means of Commodities.* Cambridge: Cambridge University Press.

Thijs ten Raa. 1983. Dynamic input–output analysis with distributed activities. *IFAC/IFORS Conference Reprints*, Washington, DC.

Walras, L. 1874–7. *Elements of Pure Economics or the Theory of Social Wealth.* London: Allen & Unwin, 1954; Homewood, Ill.: R.D. Irwin.

Weierstrass, K. 1867. Zur Theorie der bilinearen und quadratischen Formen (On the theory of bilinear and quadratic forms). Berlin, *Monatshefte der Akademie der Wissenschaften*, 310–38.

Socialism

ALEC NOVE

It is said that the word 'socialism' was first used by Pierre Leroux, a supporter of Saint-Simon, in 1832, and was quickly taken up by Robert Owen. The word has meant many different things to different people. It has been used as a synonym for communism, i.e. as a bright vision of a future in which there are neither rich nor poor, neither exploiters nor exploited, in which, to use an expression borrowed from Charles Taylor, 'generic man is harmoniously united in the face of nature'. It is by definition the solution of most if not all economic problems, the end of 'alienation'. As such it has religious overtones: Man was at one time in harmony with society, and will become so once again. For others, these utopian-sounding aims are either meaningless or a vague ideal, the higher stage of communism. 'Socialism' is, so to speak, here on earth, and can be seen (according both to Soviet doctrine and to right-wing critics) in the 'really existing socialism' of countries in the Soviet sphere, who claim to be on the way towards a communist future. Still others criticize this 'really existing socialism' from the left, declaring it not to be socialism at all; their criteria for what constitutes socialism are not always very clear, some using the marxist vision as their point of departure, others laying stress on the lack of democracy, the hierarchical nature of society, and other departures from what, in their view, ought to be. The term 'socialism' is also used, or misused, to describe the aims and programme of the British Labour Party, or the state of affairs actually achieved under a series of social-democratic governments in Sweden. The term at one time had an appeal to moderates. Thus the moderate-reforming party of the Third Republic in France chose to call itself Radical-Socialist, though its leaders, such as Edouard Herriot, had no aims which could qualify as socialist. Then, at the extreme right of the political spectrum, Hitler's party was self-described as national-*socialist*.

So one should proceed at an early stage to a definition, or rather to exclusions. Not Hitler, obviously. Nor Herriot either. If one were to adopt a definition which corresponds with Marx's vision of socialism (of which much more below), there is the evident danger of adopting an impossibly rigid criterion by which to judge any real-world society: thus, whatever reasons there may be to criticize or condemn today's USSR, it would be rather pointless to 'accuse' it of not having ensured the withering away of the state, or not having 'surmounted' (*aufgehoben*) the division of labour. Let us provisionally accept the following as a definition of socialism: a society may be seen to be a socialist one if the major part of the means of production of goods and services are not in private hands, but are in some sense socially owned and operated, by state, socialized or cooperative enterprises. 'The major part' is enough. Just as any non-dogmatic socialist would accept that most 'capitalist' countries contain sizeable state and cooperative sectors but still deserve the label 'capitalist'. This leaves three big questions unanswered:

(1) What are the relationships between management and workforce *within* the enterprise?

(2) How do the production units interrelate? (i.e. by plan, by contractual or market relations, or some combination of both).

(3) If the state or other public bodies own and operate any part of the economy, who controls the state, and how? One remembers the remark attributed to Engels, that if state ownership is the criterion of socialism, the first socialist institution was the regimental tailor.

If the word 'socialist' was coined in 1832, the idea of socialism long preceded it. Among the first to put forward principles which contain strong socialist elements was Gerard Winstanley, representing the Levellers of Cromwell's time. They believed in equality, wished property to be held in common, opposed concentrations of private wealth. During the French revolution Babeuf denounced inequalities of wealth and advocated the overthrow of the government, which he saw as representing property-owners. Robert Owen could be described as a paternalist, in that he believed in good treatment of his employees (as can be seen even today in the housing he built for his workers in New Lanark), but he also envisaged what would now be called producers' cooperatives. As essentially a practical man, he can be distinguished from those 'utopian socialists' who, before Marx have painted a series of pictures of imaginary socialist-type societies. Leszek Kolakowski (1976) analyses the ideas of men like Fourier, Saint-Simon, Proudhon, and notes certain elements of similarity with those of Marx, and also some essential differences. They have in common, inter alia, a hate for the 'bourgeois' order, a society based upon greed, profit, the mercantile spirit. The French revolution substituted plutocracy for aristocracy. Unlike Marx, they did not consider this to be a progressive stage in the history of mankind, but, like Marx, they stressed the ugly features of capitalist industrialism and wished to do away with it, substituting a new harmony, cooperation, the reassertion of the true rights of Man. They rejected Adam Smith's basic idea that common good is generally attained through the competitive profit-making process. As, for instance, was asserted by Saint-Simon, the basic cause of human misery is free competition and the anarchy of the market. The so-called utopians varied in their approach to the issue of equality: thus in Fourier's 'phalansteries' the means of production were held in common, children were to be brought up together, the family would dissolve, there would be provision of subsistence for all, but Fourier would encourage individual enrichment through work (though not the inheritance of riches or unearned incomes). Some advocated violent revolution to achieve their objectives, others hated violence and hoped to persuade their fellow-citizens to adopt freely the ideas of the good and just society of their imagination.

As will be argued later, Marx differed from his predecessors not because he conceived of a realistic alternative to capitalism: there was much that was utopian in his ideas too. However *firstly* he did not go into detail as to how a future society would function; nothing in Marx is similar to such notions as phalansteries, or radiant cities of 1800 persons with 810 different human characteristics, or the idea that dirty work that needs doing will be done by boys, who, as everyone knows, like dirt; Marx favoured the emancipation of women, but he did not follow Fourier in drawing up a 'table des termes de l'alternat amoureux'.

Secondly, and more important, he provided a set of powerfully argued historical reasons as to why the desired state of affairs must come to pass. As Engels said at his graveside: 'Just as Darwin discovered the law of development of organic nature, so Marx discovered the law of development of human history.' The class struggle, the growth of monopoly capitalism, the proletarianization of the petty bourgeoisie (peasants, shopkeepers, small business men of all kinds), the growing misery of the masses, the growth of class-consciousness, the logic and consequences of large-scale industry, the belief that, having spectacularly developed the forms of production, the bourgeois-capitalist relations of production act as fetters on the further development of productive forces, all these things will lead inexorably towards socialism. Ever-deepening crises, the falling rate of profit, the refusal of the poverty-stricken masses to accept their lot, i.e. the accumulation of capitalist contradictions, will bring the system down. The proletariat, having overthrown the bourgeoisie, would inaugurate the classless society. In the marxist tradition there are various interpretations of the relative importance of historic necessity (i.e. inevitableness, a march towards a predestined goal) and voluntariness (deliberate human action designed to achieve the goal). These two principles coexist uneasily, and they can be seen as mutually inconsistent, but they can be reconciled. To take two examples, it *is* meaningful to assert that, should a professional soccer team play a school side, the professionals would 'inevitably' win. The same would be (was) true of a conflict between the Germans and say the Luxemburg army. However, the outcome requires human action, on the part of the footballers and the German soldiers respectively.

This calls for two kinds of comments. One relates to the interpretation of history, the other to the utopian elements of so-called scientific socialism.

It hardly needs stressing that capitalism has not evolved in the manner foreseen by Marx. He himself stressed, in a famous passage, that no mode of production passes from the historical scene before its productive potential is exhausted. He believed that capitalism was reaching exhaustion already when he was writing

Das Kapital. Over a hundred years later it is still not exhausted, and ever-new technological revolutions, while certainly presenting new problems and dilemmas of which we shall speak, continue to enlarge the productive potential of capitalist society. It is also clear that the concept of 'proletarianization' was wide of the mark. Yes, great concentrations of 'monopoly-capital' do exist, but so do very large numbers of small businesses and a far larger number of 'professionals' of all sorts and grades who are, or consider themselves to be, middle class. This fact has given rise to much debate among marxists, typified by the argument between Poulantzas and Erik Wright (see for example, Wright, 1979). We need not go into this argument, which turns on who could or could not be considered to be working class. The political and social fact remains that a large and growing proportion of the citizenry of developed countries do not own the means of production and are emphatically not class-conscious proletarians.

Furthermore, the development of the forces of production has made possible a substantial improvement in the living standards even of those who in any definition are workers. Clearly, they do not have 'nothing to lose but their chains'. It is neither original nor amusing to say that men who have 'nothing to lose' except a three-bedroomed house, a car, a video-tape machine and a holiday in Spain are not very likely to be revolutionaries, or indeed particularly interested in socialism. It is true none the less. Marx himself, and some of his followers, when willing to recognize that living standards could rise, insisted that this does not remove the essential antagonism between labour and capital, the existence of exploitation and alienation. In a sense this is so, though one must avoid an oversimplified zero-sum-game approach; situations arise in which both profits and wages can rise together, as they have done in successful capitalist countries in the twenty-five years that followed the last war. Nor is there any necessary correlation between the depth of human misery and the spirit of revolt. None the less, the lack of support for the socialist alternative in developed countries cannot be treated as merely a temporary aberration. It is also true that revolutions, whatever their merits or necessities, impose grave hardship upon people, notably the masses. The association of the word 'socialism' with revolution is therefore an important reason for many 'proletarians' *not* to support the socialist idea, at least in developed countries. 'Underdeveloped socialism' is a different question, to be tackled later.

Now to the utopian nature of Marx's 'scientific socialism'. The key points to make are:

1. *Abundance.* Here Marx reflects the optimism of his century, yet natural resources are not inexhaustible. Human needs and wants increase – as indeed Marx himself recognized. Conservationist and ecological socialism can be strongly defended, but this is precisely because resources (even the air we breathe, the water we drink) are finite. It is not the case that the problem of production has been 'solved', and that socialists will not require to take seriously the question of the allocation of scarce resources. I define 'abundance' as a sufficiency for all reasonable requirements at zero price.

2. *The non-acquisitive 'new man'*. His (and her) appearance surely presupposes abundance. Marx himself was perfectly clear that a share-poverty 'socialism' would reproduce 'the old rubbish'. Men do not become good by being so persuaded, or by reading good books. If there is enough for everyone, then there is no need to strive to keep things for oneself, one's family, one's locality, one's institution. If there is scarcity, therefore opportunity cost, therefore a situation in which there are mutually exclusive alternatives, then conflict on priorities of resource allocation is inevitable. This does not in fact require any assumption about individual egoism. Even unselfish persons tend to identify the needs they know with the common good. Indeed, in a complex modern society there is no generally accepted and objectively based criterion as to what 'the common good' is. Nor can any individual apprehend the multitude of alternative uses potentially available for the resources he or she desires, either for him/her self or for the given township, library, orchestra, football team, industry or whatever.

3. *The political assumptions*. These are linked with (1) and (2), above. The state withers away, not only because it is assumed that its 'essential' repressive functions are not needed when no ruling class imposes its will on the masses, but also because, to re-cite Charles Taylor, Marx assumed a 'generic man harmoniously united in the face of nature'. Consequently there would be no need for legal institutions, coercive powers, police, indeed any politics as we know them. Civil society and individuals will have merged, the task of the 'administration of things' would not be undertaken by political institutions, would be merely technical. There *is* no marxist *political* theory of socialism.

4. *The economic assumptions.*
(a) *Value theory and economic calculation.* The suppression of the market, of commodity production, of money, seems to involve the 'withering away' of the law of value. What is to replace it? Presumably it will continue to be important to use resources economically to provide the goods and services desired by society. How are calculations to be made? On this Marx is almost totally silent. Engels, in *Anti-Dühring*, speaks of assessing use-values and relating them to the labour-time required to provide for them. This runs at once into several rather evident problems. First is the theoretical one that Marx most emphatically (at the very beginning of the first volume of *Das Kapital*) asserted that different use-values were not comparable, so could not be added up or subtracted. A pen, a cup, a book, a skirt, a light-bulb (to take a few examples at random) satisfy different needs. The one thing they have in common, apart from satisfying various needs, is that they are the products of labour. How, in any case, are Engels's use-values to be computed, by whom, on the basis of what criteria? In a book wholly devoted to marxian use-value (*valeur d'usage*), G. Roland (1985) goes at length into the basically unsatisfactory treatment by Marx of use-value, due apparently to his anxiety to distance himself from subjective value theory. This has created some awkward problems for Soviet pricing theory, or at the very least does nothing to help. The dogmatists insist

that Marxian labour-values ought to underlie Soviet prices, or alternatively that these be modified into the equivalence of 'prices of production', but both of these share the characteristic of being based on effort, on cost. This not only fails to give due weight to utility(or user preferences), but also runs into yet another problem, or rather two interlinked problems: measuring labour inputs, and the failure to take into account other scarcities. A few brief remarks are appropriate on each of these points.

Can one actually identify the labour content, including the labour embodied in machine and materials, and the 'share' in joint overheads, of hundreds of thousands or even millions of different goods and services? This is a hugely difficult if not impossible task, even if one calculated only in hours of labour. But then what of skilled labour? How is it to be 'reduced' to simple labour? Marx does not handle this 'reduction' satisfactorily in discussing value in capitalist society, and in the end one is left with actual wage ratios as the only usable criterion, which is unhelpfully circular. And then can one treat labour as the only scarce factor? What of land, oil, timber, what of time (not labour-time, but, say, delay in construction)? Novozhilov remarked that the most modern equipment would be scarce even under full communism unless it be assumed that technical progress ceases.

Space forbids further remarks about other deficiencies of the labour-theory inherited from Marx. (Thus demand or price must affect labour-content if there are economies or diseconomies of scale, or if relative prices influence choice of techniques.) And if the purist retorts that Marxian value theory is not supposed to apply to socialist economies at all, then he or she must be asked: 'What is your alternative?'. This has (so far) usually taken the form of some surrogate labour-theory (such as hours of human effort), with all the deficiencies of such an approach.

(b) *'Simplicity'*. The lack of interest – until comparatively recently – of Marx and marxists in the question of economic calculation under socialism is explicable by a grave misunderstanding, i.e. by the belief that the complexities of modern industrial society are a consequence of commodity production and 'commodity fetishism', which conceal relations which, as Marx said, were inherently 'clear and transparent'. 'Everything will be quite simple without this so-called value', said Engels. Planning under socialism 'will be child's play', said Bebel. 'To organize the entire economy on the lines of the postal service, ... under the leadership of the armed proletariat, this is immediate [*sic*] task' (Lenin, in 1917), and so on. But evidently in a modern industrial society with hundreds of millions of people, hundreds of thousands of productive units, millions of products and services (if disaggregated down to specific items, there *are* millions), it is a hugely complex task to discover exactly who needs what, and to identify the most effective means of providing for needs, especially if one bears in mind that any output requires the acquisition (or allocation) of dozens or more of inputs. Barone (in his path-breaking 'Ministry of production in a collectivist state') pointed this out in 1908, but failed to get a hearing from the socialists of his time. It is nonsense to talk of labour under socialism being 'directly social', in the sense of being applied with advance knowledge of needs – contrasting with *ex post* validation through the market under capitalism. This can also be so if perfect knowledge and foresight were assumed, and the need to test *ex post* for possible error assumed to be unnecessary. All socialists (rightly!) reject theories which assume perfect foresight, perfect markets, perfect competition, when put forward by neoclassical model-builders. So, apart from problems of value theory, there is the sheer complexity of marketless, quantitative planning, the formidable obstacles in the way of identifying requirements and providing for their satisfaction.

(c) *Political-social implications.* Lest the above be seen as 'merely technical', and so remediable by computers, the objective requirements of marketless planning in a complex industrial economy are centralizing (who but the centre can identify need and ensure the allocation of means of production?), hierarchical, bureaucratic, and concentrate immense power over both people and things in the hands of the state apparatus. The importance of political democracy is undeniable, but the officials (who else?) who plan the output and allocation of sheet steel, sulphuric acid and flour are taking decisions unconnected with democratic voting – save in the sense that such voting should affect broad priorities. There were moments when Marx, Engels, Lenin, showed that they understood the inevitability of hierarchy: thus Lenin saw the socialist economy as a sort of 'single office, a single factory', with 'a single will linking all the sub-units together' to ensure the part of the economy fitted together 'like clockwork' (Lenin, 1962, pp. 157). But whereas clockwork functions automatically (i.e. it not unlike the 'hidden hand', or maybe the hidden pendulum), in a marketless economy the parts have to be moved by human beings charged with the purpose. The contrast between 'the administration of man' and 'the administration of things' (a phrase borrowed by Marx from Saint-Simon) is a false contrast: I am quite unable to 'administer' this piece of paper, but I can persuade a secretary to type it, a postman to deliver it to the publisher, and (hopefully!) the publisher decides to tell the printers to print it! All Soviet experience underlines the political and social consequences of the high concentration of hierarchically-organized economic power.

5. *Division of labour and 'alienation'.* There is, and must surely be, a division of labour between productive units (those that produce sulphuric acid, steel or hairdressing services are unlikely also to be making hats, computer software or music). Marx's notion of a universal man, who fishes, looks after sheep and writes literary criticism, without being a professional fisherman, shepherd or critic, makes no sense, other than in the (sensible but weaker) form of aiming at a greater degree of job interchangeability. Thus the author of these lines was once a soldier, then a bureaucrat, then a university teacher, but could not be all of these at once. The vertical devision of labour (e.g. between management and those managed) could also be modified by some system of rotation or election, but management is also a skill, and human intelligence is not of itself a guarantee of tolerable administrative ability: we all know of good specialists

who could not (and would not wish to) administer anything well. One is then struck by the inherent unreality of such books as by I. Mészáros (1972). Mészáros fully and correctly sets out Marx's view, and he does state that 'the political road to the supersession of alienation and reification' is a long one and success is not guaranteed. But he still sees the 'transcendence of alienation' as a meaningful goal, as if separation of Man from his product, his subordination to outside forces, the division of labour, can be overcome through the elimination of private ownership. And Kolakowski (1976, p. 172) is surely right when he notes that for Marx 'the fundamental premise of alienation is already present as soon as goods become commodities', and that 'the division of labour leads necessarily to commerce'. So alienation appears to be the inescapable consequence of an inescapable division of labour, so how can it be *aufgehoben*? Private ownership represents a particular manifestation of 'outside' control, and it is an important part of any socialist programme to give to labour a greater influence over the work process. But what can one make of Bettelheim (1968), when he criticizes Yugoslav-type self-management enterprises for what is surely the wrong reason: that they are controlled not by the workforce but by the market. It ought to be clear that production is for use, and that *what* is produced ought in the last analysis to conform to user needs, i.e. to be controlled by a force outside the production unit itself. This could be the market, in which bargaining takes place between producer and user. It could be a planning agency, who informs the production unit what it should be doing. *Tertium non datur.*

6. *Labour, wages, 'the proletariat'.* Several distinct points need to be made.

(a) *The end of the wages system.* This is not what real workers want. Money wages give freedom of choice, including the choice of hiring the services of each other (to repair the roof, baby-mind, drive to work or whatever). Marx's idea of tokens denominated in hours of labour ('which are not money and do not circulate') makes very little sense, and not surprisingly has not been applied. If goods are distributed free, this usually limits consumer choice: you take what you are *given.*

(b) *Labour direction* is the sole known alternative to material incentives or other forms of inequality. This was understood by Kautsky, Trotsky and Bukharin, when they discussed this question. The term 'labour market' has an opprobrious sound, reminiscent perhaps of a slave market. Yet workers are freer, have greater choice, more possibility to bargain, than under direction of labour, necessarily exercised by officials with power over persons.

(c) *The proletariat as redemptor humanis* is essentially a religious concept, unrelated to the qualities and desires of the real working class. Eloquent words on this subject have been written by Andre Gorz: 'No empirical observation or actual experience of struggle can lead to the discovery of the historic mission of the proletariat which, according to Marx, is the constituent of its class being' (Gorz, 1980, p. 22). Rudolf Bahro wrote that 'the proletariat, the collective subject of general emancipation, remains a philosophical hypothesis in which is concentrated the utopian element of marxism', and he added, rightly, that 'the immediate objectives of subordinate classes and strata are always conservative' (*sind immer Konservativ*) (1977, p. 174). But if one accepts these and other similar arguments, it follows that, as Lenin said, the working class left to itself will limit itself to 'trade union' types of demands, and so it is the task of the revolutionary intelligentsia to provide the revolutionary theory. This in turn leads to what has been called 'substitutionism', i.e. party dominated at the top by non-workers, which in its turn dominates society, an outcome prophesied by Bakunin well over a hundred years ago. It is clearly not the case that, to cite Marx's letter to Weydemeyer in 1852, 'the class struggle leads necessarily to the dictatorship of the proletariat', which 'is but a transition to the withering away of classes' (letter dated 5 March 1852, Marx, 1962, p. 427).

Marxists may now be impatiently protesting that the above analysis is a vision of full communism, that no one, certainly not Marx himself, expected this to be realized quickly, or even certainly. The much-used words 'socialisme ou barbarie' show a recognition that barbarism can be an outcome if the socialist idea fails. Trotsky spoke often of a 'transitional epoch' during which money, markets, commodity production, are indeed indispensables. Soviet discussions refer to the indeterminate length of time required to move from 'socialism' (i.e. Soviet reality, which they define as socialism) to full communism. For example, a book devoted to the subject and published for the fiftieth anniversary of the revolution duly lists the characteristics of communism (abundance; from each according to his ability, to each according to his needs; the elimination of commodity money relations, and so on), but goes on to stress that communism must be preceded by the lower 'socialist' phase, and that to try to overleap that phrase is 'a harmful utopia' (Gatovski et al., eds, 1967, pp. 9, 43).

Marx himself used 'socialism' and 'communism' almost as interchangeable terms. Whether 'really existing socialism' should be seen as a transitional society or as socialist is to some extent just a terminological question. In either case it is supposed to be evolving towards fully-fledged socialism or communism. But does it? Should it? What are the signs by which such an evolution can be identified?

Bettelheim has good evidence for his view that, for Marx and Engels, when the workers acquire the means of production, 'there will be in socialist society, even at the beginning, no commodities, no value, no money, and consequently no prices and no wages' (Bettelheim, 1968, p. 32). Equally strongly, the French critic Cornelius Castoriadis roundly asserts that 'Marx knew nothing of transitional societies infinitely contained within each other like Russian dolls or Chinese boxes, which Trotskyists later invented' (Castoriadis, 1979, p. 299). Marx did specifically say, in the *Grundrisse*, that 'nothing is more absurd than to imagine that the associated producers' would choose to interrelated via commodity production, exchange, markets. We have already noted that, in his *Critique of the Gotha Programme*, Marx envisaged an immediate conversion of wages into tokens denominated in hours of labour, not despite but *because* society will still bear the stigmata of pre-socialist attitudes. In the 1920s in the Soviet Union it seemed obvious to the party comrades that reducing the area of market relations was in some sense the equivalent of an advance towards socialism. Indeed those who forced 25 million peasant households to join so-called collective farms thought that this was part of the class struggle, though the effect was to turn independent 'petty-bourgeois' households, who did to a considerable degree control their own means of production and their product, into something akin to a new sort of state serfdom. If socialism is to do with the liberation of the 'direct producers', then surely this was a march in the wrong direction.

Similarly, can we say that the Hungarian or Soviet reformers of today are wrong in advocating an extension of 'commodity–money relations'? And if the point is made that such a judgment would be premature, but that communism is still an aim to pursue when circumstances are propitious, it is legitimate to ask: what circumstances can be imagined in which communism/socialism in Marx's sense *could* come about? No wonder the Soviet orthodoxy of today is to speak of 'mature socialism' as a long-term stage, with communism seen as a remote objective of no short-term operational significance.

There were also socialist alternatives to Marx, during and since his lifetime. William Morris combined some ideas derived from Marx with ethical socialism and devotion to arts and crafts. Others further developed Christian socialism of various kinds, and indeed much could be made of the contrast between Christian ideals and the mercantile spirit, the 'dark satanic mills' ('and we will build Jerusalem in England's green and pleasant land'). The British Labour Party in its origins and for many decades afterwards was heavily influenced by Christian beliefs, especially those based on Methodist and other nonconformist creeds (thereby attracting some contemptuous remarks from Lenin). The Fabian Society (Shaw, the Webbs and others) by contrast, preached non-religious (and non-violent) socialism, opposed extremes of inequality, and advocated industrial democracy. However, though they too influenced the Labour Party, the Society remained a small intellectual group, with a tendency to believe that an elite (themselves), or even a strong dictator, would show the way. It is perhaps no accident that both Shaw and the Webbs lived to express an admiration for Stalin – even though they themselves would recoil from cruelty and killing. Mention must also be made of G.D.H. Cole and 'guild socialism', with decentralized decision-making by producers' associations.

On the continent, social-democracy nominally retained its allegiance to Marxism. However already in 1899 Edward Bernstein advocated a non-revolutionary revision of many of Marx's theories. While the leaders of German social-democracy, men like Bebel and Kautsky, rejected Bernstein's 'revisionism', it was in fact rooted in the considerable improvement of the workers' living standards, the weakening of revolutionary spirit. In the end, while retaining marxism as their nominal creed, German and other continental social-democrats (notably the 'Austro-marxists', such as Otto Bauer) adopted a non-revolutionary position which differed little from Bernstein's and become a party of moderate reform within capitalist society.

In Russia, side by side with the growth of marxism (initially preached by men such as Plekhanov and Zieber) there arose other and non-marxist socialist currents, sometimes labelled 'populist'. They believed that a Russian road to some form of socialism could be found, perhaps based on traditional communal institutions, which would enable capitalism to be by-passed. These ideas came from men such as Mikhailovsky and Vorontsov. As we shall see, Mark himself did not reject this possibility. There were also some influential anarchist socialists, owing inspiration to Bakunin, of whom Prince Peter Kropotkin was a colourful example.

Since 1945 European social-democrats have tended to abandon their already tenuous allegiance to Marx and Marxism, and it may be hard to discern the extent of commitment to socialism of any sort in the programme and policies of the German and French parties. By contrast, the recent evolution of the Italian *communist* party has put it close to a social-democratic, evolutionist position. Opinions vary within the British and the Scandinavian Labour parties. Further change may well depend greatly on what happens to contemporary capitalism.

Of course the future may reserve surprises for us all. While material resources may be finite, the scientific-technical revolution may enable us to economize labour on a big scale. The resulting high level of unemplyment may be a chronic disease. True, by freeing factory and office labour, we could, in a more rational society, greatly enlarge labour-intensive forms of providing a higher quality of life. But precisely this is opposed, and successfully so, by the New Right, by the 'Chicago' ideology, which is vehemently against public expenditures. Yet we may already be reaching a stage in which the *profitable* (privately-profitable) use of labour can cover only a portion of those available for work. A possible reading of Marx places emphasis on equating the realm of freedom with freedom *from* work (i.e. from necessity), with a much shorter working week, and Gorz too sees freedom as a situation where one can undertake handicrafts and other hobbies. This would be a paradoxical reversal of the view that the one scarce factor of production is labour, since then it would be the abundant factor, the problem being how to share it out. This would not be the era of abundance. To cite an example, fish could be caught by modern trawlers using fewer fishermen, but dangers of over-fishing would compel a strict limitation on numbers caught. This brings one back to the idea of an environment-preserving, ecologically-conscious, employment-sharing socialism as an attractive alternative to capitalism. But this was not Marx's alternative.

A case for socialism can be made, not only along the 'ecological' lines mentioned above. In the developed world, massive resources are devoted to persuading people to buy trivia, to keep up with the Joneses. Unemployment is a scourge which is a threat to public order. External diseconomies (and external economies too) frequently cause the pursuit of private micro-profit to conflict with more general interest. The 'quality of life' may not be readily quantifiable, but several economists (for instance Kuznets, Tobin) have noted that conventional measures of economic growth by GNP can conceal real losses, or indeed count real *costs* of urban living as a net addition to welfare. The inequalities of income and property-ownership have all too often no visible connection with the contribution to society or to production of the individuals concerned.

Schumpeter (cited in Brus, 1980) rightly pointed out that no social system 'can function which is based exclusively on free contracts . . . and in which everyone is guided only by personal short-term interest'. Furthermore, fanatics of the New Right are engaged in reducing essential public services, disintegrating where possible the welfare state, cutting back public transport, pursuing dogmatic monetarism, in the naive belief that primitive laissez-faire is the best of all possible worlds. It may turn out that the grave-diggers of capitalism will be those ultra-'liberal' ideologists who fail to understand how modern capitalism really works, that the so-called imperfections (price and wage stickiness, administered prices, oligopoly and so on) are preconditions for the functioning of the system. On the assumption of perfect competition, perfect markets, perfect foresight, there is no role for the entrepreneur, no reason for firms to exist, and logically enough profits tend to zero in equilibrium. The idea that rational investment decisions are possible when we face so many inflationary uncertainties (what will the rate of the dollar, or the rate of interest, be in a year's time?) is somewhat far-fetched, to put it mildly, and inconsistent with meaningful 'rational expectations'. The belief that all markets clear, that unemployment is 'voluntary leisure preference', curable by freeing the labour market, will sound very odd to future generations.

No socialist should deny the need for economic calculations. With no price mechanism it is not possible to calculate or compare cost, or to measure the intensity of wants. Microdemand cannot be derived from voting or from clamour, nor should there be 'dictatorship over needs', to cite the title of a critique of East European socialism (Feher et al., 1983). There really is no alternative to allowing choice, i.e. to 'voting' with money. Choice necessarily involves competition between actual and potential suppliers. Yet the limitations of the price mechanism also require to be clearly seen. As the Hungarian economist Janos Kornai (1971) has pointed out, major decisions are not and cannot be taken on the basis of price information alone. The currently fashionable 'methodological individualism' goes far to deny the very existence of the general interest, distinct from that of individuals composing the society, confining 'public goods' to defence and lighthouses. (Yet it is not even true that the interests of a *firm* are only the sum total of that of the individuals composing it!)

Socialism as an idea lays stress on the general interest, but has not always avoided overstressing this at the expense of the individuals, for otherwise the dangers of totalitarianism (albeit of a paternalist kind) may loom ahead. The notion that Man is at the mercy of blind forces he cannot control, or of mighty and remote corporations (faceless, *sociétés anonymes*, or worse still, inhuman computers) sets up a search for a 'socialist' alternative, more human, fairer, and not necessarily less 'efficient' in terms of human welfare. Acquisitiveness and competitiveness may be unavoidable, must indeed be utilized, but do not require to be encouraged. Individualist profit-seeking as the dominant purpose in life, can be regarded by socialists as inhuman and ultimately destructive of society. A greater – not exclusive, but a greater – emphasis on caring for others may be a precondition for survival. More directly destructive would be nuclear war.

There was a long-standing attachment of the idea of socialism to that of peace. This can be less confidently argued today, alas (when Chinese and Vietnamese soldiers shot at each other, could they both be 'socialist'?). Experience does show that states aiming to be socialist can commit aggressive acts, and accumulate immense stores of destructive weapons. None the less, the autonomous role of the arms lobby and of hate-propaganda may be particularly associated with militant capitalism.

Socialist ideas in the Third World raise some specific problems. While it is dangerous to generalize about so heterogeneous a group of countries, in many of them the logic and spirit of capitalism is rejected. There too, to re-quote Bahro, ordinary people are 'immer konservativ', and it is capitalism which is new, which threatens ties and attitudes. The effect may or may not be to provide mass support for socialist slogans: we have had such phenomena as Khomeini and Moslem fundamentalism by way of reaction. But socialist ideas do attract many, in places as far apart and as different as Chile, India, Egypt, Zimbabwe. Of course many blunders have been committed in the name of pursuing socialist policies, not least in relations with the peasantry. But there are many examples which demonstrate that there are countries where free-market capitalism, far from being associated with free and democratic institutions, requires repressive police-state measures. Pinochet's Chile is but one such example.

The relationship between socialism and economic development is a subject in itself, on which volumes could be written. It has often been pointed out that, paradoxically, marxist-inspired revolutions have occurred in relatively backward countries. Indeed, the Russian Empire in 1917 was in no sense 'ripe' for socialism. The preconditions were absent, and the Mensheviks considered themselves to be orthodox marxists when they denounced the Bolsheviks for trying to overleap the predestined historical stages. Lenin, on the contrary, believed that it was possible, indeed essential, to seize power when opportunity offered and *then* to create the preconditions, with (he hoped) the help of revolutions in developed industrial countries. Some of the less agreeable features of the Soviet system can be ascribed to isolation in a hostile world, or to 'socialism in one country', though it would be wrong, in the light of later experience (such as the evolution of the relations between the USSR and China) to regard this one factor as decisive. But, true enough, backward countries seeking to introduce 'socialism' introduce backward 'socialism'. It becomes an industrializing ideology, mobilizing the masses and imposing sacrifices for the goal of modernization, of industrialization, with a substantial admixture of nationalism. Whatever may have been their conscious aim, a strong case can be made for the proposition that Lenin and Mao re-established their respective empires, after a period of breakdown and disintegration, which in China's case lasted almost a century.

Marx's attitude to the socialist transformation of backward countries was by no means clear-cut. While his basic model did point to a socialist revolution occurring in highly industrialized capitalist countries, his correspondence with Vera Zasulich showed that he had great difficulty in applying his ideas to Russia. Theodor Shanin has edited a lively and (in the best sense of the word) provocative volume (Shanin, 1984), which does show Marx's perplexity, his partial recognition that there would perhaps be a road which by-passes capitalism. This was far from the view of Russian marxists, and the correspondence with Zasulich remained unpublished until 1924. However, on other occasions Marx took a different view, as when he regarded British rule in India as progressive, in the sense of introducing capitalist relations into a traditionalist society.

Any analysis of 'really existing socialism' would have to take account of the major role of nationalism, though this at least would have astonished Marx. It influences Soviet internal and foreign policies, it surely played a key role in the split between Russia and China, it may be seen in the treatment of the Hungarian minority by the Romanians. The Soviet author Vasili Grossman, in his major novel *Life and Fate*, put into the mouth of one of his characters the thought that the battle of Stalingrad completed the process of transforming Bolshevism into National-Bolshevism (needless to say, the book was not published in the Soviet Union). We are very far from the idea that 'the workers have no fatherland', and the proper translation of the Soviet official doctrine of 'proletarian internationalism' is 'acceptance of the leadership of Moscow on all important questions'.

There is one aspect of 'backward socialism' which has profound political and social significance. In the USSR, in China, and in many Third World countries, the peasantry formed a large part of the population and there was a sizeable petty bourgeoisie. Far from having exhausted its potentialities, the 'marketization' of the economy was still in its early stages. In Marx's model the bulk of the petty bourgeoisie has been eliminated by monopoly-capital. But in these countries, in the name of class struggle, it was destroyed by coercive state policies, i.e. by police measures. Indeed, the police have to be ever-watchful in case the banned private activities are reborn. This is one reason, among others, for there being socialist police states, which have only a remote connection with Marx's 'dictatorship of the proletariat'.

Much could be said about socialist analyses of underdevelopment, and such names as André Gunder Frank, Samir Amin and Arrighi Emmanuel come to mind. How far was underdevelopment due to capitalism and to links with the world capitalist market? Do socialist remedies require a break with that market? Is the poverty of the Third World due to 'unequal exchange' and exploitation? Is there any operational meaning in the so-called transfer of values? Thus if (say) Zaire buys a machine from the United States and a precisely similar machine at the same price from India, are 'values transferred' in the one case and not in the other?

If Amin is to be believed, such a deal would actually impoverish Zaire if the purchase is from the United States, for presumably the machine would contain much less labour than the similar machine bought from India, or than whatever Zaire exports to America in exchange fot it. Yet frankly this is nonsense. Which by no means excludes the possibility, or even the likelihood, of unequal *gains* from trade.

It is of interest, in the light of some socialist theories of development, to compare the experience of various countries which follow widely different models. In doing so it is evidently important not to select countries which suit a prearranged *roman à thèse*. Thus Cuba's record on literacy, health, the poor, compares favourably with (say) Guatemala, its economic performance is outshone by South Korea and Singapore, but it would be far-fetched to imagine that Cuba under another Batista would have equalled such countries as these; many factors are involved other than the economic system. More to the point would be to compare South Korea with North Korea: same people, same historical experience until 1945. In this instance South Korea undoubtedly out-performs the North. In Africa the free-market orientated Côte d'Ivoire has done better, even for its poor, than those of its neighbours who have opted for socialist-type solutions, but again, some African countries have achieved an appalling mess for reasons very far removed from socialism: Ghana and Uganda can serve as examples.

Those who assign to capitalism, or the links with the world market, the responsibility for income inequality, unemployment, regional underdevelopment, etc., should be made to study China. China also illustrates the correctness of the idea advanced by Arthur Lewis: the general level of wages in a given country depends not on the relative productivity of specific workers: thus an Indian or Chinese driver of a five-ton truck is probably as 'productive' as his American or British equivalent. It is determined by what he called opportunity-cost, notably (in predominantly peasant countries) the very low productivity and rewards available in agriculture. Thus wages in Shanghai, even in the modern industrial sector, are very low indeed. Were China a capitalist country, this would be the effect of the enormous 'reserve army of labour' constituted by 800 millions peasants, whose income is much lower than that of Shanghai workers. In China it is a matter of public policy that urban wages be not too far above the levels in rural areas. The effect is not dissimilar.

True enough, any comparison between China and India must note the great inequalities of income in India, and also the fact that the lowest strata of the poor in India are very poor indeed, compared with China. However, as was pointed out by Amartya Sen, India since independence has found it politically indispensable to avoid mass famine, while China suffered acutely from the politically imposed effects of the Great Leap Forward: millions died.

Now should one ignore the big regional disparities in China, or the very considerable inequalities which existed even before Deng's reform policy was adopted. Also Yugoslavia's regional inequalities persist. Of course in both these instances there are historical and geographic explanations. All that can be said is that these matters resist speedy solutions under all systems.

To return to the developed world, the Soviet model has come to serve as a negative factor, and Western socialists, and indeed Eurocommunists, have tried to distance themselves from it.

The negative influence of the Soviet example is partly due to the revelations about the Stalin terror and Gulag. But, paradoxically, it was the Stalin period which, with all its horrors, did show a high degree of dynamism, high growth rates, evoking some enthusiasm and commitment from many Soviet citizens as well as foreign observers. It was brutal, it was crude, but they were forcing through a huge industrialization programme, preparing for war, fighting it, eventually winning it. There is, unfortunately, some Stalin-nostalgia in the Soviet Union today, analysed vividly by the emigré Viktor Zaslavsky (1982). 'Really existing socialism' has become grey, dull, undramatic, inefficient, more than a little corrupt. The ruling stratum under Stalin was young and faced sizeable risks of purge and execution. People could find little to enthuse about under the Brezhnev gerontocracy; the privileged abused their privileges without fear of punishment, shortages and poor quality contrasted with official claims of successes. Of course, under Stalin, things were in fact much worse. There were indeed horrors, but they were little understood outside the Soviet Union. (Thus the brutalities of collectivization and the famine that followed it were fairly successfully concealed from view.) The result was that the Soviet Union and the 'socialism' it represented became for a time a pole of attraction for millions. 'I have seen the future, and it works', 'Soviet communism – a new civilization', to cite two contemporary judgements. Today the Soviet model no longer impresses or convinces. It is not in chaos, it is not about to fall apart, but it is no beacon, can inspire nobody either in or out of the Soviet Union. And this despite the fact that much has gone wrong in the capitalist West. We will see if the new generation of leaders can restore the lost dynamism.

A few left-wing intellectuals transferred their allegiance to Mao. As was the case with some Western admirers of Stalin's Russia of the Thirties, this allegiance or admiration was based on misunderstanding, on ignorance. The 'Maoists' simply did not know about the real Great Leap Forward and its millions of victims, or just what the 'Great Proletarian Cultural Revolution' was really about. The post-Mao reaction brought them to their senses. The Yugoslav self-management model too has had its admirers, and indeed its principles are attractive, and will be looked at below. However, grave economic problems have hit Yugoslavia. By no means all of them are connected with the self-management model, but the fact remains that the negative aspects now tend to predominate in observers' minds. Then there was Poland. The 'Solidarność' story, in the present context, is one which not only highlights governmental economic ineptitude, but more important, makes spectacular nonsense of the communist claims to represent the workers, or to be the advance-guard of the proletariat.

So, to summarize, socialism is not, at present, a politically attractive slogan, and this despite the quite vigorous efforts of the New Right to destroy 'consensus-capitalism'. Worse, the immediate political programme of (for instance) Labour's left in Great Britain may be a sure recipe for trouble, reminiscent of the tragic errors of the Allende regime in Chile (which I had the sad experience of witnessing: price control, import controls, large wage increases, the disruption of the normal functioning of the market with no coherent idea of how to replace it).

Democratic socialism, however defined, can come only if the majority of the people are convinced that the old order has outlived itself, that major changes in a socialist direction are urgently needed. In a percipient analysis, S.C. Kolm has noted a repeated tendency: a left-wing government is elected, and its economic policies begin to hurt those middle strata (or middle-class, or left-centre parties) whose votes brought this government to power. The result is a rightward shift of opinion, and either the loss of the parliamentary majority (as in France, in 1937–8, for example) or a successful right-wing coup, as in Chile. Some draw far-reaching conclusions about there not being any democratic road to socialism (although, for example, in Chile there was no left-wing majority in Congress, Allende having been elected on a 'reformist' programme and with some support from left-wing Christian Democrats). Whatever may be the actual or anticipated resistance of the powers-that-be, one can only repeat that democratic socialism requires the support over a prolonged period of the democratic majority – and right now this is not available – *except* for Swedish-style welfare state social-democracy (which has again won an election in Sweden on a welfare-state programme).

Perhaps Sweden is in fact the model we should study, if what we seek is a programme which a moderate, non-revolutionary, democratic-socialist party ought to 'sell' to the electorate. Yes, it is a high-tax solution, but one which the electorate, at least in Sweden, can be persuaded to prefer to any Swedish translation of Thatcherism. In my book on *Feasible Socialism* (Nove, 1983), I rejected the notion that Sweden is a socialist republic ('and not only because it is a monarchy'), and of course there is a large 'capitalist' sector. But there is no serious current of opinion in Sweden which would support a policy of nationalizing the privately owned enterprises, or other drastic changes of existing arrangements. So if this is in fact the practical policy recipe of moderate-socialism or social-democratic parties in Western Europe, then this might be seen as a medium-term objective. Leaving the term 'socialist' as a distant perspective, just as the official Soviet propaganda now views full communism. Just as the Soviet government does not tell people that they actually intend at any particular date to abolish wages and prices, so a Western socialist party should not be committed to 'the introduction of socialism' as a policy for today. But there should be a longer-term objective. What objective?

For reasons already examined at length, it cannot be the socialism/communism foretold by Marx. Then what can it be? Let us examine this subject, bearing in mind the three points made earlier: the relationship between management and workforce; how productive units interrelate; and what sort of state can be envisaged – bearing in mind that a state there would and must be, with important functions to perform.

So let us look at self-management. Why has its Yugoslav version lost much of its attractiveness? As already suggested, some of the reasons have little to do with the self-management model as such: centrifugal tendencies in a multi-national state with a relatively weak central authority; unwise policies on interest rates (which have been negative in real terms) and on foreign exchange; lack of any effective control over bank credits, to cite some examples. However, certain lessons can none the less be drawn.

One is that self-management is not necessarily desired by the workforce, in the sense that many wish to spend long hours sitting in committee-rooms or studying the firm's accounts. However, the formal responsibility of management to the workforce is an important principle, as is the right of participation, which can be exercised when something goes wrong or feelings run high.

A second point relates to the lack of interest of much of the workforce in the longer term. This is a consequence of the fact that the capital assets do not belong to them, and when they leave they have no saleable asset to dispose of. Their only interest is in the income they can earn. This inclines them to a short-term view, to a desire to increase current income rather than invest in the future. One effect is to increase inflationary pressure.

Thirdly, neither the workforce nor the management has any real responsibility for investment decisions, past or present. Suppose they prove disastrous, who is to blame? If indeed the initial investment decision (to set up the firm) was mistaken, and it was taken before there could be a workers' council or the election (appointment) of a manager, why should management or labour be penalized? This is one aspect of a wider problem: that of how to cope with failure under socialism (other than by assuming that it will not occur!).

Fourthly, by making the workforce's incomes dependent on the given enterprise's financial results (subject, to be sure, to a legal minimum), one ensures unequal pay for equal work, and thus a chronic source of tension and discontent. Thus suppose citizen A and citizen B both drive five-ton lorries from Zagreb to Split, but A works for a more successful enterprise than B; they may well receive very different pay. The resultant pressure for higher pay in the financially less successful enterprises is yet another source of inflationary pressure.

Fifthly, Yugoslavia suffers from unemployment. Yet material incentives based upon dividing net revenues among the existing labour force builds in a reluctance to employ extra labour, whenever such employment would diminish the sum represented by net (distributable) revenue per head. In choosing between investment variants, there is for the same reason a tendency to choose the more capital-intensive variant, in comparison with the profit-orientated capitalist or the 'plan-fulfilling' Soviet manager.

For what should be obvious reasons, self-management requires a market. The self-managed units decide what to produce by reference to market criteria, and purchase their inputs by freely negotiating contracts with suppliers. Charles Bettelheim was quite right when he wrote that 'commodity production' (i.e. for exchange) must exist so long as units of production are autonomous and not wholly integrated into the plan. Yet he criticizes Yugoslav-type self-management: the workers do not really control their means of production and the product – the market does. This presupposes the existence of some unrealizable alternative, in which what is done and the acquisition of means to do it are controlled by no outside force at all. Yet needs have to be conveyed somehow, if not through negotiating contracts then via instructions from a superior authority.

Another significant moral to draw from Yugoslav experience relates to regional questions. In a country which, for historical and geographical reasons, has a relatively highly developed north and a backward south, measures to correct these disparities have had little success. Experience elsewhere shows that such matters defy solution in very different systems (for instance, compare Italy's *mezzogiorno*, or the megalopolis problem in such countries as Mexico and Brazil). However, the combination of autonomous 'self-managed' units and centrifugal forces, with the centre in a relatively weak position, tends to perpetuate or even reinforce regional inequalities. Indeed – and Soviet experience with *sovnarkhozy* (regional economic councils) points in the same direction – one might conclude that regional power over enterprises is very likely to result in irrationalities. The reason is clear: a local authority has information about the needs of its locality and, unless prevented, will tend to give them priority to the detriment of other localities, with duplication of investments as yet another undesirable consequence. In other words, if one were to imagine a modern industrial society with complex inter-regional links, there are two possible logical solutions: central control or enterprise autonomy (the 'enterprise' could, in some circumstances, be large or even, in such cases as electricity supply, a centrally controlled monopoly). If power over resources were given to an authority covering one area, it would divert resources for its own purposes, with potentially disruptive effects.

Finally, one must refer to the very considerable literature, of which Ward's fascinating excursion into 'Illyria' is the original example (Ward, 1958), which appears to prove that self-managed enterprises, in which the workforce's income depends on the enterprise's net revenue, are of their nature inefficient. Some of the conclusions are irrelevant to the real world. Thus Ward's model shows that it would 'pay' the firm to reduce output if prices rose, but this would only be so under the assumption of so-called 'perfect competition', in which such considerations as real competition do not enter. For example, in real competition one is concerned not to lose customers to one competitors, who might not be regained if prices fall, as in future they might. Nor are self-managed enterprises likely to dismiss fellow-workers without some extremely strong reasons. None the less, as already noted, they may choose labour-saving, capital-intensive investment variants even when unemployment is a major social problem. It may be necessary (and it surely is possible) to devise fiscal means to counteract this tendency. As for efficiency, this depends (inter alia) on the attitude of the workforce. Would the sense of participation increase commitment and loyalty, and so the quality of the work effort? These considerations seldom figure in economic analysis (with Albert O. Hirschman an honourable exception). Some unimaginative model-builders would doubtless also conclude that the reluctance of Japanese firms to shed labour is 'inefficient', yet any loss can be counterbalanced by the sense of 'belonging' that goes with security of employment. A recent study of Israeli *kibbutzim* noted that one finds no resistance there to labour-saving innovations, which can be encountered in private firms, because such innovations do not threaten loss of jobs.

There are lessons to be learnt from the experience of the Mondragon cooperatives in northern Spain. Unlike the Yugoslav enterprises, they pay wages, so that there is an identifiable profit. They also ensure that the workforce has shares in the business (if necessary lending them the money to acquire them), and this also gives them a longer-term stake in its prosperity. It is, however, worth recalling that the Mondragon enterprises function in an area of strong local loyalties, just as the *kibbutz* members are committed volunteers. The outcome may be different with different human material.

Socialists must be aware that there are bound to be problems connected with property ownership and long-term responsibility, involving also risk-taking and the consequences of failure. Where uncertainty exists – i.e. in any conceivable situation – there must be the possibility of failure. A capitalist can go bankrupt, but what of 'socialist bankruptcy'? One cannot 'solve' this question simply by assuming either perfect foresight or perfect planning. The existence of genuine autonomy of decision-making is surely an aim desirable in itself, and freedom necessarily involves both uncertainty and freedom to err, to act in ways not necessarily consistent with the general interest or the national plan.

What, then, could a 'feasible socialism' be like? Should the word be redefined? Surely a non-utopian definition of socialist values should be counterposed to the crude laissez-faire ideology of the New Right. Some of the traditional slogans associated with socialism have become deservedly unpopular. There are good reasons to associate nationalization with bureaucracy, satisfying neither the workforce nor the customers. It is in a review in *Radical Philosophy* (Spring 1985) that one can read: 'A regime devoted to equality in its literal sense would have to be authoritarian, ready to crush inequalities whenever they reasserted themselves, as they inevitably and constantly would.' The New Right's view of 'liberty' may be distasteful, but one must recognize that the aims of equality and freedom can conflict with one another. Socialism cannot be happy with a purely acquisitive society. Indeed such a society would fall apart, for why should civil servants, judges, police officers, not be crude income-maximizers, i.e. behave as most doctors seem to do in America? Yet acquisitiveness is not a value to be disparaged, the vast majority of citizens do have material aspirations. Thus a conscientious doctor does his best for his patients, even if they cannot pay an economic fee, but he or she is also not averse to acquiring a country cottage and going on holiday to Greece. Furthermore, at least since the days of Adam Smith it has been rightly noted that there are worse ambitions than making money: the men who, in the process of competing for power, sent their comrades to be shot in cellars were not seeking to maximize profits. What is to be sought is a balance between (enlightened) self-interest and a sense of social responsibility. Inevitably this differs as between individuals.

Individuals also differ greatly in what might be called 'producers' preferences'. Some like to be independent innovators, others prefer routine. Some gladly take responsibility, others prefer to avoid it. Some opt for life in a commune or *kibbutz*, others would be very unhappy there. While Marx's vision of a universal Man is a fantasy, it is not at all a fantasy to provide both for variety and for the opportunity to change one's specialization if the spirit so moves one. A socialism based on one economic model might be a sort of procrustean bed for a sizeable part of the population. (Imagine, for example, *compulsory* communal

246

living!) Hence it seems desirable to redefine 'socialism' as a mixed economy: enterprises large and small, many if not most self-managed or cooperative, with some private enterprises too. If the private sector does not play a dominant role, its existence should be consistent with a sensibly defined socialism; otherwise its suppression would be the constant task of a 'socialist' police (unless, of course, it proves not to be needed, in which case it is no more necessary to ban 'privateers' than to outlaw private water-carriers when everyone has tap water). A major objective would be not only to ensure variety of choice of occupations, but also work for all, when unemployment is in danger of becoming a major social curse. Only in ideological textbooks of economics do labour markets automatically clear. One must anticipate the need to take job-creating action. One must also anticipate that freedom to organize involves freedom to form not only political parties but also interest groups which will press for additional resources. Since money will undoubtedly continue to exist, it would be possible to issue too much of it in the face of pressures, so inflation (and some species of monetarism) will not just go away. Freedom of choice implies both a market and competition, both in consumers' goods and producers' goods and services, though there must also be some large-scale natural monopolies (such as electricity, water, public transport), where responsibility of management to the users is as important as its responsibility to its workforce.

Mises, Hayek, and later on also Friedman, have argued that efficiency in resource allocation is impossible under socialism. At a formal level they were answered by Lange, Lerner, Dickinson, but there were and are major practical obstacles in realizing their socialist models, which are anchored (as are so many of the neoclassicals') in static equilibrium assumptions, and it is unclear why either the central planning board or the managers in Lange's model should act out their parts in the prescribed manner. It should be admitted that the absence of (or severe limits on) a real capital market can cause inefficiencies, that rewards for risk-taking and innovation may well sit uneasily with social or state ownership of capital assets. Nor is this all. Kornai, in his Dublin lecture (Kornai, 1985) pointed to contradictions between the requirements of efficiency and socialist ethics. But the world is full of contradictions, and one usually arrives at some species of compromise; 'maximization' in terms of just one objective function can seldom be encountered in really existing societies (a fully-fledged and devoted 'profit maximizer' would probably suffer a nervous breakdown, if not already dead of cardiac arrest). Mises and company are right to insist that economically meaningful prices are needed, wrong to assert that socialist prices cannot be meaningful (though today's Soviet prices are indeed irrational, reflecting neither use-value nor relative scarcity). But it must be emphasized how far the contemporary Western system is from the free-market model of the textbooks. Thus in his challenging 'Profits without production', Seymour Mellman notes and deplores the narrow concentration on short-term profits, by executives who have no long-term commitment to their corporation (on average they move to another one within five years or so). Current uncertainties about prices, interest rates, inflation, are hardly conducive to 'rational' long-term investment decisions.

Too often critics of socialist economics (with its imperfections) implicitly compare it with a Chicago utopia, which is in its own way as unreal as a marxist one. Perfect markets and perfect plans are equally utopian.

But in the end much will depend on the ability of contemporary capitalism to surmount its many problems, not least that of mass unemployment and ecological decline (acid rain, deforestation, over-fishing, etc.). The masses will not opt for a different system unless faced with the bankruptcy of the existing one. To repeat, it was Marx who wrote that no mode of production passes from the scene unless and until its productive potential is exhausted. Soviet-type socialism is seen as obsolete, in contradiction with the forces of production; yet it offers no alternative model. A great deal remains to be done to revive socialism as an aim worthy of effort and sacrifice.

BIBLIOGRAPHY

Bahro, R. 1977. *Die Alternative: zur Kritik des real existierenden Sozialismus*. Cologne: Europäische Verlaganstalt.

Bettelheim, C. 1968. *La transition vers l'économie socialiste*. Paris: F. Maspero.

Brus, W. 1980. Political system and economic efficiency – the East European context. *Journal of Comparative Economics* 4(1), 40–55.

Castoriadis, C. 1979. *Les carrefours du labyrinthe*. Paris: Editions du Seuil. Trans. K. Soper and M.H. Ryle as *Crossroads in the Labyrinth*, Brighton: Harvester, 1984.

Feher, F., Heiler, A. and Markus, G. 1983. *Dictatorship Over Needs*. Oxford: Basil Blackwell; New York: St Martin's Press.

Gatovsky, L. (ed.) 1967. *Zakonomernosti i puti sozdaniia materialno-tekhnicheskoi bazy kommunizma* (On legality and the means of creating a material-technical base for communism). Moscow: Akademii Nauk SSSR.

Gorz, A. 1980. *Adieux au prolétariat*. Paris: Editions Galilée.

Grossman, V. 1985. *Life and Fate*. Trans. from the Russian by R. Chandler, London: Collins Harvill; New York: Harper & Row.

Kolakowski, L. 1976. *Main Currents of Marxism: its rise, growth and dissolution*. Vol. 1, trans. from the Polish by P.S. Falla, Oxford and New York: Oxford University Press, 1978.

Kornai, J. 1971. *Anti-Equilibrium. On economic systems theory and tasks of research*. Amsterdam and London: North-Holland.

Kornai, J. 1985. The dilemmas of the socialist economy. Geary Lecture, Dublin, 1979. In J. Kornai, *Contradictions and Dilemmas*, Corvina: Kner Printing House.

Kuznets, S. 1941. *National Income and its Composition, 1919–1938*. New York: National Bureau of Economic Research.

Lenin, V.I. 1962. *Sochineniia* (Works). 5th edn, Vol. 36, Moscow.

Marx, K. 1962. *Marx–Engels Works* (Russian). Vol. XXVIII, Moscow.

Mészáros, I. 1972. *Marx's Theory of Alienation*. 3rd edn, London: Merlin Press.

Nove, A. 1983. *The Economics of Feasible Socialism*. London: Allen & Unwin.

Roland, G. 1985. *Valeur d'usage chez Karl Marx*. Brussels.

Schumpeter, J. 1976. *Capitalism, Socialism and Democracy*. 5th edn, London: Allen & Unwin.

Shanin, T. 1984. *Late Marx and the Russian Road*. London: Routledge & Kegan Paul.

Ward, B. 1958. The firm in Illyria: market syndicalism. *American Economic Review* 48, September, 566–89.

Wright, E.O. 1979. *Class Structure and Income Determination*. New York: Academic Press.

Zaslavsky, V. 1982. *The Neo-Stalinist State: class, ethnicity, and consensus in Soviet society*. New York: Sharpe; Brighton: Harvester.

Josif Vissarionovich Stalin

MICHAEL ELLMAN

Stalin (Joseph Djugashvili, 1879–1953) was ruler of the USSR (1929–53), leader of the international Communist movement (1929–53) and an important theoretician of Marxism–Leninism. A russified Georgian, his parents were born in serfdom. He was a professional revolutionary from the end of the 19th century, a Central Committee member from 1912, and General Secretary of the Central Committee from 1922. After Lenin's third stroke (March 1923) he was one of the triumvirate which succeeded to supreme power in party and state. He defeated the other triumvirs in 1925, Trotsky in 1927 and Bukharin in 1928. He organized mass collectivization in 1929–32 (and hence caused, directly and via the subsequent famine, several million deaths) and mass arrests and mass expansion of the concentration camp system in 1937–39 (and hence was responsible for a large number of additional deaths prior to the outbreak of the war). He led the USSR in the Great Patriotic War (the Soviet–German war, 1941–45) and hence was responsible both for the early defeats and also for the subsequent victories. He imposed Soviet-style socialism on Eastern Europe after World War II. His plans for a new wave of arrests and intensified terror were presented by his death (March 1953). He established leader worship, unconditional obedience to Moscow, intellectual sterility and anti-Americanism throughout the international Communist movement. At the twentieth congress of the Communist Party of the Soviet Union (1956) his theoretical legacy was publicly criticized and in a closed session his liquidation of loyal party leaders in the 1930s, and poor military leadership at the beginning of the Great Patriotic War, were severely criticized. In 1961 his policies were severely criticized at the twenty-second congress of the Soviet Communist Party. He was publicly revered in China under Mao.

Stalin's significance for economics relates to economic policy, the model of the functioning of a socialist economy, and the political economy of socialism. He implemented an economic policy based on the general use of coercion to attain a high proportion of investment in the national income, high rates of growth, rapid industrialization and the rapid development of strategic industries. Living standards were depressed and held at a low level. Everyday life was marked by shortages and fear. Food shortages, inequality, piecework, state-directed Taylorism, the rapid expansion of education, rapid social mobility, the rapid expansion of urban employment opportunities and high participation rates were characteristic of Stalinist economic policy. Trade unions functioned primarily as agencies of the state to raise labour productivity. State and collective farms were assessed primarily by their ability to meet the state procurement plans. Foreign trade was mainly valued for its *import* possibilities, for the raw materials, machinery and foreign technology, the import of which it made possible.

Stalin created, maintained and disseminated the statist model of socialism. In the statist model, private ownership of the means of production is replaced by state ownership, and the whole national economy is administered as if it were one giant firm according to the Marxist 'one nation – one factory' model. The only exception is the collective farms, which formally are cooperatives and not managed by the state. In fact in the USSR under Stalin their management was appointed by organs of the state but the state did not accept any responsibility to pay them wages or provide them with social security. The course of economic development in the USSR and the prople's democracies in the Stalinist period was supposed to be planned, by means of annual, five-year and long-term plans. In fact the five-year and long-term plans had little operational significance, being primarily used for public mobilization and propaganda. The behavioural regularities generated by the statist model and exogenous factors, were of great importance in determining the actual course of economic development. Within the state sector, the role of prices and indirect levers of control in the statist model is small and reliance is placed on direct methods of economic management (i.e. normal bureaucratic processes plus political and police measures). As far as consumption goods are concerned, in the statist model individual choice in the market is not abolished, but reduced in importance by administrative allocation and rationing. The labour market is not entirely abolished either in the statist model, but reduced in importance by forced labour camps, the internal passport system, the abolition of the right to resign without good reasons (e.g. the USSR 1940–56) and criminal sanctions for lateness, absenteeism and damage. In *Economic Problems of Socialism in the USSR* (1952) Stalin took it for granted that in the future financial relations between state enterprises would be abolished and replaced by direct product exchange, i.e. the exchange of goods without the intermediation of money. Informed public or professional discussion of economic policy in a country implementing the statist model is impossible because reliable statistics are not published, extensive use is made of misleading statistics and there is comprehensive pre-publication censorship. Public discussion is dominated by 'the propaganda of success', that is, the suppression of 'negative' facts and publication only of 'positive' facts and also of purely imaginary achievements. By the end of Stalin's lifetime, it was a trivial orthodoxy of the international Communist movement, and widely accepted outside it, that the statist model (usually referred to as 'socialist planning') was a rational and equitable form of economic organization and represented a higher mode of production than capitalism.

On the theoretical level, his main achievement was to develop and apply to the USSR the theory of 'socialism in one country'. According to Lenin, and all Bolsheviks prior to 1924, the successful building of socialism in only one country was impossible because socialism was international in its very essence. Furthermore, the complete building of socialism in Russia in particular was impossible because of the ever-present danger of imperialist attack and also because of the economic backwardness of the country. According to the theory of socialism in one country, first formulated by Stalin in the winter of 1924/25, the economic backwardness of Russia did not prevent the successful building of socialism in Russia. While the successful completion of the socialist project in Russia could not be guaranteed (because of the danger of imperialist aggression) Bolsheviks should bend all their efforts to the task of building socialism in the USSR, i.e. to the rapid industrialization of the USSR. In this way it would be possible to build up a mighty socialist industry in the USSR and hence weaken capitalism on a global scale. The theory of socialism in one country both provided an explanation of how the maintenance of Soviet power in Russia was possible in the absence of a revolution in the West and also provided a general theoretical orientation for Soviet economic policy. It also provided a theoretical basis for the merging of Marxist Bolshevism and Russian patriotism into the powerful sentiments of Soviet Patriotism. In addition it provided the theoretical basis for Stalin's defeat of the other party leaders and his emergence as the sole party leader in the 1920s.

One of the most important, influential and controversial figures of the 20th century, Stalin played by far the most important role in maintaining and spreading 'real socialism'.

SELECTED WORKS

1952–56. *Works*. 12 vols, Moscow: Foreign Languages Publishing House.

1952. *Economic Problems of Socialism in the USSR*. Moscow: Foreign Languages Publishing House.

1957. *Correspondence between the Chairman of the Council of Ministers of the USSR and the President of the USA and the Prime Minister of Great Britain during the Great Patriotic War of 1941–1945*. Moscow: Foreign Languages Publishing House, 2 vols. Also published as *Stalin's correspondence with Churchill, Attlee, Roosevelt and Truman*, London: Lawrence & Wishart, 1958.

BIBLIOGRAPHY

Brus, W. 1975. *Socialist Ownership and Political Systems*. London and Boston: Routledge & Kegan Paul.

Carr, E.H. 1958. *Socialism in One Country 1924–1926*. Part I, London and New York: Macmillan.

Davies, R.W. 1980. *The Industrialisation of Soviet Russia*. London: Macmillan.

Fitzpatrick, S. 1979. Stalin and the making of a new elite, 1928–1939. *Slavic Review* 38(3), September, 377–402.

Harrison, M. 1985. *Soviet Planning in Peace and War 1938–1945*. Cambridge: Cambridge University Press. *History of the AUCP(b) (short course)*. 1939. Moscow.

Kantorovich, L.V. 1965. *The Best Use of Economic Resources*. Oxford and New York: Pergamon Press.

Kornai, J. 1959. *Overcentralization in Economic Administration*. Trans. by John Knapp, London: Oxford University Press.

Mao Tsetung. 1977. *A Critique of Soviet Economics*. Trans. Moss Roberts, New York: Monthly Review Press.

Medvedev, R.A. 1979. *On Stalin and Stalinism*. Oxford and New York: Oxford University Press.

Nove, A. 1969. *An Economic History of the USSR*. London: Allen Lane, The Penguin Press.

Tucker, R.C. (ed.) 1977. *Stalinism*. New York: W.W. Norton.

Xue Muqiao. 1981. *China's Socialist Economy*. Beijing: China Books.

Stanislav Gustavovich Strumilin

M.C. KASER

Born Strumillo-Petrashkevich, of Polish descent, in Dashkovtsy, Russia, on 29 January 1877, Strumilin died in Moscow on 25 January 1974. He studied at the St Petersburg Polytechnical Institute under P.B. Struve and M.I. Tugan-Baranovsky and was twice sentenced to internal exile before the 1917 Revolutions. A Menshevik delegate to the Stockholm (1906) and London (1907) Party Congresses, he did not formally join the Bolshevik side until 1923. Apart from a break in 1937–43, when as an ex-Menshevik he was banished to the Urals in the Great Purge, he was on the staff of the State Planning Committee from 1921 (nominated by Lenin personally) to 1951; then aged 74, he moved to the Party's Academy of Social Sciences. An Academician from 1931, he received a Stalin Prize in 1942 for work on the wartime development of the Urals.

The expedient marshalling of economics to salvage politically determined measures, which characterized his considerable output (180 publications), was exemplified during the earliest phase of the Soviet system, 'War Communism'. To the Supreme Economic Council's committee which in 1920 considered replacing money (the rouble already being depreciated by hyper-inflation) by 'labour units', Strumilin proposed a rational price mechanism by defining (in terms of work-days of unskilled manpower) a single good as numeraire, each other good being related by the logarithm of its labour content (a surrogate for declining marginal utilities), corrected by differences in productivity and in the intensity of need (Malle, 1985; Sutela, 1984). The 'labour unit' scheme was abandoned when Lenin reintroduced a market and sound money under his New Economic Policy; Strumilin returned to his pre-revolutionary research on labour economics. Strumilin (1924) is pioneering in its sampling of wage differentials associated with educational input, measured by the cost of teaching and (for those of working age) income forgone. Invited many years later by UNESCO to update his analysis, Strumilin (1962) changed his approach from the microeconomic to a macroeconomic Cobb–Douglas-type function (without apparent acquaintance with the original) to indicate the share of the national income increment attributable to improvement in the qualifications of the labour force. Econometrically not robust, the exercise was nevertheless a *tour de force* for a man of 85 and illustrated how, as Soviet economics was released from Stalinist shackles, it was the old who led the way; his concern to widen the perspectives of the post-Stalin generation was heightened by comparison with the intellectual freedom of his own youth, as Davies (1960) perceives from Strumilin's autobiography (1957).

Strumilin (1913) is officially credited with the first 'balance method' – branch availabilities and disposals in physical quantities (*Ekonomicheskaya entsiklopediya*, 1980), as Davies (1960) also documents – but Strumilin's claim (*Selected Works*, vol. 2, p. 180) to priority for macroeconomic input–output in money terms has rightly been disputed in favour of his Planning Committee subordinate, V.G. Groman (Wheatcroft and Davies, 1985, p. 46; Jasny, 1972, p. 104). N.A. Voznesensky brought Strumilin back to the Committee as soon as he resumed the chairmanship, coincidentally with Stalin's signal that formal analysis of the Soviet economy could recommence. He took up the theory of capital efficiency – to which he had been one of the last earlier Soviet contributors (Strumilin, 1929) – by proposing an ideologically acceptable discount rate in the form of productivity change (Strumilin, 1946).

SELECTED WORKS

1924. The economic significance of national education. Trans. by B. Jeffrey in *The Economics of Education*, ed. E.A.G. Robinson and J.E. Vaizey, London: Macmillan, 1966, from *Ekonomika truda* (The Economics of Labour), Moscow, 1925. Reprinted in *Selected Works*, Vol. 3, 101–31, from *Planovoe khoziastvo* (Planned Economy), No. 9–10, 1924.

1929. K problem effektivnosti kapital'nykh zatrat' (On the problem of the efficiency of capital expenditure). *Planovoe khoziastvo* (Planned Economy), No. 7. In *Selected Works*, Vol. 2, 417–30.

1946. The time factor in capital investment projects. *International Economic Papers* No. 1, London: Macmillan, 1951. Trans. from *Izvestiia Akademii Nauk SSSR. Otdelenie ekonomiki i prava* (News of the USSR Academy of Sciences. Division of Economics and Law), No. 3. Reprinted in *Selected Works*, Vol. 4, 213–31.

1957. *Iz perezhitogo 1897–1917 gg.* (Out of my past 1897–1917). Moscow: Gospolitizdat.

1962. The economics of education in the USSR. *International Social Science Journal* 14(4). Reprinted in *Selected Works*, Vol. 5, 265–77, from *Ekonomicheskaia gazeta* (Economics Gazette), 2, April 1962.

1963–5. *Izbrannye proizvedeniia* (Selected Works). 5 vols, Moscow: Izdatel'stvo Nauka.

BIBLIOGRAPHY

Davies, R.W. 1960. Some Soviet economic controllers. *Soviet Studies* 11(3).

Ekonomicheskaia entsiklopediia: Politicheskaia ekonomiia. 1980. Vol. 4. Moscow: Izdatel'stvo sovetskaia entsiklopediia.

Jasny, N. 1972. *Soviet Economists of the Twenties. Names to be Remembered*. Cambridge and New York: Cambridge University Press.

Malle, S. 1985. *The Economic Organization of War Communism, 1918–1921.* Cambridge: Cambridge University Press.

Sutela, P. 1984. *Socialism, Planning and Optimality. A Study in Soviet Economic Thought.* Commentationes Scientiarum Socialium No. 25, Helsinki: Societas Scientiarum Fennica.

Wheatcroft, S.G. and Davies, R.W. (eds) 1985. *Materials for a Balance of the Soviet National Economy, 1928–1930.* Cambridge: Cambridge University Press.

Lev Davidovich Trotsky

RICHARD B. DAY

Born in 1879, the son of Jewish farmers living near the Black Sea, Trotsky became an important political figure by the time of the Second Congress of the Russian Social Democratic Party in 1903. Disagreeing with Lenin's centralizing view of party organization, Trotsky either favoured the Mensheviks or attempted to mediate between them and the Bolsheviks until making his peace with Lenin in 1917. In the 1905 Revolution he served as chairman of the St Petersburg Soviet, drawing upon that experience to develop the theory of 'permanent revolution' in his book *Results and Prospects*. In the 1917 Revolution Trotsky ranked second only to Lenin among Bolshevik party leaders. He orchestrated the seizure of power and subsequently organized and led the Red Army in the civil war. During the early 1920s Trotsky's political influence waned, and by the middle of the decade he became the political leader and intellectual mentor of the Left Opposition to Stalin. Defeated by Stalin in the intra-party struggle, in 1929 Trotsky was deported from the Soviet Union. In exile he edited *Biulleten' Oppozitsii* (Bulletin of the Opposition) and published numerous other writings critical of Stalinist policy, the most important being *The Revolution Betrayed*. Unable to answer Trotsky's criticisms on intellectual grounds, in August 1940 Stalin replied in the only way he knew: he had Trotsky assassinated in Mexico, his last place of exile.

In *Results and Prospects* (first published in 1906), Trotsky predicted that Russian backwardness would guarantee the revolution in permanence. Surrounded by stronger enemies, the Russian state had prevented the nobility from becoming politically independent. The nobility were mere tax collectors, extracting revenue from the peasants in order to promote development; and the bourgeoisie, likewise, were weaker than their Western counterparts, for much of the economy was built with foreign loans, serviced by grain exports. The proletariat, in contrast, enjoyed disproportionate strength. Few in number,

Russian workers were concentrated in large factories organized around foreign technology. Trotsky predicted that the proletariat would overthrow the autocracy, by-passing the bourgeois revolution, but would then confront a counter-revolutionary alliance when it implemented its programme. The counter-revolution would be supported by Germany, Austria and France, who would be anxious to prevent the revolution's spread and to safeguard their investments. When these countries mobilized, however, they would drive their own workers to revolt, thereby making the revolution permanent both domestically and internationally.

Aware of Russia's historical dependence on the world economy, Trotsky characteristically viewed economic issues in an international context. Modern industry, he believed, had become so capital-intensive that production could only be profitable through specialization in service of the world market. It was in the nature of socialism to emancipate the productive forces from the fetters of the nation state. A victory of the proletariat in the leading countries would mean 'a radical restructuring of the very economic foundation in correspondence with a more productive international division of labour, which is alone capable of creating a genuine foundation for a socialist order' (*Trotsky Archives*, No. T-3148).

When the international revolution did not come to Soviet Russia's aid as Trotsky had expected, he continued to insist that industrialization must draw upon the resources of the world market. Opposing Stalin's notion of an isolated socialist state (Socialism in One Country), he argued that 'a properly regulated growth of export and import with the capitalist countries prepares the elements of the future commodity and product exchange [which will prevail] when the European proletariat assumes power and controls production' (*Trotsky Archives* No. T-3034). Soviet Russia's relation to the West would involve a dialectic of cooperation and struggle in which the Soviet state would regulate its 'dependence' on capitalism through its monopoly of foreign trade. The alternative, the Stalinist vision of autarky, would mean reliance 'on the curbed and domesticated productive forces, that is ... on the technology of backwardness' (Trotsky, 1947, p. 53).

Uppermost in Trotsky's mind throughout the 1920s was the need not only to preserve access to foreign technology, but also to reduce domestic prices in order to maintain the trade monopoly. In 1923 he warned the party that 'Contraband is inevitable if the difference between external and internal prices goes beyond a certain limit ... contraband, comrades ... undermines and washes away the monopoly' (*Dvenadstatyi s'ezd RKP* (b), 1923, p. 372; 12th Congress of the Russian Communist Party, Bolsheviks). Without this protection for new Soviet industries, planned growth would be impossible.

For the promotion of new industrial construction, Trotsky proposed to supplement domestic tax revenues by taking advantage of Europe's need for foreign markets and by pursuing all manner of credits:

What does foreign credit do for our economic development? Capitalism makes advances to us against our savings which do not yet exist . . . As a result, the foundations of our development are extended . . . The dialectics of historical development have resulted in capitalism becoming for a time the creditor of socialism. Well, has not capitalism been nourished at the breasts of feudalism? History has honoured the debt (*Pravda*, 20 September 1925).

In addition to making use of foreign credits, Trotsky hoped to resume the tsarist pattern of exporting grain in exchange for finished goods. In 1925 he predicted that the Soviet economy would be unable to satisfy more than a fraction of its need for new equipment:

We must not . . . forget for a moment the great mutual dependence which existed between the economies of tsarist Russia and world capital. We must just bring to mind the fact that nearly two-thirds of the technical equipment in our works and factories used to be imported from abroad. This dependence has hardly decreased in our own time, which means that it will scarcely be economically profitable for us in the next few years to produce at home the machinery we require, at any rate, more than two-fifths of the quantity, or at best more than half of it (*Pravda*, 20 September 1925).

Trotsky hoped to reconcile a high level of foreign trade with socialist protectionism through strict determination of priorities. Soviet industries should economize on scarce capital, specialize in those products in greatest demand, standardize output and reduce costs, while leaving the remaining needs to be met by low-cost imports. A system of comparative coefficients should be devised by the planners, comparing the cost and quality of Soviet products with foreign competition. A poor coefficient would then signal the advisability of imports in the short run and of re-equipment in the long run, as new resources became available. 'A comparative coefficient is the same for us as a pressure gauge for a mechanic on a locomotive. The pressure of foreign production is for us the basic factor of our economic existence. If our relation to this production is [unsatisfactory], then foreign production will sooner or later pierce the trade monopoly' (*Ekonomicheskaia Zhizn'*, 18 August 1925).

In spite of his balanced approach to industrialization, official Soviet historiography insists that Trotsky was a 'super-industrializer', determined to plunder the peasantry. In reality he attempted more systematically than any of his contemporaries to avert the crisis of forced industrialization by balancing the needs of the peasantry against those of industry through a policy of 'commodity intervention'. To the extent that export-oriented growth clearly depended upon the peasants bringing grain to market, Trotsky was quite aware that the most urgent consumer needs would also have to be satisfied through imports. The world market was to function as a 'reserve' for both light and heavy industry. The 'goods famine', or the chronic shortage of consumer goods, was 'obvious and incontestable proof that the distribution of national economic resources between state industry and the rest of the economy has . . . acquired the necessary proportionality' (*Trotsky Archives*, No. T-2983). The real enemies

259

of the peasantry, in Trotsky's view, were the authors of Socialism in One Country – Stalin, who saw only the needs of the machine-building industries, and Bukharin, who urged the peasant to 'enrich' himself without seriously considering the need to provide consumer goods upon which these savings might be spent.

It was Trotsky's concern for the legitimate needs of workers and peasants alike which led him in the 1930s to reconsider the role of market forces, for a time at least, in socialist planning. As early as 1925 he had warned that it was 'impossible to push industrialization forward with the aid of unreal credits' (Trotsky, 1955, p. 186). During the first five-year plan he called for restraints upon the inflationary financing of heavy industry and 'strict financial discipline', even at the expense of closing down enterprises. A stable currency, in turn, would provide an instrument whereby the masses themselves could democratically control production decisions from below. 'The innumerable living participants in the economy,' Trotsky wrote in 1932,

> state and private, collective and individual, must announce their needs and their respective intensities not only through the statistical calculations of the planning commissions, but also by the direct pressure of supply and demand. The plan . . . [must be] verified, and in an important measure must be achieved through the market (*Biulleten' Oppozitsii* XXXI, 1932, p. 8).

A planned market, free trade unions, and restoration of soviet democracy: these were the three elements without which any talk of socialism was a mockery.

> If there existed the universal mind described in the scientific fantasy of Laplace – a mind which might simultaneously register all the processes of nature and society, measure the dynamic of their movement and forecast the results of their interactions – then, of course, such a mind could *a priori* draw up a faultless and exhaustive economic plan, beginning with the number of hectares of wheat and ending with buttons on a waistcoat. True, it often appears to the bureaucracy that it possesses just such a mind: and that is why it so easily emancipates itself from control by the market and by soviet democracy. The reality is that the bureaucracy is cruelly mistaken in its appraisal of its own spiritual resources (*Biulleten' Oppozitsii* XXXI, 1932, p. 8).

In *The Revolution Betrayed*, his most thorough critique of Stalinist 'planomania', Trotsky concluded that the real basis of bureaucratic power had nothing to do with Stalin's pompous claims of industrial triumphs; the horrible truth was that the whole bureaucratic edifice had come to rest upon nothing more profound or despicable than an ability to manufacture poverty. Queues were the foundation of Soviet power and the innermost secret of the police state:

> The basis of bureaucratic rule is the poverty of society in objects of consumption. When there are enough goods in a store, the purchasers can come whenever they want to. When there are few goods, the purchasers are compelled to stand in line. When the lines are very long, it is necessary to

appoint a policeman to keep order. Such is the starting point of the Soviet bureaucracy. It 'knows' who is to get something and who has to wait (Trotsky, 1945, p. 112).

Historians will continue to debate whether Trotsky's policies might have avoided forced collectivization and the excesses of Stalin's five-year plans. On one point, however, there can be no dispute: Trotsky was perfectly correct to conclude that Stalin's pursuit of autarky had more in common with the ideals of Hitler than with those of Marx. The Russian revolution, confined to a single backward country, did not lead to the emancipation of the proletariat. Trotsky attempted to reinterpret and apply Marxism to the unexpected conditions of an isolated revolutionary experiment. He did not win the battle against Stalin. He did, however, help to explain and attempt to avert one of the great tragedies of the 20th century.

SELECTED WORKS

The Permanent Revolution and Results and Prospects. Trans. John G. Wright and Brian Pearce, London: New Park Publications, 1962; New York: Pioneer Publishers, 1965.

Terrorism and Communism. Ann Arbor: University of Michigan Press, 1963.

The New Course. Ann Arbor: University of Michigan Press, 1965.

Towards Socialism or Capitalism? London: Methuen & Co., 1926. In *Whither Russia? Towards Capitalism or Socialism*. New York: International Publishers.

The Platform of the Left Opposition. (1927). London: New Park Publications, 1963.

My Life. New York: Grosset & Dunlap, 1960.

The History of the Russian Revolution. Trans. by Max Eastman, London: Victor Gollancz, 1965; Ann Arbor: University of Michigan Press.

The Revolution Betrayed. New York: Pioneer Publishers, 1945.

Stalin: An Appraisal of the Man and His Influence. London: Hollis & Carter, 1947; New York: Stein and Day, 1967.

Biulleten' Oppozitsii (Bulletin of the Opposition). New York: Monad, 1973.

BIBLIOGRAPHY

Day, R.B. 1973. *Leon Trotsky and the Politics of Economic Isolation*. Cambridge and New York: Cambridge University Press.

Deutscher, I. 1954. *The Prophet Armed. Trotsky: 1879–1921*. London: Oxford University Press; New York: Vintage Books, 1965.

Deutscher, I. 1959. *The Prophet Unarmed. Trotsky: 1921–1929*. London: Oxford University Press; New York: Vintage Books, 1965.

Deutscher, I. 1963. *The Prophet Outcast. Trotsky: 1929–1940*. London and New York: Oxford University Press.

Howe, I. 1978. *Leon Trotsky*. New York: Viking, 1978.

Nikolai Alekseevich Voznesensky

M.C. KASER

Voznesensky (born the son of a timber dealer in Teploe, Russia, on 18 November 1903; executed on 30 September 1950) joined the Bolshevik Party in 1919 and studied political economy at the Institute of Red Professors, Moscow, where he stayed on as lecturer. His publications – fewer than 30, his culminating manuscript being destroyed by the police – have been analysed by Harrison (1985) and Sutela (1984). In a concept later to be termed 'unbalanced growth' by A.O. Hirschman, he saw that the national plan 'must localize bottlenecks, not for adapting them, but for doing away with them'. Ranging himself against those who argued that comprehensive planning invalidated money calculations, he had by 1935 embraced the position – which was to figure in Stalin's indictment of him in 1949 – that money would have a distributive function even when all means of production had been nationalized. His association with the Leningrad circle which eventually led to his execution also began in 1935, for A.A. Zhdanov, having replaced the assassinated S.M. Kirov as Leningrad Party Secretary, invited Voznesensky to lead that city's plan organization under an Executive Committee headed by A.N. Kosygin.

Voznesensky was promoted to the chairmanship of the USSR State Planning Committee in January 1938 and brought order into the chaos resulting from the 1937 Great Purge (Voznesensky, 1938, 1940; Harrison, 1985), but so inadequate were his plans for a war economy both before and after the German attack of June 1941 that Zhdanov's rivals, G.M. Malenkov and L.P. Beria (Ra'anan, 1983) ran the newly created State Defence Committee, from which Voznesensky was excluded until February 1942. He regained chairmanship of the Planning Committee in December 1942, and achieved in 1943 a peak of armaments production and economic expansion in the unoccupied territory. He allowed market forces to operate in the household sector, alongside rations at controlled prices, absorbing some of the inflation in purchasing power through highly taxed off-ration prices in state shops, and intended to liquidate the inflationary overhang generated by free sales by farmers in a monetary reform as soon as the war ended (though famine caused postponement and retail price restructuring until December 1947).

At the height of Voznesensky's economic leadership (he was elected Academician in 1943) an unsigned editorial, 1943, condemned the 'voluntarism' which disregarded the 'objectively-determined process of development' and confirmed, as had been adumbrated in 1941 (Kaser, 1965), that a law of value operated under socialism. His postwar Reconstruction Plan evoked 'economic levers in the organization of production and distribution, such as price, money, credit, profit and incentives' (*Selected Works*, 1979, p. 465): he brought in Kosygin as Minister of Finance to oversee the cut in subsidies required by his reform of wholesale prices; the measures which took effect on 1 January 1949 would have been a major contribution to rational economic management (Kaser, 1950).

Political realignments led to Voznesensky's dismissal within weeks of his reform and his eventual execution without trial; the life of the dismissed Kosygin, in Khrushchev's later words, 'hung by a thread'. Stalin reversed the reform of both retail and wholesale prices and soon (Stalin, 1952) limited the role of 'commodity relations' to the interface of the socialist sector with non-state entities (such as collective farmers and foreigners), vilifying Voznesensky's analysis of the war economy (Voznesensky, 1948) for the very 'voluntarism' that the author rejected. The death or disgrace of those in the Leningrad circle was a triumph, albeit short-lived, for Beria and Malenkov in a political power struggle, but the open disputations were on economic issues: on one, to stop dismantling capital in the Soviet Zone of Germany in favour of current deliveries, Voznesensky had been right; in the others – where E.S. Varga argued that east Europe should be allowed to be 'state capitalist' with market relations with the West and that Keynesian policies had halted the 'general crisis of capitalism' – he had been wrong.

SELECTED WORKS

1938. K itogam sotsialisticheskogo vosproizvodstva vo vtoroi piatiletke (On the results of socialist reproduction in the second Five-year Plan). *Bol'shevik* No. 2. In *Selected Works*, 346–62.

1940. Tri stalinskie piatiletki stroitel'stva sotsializma (Three Stalinist Five-year Plans for building socialism). *Bol'shevik* No. 1. Not reproduced in *Selected Works*.

1948. *The War Economy of the USSR in the Period of the Patriotic War*. Washington, DC: Public Affairs Press and the American Association of Learned Societies. Translation of *Voennaia ekonomika SSSR v period Otechestvennoi voiny*, Moscow: Gospolitizdat. In *Selected Works*, 484–604.

1979. *Izbrannye proizvedeniia 1931–1947* (Selected Works 1931–1947). Moscow: Izdatel'stvo politicheskoy literatury.

BIBLIOGRAPHY

Harrison, M. 1985. *Soviet Planning in Peace and War, 1938–1945*. Cambridge: Cambridge University Press.

Kaser, M.C. 1950. Soviet planning and the price mechanism. *Economic Journal* 60, March, 81–91.

Kaser, M.C. 1965. Le début sur la loi de la valeur en URSS. Etude rétrospective 1941–1953. *Annuaire de l'URSS 1965,* Paris: CNRS.

Ra'anan, G.D. 1983. *International Policy Formation in the USSR: Factional 'Debates' during the Zhdanovshchina.* Hamden, Conn.: Archon.

Pod znamenem marxizma (Under the banner of Marxism). 1943. No. 7–8. Editorial.

Stalin, J.V. 1952. *Economic Problems of Socialism in the USSR.* Moscow: Foreign Languages Publishing House. (Translation of *Ekonomicheskie problemy sotsializma v SSSR,* Moscow.)

Sutela, P. 1984. *Socialism, Planning and Optimality. A Study in Soviet Economic Thought.* Commentationes Scientiarum Socialium No. 25, Helsinki: Societas Scientiarum Fennica.

Varga, E.S. 1946. *Izmeneniia v ekonomike kapitalizma v itoge vtoroi mirovoi voiny* (Changes in the economy of capitalism as a result of the Second World War). Moscow: Gospolitizdat.

Contributors

A. Aganbegyan Chairman, Commission for the Study of Productive Forces and Resources, Moscow; Chairman, Economics Section, Academy of Sciences of the USSR (since 1985); Director, Institute of Economics and Industrial Organization, Siberian Academy of Sciences (1967–85). *The Challenge: Economics of Perestroika* (1988).

A. Brody Economic adviser, Institute of Economics, Hungarian Academy of Sciences. Fellow, Econometric Society. *Proportions, Prices and Planning* (1972); *Slowdown* (1985).

W. Brus Professor, Wolfson College, Oxford. 'Stalinism and "People's Democracies"', *Stalinism: essays in historical interpretation* (ed. Robert Tucker, 1977); *"Normalization" Processes in Soviet-Dominated Central Europe* (with P. Kende and Z. Mlynar, 1982); *The Soviet Systems After Brezhnev* (with P. Kende and Z. Mlynar, 1984).

Robert W. Campbell Professor of Economics, Indiana University. *Accounting in Soviet Planning and Management* (1963); *The Economics of Soviet Oil and Gas* (1968); *Trends in the Soviet Oil and Gas Industry* (1976); *Soviet Energy Technologies: Planning, Policy, Research and Development* (1980).

Wolfgang Classen Akademie Rat, University of Bielefeld. *Probleme einer materialistischen Analyse des bürgerlichen Staates* (1979); *Faschismus und bürgerliche Gesellschaft* (1980).

D.C. Coleman Emeritus Professor of Economic History, University of Cambridge. Fellow, British Academy. *The British Paper Industry 1495–1860* (1958); *Sir John Banks: Baronet and Businessman* (1963); *Revisions in Mercantilism* (ed., 1969);

265

Courtaulds; an Economic and Social History (1969); *The Economy of England, 1450–1750* (1977); *History and the Economic Past* (1987).

Richard B. Day Professor, Department of Political Science, University of Toronto. Killiam Senior Research Fellow. *Leon Trotsky and the Politics of Economic Isolation* (1973); 'The theory of the long cycle: Kondrat'ev, Trotsky, Mandel', *New Left Review*; *The "Crisis" and the "Crash": Soviet Studies of the West, 1917–1939* (1981); *N.I. Bukharin, Selected Writings on the State and the transition to Socialism* (ed. and trans., 1982); *E.A. Preobrazhensky, The Decline of Capitalism* (ed. and trans., 1985); *Democratic Theory and Technological Society* (ed., with Ronald Beiner, Joseph Masciulli, 1988).

Meghnad Desai Professor of Economics, London School of Economics. 'Growth cycles and inflation in a model of the class struggle', *Journal of Economic Theory* (1973); 'Phillips Curve: a revisionist interpretation', *Economica* (1975); *Applied Econometrics* (1976); *Marxian Economics* (1979); *Testing Monetarism* (1981); 'Men and Things', *Economica* (1986).

Michael Ellman Professor of Economics, University of Amsterdam. *Planning Problems in the USSR* (1973); *Socialist Planning* (1979); *Collectivisation, Convergence and Capitalism* (1984); *The Soviet Economy to 1992: Stagnation, Disequilibrium and Perestroika* (1989); 'The crisis of the welfare state – the Dutch experience', *The Economics of Human Betterment* (ed. K.E. Boulding, 1984).

Gregory Grossman Professor of Economics, University of California at Berkeley. Fulbright teaching grant to Italy, 1960–1; Guggenheim grant, 1964–5; Fellow, Center for Advanced Study in the Behavioral Sciences, 1969–70; President, American Association for the Advancement of Slavic Studies, 1980–1.

Joseph Halevi Senior Lecturer in Economics, University of Sydney. 'The contemporary significance of Baran and Sweezy's notion of monopolistic capitalism', *Money and Macroeconomic Policies* (ed. M. Jarsulic, 1985); 'Structure economique et demande effective', *Economie Appliqué* 37(1), (1984); 'Lowe, Dobb and Hicks', *The Eastern Economic Journal* (April/June 1984); 'Employment and Planning', *Social Research* 50(2), (1983); 'The composition of investment under conditions of non-uniform changes', *Banca Nazionale del Lavoro Quarterly Review* (June 1981); 'On Kalecki's conception of the economic cycle and state intervention', *Annals of Public and Cooperative Economy* 46(3), (1975).

Donald J. Harris Professor of Economics, Stanford University, California. National Research Council–Ford Foundation Fellow, 1984–5. 'Inflation, income distribution, and capital accumulation in a two-sector model of growth', *The Economic Journal* (1967); 'Income, prices, and the balance of payments in underdeveloped economies: a short-run model', *Oxford Economics Papers* (1970);

'On Marx's scheme of reproduction and accumulation', *Journal of Political Economy* (1972); *Capital Accumulation and Income Distribution* (1978); 'Profits, productivity, and thrift: the neoclassical theory of capital and distribution revisited', *Journal of Post-Keynesian Economics* (1981); 'Accumulation of capital and the rate of profit in Marxian theory', *Cambridge Journal of Economics* (1983).

Branko Horvat Professor of Economics, Zagreb University. Director, Institute of Economic Sciences, Belgrade; Chief Methodologist, Federal Planning Bureau, Belgrade; Member, Federal Economic Council; Federal Council for Market and Prices; Editor, *Economic Analysis and Workers' Management*; Founder, International Association for the Economics of Selfmanagement. *Towards a Theory of Planned Economy* (1961); *Economic Models* (1962); *Business Cycles in Yugoslavia* (1969); *Economic Analysis* (1972); *The Political Economy of Socialism* (1982); *The Labour Theory of Prices* (1987).

Holland Hunter Professor of Economics, Haverford College. *Soviet Transport Experience* (1968); *The Future of the Soviet Economy 1978–85* (ed., 1978).

Michael Kaser Director, Institute of Russian, Soviet and East European Studies; Reader in Economics, University of Oxford. Professorial Fellow of St. Anthony's College, Oxford. *Comecon: Integration Problems of the Planned Economies* (1965); *Soviet Economies* (1970); *Health Care in the Soviet Union and Eastern Europe* (1976); *The Soviet Union since the Fall of Krushchev* (ed., with A. Brown, 1977); *Soviet Policy for the 1980's* (ed., with A. Brown, 1982); *The Economic History of Eastern Europe, 1919–1975* (general editor, 1985–6).

Tadeusz Kowalik Professor, University of Warsaw. 'Rosa Luxembourg's theory of accumulation and imperialism', *Problems of Economic Dynamics and Planning, Essays in Honour of Michal Kalecki* (1964).

Marie Lavigne Professor, University of Paris I, Sorbonne. *Economie internationale des pays socialistes* (1985); *La réalité socialiste* (1983); *Travail et monnaie en système socialiste* (1981); *Stratégies des pays socialistes dans l'échange international* (1980); *Economie politique de la planification en système socialiste* (ed., 1978).

Valery L. Makarov Director, Central Economic and Mathematical Institute, USSR Academy of Sciences; Editor-in-chief, Journal of Mathematics and Economics Methods. Fellow, Econometric Society. *Mathematical Theory of Economic Dynamics and Equilibria* (with A.M. Rubinov, 1973); *Models and Computers in Economics* (1979); *Computer Simulation in Analysis of Regional Problems* (1987).

Béla Martos Research Counsellor, Institute of Economics, Hungarian Academy of Sciences. *Dynamic Models of the National Economy* (with R. Andorka and

D.Dányi, 1967); *Nonlinear Programming* (1975); *Non-Price Control* (ed. with J. Kornai, 1981); *Economic Control Structures* (forthcoming).

Peter Nolan Lecturer, Faculty of Economics and Politics, Cambridge University. Fellow and Director of Studies in Economics, Jesus College, Cambridge. *Growth Processes and Distributional Change in a South Chinese Province: the case of Guangdong* (1983); *Re-thinking Socialist Economics* (ed., with S. Paine, 1986); *The Political Economy of Collective Farms* (1988); *China's Economic Reforms Since Mao* (ed., with F.R. Dong, 1989); *Markets, Competition and Small Private Business in China* (ed., with F.R. Dong, 1989).

Alec Nove Professor Emeritus, University of Glasgow. Fellow, Royal Society of Edinburgh, British Academy. *The Soviet Economic System* (1977); *Stalinism and After* (1975); *Reagan, the Pipeline and East–West Relations* (1982); *Marxism and 'Really Existing Socialism'* (1986); *Soviet Agriculture* (1988).

Domenico Mario Nuti Professor of Economics, European University Institute, Florence. 'Capitalism, socialism and steady growth', *Economic Journal* 80 (1970); *Economic Essays on Value, Competition and Utility* (ed., 1974); *Socialist Economics* (ed. with Alec Nove, 1972); 'The Contradictions of Socialist economies – A Marxian Interpretation', *Socialist Register 1979* (ed. R. Miliband and J. Saville, 1979); 'Profit-sharing and employment: claims and overclaims' *EUI Working Paper* (1986); 'Perestroika: transition between central planning and market socialism', *Economic Policy* 3(2), (1988).

Tibor Scitovsky Emeritus Professor of Economics, Stanford University. *Welfare and Competition* (1951); *Economic Theory and Western European Integration* (1958); *Papers on Welfare and Growth* (1964); *Money and the Balance of Payments* (1970); *The Joyless Economy* (1976); *Human Desire and Economic Satisfaction* (1986).

Rajiv Vohra Associate Professor, Brown University, Rhode Island. 'On the existence of equilibria in economies with increasing returns', *Journal of Mathematical Economics* (forthcoming); 'A consistent bargaining set', *Journal of Economic Theory* (with B. Dutta, D. Ray and K. Sengupta, forthcoming); 'Optimal regulation under fixed rules for income distribution', *Journal of Economic Theory* 44 (1988); 'On the approximate decentralization of Pareto optimal allocations in locally convex spaces', *Journal of Approximation Theory* 52 (with M. Ali Khan, 1988); 'Local public goods as indivisible commodities', *Regional Science and Urban Economics* 17 (1987).

P.J.D. Wiles Professor Emeritus, University of London. *Price, Cost and Output* (1961); *Political Economy of Communism* (1962); *Economic Institutions Compared* (1979); *Communist International Economics* (1968); *Economics in Disarray* (ed., with Guy Routh, 1984).